W9-BRQ-422

Omohundro Institute of Early American History & Culture

Charles Royster

A Revolutionary People at War

The Continental Army and American Character, 1775–1783

Published for the Omohundro
Institute of Early American History and Culture
Williamsburg, Virginia,
by The University of North Carolina Press
Chapel Hill, North Carolina

The Omohundro Institute of Early American History and Culture is sponsored jointly by The College of William and Mary and The Colonial Williamsburg Foundation.

Manufactured in the United States of America

Library of Congress Cataloging in Publication Data

Royster, Charles.
A revolutionary people at war.

Bibliography: p.
Includes index.
1. United States. Army. Continental Army.
2. United States—Civilization—To 1783.
3. National characteristics, American. I. Title.
E259.R69 973.3′4 79-10152
ISBN 0-8078-1385-0
ISBN 0-8078-4606-6 (pbk.)

09 08 07 06 05 12 11 10 9 8

TO MY PARENTS

Preface

While I was researching and writing this book and while I was looking for an academic job, a number of people asked me, "What is your book about?" I always found this question hard to answer—not because I did not know what my book was about but because most of my short answers seemed to give people ideas that I had not intended. If I said that my book was about the Revolutionary War, I seemed to be retelling a familiar story of generals and battles. If I said that my book was about the Continental Army, I sometimes seemed to have become a would-be chief of staff who presumably delighted in organizational charts, chains of command, and the study of logistics. If I said that my book was about the American people during the Revolutionary War, I seemed to sound like a student of the new social history, compiling socioeconomic data. And if I said that my book was about American character, I seemed to deal in elastic abstractions drawn from sources that were suspiciously literate. All of these short answers were accurate but incomplete. Through experience with the misleading effects of incomplete explanations I learned that only by a long answer could I hope to say what my book is about. To give that answer I wrote this Preface.

This book assumes that there was an American character prevalent during the War for Independence and that we can profitably analyze it. I use the word "character" because I try to understand not only the formally articulated ideas usually described by the word "mind" but also some of the most important emotions, attitudes, and conduct of Americans in wartime. I believe that these attributes of the revolutionary movement bore a coherent relationship to each other that can be reconstructed. Although my book begins by assuming that a national character existed, I hope that my analysis also contains enough evidence to show why I began with this assumption. In order to discuss these prevalent attributes without constantly repeating a stock set of cautionary phrases, I have used the words "revolutionaries" and "Americans" interchangeably to refer to the people who seem to me to exemplify this national character. Obviously, these words are not precise. If we take "revolutionaries" to be people who favored resistance to British authority during the war, we know that not all natives of America were revolutionaries and that many people's attitudes differed subtly and changed over the years. Moreover, no matter what criteria we choose for defining the group, our conclusions about it must rest on reasonable inferences, not conclusive proof of the accuracy of the word when it is applied to large numbers of people. Accepting these imprecisions as a necessary evil for the purpose of making generalizations, I have not always taken the space to qualify my conclusions by adding words like "most," "usually," "probably." At the same time, however, this book does offer evidence that allegiance to the "American" or "revolutionary" side in the War for Independence was the prevailing sentiment of people in the United States. And the book implicitly argues that the national character of revolutionaries formed one of the principal bases of their wartime allegiance. These propositions are the premises on which the book's discussion of the Continental Army and American character rests.

One of the central questions that I ask is, What was the relationship between the ideals espoused during the revolution and the actions of Americans? Because of the comprehensive ideal of citizen, society, and state enunciated by the revolutionary generation, this question, if applied to the whole era, would require wide-ranging and complex answers beyond the scope of one book. So I have addressed the question in a more specific way. I have studied the ideals that Americans defined for themselves in creating, recruiting, and fighting in an army, and I have studied the relationship of these ideals to their experience with their army. The ideals of achievement were rigorous, even absolute; the conduct was always flawed and often gravely deficient. What were the nature and the effects of this disparity? I have addressed this question as thoroughly as I could. In the process, I have touched far less systematically on the disparities in other realms—for example, religion, government, and commerce. I have done so partly because these realms affected Americans' dealings with the army and partly because I believe that my findings on the wartime lot of the Continental Army yield insights relevant to the study of other areas of revolutionary experience—areas that limits of space and competence allow me only to broach in this book.

I have found the study of the Continental Army especially rewarding for this purpose because at its center lies one of the most fundamental problems of the revolution: survival. To Americans of that era, the great fact for republics, like the great fact for individuals, was death. The selfishness of corruption, like the debility of age and disease, inevitably killed self-government. Could Americans postpone the republic's day of death? Could they, by unprecedented strength, forestall it indefinitely? The clearest, most dramatic test came in the army's resistance to British force. Here the connection between the individual's conduct and the republic's survival was most visible and direct. From our understanding of this connection we can draw insights into other kinds of conduct in which, according to revolutionary ideals, the republic would depend on citizens' strength.

In my discussion of the role of national character in the military demands of the Revolutionary War I have studied some of the mental processes and emotional crises that revealed Americans' concerns. However, I have not systematically used the concepts or the vocabulary of clinical psychology. I have tried to enhance my understanding of the people I write about by varied reading outside the field of history. But in writing history I usually do not use technical words, because neither the sources for the Revolutionary War nor my analyses of the revolutionaries fully conform to the requirements of other disciplines. Consequently, when I discuss individuals and the populace at large I try to convey insights through a vocabulary that is as widely accessible as possible. At the same time, I do not believe that traditional analytical exposition is the only useful method for portraying character in a scholarly work. Biographical narratives and other forms of reconstructing wartime experiences can help one understand the intensity of the revolutionaries' reaction to the struggle for independence. No explanation of Americans' conduct can alone explore its significance as effectively as the recreation of that conduct.

This book, however, is an analytical history, not a series of narratives. In assessing the relationship between the Continental Army and American character, I have followed a chronological outline, within which many topical questions covering a number of years are addressed. In order to emphasize the importance of changes that took place during the Revolutionary War, I have often reserved part of my analysis of recurring subjects until later stages of their development. I believe that we can best study the revolutionaries' attitudes by retracing wartime concerns in the order that Americans experienced them. Thus, I begin the book by examining the ideals of revolutionary virtue and valor to which the revolutionaries aspired. After we have seen the high value that Americans set on these ideals, we are in a better position to examine the tensions that ensued from shortcomings and failure, as well as different methods of responding to those tensions. After we have studied the ways in which Americans redefined their Revolutionary War experience, we can better understand the legacy that they shaped for their posterity. If my method of exposition succeeds, the significance of each subject will become more fully apparent as the effects of ideals and conduct unfold during the war years. Only at the end of the war—and of the book—will all the subjects have been fully developed. For this reason the book does not lend itself to short, abstract summaries of its argument. I have tried to make the presentation of facts an essential part of the understanding of their meaning so that neither the author nor the readers would lose their involvement in the revolutionaries' experience while analyzing its significance. In short, I have told a story. It is a scholarly story of ideas and attitudes, with moral lessons in the form of analysis. But the lessons, if they seem worth learning, can only be found in the story.

Contents

Illustrations

following page 238

THE INNER WAR

8. "The Soldiers in the Field doing duty," from *The Downfall of Justice* (Danvers, [1777]), plate IV.
Reproduction courtesy of The Colonial Williamsburg Foundation, Williamsburg, Virginia.

9. *The Banner of Washington's Life Guard*.
Reproduction courtesy of The Colonial Williamsburg Foundation, Williamsburg, Virginia.

10. A. Dupre, *The Battle of Cowpens*.
Courtesy Musee de la Cooperation Franco-Americaine, Blérancourt.

11. Baron Ludwig von Closen's Sketch of American Army Uniforms.
Courtesy Library of Congress.

12. James Peale, Detail of Continental Soldiers from *George Washington*.
Courtesy Independence National Historical Park Collection, Philadelphia.

13. Charles Willson Peale, Detail of Continental Soldier from *Washington at Trenton*.
Courtesy The Colonial Williamsburg Foundation, Williamsburg, Virginia.

14. Charles Willson Peale, *Baron Friedrich Wilhelm von Steuben*.
Courtesy Independence National Historical Park Collection, Philadelphia.

15. Charles Willson Peale, *Jean Baptiste, Chevalier de Ternant*.
Courtesy Independence National Historical Park Collection, Philadelphia.

16. Charles Willson Peale, *General William North*.
Courtesy Detroit Institute of Fine Arts.

THE OFFICERS

17. John Trumbull, *Colonel Howard*.
    Courtesy Free Library of Philadelphia.
18. Charles Willson Peale, *John Laurens*.
    Courtesy Independence National Historical Park Collection, Philadelphia.
19. A. Rosenthal after Charles Willson Peale, *Walter Stewart*.
    Courtesy Independence National Historical Park Collection, Philadelphia.
20. A. Rosenthal after Charles Willson Peale, *Samuel Blachley Webb*.
    Courtesy Independence National Historical Park Collection, Philadelphia.
21. *An Unknown Officer*, artist unknown.
    Courtesy Free Library of Philadelphia.
22. H. B. Hall, *Tench Tilghman*.
    Courtesy, Prints Division, New York Public Library.
23. Charles Willson Peale, *Self-Portrait*.
    Courtesy American Philosophical Society, Philadelphia.
24. Charles Willson Peale, *An Unknown Officer of the Maryland Line*.
    Courtesy The Frick Art Reference Library, New York City.
25. Gustav Behne, *John Peter Gabriel Muhlenberg*.
    Courtesy Independence National Historical Park Collection, Philadelphia.
26. Charles Willson Peale, *John Eager Howard*.
    Courtesy Independence National Historical Park Collection, Philadelphia.

27. *America Triumphant and Britannia in Distress*, from *Weatherwise's Town and Country Almanack* (1782). Courtesy The Colonial Williamsburg Foundation, Williamsburg, Virginia.

28. Charles Willson Peale, *A Representation of the Figures exhibited and paraded through the Streets of Philadelphia . . .* (Philadelphia, 1780). Reproduction courtesy of The Colonial Williamsburg Foundation, Williamsburg, Virginia.

29. John Trumbull, *The Death of General Montgomery in the Attack on Quebec, Canada*. Courtesy Yale University Art Gallery.

30. Charles Willson Peale, *Benjamin Rush*. Courtesy The Henry Francis du Pont Winterthur Museum.

A Revolutionary People at War

❦One Monday in September 1781, Lieutenant Enos Reeves rode out of Yellow Springs, Pennsylvania, toward Philadelphia, to rejoin his regiment, which was on its way to Yorktown. Lieutenant James McLean, of the Invalid Regiment in Philadelphia, rode with him. They took a back road and got lost. They came out at the Bull Tavern, near Valley Forge. After eating, they went through the grounds of the camp which Reeves had left more than three years earlier. Several thousand men had lived there for six months. People were living in some of the officers' cabins now. Other cabins had been broken up to make fence rails. But most of the hundreds of huts stood empty and decayed. Some of the camp's open space had been planted and was yielding crops. In other places, growing saplings reclaimed the ground for the woods.[1]❦

PROLOGUE

The Call to War, 1775-1783

The War of the American Revolution lasted for eight years—years that severely tested Americans' dedication to independence. In the process, the country's first war both shaped and tested Americans' ideals of national character. This trial of national character was the central theme in Americans' discussion of the Continental Army's role in the winning of the revolution. Proponents of independence agreed that the future of American liberty depended first on winning the war and second on how the war was won. Liberty could survive, many Americans believed, only if the people showed themselves to be worthy defenders of it. To make independence secure, these revolutionaries contended, rigorous ideals of national character and civil polity must be realized in the victory.

In describing the Continental Army—both from within its ranks and from outside them—American revolutionaries disclosed their understanding of how their countrymen were meeting the test of war. Besides calling each other to attain the ideal of patriotic service, they measured their wartime conduct against their unattainable ideal. Americans saw many discrepancies between the two, and these induced deep concern and prolonged tension; for, in the eyes of revolutionaries, war put to the trial the military ardor and skill as well as the moral assumptions on which they based their hopes for American independence and liberty. To fail as defenders of ideals was to fail as Americans; to succeed was to give the victors, their country, and its liberty the prospect of immortality.

When the revolutionaries encouraged each other to fight the British, they invoked the spirit of their ancestors. In resisting parliamentary taxation and ministerial rule—and finally in repudiating the king—Americans did not denounce their own loyal forebears. Rather, they claimed their predecessors as courageous forerunners in the cause that now called for independence. The enemy in those early times had been the American continent and the Indians. The first settlers, according to their descendants, had left Europe and faced such enemies in order to preserve self-government and liberty of conscience. Now British power pursued "us, their guiltless Children."[1] In 1776, on the sixth anniversary of the Boston Massacre, the orator for that year likened the revolutionaries' purpose to that of the first colonists: "Freedom is offered to us, she invites us to accept her blessings; driven from the other regions of the globe, she wishes to find an asylum in the wilds of America; with open arms let us receive the persecuted fair, let us imitate the example of our venerable ancestors, who loved and courted her into these desert climes. With determined bravery, let us resist the attacks of her impudent ravishers."[2] Today we would say that many of the revolutionaries' ancestors came to America to protect their orthodoxies from the threat of other people's orthodoxies. Even so, the revolutionaries were not altogether wrong in their memory and their pride of kinship. For they, like many of the first immigrants, saw an advanced stage of contagious corruption in the society and the government of Britain. To live an upright life in security of estate and in hope for heaven required freedom—that is, the opportunity to direct one's life without constantly accommodating the wishes of those who did not share one's aspirations, who in fact sought to destroy one's aspirations and subordinate one's life to their own worldly welfare.

The revolutionaries admired their ancestors' service in this cause when a hostile continent had threatened. British taxation, imperial administration, and the ministerial army's aggression had brought corrupt power to America, and freedom called this generation to fight. Their ancestors, while courageous and worthy of emulation, were but precursors in the struggle that the wartime generation would bring to fruition. A man who went to war against the British tyrant knew that his fathers approved his defense of what they had bequeathed him. He knew that his fathers in their time had fought well to secure him this heritage. But neither his strength nor the worth of his efforts came primarily from the superior example of his fathers. These came from his concern for his children and from his obedience to God. Although to revolutionaries the heroes of ancient Greece and Rome were the "first-born of true fame," Thomas Paine spoke the thoughts of many when he said that the Ancients should admire the Americans, not the other way around.[3]

Expecting to win more glory by accomplishing a harder task, the revolutionaries offered their own strength as the sole defense of the heritage from the past and the prospects for the future. As the crucial guardians of liberty, they could animate each other to valor by aspiring to the immortality of fame.[4] Such pride seldom deigns to admit the possibility of weakness. Rather, pride sought to prevent weakness by denying that it was possible. If Americans had been offered the chance to be only as strong as any European people, they might not have bothered to try. But if they could prove themselves stronger than any other people, stronger even than ancient heroes, they would have a cause worthy of their ardor.

Many revolutionaries believed that God had chosen America to preserve and to exemplify self-government for the world. The revolutionary generation had to fulfill God's purpose against the attacks of men who, they thought, knowingly strove to sap or smash self-government everywhere. History was full of tyrants who ruled because they alone were strong or because the people had decided to share the rulers' corruption by selling themselves into slavery. Seen in this light, the British attack was no surprise, just as America's freedom was no accident. Britain sought to subjugate America partly out of envy of America's strength, prosperity, and liberty. Britain and America were like Cain and Abel, but Americans would defend themselves. Having been chosen by God to show how self-government enabled a people to flourish—and holding this promise in trust for the world—what could Americans expect but assault? In the *New Jersey Journal*, "A Soldier" said, "We ought to rejoice that the ALMIGHTY Governor of the universe hath given us a station so honourable, and planted us the guardians of liberty, while the greatest part of mankind rise and fall undistinguished as bubbles on the common stream."[5]

The alternative to resistance was enslavement. At a Continental Army recruiting muster of North Carolina militia, the colonel said, "Since the Battle of Lexington he was convinced America was to be hard rode, and drove like slaves if the Americans were inactive or inattentive."[6] Slavery brought arbitrary taxes, alien armies and officials, false religion, distant trials or no trials, expropriation, and pervasive corruption. Fearing such a fate, Americans, according to a Connecticut minister, "seemed to have an intuitive view of the consequences" of Britain's grasp for power.[7] They often identified slavery with lethargy, sleep, and spiritual death. These failings could subject people to a tyrant and perpetuate his rule. They were the most harmful effect of slavery. Although Patrick Henry made people feel imaginary chains and although Ethan Allen's story of his prisoner-of-war shackles became a wartime best seller, slavery, to revolutionaries, did not primarily mean physical bondage.[8] It need not even mean material hardship, because a people might surrender their independent judgment in return for corrupt riches. Slavery could work "the charm of a serpent—We fall in love with that which ought to be the object of our hate, as it is the instrument of our destruction."[9]

The worst curse was resignation to the tyrant's will. Acquiescence became habit; then it became advantageous; finally, it became universal and permanent. Thus people could forget that they had ever had minds of their own. A newspaper supporter of Thomas Paine's *Common Sense* argued, "*War* may cut off thousands in the bloom of their youth; but *slavery* destroys the very seeds of generation, not only in the *animal* but *vegetable* world."[10] Americans saw this threat vividly and remembered it. Because it foretold the consequences of small surrenders, it tempered calculations of immediate advantage. An attack on American self-government meant an attack also on each American's psychological integrity—on each American's soul. A man who forfeited his birthright of personal responsibility fell into a sleep which might doom him—in this world or the one to come.[11]

If a generation enslaved itself, it enslaved its posterity, who would never know a different state. The awareness of posterity strongly moved the revolutionaries during the war. Americans liked to picture themselves as others saw them: Continental Army officers worried about what British officers thought of them; Americans sought the respect of the French in order to win allies; revolutionaries felt sure that subject peoples in Ireland, India, the world, watched for American victory. But the most popular and long-lasting mirror of their fancy was their posterity. The revolution meant the sacrifice of present convenience to prevent the irreversible enslavement of their children. The threat to posterity seemed to be the most sinister feature of the British plan for tyranny. Taxes and legislation that, for now, directly hurt some and indirectly inconvenienced others would give Britain the power to paralyze future generations. Two weeks before voting for independence in Congress, Reverend John Witherspoon preached, "Our civil and religious liberties, and consequently in great measure the temporal and eternal happiness of us and our posterity depended on the issue."[12]

The revolutionaries' self-conscious vigilance on behalf of Americans whom they would never see convinced them that defiance was right. Their concern proved that they had not disrupted an empire for shortsighted and selfish reasons. Loyalists, who said that the prosperity of the empire outweighed the risks of resistance, were the selfish ones. A revolutionary satirist could put their outlook into one tory question: "What has poster'ty done for us?"[13] In *Common Sense*, Thomas Paine warned that delaying war would make independence harder for posterity to win. A loyalist replied, "Are we to precipitate ourselves into ruinous measures, because our remote descendants are to be involved in war? We may honestly answer no; whatever political quacks allege to the contrary in support of their criminal designs."[14] To this Paine had an answer in "The American Crisis," Number I: "The heart that feels not now is dead; the blood of his children will curse his cowardice, who shrinks back at a time when a little might have saved the whole, and made *them* happy."[15]

If the revolutionaries shirked their climactic duty, they would suffer the same eternal scorn they cast onto the tories. Samuel Adams liked to quote Saint Paul: "If any man love not the Lord Jesus Christ, let him be anathema."[16] Soldiers writing to their wives could be flamboyant, like Anthony Wayne—"I expect my little son will not turn aside from virtue, though the path should be marked with his father's Blood"—or plain, like Lieutenant Samuel Cooper, who was killed at Quebec—"the Dangers we are to Encounter I no not but it Shall never be Said to my Children your father was a Coward."[17] When we read of the small numbers of men involved in revolutionary military campaigns and political controversies—there were only two and one-half million Americans in 1775—we should remember that the participants often felt the presence of tens of millions more and looked at their own conduct through the eyes of the unborn.

While such self-conscious pride throve on material sacrifice and on the difficulties of resistance to Britain, it did not achieve or even try for perfect altruism toward posterity. The revolutionaries got much pleasure and inspiration from imagining their children's gratitude for their service in the decisive years. Of course, each generation had to defend self-government anew, but the revolutionary generation knew that they would stand above all their descendants. A song copied into the orderly book of the Second New York Regiment proclaimed, "The riseing world shall sing of us a thousand years to Come/ And tell our Childrens Children the Wonders we have Done."[18] During the war, when officers started to resign, General Robert Howe reminded them that they were "actors upon that glorious stage where every incident is to become an historical fact."[19]

Diverse revolutionaries thought about becoming the historians of the memorable events they were making, and people wrote at least as much about historians to come as about historians whose works were at hand. According to the revolutionaries, nineteenth- and twentieth-century Americans could not fail to record that the country owed its freedom, its flourishing commerce, its agricultural bounty, and its advanced arts to the unequaled sacrifices of the revolution. These future historians would describe in detail the hardships and temptations that their revolutionary ancestors had faced and the strength of character that had brought victory. Even poetry celebrated the histories yet to be written:

> Historic truth our guardian chiefs proclaim,
> Their worth, their actions, and their deathless fame;
> Admiring crouds their life-touch'd forms behold
> In breathing canvass, or in sculptur'd gold.[20]

The Americans who opposed Britain clearly expected their posterity to revere them even more than they revered their own ancestors. To the revolutionaries, the struggle for independence was the greatest test of the chosen people. In it they bore the weight of both their heritage and God's promise for the future. Their responsibility for preserving freedom gave them unique stature, which they saw to best advantage when reflected in the eyes of their children. An undergraduate orator, recalling *Henry V*, predicted that "posterity shall hold their manhood cheap, to think that they had no share in shaking off the yoke of British tyranny."[21] For succeeding at great cost, the revolutionaries exacted tribute in advance from their uncomplaining descendants. But in 1776, or even in 1780, the revolutionaries had not succeeded yet. In this fact we can see one important reason for their dramatization of their own momentousness. To detect a conspiracy for enslavement in British imperial administration required a keen sense of both the importance and the vulnerability of liberty. However, to be sensitive enough to fear slavery did not necessarily make a people strong enough to defeat it. To resist Britain's malevolence and power, Americans needed to believe that resistance could succeed. They expressed this belief and perhaps revealed some of their fears by saying not just that resistance could succeed but that success was inevitable.

At the beginning of the war, Americans' pride had strong enemies. The British army called the colonials a chickenhearted race of farmers, dry goods dealers, and slave drivers. The common boasts said that ten thousand or five thousand or one thousand British troops could march through the continent at will. According to Benjamin Franklin, a General Clarke—probably Thomas Clarke, the king's aide-de-camp—said in 1774 that with one thousand grenadiers he would go through America "and geld all the Males, partly by force and partly by a little Coaxing."[22]

If anyone held a lower opinion of the revolutionary forces than the British did, it was a group of Americans—the loyalists. Like the revolutionaries, the loyalists believed that the imperial crisis grew out of a conspiracy—not among the friends of the king and his ministers, but among a small faction of republicans in the colonies who had traitorous allies in England. To make money and to wield power outside the law, this cabal, according to the loyalists, had fomented discord for ten years before hostilities began. The loyalists trusted that at last, in clear conflict, the rebels would be forced to see their own weakness. Mobs might disrupt government at times, but they could not face an army. And loyalists called the revolutionary army a mob: "A vagabond Army of Raggamuffins, with Paper Pay, bad Cloathes, and worse Spirits."[23] Whether the men were farmers, mechanics, convicts, servants, apprentices, Irishmen, Negroes, or broken European adventurers, they were a joke. A loyalist woman recalled, "Our teachers became officers in the rebel army, and everywhere the scum rose to the top."[24] According to a New Hampshire man, "*John Congress* could not give a Commission worth a snap or a fart."[25] An officer is born; a soldier is made—no amount of rum, target practice, and Presbyterian cant about liberty could overcome the defects of being a rebel and a coward. Years of columns in James Rivington's *Royal Gazette* were summarized by one of his hawkers, who walked the streets of New York, shouting in a bass voice, "Bloody news! bloody news! bloody news! Where are the rebels *now*?"[26]

Americans respected the strength of the British army. The word "regular" first meant British soldiers; only later in the war did it refer to Continentals. The revolutionaries sometimes scorned their enemy's dissolute officers and degraded privates, but when such men marched under orders, Americans feared them. The army's cohesion and power seemed to make it a fit engine of tyranny. Moreover, the revolutionaries could not feel sure that the British were wrong about colonials. After all, Americans *were* farmers, tradesmen, mechanics, and planters —not soldiers—and they wanted to remain so. The implied contrast was clear when General Daniel Roberdeau of the Pennsylvania militia warned his men, "The English army derive all their strength from a close attention to discipline, with them it supplies the want of virtue."[27] Americans might have virtue, but did they have or could they face the special strength that hundreds of years of war seemed to confer on Europeans? This question plagued the revolutionaries longer than the events of the war seemed to require. Well after Americans had survived the march of tens of thousands of British soldiers, shot many, and captured more, the former colonials wondered whether their freedom from British corruption and despotism left them weak before their enemies—"inhumane butchers, who have come above 3000 miles to destroy their neighbours that are more righteous than they!"[28]

What, for example, did the battles of Lexington and Concord and Bunker Hill prove? According to the revolutionaries, British troops—who had been stationed in Boston for seven years —marched into the country to seize military stores and rebel leaders. They shot some of the armed citizens who stood in their way, whereupon hundreds of men drove the troops back to Boston and thousands kept them there when they tried to come out again, killing many by good aim from under cover. This showed that Americans would fight. Did it not also refute the British contempt for colonial prowess? Did it not show that Americans using their wits could match the masters of military tricks? Many revolutionaries said so in 1775, but few remained confident of it for long, and those who did had to keep reminding themselves that it was true. Contrary to the widespread praise of Americans' quick mastery of essential military discipline, many of the celebrations of the first battles stressed the destruction wrought among regulars by undisciplined freemen. When Lewis Nicola published *A Treatise of Military Exercise, Calculated for the Use of the Americans* in 1776, he counseled against "pitched battles with veteran troops" and commended the use of "woods and swampy grounds," even "our fences," from which Americans could harass the enemy "on all sides day and night, officers and men killed or wounded without perceiving their enemies." The discipline required to learn showy maneuvers would be cruel and impolitic for "men, who, compelled by the unhappy state of the times, take up arms to defend their liberties, with a design to lay them down as soon as the end proposed is obtained."[29] But it was one thing to use cover to fight; it was another thing to need cover to fight. Even in these first battles, some colonists faced British soldiers at short range or hand-to-hand. Still, British officers said that cover meant cowardice, and Americans suspected that cover concealed weakness.

Although reluctant to admit it, Americans feared British power early in the war. Against the hope that liberty would strengthen its defenders stood the certainty that tyranny wielded all the resources of cruelty and corruption. Before 1776 was over, the revolutionaries showed that they felt much less enthusiasm for war than for independence. Their celebration of the fighting virtues of freemen could not dispel their fear that freemen's conduct might prove less reliable than the discipline of mercenaries. The soldier who had the freedom to hide behind fences and trees also had the freedom to flee. Tyrants used professional armies because professionalism had proven its effectiveness in destroying liberty. In calling Americans to face tested enemies while relying on unproven resources, the revolution required a great risk. The revolutionaries, though they seldom discussed the risk, saw it and tried to promote confidence that it could be overcome. They had little choice because securing a government based on popular ability to preserve liberty entailed an even greater and longer lasting risk. Facing the British army would be only the necessary prelude.

One source of the revolutionaries' confidence lay in their obedience to God. A religious vocabulary voiced many of the calls to serve in the Continental Army and to promote its cause. A belief in God's design for the future of America and in His governance over the life of the individual influenced most Americans' understanding of their activities. Explanations of conduct that today might use the language of secular morality or psychology then depended on religious teachings for clarity and conviction.

According to American ministers, war was a sin and a product of sin. God permitted it and guided it for the improvement of His people. In practice, this meant that Britons sinned in waging war, while Americans suffered the consequences of war because of their own sins, which notably did not include their resistance to parliamentary taxation and legislation. We read of sinners provoking God with the usual vices, but not of rebels provoking Parliament. By this distinction, the revolutionaries tried to absolve themselves of responsibility for causing the evils that they saw in war. Theirs were domestic, civilian sins. The king and his ministers purposefully sought war. Crimes of violence lay on their heads.

In contrast, loyalists kept saying that "Rebellion according to Scripture is, as the Sin of witchcraft."[30] To rebel was to compact with the devil to overthrow legitimate authority. Americans took pains to disavow the word, applying it to the British and to the loyalists, who were "Rebels against Liberty" and against God.[31] In 1779, Luke Swetland fell in with some soldiers on the road near Appleton, New York. "I asked them if the rebels were near." A sergeant answered. "'God damn you,' said he, 'do you call us rebels?'" Swetland saw his mistake and backed off. "I said 'no I mean the army that is coming.'"[32] For themselves, Americans took the word "revolution" and declared that their revolution would drive Satan out of America, not make deals with him. Rebellion was squalid, selfish, and sinful; revolution promised happiness. In "A Military Song by the Army: On General Washington's victorious entry into the Town of BOSTON," the soldiers said to the departing British,

"Like Satan banished from HEAVEN,
Never see, the smiling shore,
From this land so happy, driven,
Never Stain, its bosom more."[33]

In 1775 revolutionaries pointed not to rebellion but to other, long-standing causes for God's displeasure. No one could doubt the Apostle James when he said, "From whence come wars and fightings among you? come they not hence, even of your lusts that war in your members?"[34] Man was born with sin. Indeed, he willfully preferred it in his natural state and never escaped it during his earthly life. He must always work to overcome it. He achieved assurance that he would be free from it in a future life only when God gave that assurance as a gift to those whom He had chosen. They did not deserve the gift, but they got it because God loved them and wanted them to love each other. The guilt for making war lay on the heads of the British. Both peoples were guilty: Americans were guilty of many sins, but only Britons were guilty of war. God intended His punishment of war-makers only for Britons, and He entrusted its execution to Americans. In discharging this trust, Americans might also correct their own vices, which had brought them to this extremity.

This explanation obviously allowed only one outcome—American victory. Americans gave little sign that they could think themselves so sinful that God would permit Britain not just to humble them in adversity but to reduce them. How could that happen when Britain was the source of many of the corruptions that tainted America? In the years before the war, Americans saw with growing clarity that Britain not only shared mankind's common sinfulness but perpetuated a corrupt society and government, which the British ministry now was systematically fostering in America.[35] Americans could expect that "the least officer employed for the regulation of trade, and about the collection of *Revenue* will soon be a formidable *magistrate*, with a stipend of four or five hundred sterling a year: And offices and salaries increased, as fast as millions of American slaves increase, and can *earn* for them with sweat and hard labour."[36] In fact, all public offices paying five pounds a year or more would go to Englishmen.[37] The king would make Americans "perpetual soldiers if he pleases, to . . . hold their native land in subjection to proud and imperious lords."[38] Instead of striving to overcome sin, the ministry promoted it in order to corrupt Americans and to make them slaves. The revolutionaries heard the warning, "Remember the corrupt, putrefied state of that nation, and the virtuous, sound, healthy state of your own young constitution. Remember the tyranny of Mezentius, who bound living men face to face with dead ones, and the effect of it."[39] Revolutionaries did not usually say that all vice in America came from the influence of Britain and its agents the loyalists, but they could not believe—and could rarely even imagine—that God meant to subjugate them. Having chosen them to exemplify the way He wanted people to live together on earth, God would not give them into the hands of men who were collaborating in the spread of tyranny throughout the world. Thus the expectation of sure victory helped both to offset fears of weakness and to avoid guilt for making war. By promising Americans victory, God tacitly forgave them for both fearing and killing their enemies. War could not be criminal because the alternative—acceding to enslavement—was worse.

American war-making seemed to differ morally from British war-making and served a godly purpose because Americans said that they fought for self-preservation. The British army was attacking Americans, who surely had the right to defend themselves. The gospels do not contain many guides for Christian self-defense; American preachers therefore preferred to invoke the great law of nature—self-preservation—which God had instilled in man. "Self" meant the Americans as a people as well as the individual American. The British attack made the Americans' common interest in union and in personal effort seem clear. "Preservation"—the most common and most formally expounded term—differs implicitly from "defense," although Americans used both words. One might defend oneself and lose and yet survive. But if one failed at self-preservation, nothing was left. "Tyranny operates like an opiate, stilling the powers of li[f]e and checking the sallies of the mind."[40] A New Jersey minister warned that even if the British occupied the continent, there would follow "inward convulsions, struggles, and attempts for freedom, till we were either ruined or set free."[41] One who knew the value of freedom and failed to defend it committed what General Nathanael Greene called "spiritual suicide."[42] Only convulsive resistance could save Americans from killing themselves morally by succumbing to the drug of corruption that Britain was spreading everywhere. Surviving in body could not palliate enslavement. If Britain suppressed Americans' minds and spirits, they would be dead in their true self. The revolutionaries could look ahead and see that victorious British tyranny would eventually control their own and their children's lives and estates. But before then it would have overcome their ability to envision and choose the right way toward a different and far better future. This attack on the mind was the immediate threat behind routine taxes, coercive legislation, and imperial corruption. A delegate in Congress wrote, "To be or not to be is now the Question."[43]

Most revolutionary spokesmen believed that service in the Continental Army had a clear religious meaning for the soldier.[44] A recruit could enlist in two armies at once—the Continental Army for the salvation of his country and Christ's army for the salvation of his soul. Stopping the British and the tories from enslaving America, he would also escape the bondage of his soul to sin. The mental habits customary in evangelical religion suited a volunteer army well by emphasizing an individual's responsibility not only for his own soul but also for his proper service to the communal welfare. This responsibility, rather than a draft, told the private that he must serve. Failure to volunteer would mean an awful weight of guilt, like that which each man knew he bore for his wayward soul: "To shun the dangers of the field is to desert the banner of Christ."[45] The consequences of such failure would be public—enslavement of the community after the British army had ravaged it. But the fault would be his—to live with, in private, in the presence of his children, whom he had betrayed. A man could not be saved amid the ruin of his community, a ruin that he had helped to cause. Nor could a man be saved as his community prospered despite his inaction. He could hardly keep it a secret; he could never hide it from God or from himself.

A chaplain addressing six battalions of soldiers at Fort Ticonderoga while the enemy was near turned all God's promises into curses for anyone who fled:

> Let him be abhorred by all the United States of America.
> Let faintness of heart and fear never forsake him on earth. . . .
> Let him be cursed in all his connexions, 'till his *wretched* head with dishonour is laid low in the dust; and let all the soldiers say, *Amen*.

Lieutenant Rufus Wheeler called it "the finest discourse ever I heard." At the end of the sermon, the soldiers "gave three cheers which made a beautiful show."[46]

The most common and vivid religious appeal to the soldier portrayed the future that his efforts would secure and that he would enjoy. This vision rewarded his individual responsibility. The American soldier, unlike British derelicts and Hessian mercenaries, faced the invaders by an act of free choice and beat them. As the viciousness of sin lay in the sinner's wish to sin, so the virtue of service lay in his desire to serve. When God called, men would find that they loved their country; that their wills were not paralyzed by British corruption or coerced by British force; that this choice, this love, this zeal came from the regenerate will of one of the chosen. The rewards of service were clear. All knew that it might end in death. Death of any kind was better than slavery. Death in obedience to God and in service to the public meant a soul at peace. Soldiers were supposed to prize glory, and the Continental Army heard many promises of immortal earthly glory for their exploits. Christian soldiers could be confident of a greater and lasting glory after death.

The evangelical appeal worked on the revolutionary as much by its psychology as by its doctrine. Did a man have the courage to seek individual and national redemption through struggle with evil? This was a test in which few were willing to acknowledge failure. A former soldier, back in his hometown, joined the church. Two weeks before joining he had made the crucial decision to see the minister and to take communion: "But Alas what oppertions did I meet with from the Divil and my Corrupt and wicked Hart to that degree that I had thots of turning back but Considering how unsoldierlike it was to turn back I went forward."[47]

Religious and political appeals to the soldier combined the forces of the two most powerful prevailing explanations by which revolutionaries understood events. The conspiracy of tyrants threatened a whole people with subjection; the incentive to resist came not only from the political threat to the citizenry but also from the spiritual danger to any person who collaborated with oppressors or even failed to resist them strongly enough. By the time war came, the religious call to seek salvation had taken on a political concern for the welfare of America and liberty. At the same time, the effort to secure liberty had acquired the emotional urgency of a test of righteousness. The Christian whig strove for the welfare of his country because such striving promised blessings to both his people and his soul. On July 4, 1779, Chaplain William Rogers wrote in his journal, "Ten o'clock. Preached to the brigade and regiment of artillery; being the anniversary of the declaration of American Independence, took notice of the same in my sermon. . . . The discourse was concluded nearly as follows: Politically as a nation are we exhorted to trust in the Lord. God hath hitherto blessed our arms and smiled on our infant rising states. . . . Let us still under the banners of liberty, and with a Washington for our head, go on from conquering to conquer. Hark! what voice is that which I hear? It is the voice of encouragement; permit me for your animation to repeat it distinctly: 'Our fathers trusted and the Lord did deliver them; they cried unto Him and were delivered; they trusted in Him and were not confounded.' Even so may it be with us, for the sake of Christ Jesus, who came to give Freedom to the world."[48]

Both those who admired the American Protestant ministry

and those who ridiculed it could agree that preachers carried the revolution to large numbers of Americans. In Boston, Major Harry Rooke of the British army confiscated a religious book that a clergyman had given to American prisoners taken at Bunker Hill. Rooke said, "It is your G—d damned Religion of this Country that ruins the Country; Damn your Religion."[49] If we believed the British and the loyalists, we would picture a gullible public whose superstitions were manipulated by hucksters. Ambrose Serle reported to the earl of Dartmouth that one preacher "told his Congregation, that 'the Man, who was able in this Country to wield a Sword and did not endeavor to stain it with the Blood of the King's Soldiers and their Abettors, would be renounced by the Lord Jesus Xt at the Day of Judgement.' Your Lordship can scarcely conceive, what Fury the Discourses of some mad Preachers have created in this Country."[50]

But revolutionaries were not priest-ridden; nor did they obey—or even admire—a minister just because he was a minister. They obeyed God, and they wanted to hear a preacher movingly and convincingly set forth God's plan as they understood it.[51] Congress and the government of South Carolina sent preachers into the up-country of the Carolinas to explain the war. But most people probably knew the religious meaning of Britain's attack and America's future by heart. Private Simeon Lyman, on the march to Massachusetts in August 1775, evaluated a minister by standards that Lyman had developed before hearing the sermon: "We staid at Litchfield. . . . There we had a sermon preached to us by Mr. Bellowmy which I think I never heard outdone by anybody in my life for liberty."[52] Listeners wanted to hear what they ought to do now—how God's plan was to be served in the immediate crisis. Corporal Amos Farnsworth heard William Emerson preach on April 30, 1775, and commented, "An Exelent Sermon he incoridged us to go And fite for our Land and Contry: Saying we Did not do our Duty if we did not Stand up now."[53]

Perhaps even more important, Americans wanted to experience the communal sympathy that flowed from and that blessed virtue. These celebrations relieved a person from the isolation of his personal responsibility while they reminded him that he still bore it and rewarded him for his steadfastness. On Thursday, July 20, 1775—a Continental fast day known as "Congress Sunday"—revolutionaries were warmed by the fact that millions of people covering thousands of miles were worshipping God, seeking His aid, and dedicating themselves to American liberty, all in unison.[54] One young minister, who preached to a large throng in Pennsylvania, recorded his feelings: "I spoke in great Fear and Dread—I was never before so nice an Audience —I never spoke on so solemn a Day—In spight of all my Fortitude and Practice, when I begun, my Lip's quivered; my Flesh shrunk, my Hair rose up; my Knees trembled—I was wholly confused, til' I had almost closed the Sermon. Perhaps this Feeling was occasioned by entirely Fasting, as I had taken nothing."[55] Sermons addressed not torpor but anxiety. Ministers were not creating a crisis for their congregations but trying to help people resolve a crisis that almost everyone could feel. In the midst of a British assault on American liberty, preachers faced their congregations' unspoken question: "What must we do to be saved?" We can infer that the urgency of Americans' distress encouraged ministers to provide strong, plain answers. The threat to liberty, the danger of complicity with evil, demanded righteous resistance by every Christian. The more emphatically a preacher drew this necessary lesson from the crisis, the more fully he attained the stature of spokesman for God's message. *Common Sense* could achieve wide popularity not because Americans had previously been unaware of royal oppression but because the pamphlet offered a resolution of anxieties. Opposition to British tyranny, fear of British soldiers, hatred of British corruption, grief over American casualties at British hands—a welter of compounded, growing distresses —could find resolution in one clear message: American independence. Similarly, ministers' call to resistance found a wide response to its clarity. But just as American independence created new problems and anxieties beyond the ones it resolved, so the ministers' clarity made any failure to fight all the more criminal. In answering the question of what to do, the religious teachings of the revolution intensified the critical question of whether one had done his duty.

If the revolutionaries had a problem with their preachers, it was the inadequacy of many ministers in the face of public expectations. The black-robed regiment had too many dullards in it, too many men who read their sermons or spoke without animating people enough. Scholars have suggested that some of these men were social conservatives who wanted to restrain emotional excess or were theoreticians more interested in ideas of divinity than in people's experiences.[56] Much more commonly, perhaps, the failing was the unwitting handicap of men who surely meant well to the cause and tried hard to serve it. The revolution moved Americans so deeply that many of its spokesmen could not equal their subject. William Tennent wrote in his diary: "Preached extempore with more ease and freedom than common. . . . I gave them a discourse upon the American dispute of near three hours; I think I was more animated and demonstrative than usual. Its effect was very visible, the people holding a profound silence for more than a minute after I was done." But even after such effective labor, he lay awake all night, brooding: "Anxiety of mind on account of the madness of the opponents of liberty robbed me of sleep until break of day."[57] Inadequate speakers always disappoint their hearers; but in this conflict between slavery and freedom—when the future depended on the work of one generation, when each person had to feel the call yet wondered whether he could meet it—in a crisis so profound and dangerous, the revolutionaries wanted special signs that they were united. Chaplain Israel Evans paused in one of his sermons to cry, "O for glowing words! words from warm and glowing hearts! for words from lukewarm hearts can never ascend to heaven! Incense must be inflamed before it can rise to the skies!"[58] Americans wanted to feel themselves triumphing together. Then they could witness the union of their voluntary efforts, appreciate its magnitude, and anticipate its success. It is small wonder that a preacher facing these expectations might fall short, even while he encouraged them.

The preachers' call to voluntary resistance relied on two related ideas that most Americans shared and that evangelical religion presented most emphatically: benevolence and disinterestedness. Today when we hear that a person or a deed is benevolent, we usually think of a benign charity that is admirable for its goodwill. To understand benevolence during the revolution, we should think of unselfish love, of active concern for others, of eager work for the welfare of all. It was not easy to be benevolent, for Christian benevolence was not supposed to be occasional good works or even constant good intentions. It was to be a new and lasting disposition of the regenerate heart, whereby a person forswore sinful self-love and willingly, instinctively loved others, seeking their well-being at all times. Nathaniel Whitaker explained, "Every soldier should enter the field with benevolent, tender, compassionate sentiments, which is the temper of Jesus Christ. . . . These are no more inconsistent in a soldier engaging in battle, and doing his best to kill his enemies, than they are in a judge and executioner, who takes away a murderer from the earth. . . . As benevolence is the source of vindictive laws in the state, so it should ever be of defensive war; and they both tend to the same end, the happiness of mankind."[59]

Closely linked to benevolence was the idea of disinterestedness. The word "interest" was used as we use it in the term "self-interest." When a person did a disinterested act, he stood to gain nothing by it. The fullest beauty of the revolutionaries' benevolence lay in its freedom from any taint of personal profit. Americans knew how often selfishness guided people, and they knew how many devious motives concealed themselves behind generosity. Even as they called each other to thwart such motives, they did not expect universal success. But they did judge themselves according to their ideal of disinterested benevolence. Sometimes this meant extravagant self-praise for routine acts of public service; more often it meant unease as people sought the certainty that they loved individuals, their country, and mankind, free from corruption wrought by self.

To describe the state of mind the revolutionaries wished to preserve and to make characteristically American, they most often used the word "virtue." As with most widely used abstractions, it came to people's lips so readily and so often that it did not always carry a precise meaning. By the time of the revolution it had become a vogue word, even a cliché, for expressing any general approval of somebody's views or conduct. But beneath this inflation, the word had value for Americans. The main qualities of virtue were restraint and sacrifice. The virtuous person avoided excess in prosperity and did not sell out in adversity. At all times the virtuous person gave up private advantage for the welfare of others or the welfare of the whole community. This attitude assumed not unassailable purity but steady self-conscious choices by each citizen.

Benevolence, disinterestedness, virtue—these strengths gave revolutionaries the promise of defeating British conspiracy. American independence would remain secure as long as its defenders possessed these strengths. In fact, the appeals prevalent at the opening of the revolution put benevolence, disinterestedness, and virtue at the heart of American national character. And the military enthusiasm that spread through the continent in 1774 and 1775 became the first and most important way for Americans to demonstrate this strength of character. Universal readiness for armed combat had become not simply a military necessity for self-defense or a temporary resort to a rare form of battlefield valor. Rather, political writers, orators, and preachers—responding to the public's desire for a righteous course of action in the face of corrupt conspiracy—founded liberty and independence on Americans' self-sacrificing courage.

On September 16, 1775, a detached command of more than one thousand volunteers from Continental Army units arrived in Newburyport, Massachusetts. On September 19 they sailed for the mouth of the Kennebec River in Maine, from which they would march overland to attack Quebec. Before leaving Newburyport, the troops paraded in general review for the citizens on Sunday, September 17. One soldier said, "We passed the review with much honor to ourselves. We manifested great zeal and animation in the cause of liberty and went through with the manual exercise with much alacrity. The spectators, who were very numerous, appeared much affected." That same day the soldiers worshipped in the First Presbyterian Church on King Street, later renamed Federal Street. Citizens filled the galleries. The soldiers marched into the church with colors flying and drums beating. They formed two lines and presented arms. As the drums rolled, Chaplain Samuel Spring walked between the lines to the pulpit. The men stacked their arms in the aisles, and Spring preached extemporaneously on the words of Moses to the Lord, "If thy spirit go not with us, carry us not up hence."

Beneath them as they worshipped lay the tomb of George Whitefield, who had been the voice of the Great Awakening. More than any other man, Whitefield, with his preaching, had introduced Americans to the joys of a communal revival of piety and a sharing of the conversion experience on a continental scale. After Spring's sermon, some of the officers gathered around him, and they decided to visit Whitefield's tomb. They found the sexton and went down to the coffin. The officers got the sexton to take off the lid. After five years the body had decayed, but some of the clothes remained. The officers took Whitefield's collar and wristbands, cut them in little pieces, divided the pieces, and carried them away.

In the following weeks, the expedition withstood the hardest march of the war—350 miles of wilderness in forty-five days. Some starved to death along the route; three companies turned back; but six hundred men made it. Despite the defeat and disease they suffered before Quebec, they earned great praise for themselves and their commander, Colonel Benedict Arnold.[60]

CHAPTER I

1775: *Rage Militaire*

From the Battle of Lexington to the Declaration of Independence, all kinds of military exercises, uniforms, and threats aimed at the British enjoyed a wide vogue among Americans. A letter from Philadelphia assured the British that "the Rage Militaire, as the French call a passion for arms, has taken possession of the whole Continent."[1] Although commitment to American independence grew during the war, this popular *rage militaire* vanished by the end of 1776 and never returned. Even in 1776 it was a weak echo of its loudest moments in 1775. Months before the Lexington and Concord skirmishes, Americans had begun militia drills to prepare for armed resistance. As mobilization progressed, they enthusiastically celebrated the citizens' rapidly acquired skill in the manual of arms and in field maneuvers. An observer who believed what he heard would have concluded that the survival of liberty depended on widespread voluntary submission to military discipline.

After war began, the Continental Army, most of which besieged Boston until March 1776, became the focus of Americans' announced determination to surpass the British in military prowess as in virtue. Two strengths, they claimed, ensured this superiority: Americans used only the essentials of drill without an intricate, unnecessary dumb show; and Americans possessed "natural" or "native" or "innate" courage.

The printed manuals of arms and evolutions that Americans used—especially Lewis Nicola's *Treatise of Military Exercise* and Timothy Pickering's "easy" plan, adapted from an English model—emphasized simplicity, not show, by using the fewest possible movements to load, fire, and maneuver. General Charles Lee assured Americans that they could dispense with "the tinsel and show of war" and learn the essentials—to load and fire, to form, to retreat, to advance, to change front, to rally by the colors, to reduce from a line of fire (two deep) to a line of impression (four, six, or eight deep)—all in three months.[2] The Massachusetts Council adopted Pickering's plan because it was not "cloged with many superfluous motions, which only serve to burthen the memory and perplex the Learner."[3] Americans, unlike the British, would aim their muskets. In all standard commands, the Continental Army and the state militias would show that intelligent purposefulness could overcome elaborate mechanical dexterity and the superstitious awe that made such techniques formidable. "Away then," Pickering wrote, "with the trappings (as well as tricks) of the parade: *Americans* need them not: *their* eyes are not to be dazzled, nor their hearts awed into servility, by the splendour of equipage and dress: *their* minds are too much enlightened to be duped by a glittering outside."[4]

The revolutionaries could not equal the complexity of British parade and decided they did not want to, but they greatly enjoyed what they had left. Judging from a few loyalist witnesses and from the long time it took the Continental Army to learn to drill, the countless town-square parades and maneuvers of 1775 must have looked pretty poor. In the *Virginia Gazette*, Robert Washington, who wanted a job training soldiers, acknowledged that Americans' early use of firearms, knowledge of the country, and "native Courage" made them superior in the woods. But he warned, "Let us not plume ourselves with this Conceit, that we shall always have the Bush to fight behind." He went to a muster to see "the *Prussian Exercise*, as they call it" but only saw men forming six deep, turning about-face, marching eighteen paces to the rear, opening ranks, and going through slow parade motions of prime and load—"you may call it *Prussian* Exercise if you please; but . . . to lead a Body of brave men, with such counterfeit Discipline, to face a disciplined Enemy, would, in my Opinion, be downright Murder."[5] After a North Carolina muster and review, a loyalist woman at a dinner party got Robert Howe—soon to be a Continental general—to read aloud to the guests a passage of Shakespeare that she had chosen. As he began to read, he saw that it was the description of Falstaff's farcical recruits. He turned red, but, like a gentleman and a soldier, he finished the passage.[6]

Reviews and drill attracted many spectators; Congress watched parade-ground evolutions on June 8, 1775. Companies drilled by moonlight. Boys between the ages of thirteen and sixteen volunteered. They were commended but turned away. Younger boys played soldier and organized their own companies for drill. One militiaman remembered 1775, the year of his thirteenth birthday: "I obtained a pamphlet in which this exercise was fully explained, according to the best system of the day, which was the Prussian. . . . I made myself so much a master, that I had the honour of standing before the company as *fugleman*."[7] Everywhere revolutionaries reported rapid progress in discipline. Not many men had uniforms, but those who had them wore them proudly and could read descriptions of themselves in the newspapers. One diarist noted, "Numbers who a few Days ago were plain Countrymen have now clothed themselves in martial Forms—Powdered Hair[—] Sharp pinched Beavers—Uniform in Dress with their Battalion —Swords on their Thighs—and stern in the Art of War."[8] Some people who saw reviews wrote that Americans were or soon would be equal to any troops in the world.

People could believe this, despite the shortcomings in drill that they must have seen, because they thought that American soldiers were courageous by nature. The Americans' claim to have native courage later became grounds for questioning the importance of the Continental Army, but in 1775 it made the army, with its growing discipline, the main representative of American resistance. The revolutionaries' courage was bolstered by their conviction that God had given them the ability to choose and the zeal to defend liberty for themselves and for mankind. Before "a large Audience" in Cumberland County, Pennsylvania, Robert Cooper praised men who were "learning the business of war. . . . Those who have endeavoured to maintain a character for piety, ought now to endeavour to distinguish themselves as brave soldiers. . . . Shall (says Nehemiah) such a man as I flee?"[9] Revolutionaries felt sure that against such strength the British could muster only the artificial courage of force, pay, and rote, while the loyalists had no courage at all.

Far from conflicting with discipline, this native courage helped make the first awkward but energetic maneuvers seem promising. Revolutionaries could look at green recruits and see proficient soldiers because these soldiers' hearts sought freedom. In February 1776, an address drafted in Congress "To the Inhabitants of the Colonies" explained that "Our Troops are animated with the Love of Freedom. . . . We confess that they have not the Advantages arising from Experience and Discipline: But Facts have shewn, that native Courage warmed with Patriotism, is sufficient to counterbalance these Advantages."[10] For about a year most Americans found the spirit of resistance best exemplified in volunteers' eagerness to become good soldiers. Driving the British back from Lexington and Concord and making them pay so much blood for Breed's Hill seemed to confirm that native courage went far to make a good soldier.

Both the English Commonwealth political tradition and the evangelical call to arms rested the crucial defense of liberty and moral rectitude on the individual citizen's eagerness to fight for them in person.[11] The aspiration to achieve a joint salvation of soul and country, the refusal to hide behind corruptible mercenary soldiers, made war the proof of Americans' moral as well as physical survival. However, no American would have argued that he was born sanctified. He was born sinful. Even after God gave him grace, life remained a struggle against his own propensity to sin. No proponent of Americans' civic virtue would have argued that people were naturally virtuous. Constant vigilance against corruption could alone defeat the inevitable tendency of power to erode liberty—a tendency to which people were prone to submit for their own ease unless they constantly kept the public interest foremost in their minds.

Yet Americans called themselves innately courageous. Even if we discount much of the talk as rhetoric designed to inspire resistance and to influence the British, most evidence suggests that a great majority of Americans wanted to believe it. On July 17, 1775, Reverend Philip Vickers Fithian walked into Martin's tavern in Northumberland, Pennsylvania, to read the newspapers. He found "Dr. Plunket and three other Gentlemen" talking about two recent sermons—John Carmichael's *A Self-Defensive War Lawful*, preached on June 4, and William Smith's *Sermon on the Present Situation of American Affairs*, preached on June 23. One of the men said, "D——n the Sermons, Smith's and all. . . . Gunpowder and Lead shall be our Text and Sermon both." According to Fithian, "The Dr . . . gave him a severe Reprooff."[12] People urgently wanted to believe that they had the strength to secure freedom, no matter what the threat. The wartime emphasis on a test of military prowess took Americans beyond the strict formulations of their religious and political ideas—they claimed an innate ability to meet that test. Their anxiety exceeded their intellectual consistency. The man who heard the call to arms with secret fear need not wonder whether he could meet it if he could confidently rely on an inborn courage. However, in seeking to spare him doubt, this claim of national bravery could heighten his isolation if his doubts persisted. Americans' religious and political ideas of duty emphasized the need for conscious choice to overcome constant threats to virtue. Revolutionaries knew that the choice was demanding and its success precarious. But if Americans were promised an innate strength that spared them the tension of conscious, fallible choice, how could the man who faltered, short of dying on the battlefield, reconcile his fallible conduct with his claim to patriotic courage?

Americans pressed their claim to native courage extravagantly because they went to war reluctantly. Resistance to British rule became widespread years before the war and grew stronger after hostilities began, and logic said that this meant war. But logic could not make Americans want to fight full-time. By 1776 they were not reluctant rebels, but they were reluctant warriors. For militia who were facing regulars, they showed great willingness and respectable competence in 1775. They certainly surprised the British. But the revolutionaries sought more: they sought a much-needed confidence to pursue war, which was alien to their vision of the country's future and to the daily life they preferred. To gain this confidence, they united a national conceit of born courage in combat with a sudden acclaim for a superior form of military discipline, easily acquired.

One of the earliest and most common public expressions of readiness for combat portrayed mothers, wives, sisters, and belles eagerly sending the men they loved to defeat the British or to die trying. Addresses to soldiers and appeals for recruits stressed the importance of protecting women from the invader. Newspapers gave special notice to groups of single women and mothers of four or more sons. The former supposedly announced that they would avoid men who shirked service: "Go act the hero, every danger face, / *Love hates a coward's impotent embrace*."[13] The latter sent all their sons to the Continental Army at once, asking not to hear of any deaths but by facing the enemy. Better that all should die than that one should return a coward.[14] People repeated these stories privately and liked to hear them. On October 2, 1775, the *New-York Gazette* told of girls at a Kinderhook quilting frolic who stripped a young tory man to his waist and tarred and feathered him with molasses and weeds. Ten days later outside Boston, Daniel McCurtin, a Maryland rifleman, copied the story into his journal.[15] A soldiers' song ran:

> A Soldier is a Gentleman his honour is his life
> And he that wont Stand by his post will Ne[']er
> Stand by his Wife . . .
> In Shady Tents and Cooling Streams with hearts all firm and Free
> We'll Chase Away the Cares of Life in Songs of Liberty . . .
> So Fare you Well you Sweethearts you Smileing girls Adieu
> For when the war is Over We'll Kiss it out with you. . . .[16]

Revolutionaries were proud that women showed support for the war as spectators at drills and parades. They even liked to say that women demanded resistance more vigorously and unitedly than men did. After the Battle of Trenton, a corporal among the Hessian prisoners described their arrival in Philadelphia: "The old women howled dreadfully, and wanted to throttle us all, because we had come to America to rob them of their freedom."[17] Popular accounts told of women who formed military-style companies to display their patriotism or who put on the uniform or who showed the valor of a soldier in a critical moment. Women's willingness to sacrifice would match the native courage of men in the field. Selfishness, worry, and reluctance would vanish amid spontaneous dedication. Not only would women's inspiration encourage men's valor, but women's valor would threaten the weak man with an ignominious contrast.

The war rhetoric of 1775 might look like only a mixture of typical exaggeration and unavoidable ignorance of coming difficulties. After the surrender of Burgoyne in 1777 and of Cornwallis in 1781, Americans recalled how unprepared they had been and how undisciplined the army was in the first year of the war. Yet throughout the war they called for a revival of the spirit of 1775. Even as they failed at, then overcame, difficulties of recruitment, supply, and discipline, they tested their feeble steps and small, gradual successes by the standard of 1775, when, according to the rhetoric of the *rage militaire*, every breast had felt military ardor and every lip had spoken words of self-sacrifice.

Instead of understanding the exaggerations of 1775 as one of the difficulties they had overcome, the revolutionaries kept saying, in effect, If we can accomplish this much despite the weakened public spirit of 1777 or 1778 or 1779, imagine how much more we could do if we had the universal patriotism of 1775. The early discussion of the conduct and the motives of the Continental Army and its relations with the public formed a set of guiding ideas and emotions to which most Americans recurred long after the army itself had altered or abandoned them in practice.

One group of these ideas and emotions defined death. As everyone heard, the choice was liberty or death. Revolutionaries talked much more vividly about the nature and consequences of British enslavement than about the details of death by resistance. The one brought perpetual base submission to the tyrant and his lackeys, enervating the individual's will. The other brought a perpetual afterlife glorified, variously, by the beauties of songs, flowers, and angels, the company of classical deities and geniuses, heroes of antiquity, and saints and martyrs, and the sound of grateful praise by generations of free Americans. A funeral orator in Massachusetts said of a soldier's corpse, "There sleeps (he seems even now to smile in death) a friend of America, a friend to his mother country, the world's friend as far as his charity could reach. . . . Who, that hath worth and merit, would not quit a present uncertain life to live eternally in the memory of present and future ages?"[18] Liberty or death was not a rhetorical exaggeration when the choice referred to the revolutionaries' minds. British slavery would end the earthly ability to imagine the future and choose the way toward it as much as a British musket ball would. Slavery meant an infinite, hereditary misery, while death in resistance meant bliss.

Early in the war, Americans, especially revolutionary leaders, talked freely about large numbers of casualties. The revolutionaries argued not only that death in a glorious cause was rewarding and that risking death was imperative, but also that they did not fear death. They would, according to the spirit of 1775, rush to the field of combat, eager to conquer or to die: "A spirit of enthusiasm for war is gone forth, that has driven away the fear of death."[19] When the deaths came—usually by disease amid filth—the revolutionaries proved as good as their word. The first anniversary of the Declaration of Independence was celebrated with the toast, "May only those Americans enjoy freedom who are ready to die for its defence."[20] To be free required a man to risk death. What proved hard was living in the presence of death—that is, not only serving but surviving to serve further. Americans offered the Continental Army a dual immortality: heaven and posthumous fame. They were far less eloquent about, and often seemed less interested in, the intervening period of service. Revolutionaries enjoyed personal freedom and the liberty of immediate self-government. In their mind's eye, they lived vicariously for centuries in their country's happy future. But while living in the presence of the enemy, whether he was slavery or death, the revolutionaries found that their vision of a clear choice between liberty and death was an insufficient guide to conduct. We should recall that when Patrick Henry declaimed, "Give me liberty or give me death," the death to which he referred was suicide.[21] Dramatizing the choice could encourage men to fight, because the loss of liberty meant the loss of life as surely as in combat. But dramatizing the choice might also oversimplify the revolutionary's alternatives: triumph or despair. Neither living nor dying in the cause of liberty proved so uncomplicated and easy as the ideals of 1775 announced. A revolutionary would need sources of strength besides native courage or would suffer for the lack of them.

Captain Joseph Jewett found it so as he took thirty-six hours to die of bayonet wounds in his chest and stomach after the Battle of Long Island. On the last morning, he "was sensible of being near his End, often Repeating that it was hard work to Die."[22] In one of the battles of Saratoga, Captain John Henry, Patrick Henry's son, distinguished himself in combat. Afterward he walked among the American dead, pausing to recognize men he had known. Then he drew his sword, broke it, threw it on the ground, and raved, mad. Nine months later, his "ill state of Health," according to Washington, caused him to resign his commission.[23]

We can see part of the revolutionaries' attitude toward killing in their celebration of the rifle and their special fondness for riflemen. Out of the west came tall men dressed in rifle shirts—also known as hunting shirts—and armed with long, grooved barrels on their weapons. Their bullets hit targets the size of playing cards, oranges, noses, and faces at 60 or 100 or 150 or 200 yards, without fail. According to John Adams, "They have Sworn certain death to the ministerial officers."[24] The British were said to fear them so much that every Continental soldier might wear a rifle shirt with good effect. Captain Thomas Pinckney heard that "they apprehend a Rifleman grows naturally behind each Tree and Bush on the Continent."[25] A letter sent from Philadelphia to the *Gentleman's Magazine* in London warned, "Their guns are rifled barrels, and they fight in ambush, five hundred provincials would stop the march of five thousand regulars. And a whole army might be cut off, without knowing where the fire came from."[26] American sentries let privates wearing rifle shirts pass but stopped general officers.

Although riflemen remained useful auxiliaries throughout the war, especially as snipers, they enjoyed in the publicity of 1775 a fascination far out of proportion to their role. When the officers of the militia Associators of Philadelphia adopted a uniform for the privates, many Associators protested that it was too expensive; they advocated "the cheapest uniform, such as that of a HUNTING SHIRT, as it will level all distinctions."[27] Better than most Continental soldiers, riflemen seemed to unite formidable appearance, awesome reputation, unerring skill, and personal independence. Richard Henry Lee looked at the six western counties of Virginia and saw six thousand men with "their amazing hardihood, their method of living so long in the woods without carrying provisions with them, the exceeding quickness with which they can march to distant parts, and above all, the dexterity . . . in the use of the Rifle Gun. . . . Every shot is fatal."[28] Lewis Nicola's treatise recommended that riflemen be exempt from drill because they had a special purpose different from ordinary battlefield maneuvers.[29] At Williamsburg, riflemen sneered at the drilling of musketmen. A Virginian's description of riflemen later in the war also held true for 1775: "They are such a boastful, bragging set of people, and think none are men or can fight but themselves."[30]

The riflemen quickly learned, however, that fighting the British took up little or none of their time, day after day. So they fought each other. Some fought army discipline and wound up in irons. Some deserted to the enemy. The rifle shirt remained popular even after it turned out to be an especially dirty shelter for lice, the carriers of typhus. Moreover, the rifle was a fragile weapon, soon fouled, slow to load, and of little use at close quarters against a bayonet, which it lacked. The British could hardly have asked for a better war than facing an army made up solely of riflemen.[31]

As the British quickly learned, they did not face such an army. With much less public attention, Americans put the smoothbore musket to a variety of uses. The standard musket-ball mold left a rib around the ball that gave it an effect like that of a soft-nosed bullet, expanding and ripping what it hit. To enhance this effect, some men split their bullets before loading, causing them to break into four pieces when fired. Americans also fired angular bits of iron, rusty spikes, and balls with nails in them. These did not have the approval of the commander in chief. But on the advice of General Alexander McDougall, Washington did revive an old trick known by Massachusetts farmers before the battle of Lexington—buckshot.

In addition to telling their army how to face death and how to inflict it, the revolutionaries defined the place of the army as an institution. This definition began with suspicion of a standing army. The political ideology that Americans adapted from the English Commonwealth writers warned that a standing army in time of peace was an engine of oppression. In the eighteenth century the favorite example of this truism had become Oliver Cromwell's rule in the 1650s. Yet these English writers worried less about military dictatorship than about the corruption of parliamentary politics by dependents, pensioners, placemen, and others with financial connections. The army meant patronage, and patronage meant power—corrupt power, which eroded liberty by threatening to smash those whom it could not make supine. As J.G.A. Pocock's analysis of republican ideology has explained, the rise of a standing army implicated the people in the corruption of the government. Employment of military professionals meant that citizens were too selfish to sacrifice property, time, or lives by personal military service. Acquiescence in the creation of a permanent army and in the taxation to support it showed that a people were fit for the tyranny that would inevitably follow.[32] By the time war came, revolutionaries hardly needed to seek new converts to this thinking. They referred to familiar truths that few people doubted.[33] Americans could never tolerate "this *armed monster*," because "freedom at sufferance is a solecism in politics."[34] Freedom could not last wherever "the powers of hell" introduced "that infernal engine."[35]

American experience before the war had shown the threat of a standing army in the prolonged presence of British troops in Boston, in Quartering Acts, in the British ministry's pretense of taxation for imperial defense. Even before the conflicts with Parliament in the 1760s and 1770s, Americans had seen generations of military men in British imperial administration and had suffered the high-handed contempt that the British army held for provincials.[36] Americans did not intend to corrupt themselves with their own army, which had been created to prevent military subjection. The revolutionaries did not allow their support for the war to overcome their vigilance against the tendency of all people, including Americans, to yield to corruption. A few revolutionaries seem to have disapproved of a standing army in wartime. At least, they used the danger of a standing army to argue against any arrangements for the Continental Army that they opposed. A new tyranny might creep in at once, masked by resistance to an old one. But most revolutionaries did not question the need for a regular army during the war. The most prevalent wartime legacy of the ingrained suspicion of a standing army was not ideological but emotional. The revolutionaries felt a strong distaste for an army in repose, an army as an institution, an army as an organ of the state. Nothing surpassed their admiration for soldiers in combat, and no degree of admiration could allay their intuitive conviction that an officer corps must tend to subvert self-government. We scarcely overstate the revolutionaries' concern by saying that they felt that when the army was not attacking the British, it must be doing some mischief to the revolutionaries.

For national defense in peacetime, the American version of Commonwealth theory preferred the militia. Except for certain exempt groups, the militia ostensibly included all adult males, aged sixteen to sixty. In ordinary times these citizens did their own work—usually farming—without military office or public expense. They would mobilize to face a threat and become the first defenders, fighting for home and family. Their readiness to serve gave a double guarantee for the survival of liberty:

freemen's sacrifice precluded reliance on dangerous mercenaries, and the virtue that citizens proved in the field could sustain self-government.[37] Early in the war some revolutionaries argued that the militia, which had proven its competence at Lexington and Bunker Hill, could sustain a large part of the resistance to the British. By late 1776 little attachment to this idea remained. The states continued to send militia instead of recruits to augment the Continental Army for brief periods. Some declarations about citizens defending their homes accompanied these detachments, but the use of militia during the war came more from necessity than from libertarian or egalitarian theory. People in every state preferred and urgently requested the presence of the Continental Army when they felt threatened. But the states never managed to recruit a regular army as large as their delegates in Congress had legislated; so they continued to call out the militia for regular fighting as well as sudden defense.

Samuel Adams was proud of the New England militia and suspicious of a regular army in war as in peace, but in 1780 he wrote to James Warren, a former militia general, "Would any Man in his Senses, who wishes the War may be carried on with Vigor, prefer the temporary and expensive Drafts of Militia, to a permanent and well appointed Army!"[38] If revolutionaries preferred a stronger Continental Army, why did they not have one? Almost all revolutionaries agreed that a standing army—no matter how suspect and unwelcome—was necessary. Every state supported the idea that a Continental Army should bear the main fighting; every state tried to recruit and supply it; every state preferred to be defended by it. The states with the most effective militias, such as Massachusetts or New Jersey after 1777, also contributed most to the army. Early in the war revolutionaries agreed that, in theory, the standing-army-versus-militia debate could not be allowed to define the wartime need for a permanent army. Congress did not resist the idea of a large standing army and soon gave up the preference for annual enlistments. Revolutionary leaders who, like Adams, had first relied on the militia then turned more emphatically to the Continental Army and tempered their early distaste for the use of professionals. But their practical calls to use the army often failed to overcome the popular aversion to permanent military institutions—an aversion that ran deeper than the theoretical warnings against a peacetime standing army.

The ideology of the revolution, which systematically expressed a widespread intuitive suspicion of governmental power of all kinds, provided few guides for the use of an army by a free people. And those guides at hand mostly told one how to control it, not how to build it. By contrast, the ideology was rich in reasons for Americans to avoid being constrained, to avoid coercing others, or to avoid creating powerful administrative organizations, even while they announced their full support for the Continental Army. In the contest between commitment to the army and suspicion of it, suspicion had all the interior lines of communication. A person might feel the force of several strong arguments: the consequences of British victory, the need for an army, the greater effectiveness and economy of a regular army, the patriotism and reliability of men in the army. But these practical arguments did not form a coherent system of thought that encouraged and prescribed immediate individual action to support the army. The systematic thinking of the revolution instead showed one how to restrain the army and justified one's reluctance to strengthen it. The validity of the call to fight did not necessarily validate the call to build a powerful military institution. Under these circumstances, the creation, survival, and victory of the Continental Army distinctively exemplified the willingness of the revolutionary generation to experiment and innovate in their institutions. We handicap our understanding of this experiment if we identify commitment to the army with one group of revolutionaries and suspicion of it with another. In a few cases such an identification holds true, and much more so in 1783. However, most revolutionaries held both sets of attitudes during the war, and the experiment took shape according to the outcome of this internal conflict.

Granted that the revolutionaries would raise a regular army, what characteristics defined an army raised to preserve liberty? The revolutionaries relied strongly on the idea of the citizen-soldier. During the war, differences in people's understanding of this term created important divisions among Americans, especially between officers and civilians, but all could agree that the American soldier would return to civil society after defeating the British. They could also agree that while in the service he would become a soldier yet would not serve the army before all others by issuing or obeying orders that violated civil authority. In addition to these unquestioned truths, most revolutionaries expected the citizen-soldier to surpass his mercenary, brutalized enemies. Since he fought to preserve his standing as a citizen against those who would make him a slave, his pride in civil society would help to make him stronger than his opponents in combat. However, when choosing what to do at any given time, the citizen-soldier, unless he chose to do what his superiors told him to do, could not have as much independent choice as the citizen. Nor could the soldiers together choose leaders and courses of action for the group, as citizens could. Thus, although the American soldier had once been only a citizen, would again be only a citizen, and fought to remain a citizen, he could not, while he was a soldier, always conduct himself as civilian citizens might.

The ambiguity in the definition of the status of Continental Army soldiers appeared at once and reappeared throughout the war. Few people analyzed the dilemma it posed. Whether revolutionaries demanded a stronger army or feared a stronger army, they based their demands and fears on the certainty that much of an army's strength lay in its unquestioning obedience to hierarchical command. They celebrated soldiers as freemen but recruited them as subordinates. Most revolutionaries cherished their earliest expectation, strongest in 1775, that the citizen-soldier's love of liberty would accept yet withstand yet animate the discipline of an army. And they harbored their earliest fears that such a feat was impossible—that citizens must fear veterans.

"We must all be soldiers," John Adams wrote to a Boston minister in May of 1776. Seven weeks later, when a student in Adams's law office wanted to enlist, Adams advised him, "We cannot all be soldiers."[39] Perhaps in the first instance Adams spoke figuratively and in the second literally. Similarly, the citizen-soldier remained both a fact and a figure of speech. The revolutionaries' ideal of citizens in arms and the call to all citizens to take up arms conflicted with their experience, which showed that the American who turned soldier had to become a kind of citizen different from his civilian countrymen.

The historian John Shy has called General Charles Lee a "radical" who wanted "a popular war of mass resistance . . . based on military service as an obligation of citizenship." In Lee's praise of American soldiers and militia, Shy sees the general's confidence in zealous citizenship as an alternative to "Prussian" discipline.[40] Lee, like his fellow Briton William Gordon, cherished a vision of a world redeemed by liberty. America, each hoped, would restore to the world ancient Roman virtue or apostolic Christian love, respectively. Lee, a former lieutenant colonel in the British army, accepted a Continental Army command. Gordon, a minister in Massachusetts who had immigrated in 1770, began at once in 1775 to prepare a history of the revolution. But when Americans' conduct fell short of these dreams, both men grew embittered toward their protégés.

In 1775 Gordon wanted God "to make the Chronicles of the American united Colonies the favourite reading of the godly in this new world till the elect shall be gathered in." But by 1778, Gordon found, the behavior of "the sons of liberty," like that of all mankind, had shown "their depravity." He decided "to have less and less to do with the bulk of them. . . . I mean soon to withdraw myself, and, the ministry excepted, to apply myself solely to the business of a faithful and honest historian." In 1782 Gordon assured Horatio Gates that "the credit of the country and of individuals who now occupy eminencies will be most horridly affected by an *impartial* history." In fact, "Should G Britain mend its constitution . . . life liberty property and character will be safer there than on this side the Atlantic; and an Historian may use the impartial pen there with less danger than here." In 1786, two years before his four-volume work was published in London, Gordon wrote from England, "Several on this side the water have the protection of the law against libels; and as they will be likely to suffer by the truth, I must give it in that artful guarded way . . . or they may hoist me into the pillory . . . besides plundering me of all the profits I wish to gain from the History."[41]

We may find it hard to discern whose conduct lapsed more rapidly, the Americans' or Gordon's. Similarly, the rhetorical manifestos in which Charles Lee proclaimed political and military radicalism reflected only one side of a revolutionary character even less steadfast than Gordon's. A rhetorical, unanalytical confidence in the virtuous success of the citizen-soldier set Lee up for a more bitter disillusionment than Gordon experienced—a disillusionment in which Lee's radicalism was much less visible than his instability.

In 1774 and 1775 Charles Lee won great favor with Americans by telling them what they wanted to hear: that they need not fear the British army's prowess, because a militia, animated by determination to preserve liberty, could become a formidable infantry. Lee's letter to Burgoyne—reprinted in colonial newspapers—and his private letters in 1775 denied that Americans lacked courage. He praised the enlisted men and "the zeal and alacrity of the militia."[42] At New York in 1776 Lee's letters took on a new tone: "As to the Minute Men, no account ought to be made of them. Had I been as much acquainted with them when they were summoned as I am at present, I should have exerted myself to prevent their coming."[43] He hoped "that Congress will find means of establishing one great Continental regular army, adequate to all the purposes of defence."[44] Lee heard that the New England delegates favored enlistments of less than one year and commented to Washington, "They say by means of a shorter engagement the whole country would be soldiers. A curious whim, this! Who the devil can fill their heads with such nonsense?"[45] For the defense of New York City, he wanted "eight thousand, at least, regular troops"; in command at Charleston, Lee reprimanded Colonel William Moultrie for being "too relaxed in Discipline. . . . There cannot be a greater vice."[46] Although in the autumn months of 1776, before his negligence enabled twenty-five British dragoons to capture him, Lee was still praising the bravery and valor of Continental soldiers, his tone changed when he was in British hands. He wrote to a British officer, "The fortune of war, the activity of Colonel Harcourt, and the rascality of my own troops, have made me your prisoner. . . . To Colonel Harcourt's activity every commendation is due; had I commanded such men, I had this day been free."[47]

In fact, Lee was a cynic who ultimately felt contempt for almost every person he knew.[48] When people failed to live up to his image of "the glorious third or fourth century of the Romans"—as everyone eventually did fail—he turned his witty sarcasm against them all: King George III, Burgoyne, Washington, Congress, state officials, officers, soldiers, and militia. When soldiers crossed him, he hit them in the head.[49] He often said that he liked dogs better than people. According to an anecdote told after his death, a woman once asked him whether he was fond of dogs; "he instantly replied, 'Yes, madam; I love *dogs*; but I detest *bitches*.'"[50] He also detested Irishmen, Baptists, and Presbyterians. Lee explained, "If you will examine history you will find all or almost all the Enthusiasts for general liberty had the reputation of being cynically dispos'd."[51] Late in 1775 some Connecticut soldiers whom Lee tried to shame into reenlisting put graffiti on his door at night. We have little cause to dispute their judgment: "General Lee was a fool and if he had not come here we should not know it."[52]

In Gordon's and Lee's brief enthusiasm for the virtue of the American revolutionary we see one of the problems engendered by the ideals of 1775: how does one react when one's people fail to attain demanding goals? Gordon and Lee, being Britons, could give up on the faltering Americans. American revolutionaries, however, depended on the establishment of independence to sustain hope even for the future realization of their ideals. If independence could not be won solely by the republican citizen-soldier, it still had to be won. Unlike Gordon and Lee, American revolutionaries would have to find reinforcements for an inadequate enthusiasm. To that end, Americans maintained the ideal of the citizen-soldier while they relegated regular army service to long-term professional soldiers. Revolutionaries wanted to believe that they were all combatants and that being freemen gave them military prowess. But they quickly lost enthusiasm for sustained military training or for universal military service in a regular army. The short-lived *rage militaire*, on which Charles Lee's reputation as an experienced and learned officer rode high in 1775, lasted only as long as the quick mastery of arms seemed easy. When rigor, even simplified rigor, and prolonged duty seemed necessary, Americans feared that the citizen would be lost in the soldier. They preferred to retain their original figurative ideal; they could not be won over to a more literal definition of the citizen-soldier, either by Lee's call for rotating universal conscription or by other officers' arguments that long-term Continental soldiers were the most patriotic citizens.

Revolutionaries believed that the citizen-soldiers required a special kind of commander. The selection and evaluation of general officers filled much of Congress's time and attracted wide attention. The Americans' expectations of their military leaders manifested once more their early hope to fight a voluntary, virtuous, enthusiastic war. In June 1775, Congress made generals of George Washington, Artemas Ward, Charles Lee, Philip Schuyler, Israel Putnam, Richard Montgomery, Horatio Gates, William Heath, Joseph Spencer, John Sullivan, John Thomas, Nathanael Greene, and David Wooster. Possibly excepting Lee's rank in Europe, none of these men had been regular army generals before. A *Royal Gazette* verse about Sullivan could describe them all: "Make him a Gen'ral—Gen'ral strait he grows."[53] The loyalists sneered at the pretense of an unlawful legislature's fiat commissions—unsanctioned by wide experience, by professional evaluation, or, in some cases, by social position. Loyalist newspapers and verse never tired of parodying the American generals' former occupations, battlefield bumbling, and inelegant public writings. Even a delegate in Congress was reminded of paper dollars when he voted for "a new emission of Brigadier-Generals."[54] Yet these officers received immediate, widespread respect as generals. Like the revolutionary civil governments, Continental Army commissions acquired an instant legitimacy. The widespread support for resistance to Britain helped secure respect for those charged with leading it.

Continental generals enjoyed two other sanctions for their overnight professional status. First, Congress had selected them through an intentionally political process of state and sectional balancing. Experience and alleged expertise, as with the former British army officers Lee and Gates, recommended some of them as well, but delegates in Congress dickered over quotas and seniority based on political connections. Revolutionaries were not used to an American army, but they were used to American politics, an art in which they consistently outclassed the loyalists. The endorsements of Congress carried immediate conviction partly because they came out of a familiar process of reconciling varied interests and opinions.[55] Second, Americans thought that they knew what being a general meant, and these ideas encouraged the quick acceptance of the Continental Army commanders. The revolutionaries' assumptions about generals emerged more clearly in 1776 and 1777, when people began to find fault with the ones they had. We can better understand this disappointment if we know what they expected.

Apart from Washington, the American general most discussed in 1775 was not a Continental officer but a major general in the Massachusetts militia—Joseph Warren, who had been killed in the Battle of Bunker Hill before Congress had appointed generals. He was also a doctor and a revolutionary political leader in Massachusetts. Because Warren's commission as a general was not yet in force, he had declined a command and had fought in the ranks, but the poetic, dramatic, and rhetorical accounts of his service nevertheless portrayed a general leading "an inspired yeomanry, all sinew and soul":[56]

> From rank to rank the daring warrior flies,
> And bids the thunder of the battle rise.
> Sudden arrangements of his troops are made,
> And sudden movements round the plain display'd . . .
> With agile speed he hastes to ev'ry post,
> And animates Columbia's warring host.
> Chear'd by his voice, they burn with martial fire,
> From their rude shock the fiercest bands retire. . . .[57]

In the battle, many nearby soldiers never fought; many, including officers, left the fighting as soon as they could get away—for example, in squads of twenty, carrying one wounded man—and some, like Warren, stayed until the end. Throughout the action, according to accounts of the battle, breathed the spirit of the general, whose personal example and influence sustained the Americans. A eulogy credited him with "the highest act of benevolence to mankind, by dying in defence of the liberties of his country. . . . He partakes of the nature and happiness of God."[58]

On April 8, 1776, "a vast Concourse" attended the military and Masonic services at King's Chapel in Boston for the reinterment of Warren's remains.[59] Perez Morton told the mourners that Warren had "determined, that what he could not effect by his Eloquence or his Pen, he would bring to Purpose by his Sword. And on the memorable 19th of April, he appeared in the Field, under the united Characters of the General, the Soldier and the Physician."[60] In correspondence a week after Lexington, Warren had said, "We are determined at all events, to act our parts with firmness and intrepidity, knowing that slavery is far worse than death."[61] In a dramatization, his dying words were, "Fight on, my countrymen, be FREE, be FREE."[62]

Like the accounts of Warren, the other rhetoric of 1775—for example, the praise of Washington and Charles Lee—as well as the later criticisms of generals, assumed that a good general almost at once could control men's actions and their will to fight by his force of character and his expertise. Victory of course required discipline, which also depended not so much on experience under arms, or even on training, as on the general's immediate supervision and inspiration. Since American soldiers came freely to defend their liberty, their homes, and their future by fighting lackeys, it followed that a general who could command could lead them to victory. In the words of Benjamin Rush, "Good general officers would make an army of six months men an army of heroes."[63] If God, in the war with Satan, had given preachers not only the ability to awaken assurance of His grace in the soul but also the power to end sin by preaching, He would have created good generals on the American plan. American generals, in effect, were expected to perform miracles by force of personality alone. This expectation secured prompt respect for the commanders in 1775. It also promised them trouble if they failed.

As Americans tried to define their army, they clung to the conviction that a professional soldier was dangerous, vicious, and damned. He killed for money. He made war a trade and preferred long, easygoing wars that yielded him the largest gains for the smallest inconvenience. These gains came at the expense of both taxpayers and civil government, which a professional soldier necessarily corrupted or defied. General Henry Knox, who began his military studies in his bookstore before the war, said that such a man "will meet with his proper demerits in another world."[64] To confirm this judgment, Americans had the example not only of the British, who would kill people of their own blood for pay, or of the Hessians, hired to kill strangers, but also of the eighteenth-century soldiers of fortune—officers who went from army to army and war to war, regardless of nationality, trying always to climb to higher rank.

While moral censure of and distaste for career soldiers increased during the war, the revolutionaries, especially in Congress, for a short time put great faith in European officers who came to fight for America. In large part, the Continental Army commissions given to these men showed Congress's desire to secure the aid of France. When the first European officers came, their credentials and their advertisement of themselves as professionals seemed to promise special military effectiveness. Richard Henry Lee, speaking of the need for engineers and artillery officers, recalled, "The first that came had sagacity enough quickly to discern our wants, and professing competency in these branches, they were too quickly believed."[65] Americans did not confine such expectations to engineers or artillery officers but gave rank freely. Claude Robin, a French army chaplain, later described the French adventurers: "By assuming titles and fictitious names, they obtained distinguished ranks in the American army. . . . The simplicity of the Americans, added to their little experience, rendered these villainies less liable to be detected."[66]

On July 6, 1775, "a german Hussar, a veteran in the Wars in Germany," came to Congress and offered the service of fifty veterans to oppose the British Seventeenth Regiment of Light Dragoons at Boston. John Adams used almost one hundred words to describe the officer's beautiful uniform, superior weapons, and gaudy panache, concluding that the hussar was "the most warlike and formidable Figure, I ever saw."[67] Congress accepted the offer but changed its mind three weeks later. Behind the strong criticism of professionals lay the expectation that their vices would make them more effective. When European officers appeared with the well-known corrupt trappings of career soldiers—aristocratic station, arrogance, eagerness for high rank and pay—Americans took the trappings for marks of competence in war. Before long, this assumption proved groundless, and the revolutionaries despised almost all foreign adventurers—Continental officers or new applicants—who were not only mercenaries, but not even good ones.

Americans did not have to seek mercenary military impostors from abroad, however. The revolution spawned more proficient war-traders at home—an obscure group of men who appear during the war in reports written by others. They were scattered civilians who wore officers' uniforms. They did not do so because they were part of the large militia officer corps, or because they wished to be officers. They wished to seem to be officers because they were profiteers. The Continental Army used a wide variety of uniforms, and officers had theirs privately made. The support staff of the army—quartermasters, commissaries, sutlers, farriers, wagonmasters, and the like—bore military rank, though not seniority in the line. Consequently, no one was surprised to find captains, majors, and colonels, in varied but impressive military dress, riding around the countryside making arrangements for the army—no one, that is, except "A SUBALTERN in the Continental Army." According to his letter to a newspaper, while traveling on furlough he fell in with several uniformed men and found that he was the only member of the group who was in the army. The rest were buying goods and provisions from the public in order to sell them at a large markup to the army or to people in other regions where prices were higher.[68] Such men could also hold the goods and wait for prices to rise everywhere. A citizen might suspect the authenticity of their uniforms because they paid higher prices than the government authorized or because they paid cash, which the army often lacked. Suspicion was strong enough to leave a fragmentary record but not strong enough to drive such men out of business, even though real purchasing officers had credentials as well as a uniform. Law, a governor's proclamation, and newspaper articles denounced this traffic. It would be interesting to know how many buyers used a Continental Army uniform to cover their crimes. It would be more interesting to know how many of the sellers were fooled by one.

At first, Americans hoped to guard against the dangers of a wartime standing army and offset reluctance to serve in it by keeping the soldiers' terms of enlistment short. A one-year enlistment assured the citizen that he need not become the army's bondsman, even if he reenlisted as often as necessary until the war was won. The first enlistments of Continental Army soldiers ended in December 1775. Reenlistments and new enlistments were for one year, except for a few men who engaged for the duration of the war.

Before 1776 was over, almost everyone except the soldiers regretted the one-year term. Short enlistments troubled the army throughout the war. Experienced soldiers gave way to recruits or went home for a few months until they felt like reenlisting. The size and composition of the army stayed in flux. The Continental Army did not try long-term enlistments until mid-1776, partly because some revolutionaries thought that annual reenlistment and even annual review of officers' commissions would protect America from some of the abuses of a standing army. Congress could alter or abolish the military as events required with less danger that the army could become an independent interest with its own long-term resources. Also,

Congress could retain or promote able soldiers and drop the unfit routinely, without court-martial or formal proceedings. Moreover, hardly anyone thought that Americans could be induced to enlist for an indefinite term. Congress and the states used short enlistments because they hoped that the war would end soon, and they expected the soldiers to serve until it did. Joseph Warren, a week after Lexington, called for troops "enlisted for such time as is necessary."[69] But when the necessary time grew long, many Americans feared that by long or indefinite enlistments they would lose their freedom. Sarah Hodgkins wrote her husband, Captain Joseph Hodgkins, that she was afraid he would stay in the cause of liberty until he made himself a slave.[70] In Congress, Roger Sherman argued that "long enlistment is a state of slavery. There ought to be a rotation which is in favor of liberty."[71]

In 1775 recruitment did not seem to be a problem; people did not foresee that Americans would also refuse to reenlist for a definite term. Congress later said that short enlistments had been adopted "to ease the people."[72] But many men eased themselves by staying out of the army or leaving it as soon as they could. For the rest of his life, Private Thomas Painter remained glad that he had enlisted for only six months in June of 1776, instead of waiting until fall and enlisting for the duration. In December he "returned to West Haven, thoroughly sick of a Soldier's life, determined, if I went into the War again, to have my furniture conveyed without its being Slung at my back."[73] Some revolutionaries, including many enlisted men, favored rotation in service, either to share the burden or to spread military training or to prevent the growth of a military caste. But even they expected that somebody would enlist. Public officials learned fast, as regiments disbanded at Boston in the face of the enemy and as recruits came in slowly. In 1776 enlistment for the duration became popular in Congress, in state legislatures, and in newspaper appeals for recruits, but never attracted more than a few thousand men at any one time. Nathanael Greene, who in June 1775 preferred enlistments for the duration, nevertheless recommended one-year enlistments in October because "men esteem confinement, (of which the service partakes,) without any fixed period to its duration, a boundless gulf, where the fruitful imagination creates ten thousand nameless horrours."[74]

The failure of the one-year enlistment caused revolutionaries special distress, because a central element in their definition of their army was voluntarism. An army of freemen ought to consist of volunteers. In 1775 the crux of resistance to Britain was the protection and exercise of personal, conscious responsibility for the public welfare. That is, each person used his wits and his God-given will to better himself and to serve mankind because he wanted to spend his life that way—not in unthinking ease, which led to impoverished oppression. Armed service against attackers was to flow from this state of mind without a break, just as soldiers were to appear where shortly before stood farmers. Of course, they would need training, good commanders, pay; but they served as volunteers. In this fact lay their greatest moral strength, which gave them physical strength.

One recurring expression of voluntarism was also one of the least effective militarily: the volunteer irregulars, civilians who formed their own auxiliary units without enlisting in the army. At various times this kind of service attracted gentlemen of independent means, who formed light-horse companies, "substantial Yeomanry," and some who argued "for no pay at all or officers, but all marching promiscuously and on equal footing as volunteers."[75] Accepting no pay and acknowledging only such authority as they might give to elected officers, volunteers seemed to combine valor, disinterestedness, and freedom. Colonel Otho Holland Williams reported of backcountry riflemen in 1781, "They say they are Volunteers and should be treated with distinction."[76]

But when Governor Patrick Henry, unable to fill Virginia's Continental Line with recruits, offered to send volunteers in 1777, Washington refused them. Men "of the *Volunteer kind*," he said, "are uneasy, impatient of Command, ungovernable; and, claiming to themselves a sort of superior merit, generaly assume, not only the Priviledge of thinking, but to do as they please."[77] James Collins's father was willing to serve as a volunteer in 1780, "though over age for the law of my country to demand it, yet I think the nature of the case requires the best energies of every man who is a friend to liberty." But when James thought of enlisting, "My father counseled me otherwise; he said the time was at hand when volunteers would be called for, and by joining them . . . if I went to battle I stood as fair a chance; besides I would be less exposed, less fatigued, and if there should be any time of resting, I could come home and enjoy it."[78] Philadelphia volunteers who had turned out in 1776 refused to do so in 1777 without a regular militia draft because they had "found their business and customers so deranged on their return, and engrossed by those who staid at home."[79] When the British invaded Virginia in 1781, "a number . . . who turned out Volunteers on the first approach of the British, finding the life of a Soldier by no means an agreeable one, thought proper to take a hasty leave of their brother Sufferers."[80] Washington complained to Patrick Henry that "half their time is taken up Marching to and from Camp at a most amazing expence," and commanders in both the Northern and Southern departments found volunteers especially inclined to plunder citizens.[81] Voluntarism revealed not only Americans' enthusiasm but also their waywardness. Comfort, profit, pride —all could impede the ostensible military purpose of the volunteer's presence in the field. To succeed militarily, voluntarism would have to include the acceptance of stricter discipline.

As voluntarism was to be the central guide to the individual's relations with the army, the principal belief guiding the relations of governments and the army was the supremacy of civil authority. Military power and the officers who wielded it must always be subordinate to civil officials. This meant that the military received its orders from civil government and that it had no independent or permanent source of revenue or authority. To be subordinate, it must remain dependent. Only in this way could self-government protect itself against the inevitable tendency of power to grow. An army required special, explicit checks because its armed strength, its size and expenditures, and its importance to the survival of the country made it uniquely dangerous. The revolutionaries did not intend to hire saviors who would rule them. This idea commanded universal assent; Congress and the states referred to it regularly in their decisions in order to make sure that no encroachments came upon them unawares.

Among the political ideas of the revolution, civil supremacy over the military achieved one of the most nearly complete successes, in practice as well as in allegiance. Of all the principles of 1775, it came nearest to full and lasting implementation. The support of the Continental Army with men and supplies, sporadic though it often was, depended primarily on the willing contributions of the public. No officers, not even Washington at the height of his popularity, could have secured these willing contributions so consistently as civil governments did. The conduct of the army in confiscating supplies suggests that it would have secured support by force much less equitably or effectively than Congress and the states did. Civil supremacy alone could have sustained the army's existence.

The idea of civil supremacy also did important service during the many times when it was violated. Throughout the war the army seized food, wagons, and livestock without legal authority. Although the states and Congress authorized various kinds of impressment, the army also acted without such approval or failed to comply with the procedures and safeguards that were supposed to guide it. This happened when lower-ranking officers exceeded their instructions and when commanders gave orders they knew to be unlawful. In 1781 Congress ordered the army in the Southern Department to supply itself by impressment long after it had been doing so anyway. The army usually violated civil supremacy by ignoring state regulation of the impressment of supplies. General Nathanael Greene explained to Governor Abner Nash of North Carolina, "It is my wish to pay the most sacred regard to the laws and Constitution of the State, but the emergencies of war are often so pressing that it becomes necessary to invade the rights of the citizen to prevent public calamities."[82] The need to keep the army together might violate Continental authority as well. General John Sullivan seized provisions and wrote afterwards, "I know the Resolves of Congress upon this head I ever will Comply with them when possible yet it is a Maxim older than the Congress That Necessity has no Law."[83]

Yet while all of this went on, everyone knew that though it might be necessary, it was wrong. Citizens resented the army's inequitable seizures and the officers' peremptory enforcement of their own estimate of the army's needs. The army resented the public's slow and inefficient supply and the preference many people showed for profit. But even when the army balanced accounts outside the law, the two groups did not become enemies for this reason. Late in the war the quartermaster general was under civil arrest in New York, but for the most part seizures met with tacit assent. The officers' acknowledgment that their conduct was illegal, that they could not make a separate law for the army, helped to sustain cooperation amid coercion. And, in turn, the citizens' respect for the officers' intentions discouraged the growth of contempt for law. In this instance, Americans maintained harmony in the act of violating their ideology because they remained confident that they agreed on its meaning and that all parties were working to preserve and to implement it.

In discussing some officers who wanted to defy Congress at the end of the war, the historian Richard Kohn uses the word "purity" to describe civil supremacy over the military. If a "corrupting element" shatters the "aura" of civilian control by violating it, military rule thereafter "lurks in the background."[84] The Newburgh crisis of 1783 did not violate civil authority, but it challenged civilian rule far more seriously than actual violations during the war because in it some American officers abandoned the idea of civil supremacy. The "purity" that America had preserved lay in the idea and in unanimous endorsement of it, not in conduct always free from taint. During the war, as long as officers called their deeds sins and regretted that their sins had been forced upon them, sin could help save America.

CHAPTER II

1776: The Army of Israel

Faith Trumbull Huntington—known to her family as Faithy—was thirty-two years old in 1775, the mother of an eight-year-old son. Her husband was Colonel Jedidiah Huntington, also thirty-two and, beginning in July, commander of the Eighth Connecticut Regiment outside Boston. Her father was Jonathan Trumbull, who served as governor of Connecticut for fifteen years, including all of the war. Her mother, Faith Robinson Trumbull, was believed to be a great-granddaughter of John Robinson, the pastor of the Plymouth Pilgrims while they were in Holland. Her oldest brother, Joseph Trumbull, was commissary general of the Continental Army. Another brother, Jonathan Trumbull, Jr., was paymaster general of the Northern Department and, later in the war, military secretary to Washington. Her youngest brother, John Trumbull, served as adjutant to the Second Connecticut Regiment, then briefly as aide-de-camp to Washington, then as a brigade major. After the war he became the foremost artist of the revolution. Through his eyes Americans still see *The Death of General Montgomery*, *The Declaration of Independence*, *The Surrender of Lord Cornwallis at Yorktown*, other tableaus, and portraits of revolutionaries. In his autobiography John said that his sister Faith first awakened his interest in drawing while he was a child. Faith and her sister went to school in Boston, where Faith painted two portraits and a landscape. These hung in her mother's parlor and were among the first objects that caught her favorite brother's eye.

As a child and as an adult Faith was an active Christian. She made an early and serious profession of piety and remained diligent in attendance at religious services. Although she had not yet undergone a "Change of her Heart"—that is, a conversion experience, giving her assurance that she was one of the saved—her first pastor said that she had "comfortable Hopes." Her husband thought her "the best of Women" and valued her as "my best earthly friend." She was admired for her learning, her friendliness, and her open, frank, cheerful character. Governor Trumbull said, "The tenderness and affection of my daughter Faith I am apt to think are without a parallel." Although wealthy, she was not idle. She showed benevolence in acts of generosity to others.

When the war began, Faith Huntington was deeply affected by the wrongs done to her country and felt a generous love of America's rights. Yet her sensitivity—her "soul susceptible of the most tender impressions"—soon made these feelings painful.

She experienced a strong shock during the Battle of Bunker Hill. She and a party of young friends visited the army outside Boston in June of 1775, their curiosity excited by the novelty of military scenes. Instead of a great militia muster with the promise of glorious war, they saw the battle, the artillery fire—chain shot, ring shot, and double-headed shot—and the burning of Charlestown. These sights, with their threat to her husband and her brothers, "overcame her strong, but too sensitive mind." Later, at home, her health was impaired: she was not robust, and "her feeble frame almost sank beneath the weight" of her anxiety. But when her husband was given his command in July, she "cordially" consented to his departure, concealing her strong emotions. Soon, however, she fell into a despondent frame of mind, which by the first week of October had become a deeply fixed gloom and melancholy. Although she was not explicit when she wrote to her husband, in her mind everything seemed "totally inverted": "she thought she was most deservedly forsaken and hated by God, her friends and all mankind, and was the most ungrateful and wicked creature on earth; and in spite of all the efforts of her friends and physicians, these things were to her perfectly real."

When Colonel Huntington heard from his mother, his father, and his father-in-law about the illness of his wife, he felt "the greatest Uneasiness and Concern," but he was "in great straits." The eagerness of many officers to get out of camp troubled Washington and made it dishonorable to ask for a leave of absence. Huntington decided to have his mother accompany his wife to Dedham, Massachusetts, where he could visit Faith and have her treated.

They arrived at Joshua Henshaw's house on Friday afternoon, October 27. Colonel Huntington met them there and found his wife better than he expected. For several weeks, in addition to having the tenderness and care of Mr. and Mrs. Henshaw, she was treated by Dr. John Sprague. "She had intervals of calm tranquility and composure, but frequent turns of great and surprizing pain and distortion." Her husband called these turns "the Fits." Sprague visited her on Thursday, November 2, and predicted that "her Disorder will go off like a Mist." Both the doctor and the husband felt confident of her recovery. Colonel Huntington visited her for several days in mid-November and found that her intervals of calm increased daily. Faith was told that "her distempered Mind proceeds from a distempered Body." She said that she wished it might turn out to be so.

Thursday, November 23, 1775, was Thanksgiving Day in Massachusetts. The legislature called on ministers and people to praise God for giving them subsistence and health, for preserving the lives of their officers and soldiers while the enemy fell, for uniting the American colonies in "a Band of Union, founded upon the best Principles." With their thanksgiving, the people were to pray that wisdom would guide civil rulers and generals, that peace would be restored and the rights of posterity preserved, that God would "pour out his Spirit . . . bring us to a hearty Repentance and Reformation; purify and sanctify all his Churches: That he would make Our's Emanuel's Land."

Mr. and Mrs. Henshaw and Faith Huntington expected all the Huntington and Trumbull brothers in camp to gather at Dedham "to rejoice with them . . . on this Day of public Thanksgiving." On the morning of the twenty-third the men had not yet decided to go, because they expected the British to attack the new siege works on Cobble Hill. However, Jedidiah was in Dedham early on the morning of the twenty-fourth, the day after Thanksgiving. He saw Faith; she seemed well; he left. Within the hour she found a small cord, and in her bedroom she hanged herself.

Governor Trumbull wrote in the family Bible: "*Faith d. at Ded. Friday Morning*, 24*th Nov*. 1775." In a memorial sermon at Lebanon, Connecticut, on December 3, Faith's first pastor said that the reasons for her death were among the unknowable secrets of God's infinitely wise providence: "I can give you no Account of this Matter." But he did advise, "Let us all take Warning to improve our Reason, that Candle of the Lord, and his precious Gift, while we have it. . . . We have no Assurance of the Continuance of our Reason, or of our Lives: And when Reason is gone, we can do as little about working out our Salvation, as when we are dead." A newspaper obituary said, "The authors of American oppression and the public calamity, are accountable for her death, and that of thousands more." Governor Trumbull wrote to his son-in-law, "The world after all is a little pitiful thing; not performing any one promise it makes us for the future, and every day taking away and annulling the joys of the past. A few days ago I had a dear affectionate daughter Faithy. Alas! she is no more with us. Let us comfort one another, and if possible study to add as much more goodness, love, and friendship to each other as death has deprived us of in her." In camp, Colonel Huntington trusted that his wife had gone to "uninterrupted bliss"; but he recalled "the thousand agreeable and tender scenes" of their marriage and wept. He wished to see their son: "his presence might have soothed me—but it could not well be." During the war the boy lived with Governor and Mrs. Trumbull. Colonel Huntington hoped that "he may by his improvements and dutifulness make some amends to his grandparents for the loss of their lovely daughter."

Faith Huntington's body was placed next to the remains of Nathaniel Ames, Sr., in Dwight's tomb in Dedham on November 28. Four junior officers in Colonel Huntington's regiment came from Roxbury camp to attend the services. Their walk took two and one-half hours, and on the way one of them argued to the others that it was beneath the dignity of human nature to shed tears or to mourn for the dead. They all debated this at great length and then disputed on the doctrines of predestination and free will the rest of the way.

The corpse lay at the Henshaws' house, where the mourners gathered. After prayer by the minister of Dedham's First Church, the funeral procession—first the immediate mourners, then those who had lived with Colonel Huntington, then officers, then women, then men—escorted the body to the tomb, walked back to the meetinghouse in the same order, and parted. That evening the four officers were guests at the Ames home. The company dined heartily on roast turkey.[1]

I
Men at War

The army's experiences in 1775 and 1776 quickly revealed the contrasts between the ideals of 1775 and the conduct of the war. The first year of fighting the British and creating a regular army began the test of Americans' response to the problem of reconciling lapses in revolutionaries' conduct with the rigor of absolute ideals. Two kinds of failure threatened to undermine the cause: battlefield reverses, which called Americans' native courage into doubt, and the army's lack of discipline and decorum, which fell far short of the revolutionaries' hope for an army of Israel.

When Washington arrived at Cambridge in July 1775, the

Massachusetts legislature apologized for the state of discipline in the army. The representatives told him that the men were "naturally brave, and of good understanding," but "the completion of so difficult and at the same time so necessary a task is reserved to your Excellency."[2] Even before reaching camp, Washington could notice one of his difficulties: the sound of sporadic musket fire. The shots did not mean combat or even sniping at sentries. The firing was just what it sounded like—men shooting off muskets at random in camp. One of the revolutionaries' most often-repeated claims to superiority over the British army said that Americans learned the use of firearms from childhood. These claims exaggerated both American marksmanship and its usefulness in combat against a disciplined bayonet charge. Whatever the extent or the advantage of early familiarity with weapons, muskets in the hands of idle men proved very dangerous. Men used them to start fires; men discharged them to empty them; men fired at wild geese flying overhead. Some soldiers wounded or killed themselves by accident. Many men enjoyed snapping flintlocks for the fun of it; sometimes the musket was loaded and a nearby soldier was killed or wounded. In 1776 Washington was still saying in general orders, "Seldom a day passes but some persons are shot by their friends."[3]

The Massachusetts legislature had warned Washington that the soldiers were "youth . . . used to a laborious life," who had not learned "the absolute necessity of cleanliness in their dress, and lodging, continual exercise, and strict temperance, to preserve them from diseases."[4] Some soldiers felt that washing clothes was women's work; so they wore what they had until it crusted over and fell apart. Others sent their laundry home. Washington wanted the soldiers to bathe; those who would bathe wanted to swim all day and show off naked in front of "ladies of the first fashion" who happened to be crossing the bridge in Cambridge.[5] Prolonged swimming threatened the men's health, as did refusing to bathe or to wash their clothes. In 1777 a Massachusetts soldier whose regiment had been in service for two months wrote in his diary, "This day the old carter, Brown, washed his face and handes he Desired to have it seat down in the Journal the first time since he Come in."[6] Throughout the war soldiers and officers suffered from "the Itch," a product of poor hygiene and sleeping on the ground. It could become so severe as to cover a man with scabs or strip off his skin. It left large numbers of men hardly fit for duty. Soldiers "Ointed for the Itch" with hog's lard or pine tar and brimstone—a process that made "the Devil of a Stink" and, in one case, "over came them so that we Thought they would a Died in the Night."[7]

Every soldier's health was endangered by persistent problems with camp sanitation, which did most harm in the early years of the war. Open latrines for thousands of men were bad enough, but many soldiers would "Set Down and Ease themselves" wherever they felt like it.[8] The remains of slaughtered cattle often rotted unburied. When the army stayed in one place for long, it sat amid a smoky miasma rising from green wood fires, gunpowder smoke, urine, feces, and animal offal. At first Washington thought that Massachusetts men were "an exceeding dirty and nasty people"; he later found that soldiers from all states would freely foul their own camp.[9] The Continental Army became much cleaner in the years after 1777, but in 1781 Americans could still marvel at how clean their French allies managed to keep a camp.

Neglect of cleanliness, like carelessness with firearms, was a self-destructive response to the unforeseen hardships of life in camp. General Philip Schuyler put the soldiers' attitude in one word: "nonchalance."[10] We might call it anxiety. Americans' inexperience in war caused many of their early problems, and the revolutionaries' respect for personal independence worked against quick, strict obedience to orders. Men who had shared the *rage militaire* of 1775 remained reluctant to master the soldierly skills that would help to keep them alive in the army. Even those soldiers who put self-preservation first by deserting a few weeks or months short of their discharge date risked, by their departure, the self-destruction of the army. Late in June 1775, eighteen men from Captain Winthrop Rowe's New Hampshire company deserted outside Boston, saying "that they didn't intend when they enlisted to join the Army, but to be station'd at Hampton" on the New Hampshire coast. Nathaniel Folsom warned the state committee of safety that failing to send the men back might cause the whole battalion to follow their example.[11] These first flights from the pain of war foreshadowed the difficulty, not the promised ease, of reconciling voluntarism and the need for military success. The soldier's free choice had to confront his anxiety. Even though deserters did not run a great risk, a few unhappy men did not desert; they killed themselves.

Generals and doctors found that homesickness meant just that—sickness. The symptoms were loss of appetite, restlessness, and melancholy. Few of the New England soldiers had been far from their hometowns before; they would seldom have gone away for long; they would never have lived with thousands of others in new and uncomfortable constraint. The soldiers' strong local attachments came not only from their affection for family and friends but from lives wholly shaped by experience within a small area. Private Barber said of his company, "Most of us had not . . . been twenty miles from home."[12] The ardor that had moved them to defend their beloved homes against the threat of invasion could not alone sustain all of them. They fell ill, yet recovered when discharged. No doubt some were malingering, but most who suffered from homesickness must have found it as real as smallpox or dysentery. Their longing was not just the disappointment or temporary low spirits we usually mean by the word "homesick." It was a lasting obsession. Repeatedly during 1776 and 1777 newspaper advertisements for deserters described soldiers as having a "dejected" look, a "down look," a "prodigious down look."[13] One colonel reported from camp, "The Officers and Soldiers are possessed to get Home."[14]

The revolutionaries confidently expected victory—that is, concessions from Britain—even when they spoke of a long war, and they found volunteers who they believed would achieve this unquestionable, inevitable mark of God's favor. These volunteers encountered more prolonged, less decisive tests than facing death at the hands of the invader. In these tests, a volunteer's public spirit, his native courage—even the state of his soul—did not provide adequate guides for his conduct. Officers and preachers might run through the litany of obedience and sobriety, but even now their appeal for painstaking discipline sounds like mundane rote when compared to the brilliant rewards for inspired virtuous exertion. We may, as the generals did, draw a logical connection between discipline and inspiration, but we cannot infuse the one with the promise of the other.

For the soldier, the promise of success for virtuous effort guaranteed victory, yet put disproportionately great responsibility on him, while paying little notice to the shock of his trials in a siege camp. Communal voluntarism might carry an American to war, but, in taking care of himself while he was there, he was spiritually on his own. The soldiers' "nonchalance" revealed not only independent minds that loved personal freedom but also the distress of volunteers meeting surprise enemies—disease, constraint, deprivation. Since victory over the British was certain, soldiers did not always feel obliged to face these new enemies, too. The Continental Army provided the first test of many revolutionaries' ability to live continentally as well as to think and talk continentally—to put their daily lives under the control of the Union without the constant support of a familiar community. Those who became more lawless and careless than they had been at home, those who deserted, or those who went home to stay at the end of their terms could not sustain a uniquely vulnerable position solely by the strength of their patriotism.

The revolutionaries would not adopt a professional army composed of soldiers who were not expected to remain citizens. Therefore, three solutions to the early discipline problems were possible. The Continental Army used all three but relied mainly on the third. First, the army might impose service and discipline by force, without pretending that the war could be fought according to the voluntaristic ideals of the revolution. Second, the revolutionaries might modify their ideals by developing new admiration for the worth of military discipline and the value of obeying delegated authority to achieve national ideals. Third, soldiers might temporarily choose to accept military discipline, knowing that it held a very tenuous place, if any, in revolutionary ideals. The revolutionaries largely left it to the men in the army to define the citizen-soldier in practice.

When their enlistments ran out at the end of the year, the men around Boston and in Canada wanted to go home. A colonel heard that "some of the Soldiers begin to count the days they have to stay in Camp."[15] Once the men got home, people found that "the Soldiers can give no other Reason for not Enlisting, than the old Woman's, They wou'd not, cause the[y] wou'd not."[16] Although many would reenlist later, they still wanted to go home. For several months, old soldiers were leaving camp, new soldiers were entering camp, militia were entering and leaving, and old soldiers who had left were returning.

The most notorious departers were the Connecticut soldiers who refused a request to stay beyond the end of their terms. The generals tried patriotic appeals, flattery, shame, drinks, and blows, but Colonel Jedidiah Huntington found that "we shall not with all our Rhetorick be able to retain many."[17] When the soldiers marched, the generals encouraged the citizens and tavern keepers along the road to deny service to the soldiers and to express contempt for their conduct. In Connecticut people were glad to see the soldiers for a visit, but expected them to go back to camp. Many condemned the soldiers' departure from camp and shamed some men into reenlisting.

By the end of 1775, many revolutionaries had begun to see that the war would impose new, severe tests on their ability to match the ideals of personal courage and public virtue on which America's liberty depended. In addition to facing an enemy who, they believed, was bent on enslaving them, they were facing their own rigorous ideal of revolutionary conduct, and they could see that they were often failing to achieve the virtuous strength that was a mark of God's favor. Not only did the Continental Army fall short of Americans' ideal image of an army, but the difficulty of recruiting men also created a network of evasion and corruption that spread far into the populace. The expedients used to keep the army in the field disclosed the lapses of civilians as well as soldiers.

In 1776 the army again enlisted for one year. Against the wishes of the generals and the New England delegates, Congress resolved that "no bounty be allowed to the army on reinlistment."[18] During the early months of 1776 the states tried to fill their regiments without a bounty. In January the Massachusetts legislature forswore both a bounty and a draft, while the *Connecticut Courant* addressed potential recruits, "Will it not be criminal, at a crisis like the present, to bury your martial talents because more of your money is not taxed from you and returned as a bounty. . . . The pay of the soldiery, though not equal to intentions of bribery, is equal to all the purposes of comfortable and manly subsistence."[19] At first Virginia and North Carolina wanted to recruit even more battalions than Congress had asked them for. But the states failed to fill their regiments, and Congress acknowledged the failure on June 26, 1776, when it voted to grant ten dollars to men who enlisted for three years.

Men joined the army, but too few. Nathanael Greene estimated in September that since 1775 the army had consistently been short of its voted strength by more than one-third and almost one-half.[20] Short-term militia and the Flying Camp were a large part of Washington's force in 1776. There were many reasons, including high wages for laborers, high bounties for brief militia service, the hope for high returns by serving on privateering vessels, and the word of deaths by disease in the army. Men were not "obligd to resort to the Army for employment" and were not inclined to enlist altruistically.[21] So a Rhode Island delegate concluded, "The draughting of Men is vastly disagreeable to Me. . . . On the other hand I cant bear that our Quota should be wanting; I had much rather have given a Bounty than be perplex'd in this Manner."[22] By March towns in Massachusetts overcame recruits' reluctance, especially among men who had served in 1775, by offering ten dollars per man as a bounty; "others have declined giving anything, and of consequence no men can be obtained."[23] When Samuel Adams, in Congress, heard of the slow recruiting, he wrote home in May, "Do our Countrymen want animation at a time when [all] is at Stake! Your Presses have been too long silent. What are your Committees of Correspondence about? I hear Nothing of circular Letters—of joynt Committees, etc."[24] By June one did hear of bounties, voted by the legislatures of Massachusetts, New Hampshire, and Rhode Island, as well as Congress. On September 6, Congress offered twenty dollars and one hundred acres of land to men who enlisted for the duration.

In urging a substantial bounty, Washington explained that "a Soldier reasoned with upon the goodness of the cause he is engaged in, and the inestimable rights he is contending for, hears you with patience, and acknowledges the truth of your observations, but adds, that it is of no more Importance to him than others. . . . The few, therefore, who act upon Principles of disinterestedness, are, comparatively speaking, no more than a drop in the Ocean."[25] Voluntarism had not achieved the unanimity or the disinterestedness that the ideology of the revolution called for. Some men would enlist and reenlist, while others equally fit and freedom-loving would not enlist at all.

An annual pattern of recruiting began in 1777. Congress assigned a quota to each state, which then assigned quotas to the towns. The commander in chief, the delegates in Congress, and Continental Army officers from the state wrote letters urging prompt compliance. The local militia commander held a muster and called for volunteers. A few men enlisted. Then weeks of dickering started. The state or the town or private individuals or all three sweetened the bounty. Meanwhile, citizens who did not want to turn out with the militia were looking for militia substitutes to hire. Continental Army officers were in the countryside trying to build their own company or regiment. As men held out for an offer they liked, Washington and the officers in camp wrote more letters urging the state to fill its quota promptly so that men could be trained before the fall campaign. By late spring or summer, all of the men who were going to enlist that year on any terms had done so, whereupon the state found that it had not filled its quota. Washington called for militia reinforcements. Drafting began in 1777 and sent men for terms ending in December, which ensured that the whole process would begin again next January.[26]

Those who did enlist wanted to be paid. After army pay

became low, rare, and depreciated, these men sought their main compensation in the bounty given at the time of recruitment. Whether this bounty came from Congress, from the state, or from local pools, it obviously meant that those who could not or would not enlist paid those who would. When the draft began, it often did not mean selecting an unwilling man to go, but selecting from among the unwilling one man who had to pay one of the willing to go as a substitute. Even then the draftee got a bounty.

The system varied in detail among the states and grew by improvisation, but it had a consistent goal: obtaining recruits with a minimum of governmental coercion. Before the end of 1776, Georgia was recruiting throughout the South; by the end of April, Colonel Lachlan McIntosh was proud to have raised more than half his battalion despite the difficulty of recruitment. He wrote to Washington, "If the ease in which the poorest People generaly live in the Southern Coloneys and the prejudice they have to any regular service, on account of the restraint that any thing of a strict discipline requires is considered, I flatter myself your Excellency will think we have not been idle."[27]

One year's experience convinced most American officials that they needed a standing army to fight the war. They were willing in 1776 to create a dangerous institution in order to secure independence, but they were not willing to violate personal freedom by drafting men for as long a term as the revolution might require. Judging from the difficulty governments encountered in drafting men for terms of less than one year of service and the reluctance with which the public turned in deserters, the states probably would have been unable to enforce a uniform, long-term draft of the kind that Washington and others recommended in 1777.

All agreed that a regular army had to exist and that longer terms were needed to make the army both effective and economical. As long as the British attacked, American liberty stood to gain more than it risked from such an institution. However, these conclusions did not mean relaxation of civilian rule or of vigilance against military abuses. The use of three-year enlistments, enlistments for the duration, and conscription by the states did not represent a trend toward military dictatorship or toward military subversion of politics through the patronage created by a standing army. All of the states used these recruiting devices and regretted only that they were not more successful. These devices did entail the surrender of personal freedom by the recruits. In some cases, men's willingness to serve overcame their reluctance to make this surrender. In other cases, the desire for personal freedom caused men to resist all forms of surrender. More often, the desire and the public's respect for it enabled men to sell their surrender as dearly as possible.

Apart from the handling of army supplies, recruiting introduced more corruption into American society than any other activity associated with a standing army. But in this kind of corruption, we do not see a ruler taxing the people in order to employ favorites to support his rule. We see the people buying freedom from the demands of their own government. Everyone knew that this was happening, and even men who applauded the widespread suspicion of open-ended enlistments deplored the traffic in short-term recruits. They wanted men to enlist and reenlist for a fixed bounty. Some men did, but not enough.

The revolutionaries often said that freedom could not survive without virtue. If people were not willing to put the public good ahead of personal interest, power would pass to those who could, in the selfish free-for-all, buy or coerce the most support. A standing army—even one created to defend the country's freedom—brought an individual's virtue and freedom into conflict. The man willing to serve had to submit to new, harsh control. The man unwilling to be so coerced put his personal freedom ahead of the public good, which he then might or might not serve outside of the army. Revolutionary political theory could explain why citizens had to submit some of their personal freedom to civil government and, by extension, to serve in a standing army, temporarily. But the emotional gap between supporting civil government as a citizen and enlisting in the army was much wider than the theoretical gap—it was at least as wide as the difference in personal freedom. Moreover, the revolutionaries were far from having resolved in political theory or practice the problem of how to safely surrender some personal freedom to help maintain national freedom. A standing army departed so far from the Americans' ideal of personal freedom that they were unable, in conscience or in fact, to force a man to serve for as long as he was needed, even while they could explain why he ought to want to do so.

To resolve this conflict between the impulse to personal freedom and the call to public virtue, the revolutionaries relied on money. But here again they confronted a gap between theory and emotion. A central measure of a man's freedom was his right to control his own money, subject only to laws enacted by the people's representatives. Since Americans knew that money could buy loyalty, no authority independent of the people or their representatives could be allowed to control their money and use it to subjugate them. While the control over one's money was a test of freedom, the voluntary sacrifice of money was an important test of virtue. One sacrificed to serve the public good either by paying more than he had to pay or by declining to be paid as much as he could get.

Although the revolutionaries' ideology presented a consistent, rigorous call to arms, inevitably, people's individual abilities, circumstances, and ambitions varied widely and shaped their understanding of their own duty toward the Continental Army. The ideology of voluntarism said, and revolutionaries strongly felt, that the interpretation of that duty should come from the individual, not the state. People equalized their differing interpretations through the medium of money. If the revolution had depended on money as the only motive—or even the main motive—for facing the British, it would have failed quickly. But the revolution did depend heavily on money to make the recurring administrative decisions that ideology could not make and that people did not want government to make. The call to voluntarily resist the British convinced people to sacrifice some self-interest to the public welfare. Yet, voluntarism could function only by overcoming self-interest uniformly or by allowing people to negotiate the terms of their different forms of self-sacrifice.

Suppose a man who does not want to serve in the army pays another man who will serve. Both can claim to have done a virtuous act. Each can accuse the other of being less virtuous, or even selfish, for evading service or for extorting a large bounty. In fact, one man has kept his personal freedom and given up money, while the other has gained money and given up some of his personal freedom. Both parties clung to this system during the war—it was the recruits' most reliable source of pay; it was the citizens' best way to avoid conscription. A standing army did not make Americans the victims of a governmental traffic in patronage so much as it made them the practitioners of a popular traffic in personal freedom.

Though all parties claimed that their own conduct was virtuous, many people deplored the whole system as an example of spreading corruption. The corruption originated not in the love of power but in the fear of power and in the love of personal freedom. The Continental Army could not have existed amid such great personal freedom without the help of such corruption. Ideology called on the citizen to sacrifice some money or some personal freedom in order to serve the public good. We see this ideology at work in the recruiting process. But in that process we also see other impulses: personal freedom buying its way out of public service and public service making money. People obeyed their impulses while they knew that their principles called them to a more demanding course. These impulses eroded or overcame the rigorous dictates of ideology—as everyone charged but no one confessed—and, because revolutionaries took the ideology very much to heart, tainted the recruiting process and the standing army with guilt —a guilt not allayed by the sacrifices people made and repeatedly praised themselves for.

The army that civilian revolutionaries recruited and sent against the British embodied many derelictions from the *rage militaire* of 1775 besides the expedients by which it had been raised. While the ideal of popular military resistance to Britain was giving way to greater reliance on the army for defense, soldiers' lack of discipline not only was weakening their cause in the field but also was calling into question their fitness to claim revolutionary virtue. Thus, the more fully Americans turned to their army to preserve liberty, the more clearly American liberty embraced military vices, as well as the virtues of 1775. Washington and the senior officers hoped to check these vices. The generals wanted the Continental Army to become a regular army in its discipline as well as in the duration of its enlistments. When they thought of a regular army, they thought of the armies of Europe, especially Britain's, officered by gentlemen, disciplined by force, maneuvered in the field by elaborate formulas. Although the generals publicly appealed to the spirit of freemen, the American soldiers' sense of personal freedom at first seemed to be a military drawback. The generals tried to subordinate it to proper military ritual. The story of early Continental Army discipline shows for the most part the soldiers' conduct defying the officers' intentions.

The first casualty was the intricate drill, maneuver, and manual of arms that Europeans prized. The orders for handling arms and moving units in the face of the enemy were complex: the sight of thousands of men executing highly technical orders while in imminent danger of death awed the enemy with mechanical discipline. When Americans saw it, as at White Plains, the sight had the desired effect. The formulas also provided security under stress for soldiers whose spirit was questionable and who were not supposed to think. As we have seen, American military writers, such as Timothy Pickering, explained that intelligent citizens, who fought by choice and used their wits, did not need this charade. Many American soldiers refused to learn it. The Continental Army in 1776 and 1777 had no uniform standard for drill or for combat maneuvers. Commanders adopted whatever plan they liked, relying on sergeants to teach it, while the soldiers often did not try very hard to learn it. As Americans liked to point out, this shortcoming did not necessarily keep men from fighting well. However, it did mean that they had few guides for their conduct in battle other than their commanders' orders and their own spirit. One unit might renew the attack repeatedly. Another might see bayonets and run. Or the same unit might do both in turn. In combat, wits and the love of freedom needed the aid of routine. Pickering's plan contained in outline the successful philosophy of discipline eventually developed in the Continental Army. But the revolutionaries' initial distaste for the European military dumb show carried them beyond simplified drill to no reliable drill at all.

Although the Continentals resisted the discipline of a European army, they freely adopted many time-honored military vices. Desertion, for example, had many forms. Bounties inspired some soldiers to enlist several times with several units within a few days. Men bought or forged illegal discharges. Soldiers went to the enemy. More often, they went home. The army sent small detachments to catch them. Although the British and the loyalists encouraged men to desert and promised to reward or shelter them, deserters were most commonly helped by revolutionaries themselves, especially relatives. People not only refused to help army detachments apprehend deserters, but also helped the deserters escape arrest. In "many instances," according to Washington, "Deserters which have been apprehended by Officers, have been rescued by the People."[28] Citizens also bought deserters' arms and clothing. States offered rewards for the arrest of deserters and threatened to draft, fine, and flog people who sheltered them. Trying another expedient, from time to time Washington offered amnesties. None of these measures, nor the whipping of captured men, nor the execution of some deserters, had any lasting effect. The most thorough study of the official returns estimates an average desertion rate of between 20 and 25 percent.[29] The army's returns showed desertion to be declining in the later years of the war, as the army developed a core of long-term soldiers.[30] Those reports are probably correct in the pattern they portray, though distorted by the graft of recruiting officers who recorded nonexistent enlistments and desertions in order to embezzle bounty money.

Publicly, being a deserter was a source of shame. A deserter cheated his country, failed those who depended on him, and showed himself a coward. Generals' appeals to their men, newspaper advertisements in the home state, and public ceremonies of humiliation in the army used the weapon of shame. To escape it and to avoid capture, men moved to Vermont or Kentucky; they explained to newspapers and local officials that they had been fraudulently enlisted or cheated or legally discharged; a few returned to their units or enlisted again; perhaps most important, to preserve their self-respect they did not desert in the first place. When the British seemed especially cruel, as in their 1780 raid into New Jersey, or when some especially shameful act occurred, such as Arnold's treason, desertion almost stopped for a while.

The camps around Boston introduced both soldiers and civilians to a problem of discipline that followed the army throughout the war—the theft and destruction of property. The private homes and Harvard College buildings that were used for quarters inevitably got damaged. For a mile around Cambridge, soldiers pulled down every fence and cut down every tree for firewood. They threatened to start on houses until the legislature empowered the army to seize loyalists' woodlots. Soldiers also stole things on their own. Private Daniel Barber later said that "home and plenty are very different from the close quarters and deprivations to which a soldier is liable. The devil would now and then tell us, that it was no harm sometimes to pull a few potatoes and cabbages, and pluck, once in a while, an ear of corn, when we stood in need."[31] Around Boston, the army seldom lacked supplies; yet Colonel Samuel Holden Parsons had to try to stop his men from throwing stolen apples around camp and injuring each other. Orders against theft were "often transgressed," and citizens made "repeated complaints . . . of very disorderly conduct."[32] Men were flogged for burglary; a Harvard senior found his copy of Johnson's English Dictionary gone; on the march to Cambridge, soldiers stole spoons from the people who gave them food along the way.

Unlike British army plunderers, these soldiers were not abusing people whom they despised. The people of Roxbury, according to a Maryland soldier, Daniel McCurtin, had "left their houses and given them to the Soldiers for to make Barracks of them for to protect their rights and libertys."[33] In most cases the soldiers probably obeyed the devil because close quarters deprived them of "home and plenty." Though at home they had been taught to respect property and though their commanders reminded them that the army defended Americans' property, these teachings could not always replace the greatest article of plenty that the soldiers had enjoyed before enlistment: freedom of action in familiar surroundings. In a new, crowded, trying situation, this love of plenty might burst out destructively, even self-destructively. For Washington's crackdown there was a saying in camp: "New lords new laws."[34] Of Americans' shift to camp life one might say, "New laws, new crimes."

Continental generals tried European discipline because they wanted to achieve their idea of a regular army and because they thought that the vulgar could best be restrained by force. Continental soldiers often were rough men, toward the enemy or toward civilians and each other. Throughout the war, people in the neighborhood of the army felt this harshness often. They withstood three kinds of plunder: official plunder, casual plunder, and private plunder. Official plunderers, following orders, took livestock and grain and left a paper certifying that they had done so; casual plunderers burned fence rails for firewood, turned horses loose in grain fields, and fouled buildings; private plunderers beat people up and robbed them.

Supply shortages and lack of pay encouraged men to take what they could find, as commanders and civil officials knew. However, some soldiers, abetted by junior officers, stole in order to turn a quick profit. They enjoyed threatening or using force against people who seldom could resist. Soldiers argued that, since property would soon fall under British control, they might as well take it. To conceal theft from private homes, they set fire to the houses. "How disgraceful to the army is it," Washington said in one of his many futile orders against theft and destruction, "that the peaceable inhabitants, our countrymen and fellow citizens, dread our halting among them, even for a night and are happy when they get rid of us?"[35] A few of the Continental Army's casualties occurred when citizens defended their property against looting soldiers, and soldiers who met resistance sometimes fired on citizens.

Unlike deserters, plunderers suffered little shame among their fellow soldiers. Those who did not steal watched those who did with amused interest to see whether they would get caught. Everyone gladly shared the spoils and joked about arresting a goose—a "Hissian"—that could not give the countersign or about giving sheep and turkey prisoners a trial by fire.[36] Sergeant John Smith asked no questions and ate well "with the Rest of my Brother Soldiers who Seamd Hearty in the Cause of Liberty of teaking what Came in the way first to their hand Being Resolv'd to Live By their industry."[37] While Washington deplored the theft and destruction, threatening harsh punishment, Private Algernon Roberts believed that a "country laid wast" was "a natural consequence attending camps whare conveniency and ease are oftener consulted than the welfare of the neighbourhood." Roberts wished "that no one was so credulous as to believe the contrary."[38] Units of militia Associators, like Roberts's company, and other militia were even more destructive than the Continentals. Sergeant William Young of the Pennsylvania militia regretted that "there are some that cannot let anything Lay that comes in their way."[39] The enemy, as Roberts said, plundered deliberately, out of hostility and policy. "Conveniency and ease" may have been "natural" causes of plunder, but plunder was not a necessary outgrowth of military encampments. Rather, it expressed the wishes of undisciplined men with guns. The French army's stay in America showed that an army need not lay waste the countryside around it. Continental soldiers' plundering owed less to their military career than to their individualism, their lack of discipline, and their reluctance to suffer inconvenience when private initiative could ease their way.

Private Marmaduke McCain and Private William Dowers were on guard duty one day in October 1777. They sat close together, while McCain sang a song. Dowers asked him to sing it again. After McCain had finished singing, he noticed that his wallet was missing. It had a five-dollar bill in it; he accused

Dowers of stealing it; Dowers denied the charge. Later, in camp, Dowers got change for a five, which he said he had found by the fire.[40] Soldiers' property was no more secure than citizens'; theft within the army hit all ranks. Generals' quarters were burglarized; officers' baggage was rifled; some officers stole from their men or cheated them out of clothing; some soldiers stole food from officers and from each other; some sick men stole from others in hospitals.

Theft started fights—as did liquor, regional insults, and the fun of a brawl. One disease, called "Barrel Fever," had unique symptoms—"black eyes and bloody noses."[41] Soldiers often settled disputes with fights, which sometimes ended in death. Some men used a knife or a musket butt.

Much of the violence in camp took place when men were drunk. When Private James McCormick was tried for shooting and killing Private Reuben Bishop while drunk, his defense was that he had not intentionally murdered Bishop because he had meant to kill his company commander.[42] Rum—West India for officers, New England for enlisted men—was the most common drink, but all ranks took stinking whiskey hot from the still, wring-jaw cider, or whatever they could get. A week before the Battle of Brandywine, General Peter Muhlenberg said that "many Soldiers [are] making a practice of getting drunk regularly once a Day and thereby render themselves unfit for duty."[43] Men sometimes pleaded drunkenness, itself a crime in the army, as an excuse or extenuation for other crimes.

Alcohol in moderation, people then thought, promoted health. To treat "putrid fevers" army doctors prescribed, among other things, "wine, (two or three bottles a day in many cases)."[44] One gill, or four ounces, of rum was part of the daily ration when available. At Valley Forge, Henry Knox urged the commissary to provide this ration: "We have found by experience that this would support the men through every difficulty."[45] Sutlers who followed the camp sold more to those who had money; a man without cash could drink up his pay in advance. Washington tried twice to ban liquor dealers and then tried to license some, control their prices, and keep others away from the soldiers. None of these efforts succeeded for long. Men stole liquor, stole things to buy liquor, even sold their clothes to buy liquor. During the war, some of the biggest fortunes were made getting European manufactured goods for civilians, but some of the surest were made selling liquor to soldiers.

From the beginning the Continental Army disturbed many Christians because so many men swore. Today, the revolutionaries' admonitions against profanity may seem naive or futile. British soldiers had long been famous for their oaths. To Godfearing Americans, this was all the more reason for the Continental Army to reflect the righteousness of its cause by superior piety and self-restraint. Instead, all observers agreed, the Americans imitated the British more effectively on this score than on any other.

To judge by surviving examples, revolutionary profanity would sound mild to many people now. The same words were stronger then because they had not lost their religious meaning: profanity still permitted important theological distinctions. After Eli Showell was jailed for refusing to enlist, an officer came to him with a drawn sword and said, "Eli, now God damn your soul but . . . your life is your own, if you do not enlist I will run you through." Two sergeants worked the "son of a bitch" over, and Eli enlisted.[46] Anthony Wayne may have been the greatest swearer among senior officers. Lieutenant Ebenezer Elmer got it this way: "Col. Wayne . . . finding no sentry, (as we have not kept one in the day time) he damned all our souls to hell, and immediately ordered two by night and one by day, which I immediately put in execution—but shall not forget his damns, which he is very apt to bestow upon people; but my great consolation is, that the power thereof is not in his hands, blessed be God for it."[47]

Washington seldom made religious appeals to his soldiers, but profanity disturbed him. In general orders, he said that "his feelings are continually wounded by the Oaths and Imprecations of the soldiers whenever he is in hearing of them." He called it foolish, unmeaning, scandalous, shocking, disgusting, wicked, and abominable; it was "a vice productive of neither Advantage or Pleasure" and subversive of "decency and order."[48] After one of Washington's periodic orders to stop it,

Chaplain Hezekiah Smith's Saturday sermon praised the "conspicuous sincerity" of "our worthy Patron" in denouncing "this diabolical language."[49] To chaplains, to Washington, to devout citizens, profanity represented not only an impious defiance of God but also a loss of self-control, a moment of mutiny against reason. It was disorder, and it caused disorder. When a private named Robinson, in confinement for desertion, taunted Sergeant Thompson with "ill language," Thompson beat him to death with a musket.[50]

Although both state and Continental articles of war began by prohibiting profane oaths, the Continental Army never stopped or even checked the widespread swearing. Reverend Henry Muhlenberg called it "the horrible national vice."[51] Several people said that the example of soldiers made profanity more common throughout the country during the revolution. To both officers and soldiers, curses were marks of toughness and bravado. Officers wanted everyone to know that they were proud gentlemen who would not submit to any external check on their passions. In "the Tribe of Swearers" a newspaper writer saw "a wish to appear *heroic* and fearless. . . . To blaspheme the name of God, appears to them a mark of a *daring mind*, which is superior to vulgar fears."[52] In Sergeant Thomas McCarty's journal, his account of the Battle of Trenton reads in full: "Came there about day break and beat the damn Hessians and took 700 and odd prisoners." But McCarty's ideas of damnation were not always so fearless. Two days later he wrote, "In the woods, and no cover to keep off snow or rain. My time was not yet come, bless His name, or I should have been frozen."[53]

Against all these forms of disorder, officers relied mainly on one device: flogging. By British standards, which went up to 1,000 lashes, the Continental Army was lenient. Congress stuck to the Mosaic law of 39 lashes until 1776. For the rest of the war, the articles allowed 100. Officers sometimes exceeded this: Private William Dowers, the music-loving pickpocket, was sentenced to 500 lashes, got 200, and still had to pay back the five dollars. For punishment of crimes such as plundering and firing guns in camp, Washington tried to make whipping more effective by authorizing lashes on the spot. He also kept asking

Congress to raise the maximum to 500 because men could take 100 and remain defiant, leaving him no effective punishment short of death. The request, which had the support of James Madison, was never granted. Washington considered punishing men by confinement at hard labor, but this was not implemented, perhaps because it would have been hard to tell from routine service in the Continental Army.

Men were either whipped with a cat-o'-nine-tails or made to run the gauntlet. Since Washington believed that witnessing punishment deterred crime—a common assumption of the time—the soldiers were assembled and, after the adjutant read the sentence, either watched a drummer whip a guilty man tied to a post or whipped him themselves with sticks as he was marched between two lines of men. A bayonet in front of him kept him from going down the gauntlet too fast. One soldier, after undergoing the gauntlet, was "in a miserable situation . . . not able to move."[54] The 100 lashes at the post might be spread over four days, with salt rubs between the four floggings. Before 50 lashes the back was "like a jelly," and the cat got clogged with blood.[55] A dry one was substituted to cut more sharply. The soldiers had a name for the post to which they were tied: they called it "the Adjutant's Daughter."[56]

Continental soldiers had several ways to lighten the punishment of their fellow soldiers. In the lines of the gauntlet men softened or deflected their strokes or put a cut in the stick beforehand so that it would break when used. Drummers lightened the blows of the whip. If a drummer laid on the lash too well, soldiers might catch him later "in a bye place" and give him advice on the proper way to do his duty.[57] But contempt for the whip was part of the soldier's bravado; the advocates of corporal punishment admitted the ineffectiveness of 100 lashes when they asked for approval of 500. Whipping was supposed to maintain discipline through fear, and it failed. Instead, it became a running test of will between officers and men serving in the same cause. One of the Continental Army's most effective commanders, General Daniel Morgan, never imposed whipping of his own accord. Twenty years before the war, as a teamster under Braddock, he had received 499 lashes. He still bragged about cheating the British out of one lash.

Morgan sometimes did use another form of punishment common among Continental officers—hitting soldiers. This practice probably hurt discipline far more than it helped. Officers in the French Army were astonished at the frequency of whippings and canings among the Americans. One of Washington's arguments for raising the maximum number of lashes to 500 was that such authorized rigor would decrease the excesses of officers' arbitrary punishments. Most generals approved of calculated blows to correct stubborn men. However, some officers seemed to have succumbed simply to rage. At West Point one writer saw an officer and a subordinate beat a soldier bloody; "many officers gathering round, said *lay on*, and damning him that dare say otherways," until one officer stopped them. To this witness, beating a man who dared not resist was the sure sign of a coward.[58] A few officers who inflicted especially cruel beatings were court-martialed. One who was found guilty of "a malevolence of temper scarcely to be equalled" got a severe reprimand.[59]

Officers beat a man who crossed them because they could not stand to be crossed and knew nothing else to do. In a speech to his troops, General John Sullivan offered to redress any complaints they had against their officers. One soldier complained about the adjutant. As soon as Sullivan left, the soldier was severely beaten.[60] Striking a man, especially to gratify anger, undermined the self-respect of both the striker and the victim. It conveyed both the officer's contempt for the soldier and the officer's loss of self-discipline, which invited the soldier's contempt for him. The men of Captain Gerard Irwin's company petitioned the Pennsylvania Council of Safety to "see them Rightified" against their captain, who was "very much given to Drink strong Liquor; and then to Stricke and knock the men after a cruel And Barbarous Manner." The company had "been in the Continental Service . . . and in every Battle and Skirmish that has been fought in these parts of America since Bunker fight, and were always Counted by the Generals and other field officers To be men of Resolution and Courage."[61] Irwin's career as an officer was short. Under his name Heitman's *Register of Officers* notes, "omitted January, 1777."[62] But most soldiers were not so lucky, and their stories of cruelty spread their resentment among the people.

Courts-martial imposed many death sentences, but most condemned men were pardoned. Estimates of the number of executions in the Continental Army during the war range from forty to seventy-five.[63] Mutiny, fighting for the enemy, and plundering were most likely to get a man hanged or shot. Washington and his generals used capital punishment as an example to discourage others from committing like crimes. Since Washington did not intend to execute all the men guilty of capital crimes, he tried to preserve the effect of the example. Soldiers were assembled for an execution; drummers marched the condemned man to the gallows or the firing squad; the adjutant read the sentence; the chaplain addressed the condemned man and the army; and when the blindfolded man was ready for execution, the general's pardon was read. In asking for a five-hundred-lash penalty, Washington complained that through overuse this charade had become ineffective. Hardly any evidence suggests that it ever had been effective, except to excite curiosity among most onlookers, sympathy among a few, and fainting or tears among the recipients of the commander's clemency. Several of the pardoned men were later hanged for new capital crimes. Executions followed some mutinies and, the generals believed, forestalled others by catching leaders, who were eliminated while the men returned to duty, glad to escape death. Hangings had little noticeable effect on desertion or plundering. Throughout the war, the Americans' use of capital punishment fluctuated between prolonged forbearance and abrupt severity.

At 10 o'clock on Saturday morning, July 10, 1779, all the off-duty soldiers of the Pennsylvania Division marched to the gallows at Smith's Clove, New York, escorting Private Neil Magonigle, who was under sentence of death for deserting to the enemy. As he approached the place of execution, he could see, stuck on top of the gallows, a man's head.

A few days earlier, Major Henry Lee, who patrolled the outposts facing British lines at Stony Point, had asked Washington to authorize the summary execution and decapitation of a deserter, as an example. On July 9, Washington approved summary execution and forbade decapitation. But on the preceding night, one of Lee's patrols, under Captain Philip Reed, had already caught three deserters, who said "that they were tired of the continental service, and were going to make their fortunes." Reed told them "that he would put an end to their fortunes, in less than one hour, by cutting off their heads, and sending them to be exposed to the whole army." Then he proposed that they cast lots to choose one from among them for execution. The deserters refused, saying that "they would rather die together." Reed then chose the one who was American-born—a corporal—shot him, and cut off his head, which Magonigle now saw.

Magonigle had been sentenced to death once before, a year earlier, for stabbing an officer repeatedly with a bayonet. Washington had reluctantly pardoned him because of his good record as a soldier, his wounds received in combat, and the strong pleas of several officers, including the one he had stabbed. In May 1779, Magonigle had been court-martialed again—this time for desertion. He had been convicted only of absence without leave and sentenced to one hundred lashes. Now, after his third conviction, under his second death sentence, in sight of the corporal's head, Magonigle expected to be pardoned again. He said only that he forgave all the world. Then he was hanged. The commander of the First Pennsylvania Brigade said that the division "behaved as well on the occasion as I could wish."

The same day, Washington received Light-Horse Harry Lee's report of the beheading. Washington wished that it had not happened, feared its bad effect in the army and in the country, and wanted the body buried at once to keep it out of British hands. He ordered Lee not to exceed instructions by "diversifying the punishment." On July 11, Lee assured Washington that the summary execution "had a very immediate effect for the better on both troops and inhabitants."[64]

Beheading and hanging were not typical of Continental Army discipline. Yet, as extreme manifestations of a frequent resort to force, they showed some of the ways in which the army had stopped relying only on the *rage militaire* of 1775 to restrain men whose virtue might lapse. Experience gradually showed Americans that they could not draw a clear line between Europe, tyranny, brutality, and rigid military discipline on the one side and America, liberty, virtue, and voluntarism on the other. Liberty required independence; independence required war; war required combatants; and combatants were often brutal—either in their discipline or in their lack of discipline. As long as the success of the revolution depended on an army, Americans would owe the survival of virtue and liberty partly to harsh, arbitrary men.

Neither corporal punishment nor capital punishment achieved the smooth system of interlocking wheels that Washington wanted for Continental Army discipline. Yet these punishments and the soldiers' consent to serve were the main supports of the new Articles of War. The generals had complained to Congress that the first "Rules and Regulations" of 1775 were too weak, and Congress strengthened them in a new set of articles in August 1776. The new articles showed increased attention to the idiosyncrasies of American soldiers. The penalty clauses mentioned punishment by death more frequently than the old articles did, and increased the limit on flogging to one hundred lashes rather than thirty-nine. New sections tried to regulate sutlers, to stop fights, and to prevent or punish the new forms of graft that had appeared in the first year of war. Congress responded to the commanders' requests and tried to transform Americans into regular soldiers by bringing the government of the Continental Army closer to that of other armies. Congress was ready to experiment with firmer military law, but the "more severe and rigorous" articles that, according to President John Hancock, conveyed Congress's determination "to introduce obedience and regularity among the troops" could not change the independent minds of the soldiers.[65]

The army's attempt to instill discipline in its soldiers placed a heavy responsibility on junior officers. The first recruits' self-destructive carelessness received little effective correction from Continental officers in 1775. The generals at Cambridge agreed that too many of the company grade officers failed to look after their men. Instead of enforcing general orders, many did not bother to learn what the orders said. Some officers sought the favor of their men by behaving as their equals, even pooling pay and taking equal shares. This conduct may have owed less to Yankee officers' egalitarian attitudes, which southerners criticized, than to the officers' wish to keep their commissions by persuading their men to reenlist with them. The kind of scene that distressed the generals was described by Private James Stevens: "Went on the pread [parade] in the morning and Capt Poor come out and spok very rash concerning our chusing a sargent and said that we had no right to wich displesd the soldiers very much they went of[f] and did no duty that day about leven a clock we praded and capt Poor come and said that he was mis under stood and the comp[any] setld with him by his making som recantation."[66] Some officers had run or made feeble excuses at Bunker Hill. Among Washington's first orders were court-martials for cowardice, which he called "a pretty good slam."[67] In 1780, Isaac Freeman, a black private from Massachusetts, recalled that the court-martialed officers had been "a very tame set of J——k-ss-s, who live only to discourage better soldiers."[68] Some officers stole from their men and from the Continental government by keeping the men's pay and by drawing more provisions than the men needed and selling the surplus.

The survival of the Continental Army would depend not only on American soldiers' public spirit and combat prowess but also on the army's routine ability to keep men healthy, to keep them from killing each other, and to cheat them no more than they would tolerate. These needs put the heaviest burdens on the officers closest to the men, and in the face of such demands their weaknesses appeared most clearly. The conduct of able officers showed that neither orders nor ingratiation alone could lead men in battle or get them to take care of themselves in camp. A good officer needed to be constantly solicitous about details. Of course, the details of camp life were new to men of all ranks; at first, ignorance and incompetence were unavoidable. But as the needs became clear, many officers found the cost too high. In a camp of free-spirited, independent-minded privates, an officer was neither a free spirit nor a link in a clear chain of authority. When Washington issued the orders of the day, their implementation depended in large part on the junior officers' willingness and ability to persuade or force soldiers to obey.

On a recruiting trip in South Carolina in 1775, Captain Bernard Elliott met the leader of some hometown boys. The man told Elliott that he would not serve under any man he could lick. Elliott agreed to fight, used boxing, beat him, and made him a sergeant before he could recover from the wonder of being whipped by a man who wore silk stockings.[69] With less direct challenges and less clear outcomes, all captains and subalterns faced similar tests in camp. Could they get men to obey them by working harder than the men to administer the camp and to develop fighting skill, thus convincing the men that they ought to obey orders? Washington and other generals knew that officers' authority needed some external support. The commanders relied heavily on whippings for privates and marks of social status for officers. Neither worked very well. The Continental Army continued to depend on voluntarism—the soldier's willingness to obey and the officer's efforts to deserve obedience. Neither Captain Elliott's boxing nor his stockings could make a man offer to enlist or teach an officer how to know a good sergeant when he saw one.

The generals wanted stronger legal instruments of discipline, but they knew that the new Articles of War could never be properly enforced by many of the junior officers serving in 1776 and 1777. When General Thomas Conway grew peeved at an officer, he would sometimes ask, "*Did Congress see you before they appointed you?*"[70] Many, probably most, of these young men did not take pains to guide their companies in camp or in combat. Washington warned that as long as "every officer is glad to throw the irksome drudgery of obedience, upon his inferior, nothing but disorder and ruin can ensue."[71] Officers left camp on furlough, especially during the winter, when they should have been supervising their men and training them for the ensuing campaign. Lieutenant James McMichael, who did not get promoted above first lieutenant in seven years of active duty, disliked the temporary commander of the Seventh Pennsylvania Regiment; so McMichael announced that "he did but little duty in the regiment, and that he would do no kind of duty in the regiment that was in his power to avoid, during Majr Moore's command."[72] Frequently, officers left camp or played sick in their tents during battles or alarms; even valor in combat did not mean competence in leading others.[73] Many were negligent in routine duties of command—attending to the troops' cleanliness and health, to camp sanitation, or to the whereabouts of their men. In March 1777, Washington toyed with an idea that he never put into practice but that must have tempted him often: "Nothing I am convinced, but the breaking of Two or Three officers in every regiment will effect a radical *cure* of their negligence, inattention, and in fact downright disobedience."[74] From the conduct of many and the comments of others, we can infer that junior officers could not persevere under the daily strain of working with men who often would not do at once what they were told to do. As we have seen, the independent minds of the privates and the army's inability to coerce them put much of the burden of securing obedience on the officers closest to the men. Large numbers of these officers shirked that burden by avoiding their men as much as they could and by neglecting necessary orders that were difficult to enforce.

After the early complaints about wax-nosed New England officers, who curried favor by affecting equality with their men, a leveling spirit rarely appeared among officers. Diaries and memoirs of enlisted men do not speak familiarly of officers; nor do they suggest that privates wanted social bonds across the ranks. Privates did not think that there ought to be no officers or that officers ought to be subject to formal review by enlisted men. Men in the ranks showed contempt for officers' incompetence, hostility toward their harshness, and disobedience of their commands, but expressed no idea that the enlisted men should run the army. For the most part, enlisted men wrote about officers as distant, different figures who had duties and attitudes separate from the privates. Officers' diaries seldom mention specific enlisted men and sometimes go for long stretches without mentioning enlisted men at all.

Continental Army officers sought this distance from their men because they believed, as did officers in European armies, that social hierarchy sustained military hierarchy. To have the proper authority over enlisted men, they thought, an officer had to be a gentleman. The French and the Prussians required that an officer be—or claim to be—a nobleman. The British settled for gentility, gauged by having the money to buy a commission and to spend like a gentleman while drawing low pay. To judge by the conduct of Americans, the gentleman officer dressed richly; he had an enlisted man as a body servant; he shipped around a lot of personal baggage with the army; he preferred to ride a horse rather than march; whenever he could, he dined at taverns rather than field messes; he preferred not to drill or train his men personally but left that duty to sergeants. All of these marks of distinction showed, in theory, that he was part of a superior order of society, entitled to unquestioning obedience from military subordinates.

The Continental Army had young officers who brought high social status to their commands: we shall see, for example, Jedidiah Huntington, Henry Beekman Livingston, and Henry Lee. But, leaving aside for the moment the question of whether American enlisted men would obey gentlemen more readily, several snags obstructed the theory before it could get a full trial. First, the revolutionaries did not have enough gentlemen to go around. The army had far more field and company grade positions than America had Huntingtons, Livingstons, and Lees. Officers usually did come from families that owned more property than privates' families did, but such differences in possessions did not securely establish the officers as a superior order of society on the European model. Their property had not given them gentility.[75] One officer recalled his colleagues: "They were generally the Sons of Farmers or Mechanicks, who had quit the Plow or the Workshop."[76] Second, young American men, whether wealthy or not, kept turning the theory around. While they were eager to serve their country as gentlemen officers, they worked harder to make their military rank prove that they were gentlemen than to use their social status as an instrument of command.

By upholding standards of ostentatious conduct, with a pay scale to support it, senior officers and their allies in Congress tried to create a corps of gentlemen. Washington hoped that giving officers pay and status would make their rank an obligation conferred on them and would abolish the notion that by serving they were doing their country a favor. Then, "the Sloth, negligence and even disobedience of Orders which at this time but too generally prevails, will be purged off."[77] Thus, salaries would make gentlemen. General Hugh Mercer complained that junior officers were too poor to be fit for polite society: "there is no one beneath a field officer whose pay gives him a right to company above a shoe-black."[78] The European officers whom the generals emulated probably would not have conceded that an officer derived his claim to genteel company from his temporary access to the public treasury. In American society, social division by birth, though of long standing, was not nearly so uniform and thoroughgoing as military hierarchy sought. It was less pervasive, less rigorous, and more suspect. This newness meant that many American officers who wanted to be gentlemen did not know how. They rightly feared that everyone detected their ignorance. They had daily proof that their rank did not command respect. Some quit; some turned to graft; but most tried to become gentlemen.

The effort to base military discipline mainly on marks of social status failed. To enlisted men, the officers' gentlemanly pretensions looked like a miniature drama within the war. The officer's demeanor evoked, at different times, resentment, respect, puzzlement, laughter, revolt, and indifference. The primary standard by which men formed such reactions and judged their superiors' behavior was competence in guiding a company.[79] The soldiers in Captain Peter Mills's company of artificers stopped waiting for him to learn his duty. Private Elisha Stevens wrote on May 6, 1778, that Mills rejoined his company after a furlough, "and He Seamed to be Voyd of all Grace and He Car[ri]ed on to a very High Rate Singing all manner of Bordy Songs I think it is a Shame for Soldiers Much More for offesors." A month later, Mills kept everyone near him awake all night with his carousing, and in the morning he stole a pig. "Littel Did He think that His Compeny took too much Notis of it But . . . we Had Sufered it Long a Nuf for we thought . . . in Contience we Could not over Lok it and Soe Entered Complaint."[80]

When Continental soldiers respected an officer, they usually did so in spite of his airs and arrogance, not because of them. Private Daniel Barber remembered Lieutenant E. Fitch Bissell this way: "He was a gentleman, though not of the most easy and familiar turn; yet, for his steady and correct attention to the duties of his station, was well respected."[81]

For most officers, being a gentleman meant more than social status, liberal spending, and personal authority. A gentleman had refined feelings that kept him constantly aware that he was different from the ordinary people around him. Foremost among these feelings was a sense of honor. Honor not only required a man to uphold his rank, keep his word, and demand the same of others; it also required that he resent any insult. As we shall see, duelling grew common after 1778, but resentment long preceded it. Honor kept a gentleman's self-esteem inviolable; and, since he felt his own worth so keenly, the slightest indignity or affront struck him as an attack on his rights as a gentleman.

American officers compounded their sense of honor with constant awareness of their own patriotism. They took pride in fighting for the liberty of their country and the welfare of posterity—in fact, they began to feel that they personified these goals. One of them later recalled, "My Patriotism was pure and irristable, including all the principles of social and Public virtue, imbracing an Enerjective devotion to support the liberty, the

Independence and political safety of my native Country. . . . My carreer was not to be controled. . . . Thus wound up in the Political inthusiasm of the times, to be inactive was to me an intolerable burthen."[82] Another officer described his stagecoach ride toward the army: "Indifferent to all around me, I sat ruminating on scenes of happiness departed, cheerless and lost to every hope of their return. Dreams of glory . . . sometimes crossed my imagination, but . . . the images were painful, and deeply tinged with despair. In so desolating a frame of mind, I perceived the necessity of active duty, which should leave me no time for reflection."[83] Their sacrifices in public service helped convince them that their pride was unselfish, that an attack on them was an attack on a righteous cause.

But even when no one challenged a gentleman's honor, he cultivated sensitivity—which people in the eighteenth century called "sensibility." He looked for things to feel: friendship with other gentlemen, love for a woman, delight at scenic beauty in nature, compassion for the unfortunate, ardor for his country, nobility in self-sacrifice. Such refinement increased his awareness of his duty to his country and demanded that he fulfill that duty in a status commensurate with his personal distinction. In February 1776, Philip Brooks decided that "as a young, unmarried man, I can neither think myself excusable, nor a useful member of society, while content with indifferently examining the public prints at home." When he applied for a subaltern's commission, he told the New York Congress that enlisting as a private "would be agreeable, could the generality of my companions be formed to the agreement of religious, or even genteel behaviour; but the contrary, which is often the case, would be very disagreeable to a person of any sensibility."[84]

On July 1, 1775, Philip Vickers Fithian, who exemplifies the outlook of many young officers, recorded in his diary the beginning of his decision to become a Continental Army chaplain: "Last Night on the cool dark Bank of the River I wandered pensive, slow, and alone, ruminating, with my Arms folded on my Breast, and my Eyes sometimes on the smooth, gently-moving Water, and sometimes on the Ground before me, upon the melancholy State of our dear Country! O if Tears driven out by Grief and real Sorrow could bring any Help, I would with much Pleasure and Desire have passed the Night and wept with the Genius of this Water, til our Tears had increased the Flood! If Grief and Sympathy will not do, I stand ready, and am willing to hazard *Life* and *Credit* and *Property*, in the general, and needful Contest for what is our *All*." Then he copied a poem from the *Pennsylvania Packet* of June 12. It ran, in part,

> While FREEDOM's daughters all their aid afford,
> And deck the Warrior with the gorgeous sword;
> Do THOU, great HANCOCK, all their ranks inspire,
> With PATRIOT virtues, and the HEROE's fire.
> Form'd by THY blest example—they shall claim
> The FAIR one's fondness, and the conqueror's fame.[85]

Sensitivity—or, in Nathanael Greene's words, "Pride and sentiment"—was supposed to inspire the gentleman-officer to occupy his highly visible, vulnerable station without discrediting himself.[86] And by carrying such keen emotions with style, though surrounded by squalor and danger, he was supposed to command respect and to attract recognition of his prowess. Major William Pierce, Nathanael Greene's aide-de-camp, regretted being unable to talk with his friend St. George Tucker, who served with the Virginia militia at the siege of Yorktown. He could only write to Tucker: "What a scene for a poet! I can easily conceive the delight of your spirits upon that occasion, and the infinite deal of pleasure which your poetic genius must have enjoyed. Every cannon ball no doubt was accompanied with a flight of figurative ideas, and the bursting of every shell served but to expand and scatter the sparks of an elevated fancy."[87]

The young officers came to the army as naive as the privates, if not more so, and carrying the extra freight of gentlemanly ideals. John Lacey, a captain at the age of twenty-one, said later, "We were all young, and in a manner unacquainted with human nature, quite Novices in Military matters, had every thing to learn, and no one to instruct us who knew any better than ourselves."[88] In fact, they were slow to admit that anyone knew better than themselves. Early in 1777, Colonel

William Richardson complained that the new officers of the Fifth Maryland Regiment were "perfect novices, and but few removes from idiots."[89] The officers' green dignity fell under attack from several directions. The privates kept behaving like churls who did not recognize superior honor when they saw it. And many senior officers, to protect their own status, kept aloof from company grade officers—not inviting them to dinner, addressing them brusquely, even showing open scorn for their lack of polish. The profusion of rank among non-line officers of the support staff meant that the camp was full of majors and colonels. Generals and field grade officers in the line felt hard put to establish their own dignity. In addition to complements of aides, honor guards, and servants, senior officers displayed their stature by separating themselves from their juniors. This was an American innovation that surprised officers of the French army. French noblemen and British gentlemen prided themselves on an easy social intercourse and fellow-feeling among officers, which respected but transcended rank. America's would-be gentlemen did not always recognize one another.

From 1775, when the officers of the Second Connecticut Regiment tried to blackball Lieutenant Ebenezer Huntington, through 1782, when the officers of Lee's Legion tried to freeze out Lieutenant Colonel John Laurens as Light-Horse Harry's replacement in command of the infantry, junior officers vented their pride in cliques, squabbles, threats to resign, and frivolous court-martial charges made out of pique. At the same time, they seemed prone to suspect that others, especially their commanders, had a fixed design to persecute them. When they were thwarted—by orders they disliked, by neglect of their talents, or by being out-politicked in the push for rank—they saw sinister malice at work. When General Nathanael Greene gave a Maryland captain command of a special detachment "with secret orders," he raised the ire of a majority of the officers of the Pennsylvania Line. One of them wrote in his journal, "We are filled with the thought of our being slighted."[90] In October 1776, Chaplain Lewis Beebe said of the men he usually called "gentlemen officers": "The whims, caprice, and vanity of this set of beings is rediculous to the last degree." Seven weeks later he had decided that "the child, the boy and the fool, is so obvious in many of our officers, that I am weary of their Company."[91]

Captain Lacey began to learn about "human nature" in June 1776, when Colonel Anthony Wayne gave Lacey's company to another officer—"his Pett"—and asked Lacey to serve as a volunteer without command. "This was a Thunder Bolt . . . an Electricity that vibrated through every nerve." Wayne even invited Lacey and other officers to dine on roasted pig: "The Pig was well Cooked and very nice; but I felt such a load of Degradation, of injured innocence, of the purest Motives of Patriotism, such a deadly blow to all my future hopes of Comfort or preferment . . . I had no appetite. . . . Dejection and dispair was evidently visible in my Countenance. Having embarked at the resk of my Life to oppose a foreign Tyrant, and, then meeting an implacable one at Home, my mind was inextricably enthralled."[92]

The officers' aspiration to a privileged position at the head of a disciplined hierarchy seems to conflict with the revolutionary impulse toward liberty and equality; yet, in the officers' character we find important manifestations of the character of the revolution. Several strong currents of ideas and emotions converged to widen the officers' concept of a gentleman beyond a social class, born or made. Anxious to defend American liberty, convinced that such service showed one's virtue, and eager to lead men by force of courage and preeminence, the officers freed their audacity. In their drive for absolute proof of their superior patriotism, courage, and status, we can recognize a state of mind comparable to that of other Americans, who sought lasting assurance that they were free from the tyrant's weapons of corruption and fear. Any impediment to these aspirations threatened the revolutionary's attainment of the primary goals of independence. In striving for such rigorous—even absolute—goals, both officers and civilians inevitably experienced setbacks, not only from enemies of their aspirations but also from their own inadequacies. Army officers were not the only Americans who often reacted with desperate fervor to these setbacks, determined to prove that nothing could make them fall short of the glory the revolution had promised. The careers of the would-be military gentlemen embody one version of the revolutionaries' search for immortality.

This search put great strain on American officers, some of whom went to extravagant lengths to establish their status. They saw threats and slights everywhere and reacted with fury. In June 1777, Lieutenant Colonel William Palfrey accused a young major in the Second Maryland Regiment, John Stewart, of abusing the inhabitants and encouraging soldiers to plunder. Nathanael Greene sent his aide to inquire "in the politest manner but the Major insulted him and abusd all the General Officers of the Army." Greene told Stewart's division commander that Stewart "wrote me a letter demanding an explanation of his crime Publishing himself as a man of fortune and a Gentleman of Liberal Education and insisting upon an immediate tryal. If the Young Gentleman thinks his being a man of fortune or having a liberal education authorises him to insult and abuse People with impunity—he will find himself mistaken—the more liberal a Gentlemans education the more polished his manners should be."[93] Of course, Greene, speaking with the wisdom of his thirty-five years, was right. But before a gentleman could develop polished manners under stress he needed to establish that he was unquestionably a gentleman. In their eagerness to secure this cachet and their uncertainty about where they stood, American officers stayed so touchy that they often behaved like boors while they were trying to make someone acknowledge their gentility. We repeatedly read of officers whose tempers exploded with privates, with civilians, with each other, and alone.

Such loss of self-control reveals these officers' preoccupation with themselves, sometimes at the expense of effective service to the cause. Who was a gentleman? How could one be sure? John Stewart was the son of Stephen Stewart, a Maryland merchant. In September 1776, when he was a lieutenant, he was court-martialed for striking a sergeant and threatening the life of a colonel. According to the prosecution's testimony, he called William Phelps "a damned coward" for running from the enemy—Phelps was later acquitted by a court-martial—and then, mistaking Phelps's rank, "told him he was not fit for an Ensign." Sergeant Phelps replied that he "was as fit for an Ensign as he (Stewart) was for a Lieutenant." Stewart slapped Phelps in the face. When Colonel Gold Selleck Silliman, commander of Phelps's regiment, "very mildly" told Stewart that "he ought to have taken another course," Stewart "grew warm." Silliman ordered him under arrest. "On this, Lieutenant Stewart took his hat and flung it on the ground, and said, 'I'll go to my tent—all you can do is to take my commission, but I am a gentleman, and will put it out of your power, for I will resign it, and in less than two hours will be revenged on you, God damn you.'" The court found that Stewart had provocation for striking Phelps and that he was not guilty of threatening Colonel Silliman's life. Eleven of the fourteen officers on the court were captains. One of them later wrote, "The dashing manner of Stewart, and indignant tone of Captain Smith . . . who testified in his behalf, impressed the court, I remember, with a high idea of their military qualities."[94]

Washington assumed that being a gentleman would help a man to be a good officer. Many of his subordinates altered the concept of a gentleman and then often seemed to assume that being a gentleman was being a good officer. They often failed at both; military hierarchy and social status became instruments of an officer's vain attempts to prove his worth according to the standards of an ideal that found him wanting. Of course, lack of earlier training left the officers as much novices at gentlemanliness as at warfare. They soon saw how vulnerable they were. We can infer a reason for their lack of resilience and their failure to extemporize: they did not see that the gentlemanly ideal was an act, a ruse de guerre—useful, perhaps at times necessary, but still a device, not an identity or an allegiance or an earthly sanctification. They did not know how to act partly because they did not know that they were acting. Many Americans resented the officers' haughty, self-righteous pretensions; and even those closest to the officers could not follow them in their attempts to live their own soliloquies literally. Lieutenant Colonel Richard Varick, when he was only twenty-four years old—before he became Arnold's aide, then Washington's secretary, then a business attorney, then the Federalist mayor of New York, and long before he died at the age of seventy-eight—wrote his sister a letter in April 1777, touching with elegant tristesse on his imminent death. Jane Varick, however, was no Ophelia. She answered, "I wish you'd inform me what you meant by writing in your last you'd bought me some yds of Muslin for a Morning Dress when you should be so lucky as to go and see tother Country. What tother Country do you mean or do you want to see[?] I did not quite understand your meaning in that. Wish you'd write it Plainer in your Next."[95]

On July 15, 1779, Major John Stewart led an advance party following the forlorn hope in the assault on Stony Point. He often said that he did not want to live to be an old man, but Crazy Jack Stewart and Mad Anthony Wayne and the Light Infantry carried the fort and lived to hear their countrymen's praise. Congress voted Stewart a silver medal. It showed America, personified as an Indian queen, giving him a palm branch. In 1789 Thomas Jefferson brought the medal from France—too late for Stewart to receive it. In 1790 President Washington sent it to Stephen Stewart, saying that "it must afford some pleasing consolation when reflecting upon the loss of a worthy Son."

Two years before the action at Stony Point, Stewart had been taken prisoner by the enemy on August 22, 1777, while commanding a detachment covering the withdrawal from Staten Island following General John Sullivan's unsuccessful raid. Lieutenant William Wilmot said that Stewart "had never gave them an inch before he found that he had nothing left to keep them of[f] with." Placing a white handkerchief on the point of his sword, he walked forward to surrender, "as cool as if he had been going to shake hands with a friend." But Stewart did not long remain a prisoner. While confined aboard a prison ship, he "made his escape by descending silently to the water, and swimming to the New Jersey shore."

Already in 1776, when he was a lieutenant, Stewart had become known for "the most fashionably cut coat, the most *maca-*

roni cocked hat, and hottest blood in the union. . . ." He was six feet tall, well made, "handsome," and had "a fine presence for an Officer." Fifteen months after Stony Point, he almost got married. According to a friend, he "was damn'd nigh it, How he escap'd I know not . . . her wedding Cloth[e]s are made, but . . . poor Kitty Crane, you must hug your sheets."

Stewart went south with the Maryland troops and made lieutenant colonel. He was well known and "much beloved" among officers of the southern army, who told "many extraordinary stories" of his bravado. Citizens who crossed him got arrested or beaten up or horse-whipped. He commanded the First Maryland Regiment at the liberation of Charleston in December 1782.

On Friday, March 21, 1783, a few weeks before the southern army was to disband, Stewart rode down a steep hill at a hard gallop in a stunt that looked certain to kill him and his horse. But he made it. Saturday evening, Colonel William Washington invited the officers to an entertainment near Sandy Hill, South Carolina. Stewart was riding there, on a level road, when his horse fell and threw him head first into a ditch, injuring his neck. Sunday morning Stewart died, at the age of twenty-five.[96]

II
The Vine and the Fig Tree

By the end of the first year of hostilities, the Continental Army had begun to develop the character that it retained throughout the war. We see fewer signs of a whole populace marching against the invader and more calculated measures to raise a distinct body of soldiers; we hear less about ardent volunteers for regular army service and more about negotiations for pay, bounties, and conscription; we read less about young gentlemen who wanted to be privates and more about youths who wanted to become gentlemen; we find less hope for the soldiers' constant self-restraint and more fear of their casual violence. In the remaining years of the war, the army's survival, discipline, and patriotism helped to sustain the revolutionaries' perseverance. But in several troubling ways that army grew more like other armies than like the popular *rage militaire* of 1775. Some recurring elements of the soldiers' conduct violated the ideals that the Continental Army was supposed to promote. Before 1776 had ended, the war had permanently linked the achievement of American independence to this flawed military institution. Americans' reactions to both the victories and defeats of that year claimed to distinguish the revolutionary cause from the army on which it depended. At the same time, the public's response to battles and marches made that dependence ever clearer. Thus, the second year of war left the ideals of the revolution inextricably tied to the vicious as well as the virtuous elements of the Continental Army.

In March 1776, the British left Massachusetts without renewing combat. Although they would soon reappear at New York, the withdrawal brought out extravagant celebrations of Americans' might and Britons' cowardice. A broadside announced, "The British troops are completely disgraced. They went off in an amazing hurry, and evidently under a panic."[97] It was a victory for the innate courage of the chosen people, whose prowess blasted the invader. On the afternoon of March 17, Washington and other leaders attended church services in Cambridge. Chaplain Abiel Leonard preached "an excellent sermon" on a text from Exodus: "Let us flee from the face of Israel, for the Lord fighteth for them against the Egyptians."[98] Congress voted Washington a gold medal and promised him that "the Annals of America, will . . . inform Posterity, that under your Directions, an undisciplined Band of Husbandmen, in the Course of a few Months, became Soldiers."[99]

At Charleston, in June, American artillery crippled the attacking British vessels and helped prevent a landing. The Americans' skill and dedication in serving their guns surprised the British and gratified the revolutionaries, who—with the help of the commander, General Charles Lee—circulated throughout the continent stories of individual soldiers' valor. Congress told Colonel William Moultrie that "posterity will be astonished" to read that "an inexperienced handful of men, under your command, repulsed with loss and disgrace a powerful fleet and army of veteran troops, headed by officers of rank and reputation."[100]

Americans' efforts at Charleston and in the siege of Boston deserved much of the praise that the revolutionaries gave themselves. But the exaggeration of American superiority did not inspire people to greater effort; it made the coming hardships and reverses more surprising than they need have been. The revolutionaries kept expecting quick victory long after their difficulties became clear. When reverses came, people continued to demand the kind of victories they thought they had won in 1776. In these images the facts took second place to the ideal. Like any combatant, Americans embellished the battle story to stress their own superiority. Yet even when the facts did them credit, they seemed less interested in measuring their gains and preparing for further efforts than in celebrating their attainment of the heroism and righteousness they believed was their birthright. By linking military victory with such an ideal, they made the war a moral test that hardly anyone could pass.

If eloquence could have defeated the British, revolutionaries would soon have completed the triumph of virtue. Perhaps the eloquence was especially fervent on behalf of American prowess because the desire for a sudden triumph had become more urgent. A quick victory not only would demonstrate the native courage of Americans but also would forestall the increasing signs of failure. The growing threat that the *rage militaire* of 1775 would not win the war by itself may have seemed more likely to come true and more troubling for the future than the remote threat that America would not win at all.

At the same time that Americans rejoiced over the liberation of Boston and the defense of Charleston, their invasion of Canada ended in collapse. The conquest of Canada would have helped the revolution by securing New York and New England against both British and Indian attack. But strategic reasons alone cannot explain the fervor with which revolutionaries pressed the invasion forward and insisted that it must succeed.

The Roman Catholicism of French Canadians had long been a symbol of the tyranny that threatened American liberty and religion. Most recently, the British government had itself joined the forces of Antichrist by enacting the Quebec Act, which protected and propagated this engine of assault on Protestant freedom. In the tense, rumor-ridden months of 1775 before war with Britain began, Americans feared an invasion of armed Catholics from Canada. When, instead, the revolutionaries invaded Canada, they felt a strong desire to redeem the rest of the continent from both Catholic tyranny and British tyranny, as the thirteen colonies were being redeemed.[101] Advancing into Canada with the last of the reinforcements, a chaplain wrote in his diary: "Had pleasing views of the glorious day of universal peace and spread of the gospel through this vast extended country, which has been for ages the dwelling of Satan, and reign of Antichrist."[102] But the revolutionaries sent too weak a detachment of short-term soldiers to accomplish their purpose. Even if their attack had succeeded, the Americans could not have held Quebec against the British forces that arrived in 1776.

The Quebec expedition marked the farthest limit of Americans' reliance on their zeal for freedom, their innate military courage, and their enemy's inevitable fall. In October 1775, John Adams said that although the American soldiers were "not the best accoutred or disciplined," they were filled "with that spirit and confidence that so universally prevails throughout America, the best substitute for discipline."[103] However, when the Continental Army reached Canada, the Americans could not persuade enough French Canadians to persevere against the British. Nor would American soldiers stay beyond their terms of enlistment; some left before their terms expired. In Arnold's remarkable march across Maine they accomplished feats rare in the history of war, but such exploits were not enough to liberate a continent. The Americans' military force fell far short of their vision. Canadians could see what many Americans could not: the invaders were too weak.

After Quebec repulsed the December 31 assault, the Americans for five months tried to maintain a siege against a stronger

British garrison. Congress tried to hurry reinforcements. One delegate said in February, "We are determined (God willing) to have Quebec before the frost breaks up."[104] In the last week of May, Congress "*Resolved*, That the commanding officer in Canada, be informed, that the Congress are fully convinced of the absolute necessity of keeping possession of that country, and that they expect the forces in that department will contest every foot of the ground with the enemies of these colonies."[105] Smallpox ran through the camp: on June 2, 1776, it killed the commander, General John Thomas. By the time Burgoyne and his reinforcements pushed the Americans back to New York in June, the Continental Army had lost five thousand men in the invasion of Canada.[106] Along the line of retreat, at Isle-aux-Noix—a swampy, insect-infested island—and at Crown Point, the army paused while fifteen to thirty men died each day from smallpox, malaria, and dysentery. In foul sheds, lice fought maggots over the sick and the dead, while men yelled, sang, cursed, prayed, and died unheeded.

Those who had ordered the invasion never regretted it. Samuel Adams looked forward to attacking again the next year. "To be acting merely on the defensive at the Time when we should have been in full possession of that Country is mortifying indeed. The Subject is disgusting to me. I will dismiss it."[107] Although they saw that large undertakings needed long-term troops, more reliable supply, and an effective hospital department, they felt sure that some individual misconduct had caused the failure. Perhaps the guilty ones were in the army—Philip Schuyler or John Sullivan. Perhaps they were in Congress—the delegates who had delayed the Declaration of Independence. Plans for "emancipating Canada" revived in 1778, and later in the war people in New York and New England repeatedly urged quick conquest.[108] A series of toasts might include: "May the fourteenth String be added to the Harp."[109] Washington, who had favored the 1775 invasion, rejected later proposals because the army could not raise a sufficient force.[110]

The deaths during the first year of war—especially those at Lexington and Concord, Bunker Hill, and Canada—shocked the revolutionaries but did not dispirit them. In fact, Americans' acceptance in 1776 of their own movement toward independence owed much of its emotional conviction to the force of that shock. Undertaking an invasion of Canada soon after hostilities began suggests that Americans' reluctance to separate from Britain did not run very deep. Their eagerness to build a free, righteous, and powerful America ran much deeper. Far from augmenting any reluctance to separate from Britain, the failure of the invasion and the casualties of the first year's campaigns strengthened Americans' demand for independence and conquest. The wartime deaths proved the oppressor's plan to kill those whom he could not subjugate. Only one course could keep faith with those who had died: vindication. In the words of *Common Sense*, "The blood of the slain, the weeping voice of nature cries, 'TIS TIME TO PART."[111] When the revolutionaries faltered in strength and when they suffered reverses, they did not give up belief in their own virtue. Any fear that their native courage had lapsed could be resolved by an even greater assertion of America's righteous destiny: continental independence. The cost of the first year of war, both in deaths and in strains between ideals and deeds, pressed revolutionaries to justify their struggle more emphatically. In doing so, they would not succumb to weakness but would prove that an American nation could summon even greater resources of virtuous courage than loyal colonies could attain.

On July 21, 1776, Matthew Patten of Bedford, New Hampshire, received news of his son, Lieutenant John Patten, and wrote in his diary: "I got an account of my johns Death of the Small Pox at Canada and when I came home my wife had got a letter from Bob which gave us a particular account . . . they moved him to Isle of Noix where he died on the 20th day of june . . . whether the moveing him hurt him he does not inform us but it seems probable to me that it did He was shot through his left arm at Bunker Hill fight and now was lead after suffering much fategue to the place where he now lyes in defending the just Rights of America to whose end he came in the prime of life by means of that wicked Tyranical Brute (Nea worse than Brute) of Great Britan he was 24 years and 31 days old."[112]

Through the remaining years of fighting, the war dead sealed the intention of the living to be free. The voice of the dead that revolutionaries heard called not for surrender or accommodation or hesitation but for revenge. In 1777, William Smith, a New York loyalist who hoped for reconciliation without military victory by either side, tried to win over Margaret Beekman Livingston, mother-in-law of General Richard Montgomery. Smith recorded the dialogue:

Smith: "there [can] be no Peace expected unless there [is] a Negotiation opened for renouncing the Independency."
Livingston: "precious in the Sight of the Lord is the Blood of his Saints."
Smith: "But a Protraction of the War will spill more."
Livingston: "They can never recompence us for what they have shed, and we ought to have no more Communication with that Nation—The Lord is just and will avenge the Sufferings of his People who must patiently trust in him."
Smith: (*aside*) "Upon other subjects I scarce know a more reasonable Woman."[113]

The war for independence had become one of the obligations of a contract between the living, the dead, and the unborn: America must be the kind of nation that, in the ideals of 1775, she had promised to her sons now dead.[114]

The Declaration of Independence imposed a more demanding test of achievement on revolutionaries than simply the accomplishment of political separation from Great Britain. The primacy of the people and not the government; the dedication of the people to equality, liberty, and happiness; the vigilance against any government that might threaten these goals—all of the motives for American self-preservation demanded independence. Early in 1776 Thomas Paine's *Common Sense* enjoyed immediate, overwhelming popularity partly because it demonstrated the contradiction between self-preservation and attachment to Britain. Paine showed that Americans' most deeply felt ideals demanded liberation from a government that thwarted them. As Joseph Montgomery had said in a sermon to Delaware officers on the Continental fast day, July 20, 1775, "Common sense, and the feelings of mankind, have long since reprobated the absurd doctrine of passive obedience and non-resistance."[115]

To most revolutionaries, governmental power seemed inherently arbitrary and alien. They did not believe they could eliminate government, but they certainly wished they could. In Americans' ideal vision of the righteous future and of the perfect past, people were free. One of the most popular revolutionary metaphors, recurring in public rhetoric and private correspondence, came from the prophet Micah's vision of Zion: "They shall sit every man under his vine and under his fig tree; and none shall make them afraid."[116] Looking backward, in the kind of sentence that Americans loved to hear, Thomas Paine rued the loss of Eden: "Government, like dress, is the badge of lost innocence."[117] So is farming, a loyalist pointed out.[118] But the revolutionaries, while knowing that man is fallen and while suspiciously watching for his innate sinfulness, looked forward beyond sinful man to freedom from the alien, arbitrary rule that had almost always prevailed since the invention of government. Immediately before the prophet described the vine and the fig tree, he told of the coming peace of Zion: "They shall beat their swords into plowshares, and their spears into pruning-hooks: nation shall not lift up a sword against nation, neither shall they learn war any more."[119] Americans knew that before such days came, they had to learn war and perpetuate government. But independence would bring them nearer to the promised day. When revolutionaries spoke of freedom, they meant, in part, the libertarian, representative self-government that they sought to create in the newly independent states. But they also meant Eden and Zion where there was no fear because there was no power. Then a free man would enjoy the full promise of independence from all enemies of his happiness. An end to enemies meant an end to the host of worldly shortcomings that alloyed even the successful defense of happiness: the delegation of coercive authority, the use of force, the temptation of corruption, the danger of weakness

—even the restless vigilance needed to forestall lapses. Escape from these offered a pure freedom toward which the appeals of the revolution often aspired.

We can see the attraction of this pure freedom as we watch Americans' voluntary engagement in war decrease at the same time that their enthusiasm for independence increased. A reasoned defense of civic freedom would call the revolutionary to the field, but the longing to enjoy at once the promised freedom of Zion turned him against the alien instruments of state and army, even when they belonged to his nation. The political ideology of the revolution offered a freedom that kept the strength of the state under the unceasing vigilance of the citizen. The revolutionary vision of the future offered a freedom from all trials of strength and fears of failure.[120]

Scholars' studies of the coming of the revolution, like the writings of the revolutionaries themselves, can sometimes leave the impression that the crucial revolution had been accomplished by 1776, when Congress declared independence. The critical decision seemed to lie in Americans' minds, as they turned from professing loyalty to breaking away. In this interior struggle, people could conjure a conspiracy of enslavement, which they could constrast with their vision of a future freed from this external source of corruption. They could choose freedom in their minds and call for the defeat of its enemies. Once they had made the choice, they had accomplished the revolution. The war would only ratify the decision. Nine days before Congress declared independence, John Adams assured Professor John Winthrop that a committee was drawing up a declaration, another committee was drawing up a confederation, and other committees were working on equally important projects. "These committees will report in a week or two, and then the last finishing strokes will be given to the politics of this revolution. Nothing after that will remain but war."[121] However, the British and the loyalists refused to see the self-evident fact that the revolution had been accomplished by 1776, and the revolutionaries rightly feared that war, even more than the routine conduct of government, would threaten their ideal of the future after independence. The deaths of American soldiers pushed their countrymen ever farther toward separation from the killers, but the engines of war—bloodshed, regimentation, governmental power, public corruption, vice in the army, the enemy's sinister overtures—threatened to taint the future with the sins of the past. For this reason, in part, many undoubted supporters of independence tried to stay clear of the war and especially of the Continental Army. Their minds, no matter how revolutionized by 1776, could hardly escape the anomaly of wanting independence but not staying in the field until independence was won. They turned to other activities to support the cause, especially the enforcement of declarations of allegiance, and they persisted in a belief that defied the facts year after year: the belief that the British would soon lose or leave.

By requiring oaths of allegiance in regions suspected of loyalism, the revolutionaries may have tried to test the souls of the doubtful or to win over the wavering, but the main purpose of an oath was to compromise people in the eyes of the British and to deter them from fighting for the British. A man who swore loyalty to Congress and his state would be a documented rebel if he fell into British hands. Worse still, if he served the British and then fell back into American hands, he would be a documented traitor. The military significance of the oath became even clearer when revolutionaries confiscated the arms of suspected loyalists and of persons who would not take the oath.

Enforcing oaths was a form of service to the revolution; sometimes it seems to have become an alternative to military service. According to the minutes of the 1778 Albany County sessions of New York's Commission for Detecting and Defeating Conspiracies, "Benjamin Baker was brought before the Board and nothing specially appearing against him, we have thought proper to set him at Liberty on his entering into Recognizance and enlisting in the Continental Army."[122] By testing and enforcing loyalty one could support the cause without going far from home. One could both enjoy freedom and promote it. Some revolutionaries argued that loyalists should be drafted to fight for independence before or instead of patriots. Such inverted reasoning reached its culmination late in the war in Connecticut and Virginia when people who favored independence swore loyalty to Britain and kept documents certifying British "protection" in order to be exempt from the Continental Army draft.[123] In New Jersey and South Carolina the British found that Americans who had taken such protections were shooting redcoats. Oaths alone proved nothing about the oath-takers; however, the revolutionaries used them to prove the activity as well as the authority of the oath-givers.[124]

Apart from vengeance killings in the Carolinas and between the two armies' lines in New York and New Jersey, revolutionaries did not indulge in widespread pillorying and execution of suspected persons. Yet they talked about doing so. In 1777 Nathaniel Whitaker preached that those who "thought it their duty not to take up arms against their king that ruled over them but to submit to the higher powers" sinned against "the great law of love and light of nature." Everyone ought "to curse those cowardly, selfish, cringing, lukewarm, half-way, two-faced people, and to treat them as out-casts."[125] John Van Cortlandt, a member of the New York Convention, said in April 1777 that "the Tories . . . are plotting from New Hampshire to Carolina, but that a Thousand of them must in 2 or 3 Months be hanged and then all will be Peace."[126] When we read the fierce denunciations of internal conspirators and enemies of the people, the revolutionaries' moderation in deeds might come as a surprise unless we consider their fervor as itself a form of revolutionary service.

Two weeks after the Declaration of Independence, Joseph Hawley, a leader in western Massachusetts, urged Congress to define high treason and to authorize capital punishment for "exterminating traitors." He was amazed that the lack of such a law had not already enabled "our intestine enemies" to ruin the cause, which was "every moment in amazing danger" for want of one. "The common understanding of the people, like unerring instinct, had long declared this; and from the clear discerning which they had had of it, they have long been in agonies about it. They expect that . . . all those who shall be convicted of endeavouring, by overt act, to destroy the State, shall be cut off from the earth." At the same time, he said that despite his most earnest efforts to get men to enlist for the duration of the war, New Englanders would not engage for more than two years—"I fear for no longer time than one year." And they would not stay after their time had expired.[127]

These two instincts of the people did not seem to conflict: neither short-termers nor those who stayed at home regarded themselves as intestine enemies. Yet we can infer that anathemas against traitors embodied zeal these revolutionaries were not expressing by sustained conflict with identifiable, uniformed enemies. As Bernard Bailyn has shown, the revolutionaries' effort to win the psychological victory of popular commitment to independence could move them to change their institutions to implement the ideals of independence.[128] But that mental victory could also create a rhetorical refuge where people could strike vivid, intangible blows for independence while the enemy ranged over the land. Wishing that the revolution could be accomplished by conversion rather than by killing the unconverted, many revolutionaries tried to win independence by declaring it over and over. In the search for signs of grace, they often convinced themselves, for a while, that words were works. They could hardly have avoided such a lapse or escape as long as they judged their present state partly according to visions of a lost Eden or a future Zion. The army and the warfare to which the cause of independence called them differed too much from the revolutionaries' ideal life. They heard the promise that by undertaking sustained, regimented combat they might achieve their vision of the future through their own deeds. But behind this promise lay the fear that sustained, regimented combat would take them so far from the vision as to make it unattainable. Instead of forswearing the unattainable vision they settled for nearing it in the mind alone.

The Declaration of Independence had hardly been circulated and celebrated when America's military fortunes began to decline rapidly. Even though the invasion of Canada had already failed, the reverses in the summer and autumn of 1776 came as sharp, unexpected blows to the assumption that declaring independence was the paramount step to its accomplishment.

Almost all the revolutionaries, including the Continental generals, overestimated the Continental Army's abilities. On July 22, 1776, Nathanael Greene wrote from Long Island, "We are strongly fortified here everything in readiness and the troops in good Spirits. I have not the most distant apprehensions for this Army."[129] They thought that they could hold Long Island and Manhattan against the royal army and fleet. They were wrong. And on August 27, 1776, on Long Island, as the British marched into their midst through a neglected American left flank, the generals matched their confidence with their incompetence. Some patriots said that Washington's silent, foggy withdrawal to Manhattan on the night of August 29 showed the intervention of Providence to protect the Americans from the British who surrounded them on land and water. If so, God must have given the Americans generals, especially a commander in chief, who would put their army in an untenable position in the first place, all the better to show that Providence was their sole firm hope.

Washington reported that the defeat, which he called a "Check," "has dispirited too great a proportion of our Troops and filled their minds with apprehension and dispair. . . . With the deepest concern I am obliged to confess my want of confidence, in the generality of the Troops."[130] The soldiers returned this lack of confidence. Many of them believed that only sabotage could have stopped them, that a conspiracy among American generals had betrayed the troops into defeat. Through the camp went the cry, "We are sold!"[131]

In mid-September, as the soldiers saw that the army would withdraw from the city too, graffiti appeared on houses and tents: "Let us fly no more."[132] On September 17, at Harlem Heights, Nathanael Greene said, "I would not evacuate one foot of ground, as it will tend to encourage the enemy and dispirit our people."[133] In November, Washington, who knew better, irresolutely allowed Greene's advice to prevail: Colonel Robert Magaw tried to hold Fort Washington on the northern end of Manhattan, even after British ships had passed all the obstructions on the Hudson. The fort was inexpertly defended, and on November 16, 1776, the British made prisoners of twenty-six hundred American soldiers, most of whom eventually died due to mistreatment. The next day Greene wrote to Henry Knox, "I was afraid of the fort. . . . I feel mad, vexed, sick, and sorry. Never did I need the consoling voice of a friend more than now. . . . Pray, what is said upon the occasion?"[134]

The soldiers' eagerness for combat proved its fighting value in resolute stands within the battles at Long Island and White Plains on October 28. At the same time, men's spirits fluctuated sharply—depressed by the rout at Kip's Bay on September 15, elated by the skirmish at Harlem Heights on September 16. They said that they wanted to stand; yet they also said of the enemy, "As soon as we can get them out of reach of their shipping we will beat them."[135] After the flight at Kip's Bay, Southerners taunted New Englanders with "standing terms of reproach and dishonour" such as "Eastern Prowess" and "Camp Difficulty," which also meant diarrhea.[136] But despite tall talk, entire units folded quickly at Long Island and White Plains. In a private letter, Washington referred to his "Mixed and ungovernable Troops" this way: "A parcel of —— but it is best to say nothing more about them."[137]

The Continentals had expected to beat the British on Long Island, but after the withdrawal to Manhattan, according to one diarist, "It seemed a general damp had spread; and the sight of the scattered people up and down the streets was indeed moving. Many looked sickly, emaciated, cast down. . . . Many, as it is reported for certain, went away to their respective homes."[138] The skirmish at Harlem Heights raised their spirits, but a week later another journal reported, "Our Lads grow tired, and begin to count the Days of their Service which yet remain."[139] The soldiers' war spirit demanded victories to confirm their risky undertaking. Neither they nor the revolutionaries at large yet knew how deep ran active commitment to independence and war. They tried to gauge that commitment by ground held or lost, by events of the moment. Confidence in America's future, which revolutionaries expressed through their enthusiasm for independence, could not alone guarantee that future. Revolutionaries would have to mobilize the tangible instruments of governmental authority and military force. By the end of 1776, Americans' capacity to create, sustain, and wield these instruments on a continental scale under prolonged assault was becoming both more crucial and less certain. Even the most active and exposed defenders of independence—Continental soldiers—had not committed themselves to stay with the fight as long as the British attacked. Nor had they developed enough expertise to assure that they could fight and lose and yet fight again. The military reverses of 1776 were testing the workings of American self-government at once. After Paine and Jefferson preached the sermons, the British army passed the collection plate.

In December 1776, the Continental Army's troubles all came together. Washington had given away twenty-six hundred officers and men by leaving them in Fort Washington; we can imagine what effect that death sentence had on the militia, the auxiliary troops of the Flying Camp, and the short-timer Continentals who took the opportunity to leave. The force under Washington shrank to three thousand men or fewer. New Jersey seemed to welcome the British: many people hurried to swear allegiance to the king and take protections. One Jerseyman later said that the British could have bought the whole populace for eighteen pence a head.[140] Some of these people were active loyalists, but most probably hoped that collaboration would secure their main desire—to be left alone. Washington fled across the Delaware, and Congress fled Philadelphia.

As these events became known, revolutionaries all over the continent felt deep distress and anxiety. Washington said that if recruitment of a new army in 1777 failed, "I think the game will be pretty well up."[141] Even so, the British capture of Philadelphia and the complete dispersal of Washington's army probably would not have ended the revolution. But Americans, who had claimed not to fear the consequences of revolution, now feared the consequences of such defeats. In October, President John Hancock, sending reenlistment instructions to the states, had said, "The Congress, for very obvious reasons, are extremely anxious to keep the army together. . . . Were this barrier once removed, military power would quickly spread desolation and ruin over the face of our country."[142] In November and December, the British and their German auxiliaries were plundering their way across New Jersey—stealing, destroying, beating, and raping, without regard to protections or political sympathies. If we imagine the total dispersal of the Continental Army at the end of 1776, we could guess that, in response to such treatment from the enemy, Americans might have become more militarily active revolutionaries and might have built stronger, more reliable militias, as New Jersey later did.[143] But we cannot conclude that they would have welcomed the prospect. They certainly did not in December of 1776. The jubilation that followed Washington's victory at Trenton celebrated the survival of the war as Americans had known it—fought primarily by the Continental Army. They would not have to choose between giving up and fighting a dispersed war of havoc.

To better understand why "A Shudder went thro' the Continent in Oct. and Nov.,"[144] followed by dejection in December, we need to consider an image or impulse that sometimes helped to express Americans' love of freedom: the urge to flee the immediate threat and find unalloyed freedom in escape. In their use of the image of flight, we can detect the revolutionaries' fear that prolonged warfare might rob them of their visions of earthly happiness, no matter who won. Within their image of freedom, two themes recurred: first, the need for perpetual struggle to win and to defend freedom; second, the attractiveness of achieving a freedom that would mean the end of all struggle. The two themes conflicted; while the first offered duty, the second offered pleasure. When British victories threatened Americans with either a long war or a quick defeat, flight could promise a freedom that struggle was unable to preserve. "The American Liberty Song," one of *Two Favorite Songs of the American Camp* in 1775, included this stanza:

With the beasts of the wood
We will ramble for food
And live in wild deserts and caves,
And live poor as *Job*
On the skirts of the globe,
Before we'll submit to be slaves.[145]

In the same year, Philip Freneau wrote, in *American Liberty, A Poem*:

> Bear me some power as far as winds can blow,
> As ships can travel, or as waves can flow,
> To some lone isle beyond the southern pole,
> Or lands 'round which pacific waters roll,
> There should oblivion stop the heaving sigh,
> There should I live at least with liberty,
> But honour checks my speed and bids me stay,
> To try the fortunes of the well fought day,
> Resentment for my country's fate I bear,
> And mix with thousands for the willing war.[146]

When active in resistance, the same vision of flight lingered. In his history of the revolution, David Ramsay, a revolutionary leader in South Carolina, later described the spirit of 1775: "The animated votaries of the equal rights of human nature, consoled themselves with the idea, that though their whole sea coast should be laid in ashes, they could retire to the western wilderness, and enjoy the luxury of being free."[147] After the loss of Fort Washington, Lieutenant Samuel Shaw wrote to a friend, "Don't let us be discouraged. . . . I heartily pray, rather than renounce that child of our hopes, that darling Independence, that we may suffer the extremes of war and desolation in all their horrors, and, after being driven from one post to another till we are pushed to the utmost point of creation, gloriously launch into the immensity of space, firm in our opposition to tyranny."[148]

As military resistance seemed to collapse, as Americans—personally or vicariously—faced desolation, freedom might, for a moment, call one to flight rather than to stubborn war on the ground. Sometimes the idea of escape was literal. In Plymouth, Massachusetts, "many devoted Whigs" gathered one evening to hear an officer just back from camp describe the retreat through New Jersey. One of them later recalled, "The young men present determined to emigrate, and seek some spot where liberty dwelt, and where the arm of British tyranny could not reach us. . . . The agitation and despondency produced, will hardly be appreciated by those unacquainted with the deep excitability of the public mind at that period.[149]

But the more dangerous flight was an interior one toward, in Freneau's word, "oblivion." As we have seen, oblivion, or permanent sleep, was the state of mind that Americans attributed to slavery. For most revolutionaries who faced the threat of a coast in ashes, attaining the poetic freedom of deserts, wilderness, islands, and space would have been, in fact, an attempt to preserve the vision of liberty in the mind while the country gave way to the tyrant. They knew that such an attempt was doomed; so they expressed the idea in images of physical escape—but knowing that the attempt would be hopeless deepened their temporary dejection. In that dejection we can also see the revolutionaries' fear that they, like many in New Jersey, might choose collaboration or surrender. Far from showing that American independence was common sense, events seemed to confirm the worst that the British and the loyalists had said about American weakness: lost battles, lost forts, thousands of prisoners, Generals Sullivan and Stirling taken in battle, General Lee—the respected military mind—captured in his quarters, the army and its militia auxiliaries reduced by dispersal and disease. A loyalist with the British army later said, "What was called their flying camp was literally so."[150] The imminent fall of the capital and the army seemed to mean that American independence would require more widespread, harsher sacrifices than all these.

The revolutionaries had assumed that the love of freedom strengthened them against the tyrant. However, fear of losing the struggle and delight in escaping the struggle might together cause Americans to question their strength rather than trust it. William Hooper, a North Carolina delegate in Congress, held the American cause as "dear as my Religion" and said that "no sacrifice that I can make can be too valuable a consideration" for American success. But with such dedication in April 1776 went a "wish for peace, that we may once more under our own Vines and Fig trees enjoy the blessings of domestic peace, that I might enjoy in my own Cabin, eat my Hogg and Hominee without anything to make me afraid."[151] If freedom's call to struggle, as expressed in the *rage militaire* of 1775, could not secure Americans' homes, would they fight a new, deadlier form of "willing war"? Or might they send their vision of freedom to some distant place in the mind while they made peace with the crown? They well knew that the alternative to self-preservation was oblivion, but in their discussions of freedom and happiness, the revolutionaries never fully convinced themselves that vigilance and struggle had to be as constant as their own warnings said. Their ideal included an eloquent strain of tranquility and enjoyment. The luxury of freedom sometimes promised an ease that required no contention, just as the luxury of slavery permitted none. The revolutionaries knew how attractive they found escape from struggle, not only when they hoped for such an escape in America's future, but also when they warned against it as the poisoned promise in slavery. They were sure that they rejected the tyrant; they were less sure that they rejected ease. The prospect of a war of desolation tempted Americans to flee toward ease and oblivion at the same time that it called them to resist. The survival of the Continental Army saved most revolutionaries from having to face the enemy in person and choose.

Few revolutionaries outside the army concluded that Americans would have lost their independence without the Continental Army. Army service was one important manifestation of revolutionary virtue, but independence rested on public virtue, not on institutions that Americans reserved the right to alter or abolish. Did the army embody the revolution? Would the nation fight on without an army? The retreat across New Jersey dramatized both questions; they persisted throughout the war. Some revolutionaries, especially army officers, assumed that as long as the British tried to prevent American independence, the Continental Army was the central embodiment of the American Revolution. Many officers grew convinced that without the army, independence would not survive.[152] As lack of pay and supplies increased their hardships, officers decided that the army and especially they, its leaders, manifested unique patriotism in both the risks they ran in facing the enemy and the sufferings they underwent due to their heedless countrymen. The commander of the Fifth Pennsylvania Regiment, Colonel Francis Johnston, said in May 1779, "I am certain nothing but the *Harmony, Fortitude*, and *Virtue* of the Army can possibly save the Country."[153] All revolutionaries wanted the army to survive, and almost all preferred that soldiers rather than civilians confront the British army. But many civilians, like Thomas Burke in June 1776, regarded the war as "the cause in which . . . I have unremittingly struggled since the stamp act."[154] The army was a central instrument in this cause, and it was better to have it than not to have it. However, it could not claim to be the repository of Americans' hopes for independence. In January 1777, Thomas Paine told Lord Richard Howe that if the Continental Army disbanded, planning to reassemble later, the British would be no nearer conquest because "you have both an army and a country to combat with."[155]

The urge to resist British rule ran deep in revolutionaries. It found one level of expression in the rhetorical celebration of the army. In addition to that vicarious, corporate resistance, many revolutionaries expected to remain defiant no matter what happened to the army. At the same time, they persisted in believing that Britain would soon give up. Consequently, the urgency and sense of crisis that officers and public officials felt during the army's prolonged difficulties alarmed the public only sporadically. Revolutionaries at home, though concerned by repeated warnings about the army's precarious state, often refused to act as if the army's survival depended on their efforts or as if they thought the army were essential to American independence. Five days before the Battle of Trenton, Benjamin Rush warned, "We must have an army; the fate of America must be decided by an army." Nine months later he wrote, "The militia began, and I sincerely hope the militia will end, the present war. I should despair of our cause if our country contained 60,000 men abandoned enough to enlist for 3 years or during the war."[156]

Popular virtue entailed popular resistance to tyranny. Not only did army operations conflict with the revolutionaries' ideal for America, but to acknowledge that Americans would have lost their independence in the absence of an army would have conceded the collapse of public virtue. Instead, the prevalence of public virtue was symbolized by the unconquerable American continent. From the beginning Americans announced that their continent gave them an advantage the enemy could not overcome. The British could march but not control. The *Boston Gazette* reprinted a British pamphlet's warning against a war "at more than 3000 miles distance, against an enemy we now find united, active, able, and resolute . . . in a country where fastness grows upon fastness, and labyrinth on labyrinth; where a check is a defeat, and a defeat is ruin. It is a war of absurdity and madness."[157] The proper American strategy was resilience, avoiding single-battle decisions while checking and hurting the British whenever possible until they gave up their vain efforts. But army officers and civilians interpreted the strategic strength of the American continent differently. Washington did not adopt his Fabian strategy for the Continental Army until after the loss of New York, and he never adopted it fully or preferred it. He wanted a regular, eighteenth-century army that could defend the capital, meet the enemy on the plain, or take New York back by siege and assault. Even so, the campaigns against Howe in Pennsylvania, Burgoyne in New York, and Cornwallis in the South followed this strategy, which sought to preserve the army in order to prolong the revolution. From Valley Forge, Nathanael Greene defended Washington's Fabian conduct by saying, "We cannot conquer the British force at once, but they cannot conquer us at all. The limits of the British government in America are their out-sentinels."[158]

In September 1776, a British officer recorded an adage current among revolutionaries: "If Great Britain cannot conquer us, she cannot govern us."[159] Revolutionaries outside the army assumed that they could rely on popular defiance throughout a vast continent when their army was not near or even if there were no Continental Army. Americans need not defeat the British army on the battlefield as long as they could keep the British army from defeating their resistance to being governed. A British report showed how such civilian resistance worked: "While in our power they conceal their arms, and secret whatever would be of use to us, appear friends and pretend to be good subjects but the moment we move harrass and annoy us. . . . Altho' this army can go wherever the General pleases—yet leaving the Country as we hitherto have done, the business is still to do over again."[160]

Yet, even though Americans praised and practiced this calculating, supple defiance, nothing aroused them so much as the loss of fixed posts and cities: New York in 1776, Fort Ticonderoga and Philadelphia in 1777, Charleston in 1780. Part of the horror of Benedict Arnold's plot was the prospect of losing West Point, which was widely considered the main defense of communications between New England and the rest of the continent. Revolutionaries who raised an outcry, full of anxiety and recriminations, in response to these reverses did not receive a satisfactory answer in being told that cities and posts did not measure the success of America's continental strategy. Revolutionaries could sometimes be nonchalant about the loss of fixed positions only because they were ignoring the war, not because they were preparing to resist in the countryside. In 1780 a newspaper's appeal to the people of the southern states reminded them, "We heard of the capture of Savannah, in Georgia, with the same indifference as if it had been a town in Asia."[161] Americans practiced the continental strategy that they advocated, but they judged the war by visible standards of ground held, strong points won and lost. Only after Burgoyne was trapped did the people who had wanted to hold Fort Ticonderoga against him to the last man discover their own masterly wisdom in entangling him in the woods.

In their anxiety about holding forts and cities, the revolutionaries showed that they were not so confident of popular resistance against immediate powerful attacks as their advance proclamations of defiance alleged. If the British army came and stayed, would they only "pretend" to be good subjects or would they insensibly slide into easy acquiescence? The survival of the Continental Army gave revolutionaries the prospect of protection, and they wanted it. Even when it left some of them unprotected, its survival assured them that a strong, cohesive force could eventually secure the country, with the help of citizens' piecemeal resistance. The fullest test of the continent's infinite ability to thwart the invader would have come when revolutionaries had no strength on which to rely but their isolated will to revolt. They believed that they could pass the test, but they were eager to avoid it.

To the generals, the Fabian strategy of keeping the army together at the expense of posts and territory seemed essential to a continuation of the war. To them, the revolution depended on the army. Most civilians acted as if the Continental Army carried with it their hopes of victory, which they measured by the ground the army occupied. But in their history of prewar opposition to British tyranny, in their ideology of popular zeal, and in their popular version of a strategy of continental resistance, the army was only ancillary to the revolution. This split view among revolutionaries at home enabled them to rely on the army more than they liked and to support it less than it required, while after victory they could say that they had needed it less than its officers claimed. In this way, Americans could try to offset the army's corrupting effect on the revolution. They could not deny that they had used it to gain independence, but they could deny that they had needed it. Perhaps this minimizing of their reliance on institutionalized force could keep independence unsullied by military vices.

Washington and his small force received ardent praise for the capture of the Hessians at Trenton on December 26, 1776, followed by the engagement at Princeton and the British withdrawal from most of their winter posts in New Jersey. Unlike the departing soldiers of 1775, Continentals this time extended their enlistments to pursue their victories. Washington persuaded men to undertake stormy winter night operations and to stay beyond their discharge dates for further combat. He had less trouble with such persuasion than he usually had in enforcing routine obligations of military service because he could promise money, movement, and results. Fife Major John Greenwood later said that the soldiers marched readily because "it was all the same owing to the impossibility of being in a worse condition than their present one, and therefore the men always like to be kept moving in expectation of bettering themselves."[162] In this perseverance despite hardship—as well as in the promise of money, the call to voluntary sacrifice, and the enjoyment of victory—we can discern the beginnings of the professionalism that enabled the army to stay in the field throughout the war. Private John Howland remembered his unit's decision to stay for the January campaign: "This was the time that tried both soul and body."[163]

Victory inspirited the remaining Continentals, and it transported the public. No later victory equaled the effect on the public mind of Trenton, Princeton, and the British withdrawal. Elation replaced dejection. Captain John Chester, who was traveling home to Connecticut from the army early in January, wrote to a colonel at the end of the trip, "You Cannot conceive the Joy and Raptures the people were universally in as we passed the road. 'T is good to be the messenger of Glad Tidings."[164] A year later Chaplain David Avery recalled that "the tidings flew upon the wings of the wind—and at once revived the hopes of the fearful, which had almost fled! How sudden the transition from darkness to light; from grief to joy!"[165] Some people expected Washington to march back through New Jersey and capture Howe's army or drive it out of New York.

The commander in chief and the soldiers who had shown the soundness of Thomas Paine's appeal received eloquent praise for saving their country. Even more important, people could see from the course of events that God's Providence intended American independence no matter how great was Britain's earthly strength. God and Washington had turned the armies around without leaving America to the severest test of her independence: self-preservation without an army. Thus, the celebrations managed to make Washington's stroke both miraculous and inevitable, conveying at once the revolutionaries' relief from great anxiety and their confidence in victory. Because Americans wanted the Continental Army to bear the main weight of defending independence from British attack, they devoted strong concern, high praise, and critical scrutiny to the army's operations. But their underlying conviction that

American independence was self-evidently, commonsensically inevitable detached them from their own immediate dependence on the army. The revolutionaries' suspicion of any hierarchical elite, especially a military one, may have combined with their intimations of their own weakness in relying so heavily on the army, thus producing deep vicarious involvement with the army's fortunes and at the same time a desire to remain aloof from the army's evils.

Janet Livingston was thirty years old when she became Janet Montgomery by marrying Richard Montgomery in 1773. She had briefly met Richard ten years earlier when he was a captain in the British army, participating in the British conquest of Canada. He was, Washington Irving later wrote, "the *beau ideal* of a soldier." In 1772, after failing in his attempt to buy a major's commission, he resigned and came to New York to be a farmer. He was thirty-six when he married Janet, who was the daughter of Judge Robert R. Livingston of Clermont. The Livingstons were important landholders, manor lords, and political leaders of the revolution in New York. One of Janet's brothers, Henry Beekman Livingston, became a colonel in the Continental Army. Another, Robert R. Livingston, became a delegate to the Continental Congress and secretary of foreign affairs. Another, Edward Livingston, became secretary of state under Andrew Jackson.

In her "husband, friend and lover" Janet Montgomery found "my every hope of happiness"; at Rhinebeck he built a mill, stocked a farm, and laid the foundation of a house, while, Janet said, "I laid off the fine lady." Surrounded by family and friends, she enjoyed "the feast of reason and the flow of soul."

In the autumn of 1773, after agitation against the Tea Act had begun, her husband woke her one night as she cried in her sleep. At first she did not know him because she had been dreaming that he was dying, mortally wounded in a sword fight with his brother. In the dream, Richard's last words to her had been, "No other way, no other way." On his deathbed she had asked him whether he knew her. He shook his head. After she described the dream, her husband reminded her that he knew his happiness would not last. "It has no foundation. Let us enjoy it as long as we may and leave the rest to God." Once, when she expressed an earnest wish for a son, he put her off with banter: "Be contented, Janet. Suppose we had a son, and he was a fool. Think of that!" They had no children.

The Coercive Acts of 1774 convinced Richard to support American resistance. In 1775 he was elected to the New York Provincial Congress, and in June the Continental Congress named him one of the first eight brigadier generals. Washington, on his way to Cambridge, brought the commission to New York. Janet first learned of it when her husband gave her a black ribbon and with a half smile asked her to tie it in a cockade for his hat. She later said, "I felt a stroke at my heart as if struck with lightning." When Richard told her that his engagement depended only on her wishes, she said that she would never consent. But he persuaded her. He told her that a just cause needed him, that he had been a soldier from his youth, that her family would shelter her, and that his honor called him. He left the decision with her: "Say you will prefer to see your husband disgraced and I submit to go home to retirement." She took the ribbon.

Richard wanted to go with Washington to Cambridge, but he was ordered north as Philip Schuyler's second in command. He led the invasion of Canada. Janet accompanied him to Saratoga, where they parted. Richard, Janet, and her eleven-year-old brother Edward sat silently together in a room—Janet sad, Richard musing, and Edward admiring the general's uniform and martial bearing. Richard suddenly thought of an old Thomas Middleton comedy. His deep voice broke the silence, as if from a dream: " 'Tis a mad world, my masters,' I once thought so, now I know it." Edward left the room. Janet later said that her husband's last words to her were, "*You shall never blush for your Montgomery*."

The couple corresponded while they were apart; Richard wanted more letters from his wife but not like the ones she first wrote: "I must entreat the favor of you to write no more of those whining letters, I declare if I receive another in that style, I will lock up the rest without reading them. I don't want anything to lower my spirits; I have abundant use for them all, and at the best of times I have not too much."

General Montgomery found fault with his New England troops: they were homesick; they deserted; their officers had no authority. "The privates are all generals but not soldiers." The First New York Regiment was even worse. At the head of "troops who carry the spirit of freedom into the field, and think for themselves," he could not count on obedience or perseverance, but he spoke to the Canadians boldly: "The Continental army came into this province for its protection; they, therefore, cannot consider their opposers as taking up arms for its defence."

The Americans took St. Johns, then Montreal. Richard wrote home, "I have courted fortune and found her kind." Congress promoted him to major general. Still, he knew that "till Quebec is taken, Canada is unconquered." But when his brother-in-law, Captain Henry Beekman Livingston, said to him, "Now, General, for Quebec," Richard replied gravely, "Oh! Harry, that is impossible."

While Richard prepared to attack Quebec, he planned to resign his commission. He wrote to Janet on December 5, "I wish it were well over, with all my heart, and sigh for home like a New-Englander." He would be willing to serve again in the future if America were in a critical position, but affairs would have to be "much worse . . . than they are at present." In his last letter to Janet, he asked her whether she would like to take his place: "Shall I recommend you for a Brigadier?"

In the early morning of December 31, 1775, he led a forlorn hope through two barricades into Quebec's Lower Town, attacked a fortified house, and fell in the narrow street, shot through the head.

Like Joseph Warren, Richard Montgomery became in death the revolutionaries' ideal of valor, command, patriotism, and self-sacrifice. Commemorations, eulogies, and verse celebrated his union with the heroes of antiquity and called Americans to equal his ardor. College students promised their countrymen that "heav'n will avenge your wrong; / MONTGOMERIES raise unnumber'd in his room." Thomas Paine wrote a dialogue in which General Montgomery's ghost came to Philadelphia to persuade a delegate in Congress that the time for independence had come. When public spirit faltered later in the war, a call to arms in the newspapers was signed, "THE GHOST OF MONTGOMERY." Janet Montgomery appeared in rhetoric and song (William Smith's *An Oration in Memory of General Montgomery*), in drama (Hugh Henry Brackenridge's *The Death of General Montgomery*), and in poetry (*America Invincible*). Both the poem and the play gave her a child. After the war, Janet's friend and correspondent Mercy Otis Warren put Richard's parting words in her *History of the Rise, Progress and Termination of the American Revolution*—words that Janet had repeated to her in 1777.

After his death, Janet called her husband "my General" and "my soldier." One night she dreamed that they were walking along a road on a boundless plain. At a crossroads he stopped, turned to her, and said, "Janet, here we part. This is my way, and you must tread for many years this weary path alone." Always, in her letters, she kept returning to "the idol of my warmest affections," the "angel sent us for a moment." She said that she did not want to appear "like a memento to my friends," but her loss caused reflections that "imbitter continually each day as it passes." The subject "always obtrudes itself let me begin with what I will and unfits me for every other Duty." She wore mourning for the rest of her life.

In her sorrow she had the support of her friends and of her confidence that after death she would rejoin her husband and her father, who had also died in 1775. From Ireland, Lady Ranelagh, Richard's sister, sent her the only portrait of Richard from life, made when he was twenty-five years old. Janet's letters expressed not only grief but strong patriotism. She nearly quarreled with two of her relatives when they began to favor reconciliation with Britain. Janet said that such a wish meant they were not "Whigs." In Livingston family conversations, she censured Schuyler for weakness; she spoke slightingly of Putnam; she called Gates a fool.

Janet Montgomery "possessed a very strong mind." After the war, she managed estates and enjoyed holding the center of attention at social events—though not in the Christmas season, which always remained "the anniversary of the deepest affliction." She told a woman whose son had died that God "did not permit me to sink under the weight" of losing a father and a husband, "but bid me look forward to the high reputation they had left behind." She enjoyed hearing from the boys who were named after General Montgomery. She urged a member of Congress to speed the shipment of the long-delayed monument to General Montgomery that Congress had ordered in 1776. In 1784 she turned down a proposal of marriage from General Horatio Gates, adding her hope that he would find a wife who could give him "undivided affections." Later she copied her letter of refusal into her "Reminiscences." Gates pleaded for her to save him from wretchedness, distress, mental agitation, "Chaos," and "irrevocable Doom." He had been a widower for less than a year, and within two years he married a merchant's daughter worth almost half a million dollars. Meanwhile, Janet was buying real estate on the lower East Side of Manhattan.

In 1789 she went to Ireland to visit Lady Ranelagh. Before leaving, she wrote to Mercy Otis Warren, "When I return, I hope to find my dear country, for which I have *bled*, the envy of her enemies and the glory of her patriots." While staying in New York City before her departure, Janet was the frequent guest of President and Mrs. Washington. She tried diligently but unsuccessfully to get her brother Robert appointed secretary of the Treasury or chief justice in the new federal government. In Ireland, with a letter of introduction from Washington, she visited Sir Edward Newenham. He took her into his "American room, which gave her much satisfaction"; there she saw portraits of Washington and "all the respectable characters in America. She remarked with pleasure the picture of one Arnold *reversed*, and his *treason* wrote under it."

In 1802 and 1803, when she was sixty years old, Janet built a mansion overlooking the Hudson River. On a broad lawn within three hundred acres of shrubbery and forest, the house commanded a view of the river and the Catskill Mountains. Washington Irving visited her there. Her house had high ceilings, great windows, and stone walls two feet thick. She called it Chateau de Montgomery. The high peak directly in front of the house had a summit shaped like a bowl. Formerly called Liberty Cap, it became known to local people as "Mrs. Montgomery's Cap," in honor of the widow's cap she always wore.

In 1818, mainly through her influence and letter-writing, General Richard Montgomery's remains were removed from Quebec and brought back to New York. The skeleton was well preserved except for the lower jaw, which had been shot away. In Albany, in New York City, and along the Hudson, parades, veterans, military bands, and minute guns gave the general the most impressive public display since the death of Washington. Edward Livingston, whose son escorted the remains, called it "a great act of national piety." Governor DeWitt Clinton told Janet what time on July 6 the steamboat *Richmond* would pass Chateau de Montgomery, carrying the plumed coffin canopied with crape and "overshadowed by twenty star-spangled banners." She asked her guests to leave her alone on the porch. As the boat approached, she watched it through a spyglass and thought of her "beloved husband, who left me in the bloom of manhood, a perfect being. Alas! how did he return!" The steamer stopped before the house; the band played the Dead March from Handel's oratorio *Saul*; the troops fired a salute; and the boat passed on. When the guests returned to the porch, they found that she had fainted.

The public attention to the return of the body made this a favorable time, in Janet's opinion, to publish a biography of her husband. In August a Philadelphia monthly printed a short memoir and an engraving of the monument erected by Congress. A biography did not appear until 1834. It was written by John Armstrong, Jr., Janet's brother-in-law. Late in life, when she saw a silhouette of General Montgomery, she said, "Hard was thy fate most amiable of men! But alas—how much more so, the lott of thy unhappy wife—condemned to live and live without thee, whilst cruel remembrance is continually comparing the past with the present and imbittering the whole." In 1820, when she was seventy-six, she wrote her "Reminiscences."

In 1824 the marquis de Lafayette toured the United States as America's National Guest. Everywhere crowds eagerly greeted the friend of Washington and the hero of the Revolution. In

September, on his steamboat trip up the Hudson and back, he visited Janet, his correspondent of forty years past. Three days before this visit, Lafayette attended a supper and ball given in his honor by the Livingstons at Clermont. Among the many guests was Janet Montgomery. The marquis gave her his arm, and they opened the dance by walking twice around the floor together.

When Janet Montgomery was in her eighties, she received through her brother the compliments of Andrew Jackson, who said he wished for "the honor of shaking by the hand the *revered relict* of *the patriotic Genl. Montgomery*, who will ever live in the hearts of his country." A European visitor to her home found her, at the age of eighty-two, "still in possession of her mental faculties, although her eyes were somewhat dim. I noticed on the wall among the family portraits for which American[s] cherish a great respect a portrait of the General. He must have been a very handsome man."[166]

CHAPTER III
Jericho

By 1777 the Continental Army's place in Americans' understanding of the revolution had changed markedly from the *rage militaire* of 1775. The year between the Battle of Trenton and the winter at Valley Forge, marked the development of a new, more complex relationship between the army and the public. As the lapsing of the popular *rage militaire* became ever more conspicuous, the army's need to recruit and retain soldiers and improve their competence grew more pressing. Clearly, citizens would not be taking the places of all soldiers whose short enlistments or lack of training ended in departure or death. Yet, citizens were not reconciled either to the prospect of a long war or to dependence on military professionalism for victory. Even as they followed the army's career with intense concern and fear, they sought a quick conquest that would preserve the republic by means of the virtue and courage of its citizens.

In the campaign of 1777, this virtue and courage won a measure of confirmation in the capture of the invading British army under the command of General John Burgoyne. At the same time, however, both the American army and the populace revealed, under the strain of a lengthening war, the ways in which their war spirit was not attaining the courageous virtue they sought. Their ardor, though enthusiastic, proved to be unpredictable. For a long war, the revolutionaries would need new resources for perseverance.

The diaries and memoirs of several soldiers end with the January campaign in New Jersey. Their terms expired, and they went home. Two of them, in their old age, recalled that their officers had promised them commissions under the new establishment, but to no avail.[1] The soldiers did not believe that they ought to apologize for their departure; nor did they consider it any discredit to have left the army long before victory. Many of those who left probably reenlisted before the summer was over, when the price was high enough. Others insisted that they had served their turn. Although the soldiers' services almost always exceeded the demands of their enlistment contract after the government defaulted on the promised pay, clothing, or food, they resorted to the contract to distinguish their hard service from the easy time of the stay-at-homes. Their notions of equity distinguished military service to the revolution from other revolutionary activities and assumed that if they reenlisted before other men had served even one term, such effort put their home state in their debt. They believed that even if they did not reenlist, they still had done more for the revolution than most of their countrymen. Late in the war, according to the memory of an eyewitness, a Virginia regiment refused Lieutenant Colonel John Laurens's request to stay three days beyond the regiment's allotted time to help with a planned attack. "One soldier, I well remember, exclaimed, 'our zeal in the service cannot be denied; we have strictly adhered to the performance of every duty required of us, and our thinned ranks sufficiently proclaim, that in encountering danger, we have shown no backwardness, nor inclination to shrink from battle. We were eight hundred strong when we joined the army—we can now scarcely muster three hundred. Five hundred men have fallen by sickness and the sword—it is time that repose should be ours. We retire with the consciousness of having deserved well of our country. The want of zeal to the cause can never be justly imputed to us.' And they left."[2]

By 1777, many citizens, while insisting that the hardships at home were comparable to those in the field, tacitly shared the soldiers' idea of military service as a distinct activity but drew from it a different conclusion. They began to assume that among men between the ages of sixteen and fifty, some were suited to be soldiers and some were not. These citizens acted as if society had the right to expect those who were suited for the army to stay in it as long as need be, while others stayed home and served the cause in their appropriate ways. That is, the revolutionaries wanted to create an army of professional soldiers for the duration without having the citizen-soldier speeches of 1775 thrown in their faces. Once a long-term army became necessary, the public decided that it was the duty only of some men—mainly unmarried sons of farmers, farm laborers, servants, apprentices, slaves, and mechanics—to fill its ranks.[3] As we have seen, the states' great reluctance to conscript and their intricate calculations to raise large bounties from among citizens staying at home suggest the guilt with which the public implemented its decision.

This background to the war news helps us to understand a recurrent characteristic of the public temper that many observers —European, British, loyalist, and revolutionary—noted at different times. Americans followed events with extravagant seesawing moods. Joy and optimism took turns with gloom as one story or rumor followed another. People tried to escape their susceptibility by disbelieving unwelcome reports and by charging that those who believed them were false whigs. If a report proved true—for example, the fall of Charleston in 1780—the subsequent distress was all the greater. The extravagance of Americans' fluctuating spirits may have come from their state of dependence. Moved by an appealing vision of the life they wanted, they found their prospects for its attainment in the hands of men, especially soldiers, over whom they had little influence and whose activities they understood only as victories or defeats, imminent triumph or imminent ruin. The revolutionaries were eager to form their own governments and suppress disaffection. They were willing to mobilize when necessary. But they wanted to enjoy independence at once, to achieve their vision and leave its defense to those who were called to that duty. The slow recruiting in 1777 distressed Richard Henry Lee because, "If the 88 Batallions were once complete, adieu to British Tyranny and every chance for its succeeding."[4] People who relied on Continental Army battalions to defeat British tyranny often expressed their desire for American victory more by their anxiety than by their personal effort. Long stretches of wishful confidence that war's end was near gave way to sudden panics after a reverse. Following a few days or weeks of gloom, military events or ingenious explanations restored the hope of quick victory.

Citizens' vicarious involvement in combat they did not see or share left them especially susceptible to the pervasive rumors, and this helped induce wide fluctuations of mood. Rumors circulated constantly on both sides of the lines. Perhaps people could more easily expect Washington to smash the British because they periodically heard that he had done so. The term "camp news" meant rumors likely to be false.[5] Despite many skeptical comments about floating stories and the "regular lie of the day," these rumors intensified public emotions.[6] People could not help but fear or hope that they were true. A letter from Eliza Wilkinson described people at Wadmalaw, South Carolina, where relatives waited for news of the defense of Charleston against a British incursion in 1779. "Once we heard that the enemy had surrounded the town . . . and that our troops there were in a starving condition. Such reports as these were constantly circulated about, and half distracted the people. Some believed, others disbelieved. I was one of the unbelievers. However, it was the constant topic of conversation."[7] Both Congress and state officials tried to blame the circulation of untrue stories of defeat or discouragement on a network of tory agents seeking to dispirit the public. In Number III of "The American Crisis," Thomas Paine revealed that "the whole race of prostitutes in New York were tories" and that the schemes to promote loyalism in Philadelphia were carried on in brothels.[8]

Loyalists and the British did spread false news among the revolutionaries, just as revolutionaries manufactured fictions for both friends and foes. But rumors derived their main strength from uncertainty and credulity. Most tale-tellers could sound convincing because they believed their own fancies. General De Kalb, after hearing the false rumor that Newport had been recaptured from the British, complained that the public heard news before Washington did "because the couriers or express messengers spread along their route the news of which they are the bearers and sit down and drink and talk politics with all their acquaintances."[9] As recruiting continued to fall short in June 1777, a newspaper address "To the Inhabitants of New England" explained the public's willingness to believe *"magnificent accounts of our own strength and diminutive ones of the strength of our enemies. . . .* We believe it indeed because it is what we wish, and we hope it, when, without prejudice, we should know it to be false."[10] Perhaps this wishful thinking was one way for the revolutionaries to play down their reliance on the army and to extenuate their reluctance to man it. Victory was imminent; thus, the *rage militaire* had not dwindled so far as to endanger the cause. But what if defeat were imminent? Then how culpable the failure of the *rage militaire* would leave Americans. Fortunately, though, victory was imminent once again. Within the flux of hearsay, some recurrent rumors were notable for their survival without support by fact. The revolutionaries kept saying that the Continental Army had smashed its opponents; the loyalists kept saying that Washington was sick, wounded, or dead. Thus, each side identified one of its enemy's main strengths and one of its own main weaknesses.

The Continental Army was larger in 1777 than in any later year. Yet, it was much smaller than the numbers Congress had voted and apportioned to the states. The process of recruiting, both in its successes and in its failures, revealed the revolution's dependence on the army and the consequences of that dependence. Large-scale recruiting began again late in 1776 and early in 1777. This time, however, the standard term of service was not one year but three years. Congress offered a bounty of twenty dollars and, to those who enlisted for the duration of the war, a postwar land grant of one hundred acres for enlisted men. Still, recruiting went more slowly than either states or Continental officers expected. Returning soldiers' hometown accounts of hardship and disease discouraged enlistment—as, no doubt, did the failure of many soldiers to return at all. Beginning in 1775, soldiers had taken disease home with them. Typhus, typhoid fever, and dysentery decimated towns and were especially deadly to small children. Everywhere the diseases were called the "camp fever" or the "camp distemper" or the "camp disorder."[11] In the four hundred families of the First Church in Danbury, Connecticut, one hundred people had died of the camp distemper by November 1775, and according to the minister, many other towns had been similarly stricken.[12] In the winter of 1776/1777, released prisoners of war and discharged soldiers, especially those from the invasion of Canada, spread disease that caused many deaths in Connecticut and Pennsylvania. When citizens claimed that their sacrifices were comparable to those of the army, they must have meant, in part, this scourge.

Even those men who had decided to enlist or reenlist had learned their lesson about pay and waited for the bounty to rise. Sure enough, New England states added their own bounties to the Continental one. Towns added bounties to the state bounties. People who wanted to avoid militia service were offering more than the total Continental Army bounties for a few months' service as a militia substitute. Washington was sure that these practices would ruin the cause by bankrupting the government. He favored a long-term draft. The bounty went still higher when militiamen drafted for the Continental Army hired substitutes. The bounties did not do as much harm to state and Continental finance as Washington feared, for the army could not get any number near the 75,760 men Congress had apportioned to the states. In October, the combined strength of Continentals present and fit for duty under both Washington and Gates was reported as 21,437. Their total strength on paper, not counting militia, was 29,608.[13] The volunteers were fewer and cagier than Congress had anticipated because for the first time they would be long-term soldiers in a standing army. Soldiers knew that they were going into the army to stay, and they wanted money in advance—in some cases to provide for their families, in other cases to enjoy themselves. The money offers from all sides to potential recruits meant, Robert Morris said with alarm, that "they are more their own Masters."[14] Men wanted to serve under commanders they admired and waited to see who would command them before they enlisted or reenlisted. They also sought assurances that the army or the states would provide better medical care, more clothing, and better food. Everyone hoped that the citizen would not be lost in the soldier, but the hope for interchangeable citizens and soldiers no longer described the Continental Army. General Henry Knox, whose artillery especially needed skilled men, looked forward with satisfaction when he told his wife that, once recruits arrived in camp, there would be "no going home to-morrow to suck."[15]

The experiences of 1776 had convinced state leaders and most revolutionaries that they needed a long-term army, but widespread support for its formation did not extend to full enlistment. New England, the main source of Continental soldiers, was especially slow in the spring. After receiving early, optimistic reports, Washington was doubly surprised when so few men came to camp. By all accounts, 1777 was the high point of graft among Continental Army recruiting officers. Officers drew bounty money, reported enlistments and disbursements, then reported the desertion of the recruits. No doubt, such reports were often true, but many of the reported recruits had never existed. Officers gambled away public money or spent it on their own pleasure during their ostensible recruiting trips. In April, Congress recommended that state executives supervise recruiting officers and replace delinquent ones. In July, Congress established district recruiters, who received a bounty of eight dollars for each recruit and five dollars for each deserter apprehended.

The officers' graft was crude and unimaginative compared to the inventiveness with which towns and citizens cheated quotas and conscription in the war years. They sent British deserters, prisoners of war, bounty jumpers, and the physically unfit; several towns charged the same man to their quotas; towns claimed credit for enlisting men who were already in the army; people bought recruits from entrepreneurs. Enterprising businessmen could pay a willing recruit the official bounty and then offer him to draftees as a substitute. The high bidder among the draftees sent the recruit to the army, and the entrepreneur pocketed the difference between the private payment for a substitute and the public bounty for a recruit. Congress stimulated such deviousness by encouraging states to grant exemptions from active militia duty to any two citizens who supplied one Continental recruit for three years or the duration. The exemptions lasted much longer than the recruits; men obtained exemptions for recruits who had enlisted before the exemptions were offered; men recruited prisoners of war; men enlisted a soldier for three years but got an exemption for the duration of the war; several men got exemptions for the same recruit; men got exemptions without providing a recruit. Moreover, the high sums that militiamen paid to hire recruits made other recruiting more difficult and more expensive. Only those "in easy circumstances" could take advantage of the exemption legally.[16] After two and one-half years, the offer was withdrawn. Sometimes local officials refused to implement state laws prescribing their duty to draft men—the state's only recourse was to fine the officials and levy extra taxes on the town for the expense of recruiting men elsewhere. Some towns sent children. As Abigail Adams wrote from Braintree, Massachusetts, in August 1777, "They make strange work in this Town in procuring their Men as usual, it always was a croocked place."[17]

In the army, drummer and fifer boys were customary, and both recruiting and drafting included boys of sixteen and older —but officers and visitors to the army also noticed boys who had volunteered or had been sent as regular soldiers. Sometimes towns or individuals sent a boy, knowing that he would be sent back but expecting to be credited for a recruit. The army seems to have had no fixed policy on whether minors under sixteen could serve as soldiers. Some stayed in the service; some were sent home. Officers may have judged the youngsters' willingness and size as qualifications or weighed the army's need. No one suggested that boys were recruited because too few men were left. Instead, sending boys decreased the number of men who had to be forced to go. Army doctors knew that soldiers under twenty years old were most likely to contract camp diseases, while men over thirty were hardiest.[18] The recruitment of boys did not result from high mortality in the army; instead, making them soldiers increased the number of deaths.

The Continental Army also contained loyalists—we cannot

know how many. Loyalists enlisted to expiate the crime of helping the British. State and local officials not only required some suspected persons to enlist in order to avoid jail, but also purposely drafted loyalists in order to spare revolutionaries from military service. Some citizens complained that this was not done often enough. In their argument, patriotism became not a promise of service or a form of service but a substitute for service. Although some contended that their taxes and other sacrifices ought to excuse them, others acknowledged that army service was an unwelcome necessity. In deciding who would do it, patriots ought to have an exemption that loyalists did not deserve.[19]

A writer in the *Connecticut Courant* summarized much of the recruiting story in one sentence: "The officers on the recruiting service enlisted soldiers at assemblies and balls, and the inhabitants were busily employed in recruiting the children and servants of their neighbours, and forbidding their own to engage."[20] When Peter R. Livingston wrote a gloomy letter in April 1777, predicting the loss of Philadelphia, he depressed his father and caused friction between his sister and his wife. Mary Livingston Duane, his sister, "said it was no Wonder Mr W[ashington] was so weak since Gentlemen did not order their Sons into the Army." In the presence of Peter's wife, Margaret Livingston, Mary advised her nephew—the son of Peter and Margaret—to enlist "whether his Parents consented or not." According to another member of the family, "This occasioned a little Sharpness among the Ladies."[21] For every noble wife or mother in newspapers and sermons, eagerly sending her husband or sons to battle, other women who favored independence reluctantly consented to enlistment or tried to persuade their sons and husbands to stay home or begged them not to reenlist.

Yet people wanted to believe that American women demanded independence and patriotic service even more strongly than men, and women acted out this belief in societies and charities and in their mockery of cowards. In public groups women urged military service. Some sustained this call in private. Eliza Wilkinson, a widow, wrote to a friend, "I've no husband to fight against them (though, by the bye, if I had one who refused to enter the field in his country's cause, I believe I should despise him from my soul.")[22] Militiaman John Hempstead remembered mounting his horse to answer an alarm: "After I got Under Way my wife Called to me prety loud. I Stopt my hors and ask'd her What she wanted. Her answer was Not to let me hear that you are Shot in the Back."[23] However, many tried in private to keep their loved ones out of danger or argued that their family had done its share or that their family had special reasons for exemption.

Besides those who asked men to stay home or to come home, other women—like Janet Montgomery—reluctantly agreed to the call of the war and then wrote letters of lament, complaint, and regret over the hardship of the unwelcome separation. Sometimes husbands replied as Richard Montgomery did—curtly. A few men said that such privileged women knew nothing of the suffering in invaded regions or among families who had no money.[24] Yet these women did not believe that their reluctance to risk their families made them less dedicated to the American cause. New Hampshire wrote this contradiction into law: "If any person or persons within this state, shall in anyway whatsoever discourage or attempt to discourage any person or persons from enlisting in the American Army . . . or from continuing in such service after being engaged therein—such person or persons shall be deemed guilty of a misdemeanor against this State, unless the party accused shall make it appear upon the Trial that he was not influenced by any motives inconsistent with the public-good but was a friend and well-wisher to the common cause aforesaid—upon which he shall be acquitted and discharged."[25] That is, discouraging enlistment was unpatriotic except when done by a patriot.

The kind of care that tried to keep a son or a husband out of the army worked on the populace in other ways, as well. They not only hid from the rigor of their own call to arms; they also hid from the enemy and from American authorities. Where the armies passed, people concealed or buried valuables—money, plate, wine, tools. When a refugee did not return or an owner did not remember, the goods stayed hidden. After the revolution, Americans who were tearing down old houses, removing fences, or digging in cellars came across these forgotten tokens of fear and caution.

In woods and swamps throughout the United States, deserters and draft evaders tried to stay near home yet avoid the law. On June 10, 1777, Colonel John Patton advertised for the apprehension of a deserter, Private Richard Swift, shoemaker: "He is a great coward, and took to the swamps to avoid going to camp."[26] Some of these men turned to robbery. In Virginia, runaway slaves, deserters, and draft dodgers terrorized whole counties. More commonly, the fugitives probably led isolated, unhealthy lives. We can see them only through the eyes of others, but we can infer that their freedom from the demands of the revolution did not reconcile them to a life of "lying out" or "lurking." A traveler in North Carolina was stopped by three men, who took his cloak and other things. Then, as he was riding away, they called him back and returned it all. In politically divided areas, loyalists and revolutionaries often hid in the woods to avoid the raids and reprisals that both sides carried out. But, within territory controlled by the United States, life and property often went into hiding to survive the push for independence.

Americans' most common escape from their own war, however, was quite open and conspicuous. People tried to live as if there were no war. We shall see the increase in moneymaking and spending, which accelerated as the supply of money grew. But, apart from the much-deplored growth of luxury, many people—especially those distant from the scene of fighting—followed their peacetime routines as closely as they could. They put independence into practice at once. This was the boldest and most widespread of all the evasions of the revolution's call to sacrifice: people began to enjoy the promises of the revolution as soon as they could get out of the struggle. The call for vigilance had to compete with the desire for peace. Much of the esteem for the Continental Army depended on its ability not just to protect but even to exempt the populace from the hardships caused by the British. The army's greatest victory of 1777, the defeat of Burgoyne's invasion, was doubly offset: the militia had to turn out, and Washington lost Philadelphia. Because the Continental Army had been unable to win alone and to shield the citizens from war, the public could take credit for American victories and censure Continental generals. However, before Americans could interpret their victory, the people of New England and New York got their turn at facing invasion and desolation. Under this stress, they censured the Continental Army for not being as strong as they had wanted it to be but had failed to make it.

At the approach of Burgoyne's force, the Continentals under General Arthur St. Clair abandoned Fort Ticonderoga on the night of July 5, 1777. Americans, especially New Englanders, covered St. Clair and the Northern Department commander, Philip Schuyler, with abuse. Schuyler privately criticized the withdrawal, but received almost an equal share of blame from the public. Rumor said that the British had bought St. Clair and Schuyler by firing silver balls into the American camp; St. Clair had them collected and then divided them with his fellow conspirator. Some New Englanders accused Schuyler of sending too many supplies to Ticonderoga so that provisions would be lost to the British with the fort; others accused him of sending too little so that the fort could not hold out. Governor Jonathan Trumbull, repeating the words of his son, told Washington and Schuyler that "some cry, Treachery; others, Cowardice; all blame."[27] St. Clair's private letter of explanation to Governor James Bowdoin was published in the *Boston Gazette* with the italicized comment, "*Believe it who may*."[28] Newspapers would not accept fear as an excuse for retreat; an article printed in New England and New York declared that "fear was treason."[29] Revolutionary ideals required Americans to escape the flaws that had marred the history of other peoples. There could be no permanent weaknesses that the revolution must accommodate. Weakness was unpatriotic.

If fear was treason, New England was now full of traitors. Those who had believed that Ticonderoga was well manned and impregnable realized that the barrier between Burgoyne and their homes had fallen. Weeks before the retreat, Governor Trumbull had called Ticonderoga "the Key of New England on that side"; and Josiah Bartlett, a New Hampshire delegate in Congress, had appealed to the militia colonels along the Connecticut River, "Reflect a moment on such a scene as this: Suppose your House in Flames, your wife, your daughters ravished, your sons, your neighbours weltering in their Blood, and the appearance of a few moments bringing you to the same Fate."[30] But few militia had left home in May or June. In April 1777, one could hear rumors of an attack on Ticonderoga, made worse by the warning that it was "in a weak state, and in great danger if attacked."[31] The revolutionaries' habit of publishing inflated strength figures and conquer-or-die manifestos had subsequently encouraged people to believe that the fort would halt the invasion. Now the warnings seemed about to come true, and New England faced the fate New Jersey had suffered.

The *Connecticut Courant* published extracts from the journal of volunteer chaplain Thomas Allen, who five hours before the retreat had preached an ardent call for soldiers to fight to the last man. In the retreat he saw regularity, rank, and courage collapse: "Now we are the derision and scorn of the world! . . . Oh how happy had these states been to what they now are had we been half slain in a glorious defence of that fortress, and the other half captivated."[32] "LIBERTUS" argued in the *New York Journal* that even if most of the garrison had been killed, the British losses would have benefited the Americans. If St. Clair had possessed "a noble and heroic soul," he would have preferred to be "gloriously unfortunate" rather than "spin out the remainder of his life, in obscurity, derision and contempt."[33] After the army's retreat from the fort, wishful rumors spread, saying that Ticonderoga had been retaken.

For a while, these emotions hid the fact that the retreat, though late and poorly done, was wise. St. Clair correctly predicted on July 14, 1777: "By abandoning a post, I have eventually saved a state."[34] After New England militia under John Stark defeated a detachment from Burgoyne's army at Bennington in mid-August, the saying became popular, "Let us get them into the woods."[35] Perhaps never was a more successful strategy adopted more reluctantly by the people who claimed credit for it. That reluctance had been conspicuous throughout the spring; at the end of April, Horatio Gates, whom the New Englanders wanted to replace Schuyler, had asked, "What infatuation has seized my Yankees? . . . They take the Field as Tardily as if they were going to be Hanged."[36] Even though New England's recruiting had gone very slowly and had fallen far short of its quota, people who had raised Continentals resented the prospect of having to go with them or ahead of them as militia when Burgoyne moved south. When they did take the field they wanted to hang the Continental generals who, they thought, had forced them to do so.

Civilians who wanted to fight the war vicariously were not the only revolutionaries whose conduct left a gap between pretensions and performance. More directly than that of most civilians, Continental Army soldiers' experience demonstrated both the importance and yet the insufficiency of Americans' enthusiastic confidence in their own native courage. The generals' effective appeals to soldiers' ideals, some of the soldiers' own diaries and songs, reports of the soldiers' spirits, and above all the soldiers' persevering service in adversity revealed the prevalence of the ideals of 1775 in the army's ranks. But the fluctuation of Continentals' spirits and conduct left their effectiveness lower than their dedication. The revolutionary populace seemed to hope that the army's quick victory would resolve the disparity between Americans' claims of inevitable righteous victory and Americans' military weaknesses. If the public turned to the army for relief, where could the army turn to remedy its own weaknesses? By the end of the Valley Forge winter, the Continental Army had begun to add military professionalism to its other resources for dealing with the failures of the first years of war.

Professionalism became a necessary recourse after the army's volatile spirits and changeable conduct left it unable to expel the British in the third year of war. Friction between soldiers from New England and those from the middle and southern states sometimes made it hard for the army to direct its hostilities toward the enemy. Washington, who had hoped to create a national army, wound up in 1780 and 1781 using Pennsylvania troops to quell mutiny in the Connecticut Line and New England troops to quell mutiny in the New Jersey Line. But the antagonism was worst in the losing days of 1776. Would-be gentlemen of the middle states scorned the Yankee officers' lack of dash and grace; privates picked fights. At Fort Ticonderoga, on Christmas night, 1776, Lieutenant Colonel Thomas Craig of the Second Pennsylvania Regiment got drunk and decided to demolish the shoemaker's bench in the quarters of Colonel Asa Whitcomb, commander of the Sixth Continental Regiment from Massachusetts. Colonel Whitcomb had drawn "the contemptuous sneers of the gentlemen officers" by allowing one of his sons, a soldier whom he made his servant, to work as a cobbler in the commander's own room. Having dispatched the bench, Craig beat up the colonel. The noise attracted Pennsylvania officers and soldiers, who took to arms, "dared the *Yankees*," and attacked the Massachusetts barracks, firing thirty or forty rounds. They drove out the Sixth Regiment soldiers, wounding several severely. One diarist called it a "singular kind of riot"; another called it "a drunken frolick."[37] Later, Craig made it up by sending his soldiers into the woods to shoot a fat bear, on which the officers of both regiments dined.

More frequent than fights were recriminations by both soldiers and civilians, people from each section charging the other with cowardice or coolness in the cause. Each group professed to be surprised when the other turned out very many men or fought very well; each suffered mortification when its own people's conduct seemed to confirm the criticisms that they resented and disbelieved. Washington correctly saw that, since he could not make a national army, he could turn this sectional conflict to good account by encouraging the regiments to vie with one another for superior prowess and reputation. Before this approach could work well, the army would have to grow surer of its own perseverance.

Part of the public's confidence in the Continental Army's ability to protect the countryside came from the soldiers' confidence in their own prowess. The reports of high spirits in the army and the promises of quick victory—like the exaggerated numbers—sought to reassure the populace and mislead the enemy. The soldiers did have high spirits and confidence at Ticonderoga, Bemis Heights, Freeman's Farm, Brandywine, and Germantown—winning or losing, charging or running away. Their conduct varied widely from unit to unit and from one battle or march to another, while they remained sure that they could beat the British. Although they were eager to win and showed that they could fight well, they lacked the discipline that would have helped make their conduct reliable. Of course, no army could always behave as predictably as its commanders would like, especially in battle, but the Continental Army of 1777 had far more spirit than it had discipline and suffered because of the discrepancy.

When we read what soldiers, officers, and observers wrote about the conduct of the army in the summer and autumn of 1777, we find that spirit was much less reliable than discipline. A disciplined unit took measures to preserve its health and safeguard its weapons; it would march, stand, or attack on order. Discipline had known effects on conduct. Spirit came and went, performing wonders but guaranteeing nothing. Three days after the Battle of Germantown, Nathanael Greene's orders of the day said, "The Genl has the highest confidence in the Troops of his Division and in the Spirit and good Conduct of the Officers. He . . . has the mortification to assure the Troops they fled from Victory, and he wishes most ardently, that the Troops may be convinced . . . that a partial Retreat, to change a position is often necessary and therefore a Particular Retreat is not to be Considered general, without the order is such."[38] In his memoirs, former Private Joseph Plumb Martin paused after mentioning the Battle of Germantown to deliver a short discourse on running from the enemy—or, as he called it, "quick retreat." He explained that he preferred to run only far enough "to be beyond the reach of the enemy's shot." Going further "always galled my feelings." Unfortunately, his fellow soldiers were "very nimble of foot," and he was therefore "obliged to run till I was worried down."[39] The day after a unit broke and ran, it once again had high spirits and was reportedly eager to meet the enemy. The same unit that pressed a thousand-yard bayonet charge at Germantown undercut its own health by willfully bad sanitation. A unit's high spirits did not enable one to know whether the unit would stand or run or decimate itself into the hospital, all the while proclaiming its ardor.

Despite the widespread praise of soldiers' patriotism, many revolutionaries were slow to admit that privates stayed and fought to secure independence and freedom. Officers eager to equal Europeans liked to see themselves as the brains in charge of unthinking tools. Some civilian leaders were convinced that armies always consisted of automatons hostile to liberty and in need of constant civilian restraint. Citizens who had raised bounty money thought that local boys had held them up for the top dollar. Although soldiers often pursued excitement and adventure, the young men in the army also took the righteousness of their cause seriously. Witnesses agreed that nothing except this conviction, not even the most stringent discipline, would have kept them on duty when clothing, food, and pay dwindled or gave out. The Continental government could not rely solely on European discipline because, among other reasons, it could not keep its end of the bargain. In addition, most commanders soon learned that the soldiers' convictions could give strength in combat, and the commanders used this appeal. Lieutenant Colonel John Brooks, looking back over 1777 in the first weeks of the new year, recalled "our poor brave fellows . . . bare footed, bare-legged, bare-breeched," complaining of short rations and "two months pay for twelve months past. . . . Under all those disadvantages no men ever shew more spirit or prudence than ours. In my opinion nothing but Virtue has kept our Army together through this campaign. There has been that great Principle, the Love of our Country, which first called us into the field, and that only to influence us."[40] The campaign of 1777 showed, however, that patriotism and self-confidence, though essential, could not alone sustain the army in the future. They might bring victory or near-victory in combat or dispel gloom after defeat, but the army would have to survive many months of hardship without combat, and such survival required not only spirit but also expertise.

The first long-term regular soldiers lacked this expertise in 1777. Their camps were laid out without a clear plan for the location of each unit; sentries were posted, then forgotten, while they in turn neglected their duty; the firing of muskets in camp continued; sanitation remained bad due to carelessness; men left camp to wander or plunder in the countryside; on the march the army straggled in long, loose, slow lines, with men leaving the column to drink or to steal; many soldiers got drunk every day, and men sold their clothing and equipment to buy liquor; soldiers handled muskets carelessly, throwing them in wagons to lighten the load in marching and throwing them away to run from the enemy faster; units adopted separate systems of drill and maneuver and mastered none of them; the only uniform step in the army was the quick step—diarrhea. By the autumn of 1777, discipline had begun to make the army more orderly than in 1776, but most of the army's work in the last five years of the war lay in fixed camps or on hard, fast marches. For high spirits to survive such tests, soldiers would need new skills.

The Continental Army, like almost every other army in history, had a temporary source of ardor: soldiers fought under the influence of alcohol. The Continentals imitated other armies more successfully in drinking than in discipline. Some soldiers, as one of them said, "tried powder and rum . . . to promote courage."[41] Liquor in moderation was thought to relieve fatigue. In addition to its routine place in camp life, it helped raise combat spirits, and officers informally encouraged its use for that purpose. Colonel Otho Holland Williams said that as the southern army marched toward battle at Eutaw Springs, a few hours before meeting the enemy "we halted, and took a little of that liquid which is not unnecessary to exhilarate the animal spirits upon such occasions."[42] Congress rewarded victory with rum. These practices risked more in the American army because fewer restraints existed to check or to guide the soldiers, drunk or sober. Liquor aggravated mutiny as well as valor. Like the love of freedom that moved Continental soldiers, rum and whiskey seemed to reduce or remove opposition, bringing wishes and performance closer together in the mind. But a battle spirit that relied solely on such unpredictable impulses might not be able to keep soldiers in the field after excitement gave way to hardship. An advertisement for a deserter from the Ninth Pennsylvania Regiment said that he was "fond of drink, and boasts much of his abilities when in liquor."[43] Presumably, he deserted while he was sober.

The soldiers' use of undependable aids to ardor had its equivalent in the war spirit that moved revolutionaries at home and in the army. This spirit relied on the workings of enthusiasm, which was the religious counterpart of patriotic zeal. Americans set a high value on enthusiasm during the war. In the controversies that the religious revivals of the Great Awakening had stirred, the word "enthusiasm" meant an ecstasy in which one lost sight of true religion and pursued emotional excesses for their own gratification, perhaps claiming immediate divine inspiration. Opponents of the revivalists charged that much of the awakening was such irreligious excess; revivalists disavowed enthusiasm and believed that their opponents loosely applied the word to genuine, strong conversion experiences. During the revolution, some people, especially loyalists, called some instances of public defiance of Britain enthusiastic, by which they meant to deplore such conduct as a sign of disorder, even mental unbalance. But the most common use of the word carried today's meaning: praiseworthy ardor. Two days after Lexington and Concord, a twenty-one-year-old man who would soon become a Continental Army surgeon wrote in his journal, "There is an enthusiasm in religion, in politics, in military achievements, and in gallantry and love, and why not an enthusiasm in the love of country? No species of enthusiasm surely can be more laudable, or more honorable."[44]

Thirty-five years before the revolution, most Americans would have deplored enthusiasm in religion, though not fully agreeing on what conduct deserved the term. During the revolution, most Americans approved of enthusiasm in politics and war. We can infer that this difference entailed not only a shift in meaning—that is, using the word to describe less extravagant states of emotion—but also a shift in value—that is, greater approval of heightened emotion. When "A JERSEY SOLDIER" looked back over the troops' sufferings and depreciated pay for the preceding two years, he said in 1779, "Nothing but a kind of enthusiasm, in the sacred cause of freedom, could have secured their continuance in the army until this time."[45] Yet, amid applause, enthusiasm had drawbacks. In the Continental Army, the characteristic drawback was not an esprit de corps that threatened to become militarism, nor a radicalism that might encourage enlisted men to seize power and turn the revolution in a new direction. The characteristic abuse of enthusiasm, whether aided by the love of freedom or by alcohol, was to be satisfied with the feeling while giving up the effort. Enthusiasm enabled men to overcome adverse facts by charging a superior enemy and withstanding immense suffering; it also enabled them to ignore adverse facts by convincing themselves that they were good soldiers after they had fled and good patriots after they had gone home.

Revolutionaries expected the commanders of the army to imbue its efforts with enthusiasm. Generals faced a severe test in the autumn of 1777. The two main battles of the campaign against Sir William Howe and the British army took place at Brandywine, September 11, 1777, and Germantown, October 4, 1777. Both times the Americans lost, and between the two the British took Philadelphia. At crucial moments in both battles, entire American units had turned and run, but soldiers, generals, and civilians were glad that the army could survive defeat, and they expressed confidence. Some historians agree with Washington and Nathanael Greene, who said that the Continental Army almost won at Germantown.[46] Washington's intricate, four-pronged, pre-dawn attack did not achieve the clockwork synchronization he planned, but the Continentals pushed back the British until the Americans turned and were themselves driven.

In spite of the soldiers' uneven conduct, critics blamed the Continental generals for the setbacks. We shall return to the criticism of Washington later; almost all of the major generals met harsh censure. Here is Benjamin Rush's rundown of part of the high command: "4 Major Generals—Greene, Sullivan, Stirling and Stevens. The 1st a sycophant to the general [Washington], timid, speculative, without enterprise; the 2nd, weak, vain, without dignity, fond of scribbling, in the field a madman. The 3d, a proud, vain, lazy, ignorant drunkard. The 4th, a sordid, boasting cowardly sot."[47] In November, General Adam Stephen, Rush's fourth major general, was dismissed for frequent drunkenness and for unofficerlike behavior at Germantown, where his division had collided with Anthony Wayne's in the fog. General John Sullivan engaged in a long controversy with a member of Congress, Thomas Burke, who was on the field at Brandywine and who blamed him for the defeat. The civilian critics received information and encouragement from some junior officers. Beginning with the outcry against St. Clair's withdrawal from Fort Ticonderoga, the campaign of 1777 was the high point of Americans' dissatisfaction with their general officers.

The prevailing censoriousness is interesting not so much for its inaccuracy as for its assumptions. The generals were inexperienced and often overweeningly vain—failings they shared with their critics. The complaints linked a general's character with his competence. They assumed that the soldiers were undisciplined and unsuccessful primarily because no inspiring leader had tapped the men's well-known eagerness and ability to fight for freedom. The Continental Army, according to this line of thought, had less need for stable routine, hierarchy, and European expertise than for charismatic commanders who could take men on to victory or death.

The critics drew an implicit analogy between fighting the British army and resisting the British administration before the war. Success came from awakening the love of liberty in the combatants and mobilizing them to defy the enemy, whereupon the British had to give up. A better analogy would have likened the war to the work of governing the United States after independence. No great leader would ever so inspiringly attract the public's support that he would end the need for institutions of government. Indeed, the security of liberty lay more in the reliability of those institutions than in the public's admiration for any man's character. Similarly, the Continental Army's ability to preserve independence against the British depended on the continuity of the army, the development of loyalty, skill, and supply that would sustain resistance even when charismatic leaders negligently fell into enemy hands (Charles Lee) or turned traitor (Benedict Arnold).

The most remarkable trait of the generals' critics is their impatience. More than ten years of sporadic resistance and quiescence had passed between the first of the current British attempts to tighten imperial administration and the beginning of the war. Even then, a year of fighting had preceded the Declaration of Independence. Yet only fifteen months after the Declaration, many Americans thought that the Continental Army ought to have conquered Canada and driven the British back to the fleet. This haste reflects in part Americans' tendency to believe that conflicts were decided in the hearts of the participants and that events merely confirmed the foreordained triumph of good over evil—that deeds were a sort of charade by which the decision of the heart was acted out, the sooner the better.

The impatience also reveals a distaste for the fallible instruments of independence, especially military institutions, which revolutionaries needed yet distrusted. John and Samuel Adams only repeated a current popular saying when they accused American officers of wanting "a long and moderate War."[48] John had already formed his attitude toward Fabian caution during the siege of Boston. He told Mercy Otis Warren, "The inactivity of the two armies is not very agreeable to me. Fabius's *cunctado* was wise and brave. But, if I had submitted to it in his situation, it would have been a cruel mortification to me. Zeal, and fire, and activity, and enterprise, strike my imagination too much. I am obliged to be constantly on my guard; yet the heart within will burst forth at times."[49] "My Toast," John said in 1777, "is a short and violent War."[50] Such a war would rely on republican zeal animated by some bold commander whose victory would cause the war, the British, and the army all to go away. As it turned out, when the war grew long, many of the critics went away. The war went on for five years after the winter at Valley Forge, but many revolutionaries turned to other concerns, trying neither to forestall nor to assist the slow creation of a regular army.

The unlikely combination of personal political influence, seniority, alleged competence, and home-state recruiting strength that lay behind the choice of general officers had not promoted a collection of losers. We may marvel at the pompous ineffectiveness of Heath and Sullivan or at the self-advertisement of Putnam and Stephen, but we could as readily marvel at the advancement of untried men like Greene and Knox, who proved very able. During the heaviest criticism of Continental generals in 1777, the army was pleased to be fighting so much more effectively than it had in 1776. The generals were glad to be able to hold the field with troops who had come to the army too late in the year for much training. The Continental Army had a few officers who could be called born soldiers—Henry Lee, Anthony Wayne, Francis Marion, Benedict Arnold—but most of its best leaders, including the commander in chief, developed their skill gradually, by experience. Since this experience included costly mistakes, such as the loss of Fort Washington's garrison and the lack of reconnaissance at Brandywine, many people were slow to understand or to forgive. In defending their own abilities, generals argued that they could not alone determine the outcome of every engagement. To justify John Sullivan's decision not to assault the British in Newport, Rhode Island, in 1778, Nathanael Greene said, "I have known people foolish enough to insist that it was only necessary for a general to lead on his forces to insure success, without regard to the strength or situation of the enemy, or the number or goodness of his own troops. . . . People, from consulting their wishes rather than their reason, and by forming an estimate of the spirit and firmness of irregular troops more from general orders sounding their praise than from any particular knowledge of their conduct, are led to expect more from such troops than is in the power of any person to effect."[51] In addition, few men had the ability of Lee, Wayne, Marion, or Arnold to secure prompt obedience on the battlefield, and all officers had trouble keeping their men orderly, healthy, and present for duty in camp or on the march. The critics believed that the right kind of men could make Americans behave like good soldiers. At best, generals could only tell recruits how to do so. The decision lay with the men, and in the fall of 1777, they, like their commanders, had only begun to learn what they had gotten into.

In August 1777, General Horatio Gates and his supporters won their long campaign to remove General Philip Schuyler from command of the Northern Department and to replace him with Gates. This victory illustrated the attachment of both Congress and the public to the ideal of an inspirational general. Although Gates used Continental soldiers to do the main fighting against Burgoyne, the Americans' capture of the British invading force was widely credited to the spontaneous virtue and prowess of citizen-soldiers, whom only Gates could lead. Since the beginning of the war, Gates's close ties with New England politicians and his praise of New England soldiers had won him a reputation as the general who could carry untrained men to triumph. William Wolcott, in his *Grateful Reflections* on Gates's victory at Saratoga, believed that even Burgoyne

> Confesses that the generous zeal,
> The sons and heirs of freedom feel,
> Inspires their souls with firmer might,
> Than all the learned rules of fight.[52]

Schuyler, according to his critics, had relied on hierarchy, brutality, and tedious logistical preparations rather than on this native courage. The criticism of Washington, especially after Gates's victory, said that the commander in chief also was too aloof and too cautious. Despite his many virtues, he failed to inspire his men to the victory that lay within their power.

In the revolutionaries' censure of their generals, we can see the reluctance with which Americans accepted the implications of their reliance on a regular army to secure independence. If they had to use soldiers, they wanted to believe that those soldiers' strengths exemplified the people's strengths and that the soldiers' victories were also citizens' victories. The success of the revolution would then be a popular triumph, not the work of a professional hierarchy. How better could Americans achieve this triumph than by demanding that each general be like a Joshua? As the Lord had promised, when the priests and the people and the ark of the covenant faced the enemy, at Joshua's command the priests blew the trumpets, the people shouted with a great shout, and the walls of Jericho fell down flat. The revolutionaries did not expect a general to bring them quite such a physical miracle, but they did want the moral miracle of a quick victory that came from this virtuous ardor of a chosen people.

CHAPTER IV

The Promised Land

Jonathan Trumbull did much of his work as governor of Connecticut in a building in Lebanon that he called the War Office. A visitor to his office might find him at prayer. Trumbull believed that "We are in the latter end of the last days." God was creating "a rising empire in this western world, to enlarge our Redeemer's kingdom and to pull down the Papacy."[1] Many revolutionaries besides Trumbull saw the War for Independence within an apocalyptic setting, and their religious beliefs gave the revolution a larger meaning than simply the accomplishment of independence from Britain. According to a widely shared vision of America's future, the Revolutionary War was to play a central role in the redemption of the world. Americans could be God's instruments to smash tyranny and to cast out the vices on which tyranny had long battened.

The union between such absolute moral ideals and American national identity had important psychological origins in the continent-wide religious revivals of a generation before the revolution. The Great Awakening left no single doctrinal or institutional heritage that would thereafter define American character exclusively, but it did foster a communal concern with righteousness. A people's capacity to achieve righteousness became an important criterion by which to evaluate individual and communal conduct. The national ideal for which the revolutionaries strove borrowed important elements from prevailing religious beliefs. Moreover, the pattern of self-examination by which revolutionaries expressed their concern over righteousness in war may have owed much to the impact and example of intense evangelical religious experience. The revolutionaries' recurrent weighing of their own patriotic merit seems often to have followed the familiar pattern of the personal conversion experience that lay at the heart of religious revivals. The anxious patriot, like the anxious Christian, must test his own spiritual state, while each person stood subject to the community's estimation of his worth. The popular aspiration to attain an absolute ideal for a whole nation and the examination of the heart's conformity to that ideal were revolutionary legacies of the Great Awakening. As we examine the vision that the revolutionaries sought to realize through American independence, we see this Awakening cast of mind at work.[2]

The prevalent wartime description of America's future revealed the revolutionaries' aspiration to an absolute national happiness that went beyond the implementation of the Commonwealth ideology. The abolition of tyranny, the permanence of liberty, the security of public virtue would be only the beginning. In their portrayal of the nation's coming glory, Americans expected the revolution to inaugurate not just a period of greater public morality but a new era of harmony never before known. As they foresaw the enjoyment of this new order, difficulties and contradictions disappeared. Almost all the descriptions were alike: America would have political freedom, artistic and scientific greatness, and immense wealth. Agriculture and commerce would thrive; poverty and ignorance would fade. The revolutionaries' detailed imagining of their country's future matched their concern for posterity. Indeed, even though it contradicts other teachings of the revolution, we can hardly escape the conclusion that, by the light of Americans' assumptions, posterity would not have to struggle continually for these blessings; future generations need only enjoy the gifts of independence. Thomas Paine expressed it with his customary felicity when he encouraged American independence by saying, "We have it in our power to begin the world again."[3]

This idea agreed with the revolutionaries' conviction that their children would look back gratefully to the unique generation that had borne the hardships of saving America from slavery.

A political ideology that explained events, motives, and the future in historical terms in order to prepare people for continuing the struggle could not suffice for revolutionaries who sought to escape the repetitive restraints of history. In their vision of the harmony and happiness of the children of the revolution, Americans slighted or omitted the ancient enemies of republicanism and foresaw an uncorrupted promised land. In the *New Hampshire Gazette* in November 1776, "a Soldier" promised that in return for continued exertions, "*Liberty* will soon triumph, wealth flow in through ten thousand channels, and America become the glory of all lands."[4] Prosperity will come from ability and enterprise, not favoritism and privilege; riches will support human betterment through culture and intellect, rather than dissipate in vanity; freedom will nourish Americans' wealth and improvement because private interest and public welfare will join, not conflict. Chaplain Israel Evans encouraged soldiers to imagine future inhabitants "at ease in their elegant seats, and in the possession of luxuriant lands."[5]

Clearly, this ideal for the future contained a broad strain of worldly ambition, and the appeal of the vision did not necessarily arise from a revolutionary's religious beliefs. Even so, the thoroughness with which Americans expected to change human conduct and the ardor with which they avowed their expectations left their behavior subject to a scrutiny no less keen than that by which the anxious Christian measured his sins. For the criterion against which the revolutionary had to measure his service on behalf of the promised future was not a relative, expedient, political one, but an absolute call for the attainment of permanent happiness. The continent, like the individual Christian, would be saved or it would not. Revolutionaries, then, must fulfill this promise and share its glory or betray it and suffer the permanent enslavement that they would thereby deserve.

The invasion of Canada in 1775 was one of the first attempts to achieve God's promises to America as quickly as possible. Few Americans expressed doubts that the United States would someday cover the North American continent, and the vision of some people included the whole Western Hemisphere. The revolutionaries knew that small battles that in European warfare would hardly count as skirmishes were deciding the future of regions vaster than whole European countries. They also knew that the American wealth and civilization they envisioned would rely on the resources and the future population of these unseen lands. The prospect of a truly continental nation not only underlay the plans and inspired the efforts of many revolutionaries; it also redressed their awareness of America's conspicuous weaknesses and troubles during the war. Conquest, like riches, lay at the heart of America's future freedom; yet, a strong army and military planning had little place in the eloquence that described the nation's expansion. John Adams believed that an earlier Declaration of Independence would have secured Canada; the New Yorkers and New Englanders who, later in the war, wanted to attack Canada again seemed to think that an announcement and an invasion would be sufficient for victory. Since the revolution was preserving liberty for an enslaved world, the revolutionaries expected to conquer more by promises than by troops.

America would change in character as well as in extent. The religious beliefs of many revolutionaries encouraged them to prepare and strive for the imminent coming of the promised thousand-year rule of Christ's law on earth—the millennium. This era would bring the final and perfect earthly achievement of the national righteousness and Christian love that the revolution expressed. The millennialism of the American Revolution did not always conform either to strict computations from the book of Revelation or to the unworldly emphases of other millennialist teachings.[6] Americans sacrificed doctrinal rigor in order to incorporate both earthly prosperity and Whig politics into Christ's promise of happiness. The certainty of the millennium's coming relied not just on prophetical calculation but on God's promise of American victory. Some learned opinion set the beginning of the millennium around the year 2000, but juniors at Yale and an anonymous pamphleteer said "e'er long" and "nigh even at the very door."[7] Chaplain William Linn prayed for the Sixth Pennsylvania Battalion in March 1776, "May your summer's campaign be great and glorious, and may you be returned in safety to the bosom of your country, and meet the congratulation of your friends. Above all, may the peaceful reign of king Jesus soon commence, when the earth shall be filled with the knowledge of the Lord, and the inhabitants thereof learn war no more."[8]

A millennium-like vision of peace, love, and ease shaped the expectations of many revolutionaries who did not speak of the Christian millennium. The union of religious and political ideals in the call to revolution did more than exploit religious teachings to make Britain Satanic or liberty sacred. This union also made political striving a means to the redemption of the world from age-old politics, a means to the achievement of happiness based on righteousness.[9] This demand for a national change of heart, this desire not simply for a just order but for a sanctified one, permeated the popular aspirations that embodied hope for the lasting success of the American Revolution. When the millennium came to an independent America, people would be united by love and would be free from former evils. They would fulfill their duty and achieve their greatest pleasure simply by living a righteous life. The crude contrivances of human coercion and competition would pass away. So would the hardship and inequity they fostered. When God's law ruled and not man's, men's God-given worth would gain its just reward in harmony and ease, no longer divided, cheated, and ranked by the artifices of sin. Fighting in the war against "the world, the flesh and the devil . . . as good soldiers of Jesus Christ, we may be thought worthy to enter into the kingdom of the prince of peace: Even into that kingdom which cannot be shaken; where are no wars, nor rumours of war, but an everlasting rest for the people of God."[10]

If some of these religious expectations resemble the more secular description of America's future, we should not be surprised, because, according to a number of thinkers, the American continent was the chosen spot for Christ's reign. As an imminent fulfillment for many Americans and as an inspirational expression of hopes shared at least in part by almost all revolutionaries, the millennium pervaded people's understanding of the revolution. The wealth, harmony, creativity, and ease Americans anticipated for their continent in worldly terms appeared in visionary eloquence that hardly differed from and sometimes led to anticipations of the millennium. The revolutionaries' future relied not on calculations of relative national advantage but on an absolute national ideal. All who wished for the United States to escape the corruption that had enslaved the rest of the world, all who longed for human nature to be freed from the restraints and misery caused by selfishness, tapped the strong appeal of this vision by seeking to transform the world. These aspirations made the revolutionary goals of virtue, freedom, and happiness achievements that had been imperfectly known in the past but that would now come ever nearer to perfection. Americans could look to the future with the hope that it would differ from the past not just in detail or degree, as one country's history differed from another's, but in disposition, as the redeemed differed from the damned.

This hope infused the diverse appeals of the revolution with a unique enthusiasm that encouraged Americans to defy rational calculations of the probability of success. When Chaplain Ammi Robbins accompanied the last Continental Army advance into Canada, down the St. Lawrence River, he responded to the ever greater hardships of the doomed campaign in a manner characteristic of the revolution's most visionary cast of mind. Here are extracts from two days of his diary—May 4, 1776: "I never had so clear an idea of the hazards and fatigues of soldiers and sailors as this day. Poorly and weak, and the sea made me very sick, vomited till I could vomit no more." May 5, 1776: "Discoursed to the people in *our* boat, on the millenium."[11]

The revolutionaries' vision of the future included the spread of their victory and liberation to other countries by people who would emulate American resistance to tyranny. Some Americans expected a revolution in Britain that would overthrow the corrupt ministry that had begun the war. In 1778 Patrick Henry warned that America would not be safe until Britain had been "deluged with blood, or thoroughly purged by a revolution, which shall wipe from existence the present king with his connexions, and the present system, with those who aid and abet it." To remain free, America must separate completely and permanently: "The old leaven still works. The flesh pots of Egypt are still savoury to degenerate palates."[12] In Trenton the people celebrating the victory at Yorktown toasted "the great and heroic Hyder Ali," who would, they hoped, "check the insolence and reduce the power of Britain in the East Indies."[13] Although America alone had preserved liberty in an enslaved world, the revolutionaries believed that other peoples wanted liberty and would fight for it when they saw Americans win. On July 4, 1778, David Ramsay's oration anticipated "the nations of the Old World emulating our successful efforts in the cause of liberty. The thrones of tyranny and despotism will totter, when their subjects shall learn that the happiness of the people is the end and object of all government." The American example, "like a wide-spreading conflagration," might then move people and nations "till tyranny and oppression are utterly extirpated from the face of the earth."[14] God had chosen the United States to show the course His Providence would take. From Paris, John Adams proudly wrote to Nathanael Greene, "America is the City, set upon a Hill."[15]

The revolutionaries expected imitation by foreigners, like gratitude from posterity, and thus created millions more supporters in their imagination than they could ever see or hear about in fact. We find more instances of uncertainty among revolutionaries when they were weighing the facts than when they were describing the future. Anyone could see that God had withdrawn His favor from the old rulers and had begun the campaigns that would redeem the world from rule by corruption. When the revolutionaries who sought this end analyzed events, they did not ask whether or not events confirmed their reading of God's plan. Rather, they asked whether or not events furthered God's plan sufficiently. If not, some people were falling short of the effort to which God had called them. American writers leafed through histories to find the crucial points at which liberty had been lost because of identifiable, recurring mistakes; they listed the timeless techniques for preserving liberty against encroachments.[16] Similarly, they looked over the world to find signs of revolt they could liken to their own. Out of the evidence of almost unrelieved tyranny throughout the world in the past and in their own time, they drew the signs of tyranny's inevitable overthrow and the tests by which to judge their own success in avoiding the errors of the past. On the rare occasions when someone suggested that the revolution might fail, he did not say that the plan first to escape the world of slavery and then to transform it might be unattainable; he said only that, if it failed, the blame would lie on Americans who had not loved liberty enough to follow the clearly marked path of virtuous effort leading to victory. The great question was not the meaning of the present or the shape of the future, but the will, the ardor, the enthusiasm of the revolutionary generation. To their aid they called the future zeal of the rest of the world.

The anticipated future union of America and the millennium offered assurance that Americans as a people were escaping the fate of other peoples, whose selfishness made their ruin inevitable. Fear of this fate helped make the revolution. The millennial vision of the future enjoyed wide appeal because its assurance responded to the threat that selfishness would ruin Americans' hope for national and individual happiness. Such anxiety demanded a surer promise of immortality than the security of political institutions could alone provide. Not only must republican government be safely established, but also the character of the people must be proven uniquely blessed with the capacity to desire and deserve public happiness above all else. The American nation derived its character from the future glory it would attain; the individual's character derived its fullest claim to be American by its contribution to that future glory. Did the individual's soul share the general awakening?

This cast of mind, whether expressed in its original Christian vocabulary or not, lay at the heart of American revolutionary identity.

When revolutionaries talked about the meaning of being an American—a citizen of the independent United States—they demanded that character match ideals. The test of patriotism bore some likeness to the test of evangelical conversion: one did not ask, "Was I born an American?" or even, "Do I choose to be an American?" but rather, "Am I worthy to be an American?" As long as Americans hoped to embody their ideals in full on earth very soon, the answer to their question had to remain provisional. One's worthiness was always open to question—subject to the measure of one's attainment of freedom, one's public virtue, and one's righteous pursuit of happiness. In the *Massachusetts Spy* of July 30, 1778, "AN AMERICAN," expecting imminent victory, explained why loyalists must not be allowed to return to their homeland after the war: "Is there an honest man that can brook the idea of admitting such to their country again to enjoy in *freedom* those *estates* they refused to defend? Whoever is afraid to support the cause of liberty and his country is unworthy to enjoy them, unworthy to be a member of the UNITED STATES OF AMERICA."[17] That is, "Fear was treason."[18] Such questioning instilled a recurring anxiety that took two forms: first, repeated self-examination and mutual examination to weigh the worthiness of a person's aspirations or services; second, extravagant claims of merit or accomplishment, made in the vain hope of proving one's worthiness beyond further question. This anxiety, in its first form, stood ready to strip anyone of his national identity not just for conspiracy against the revolution, but even for insufficient attainment of its ideals.

This threat was enforced, in part, by public scrutiny, official or popular. The secretary to the French legation said of the press, "Though they do it much more nobly, the newspapers in America perform the office of the lion's mouth in the Doge's palace in Venice," wherein one could anonymously inform against enemies of the state.[19] But the threat derived its greatest strength from within the minds of the revolutionaries—every man was his own inquisitor. Having compared his achievements to the ideals of the revolution, he would be forced to inform against himself. One could seldom bear such anxiety for long; people escaped it for a while by increasing their efforts for the cause and for themselves, by denouncing Americans whose unquestioned criminality made the conduct of others look worthy in contrast, or by filling the gap between conduct and ideal with rhetorical claims.

American political thought was vigilantly aware of Americans' susceptibility to corruption, love of power, and selfishness —all the more so because American ideals allowed no place for these crimes. Nor did American ideals allow any plan of conduct to be evaluated primarily by facts. Facts always ought to be subordinate to and judged by their conformity to ideals. Although the revolutionaries, as they saw it, tried to administer chattel slavery, a standing army, covetous commerce, and government itself by a balance of practical possibilities and ideals, such compromises could be justified, if at all, only by necessity. When human weaknesses conflicted with the vision, they were alien, not American. During the trial of Samuel Fisher—a loyalist Quaker whom the Pennsylvania authorities sent to jail on a false charge of aiding the British—Jonathan Sergeant, the state's attorney general, accused Fisher of "longing for the Onions and Garlick of Egypt," as the children of Israel did when they grew tired of manna.[20] Having been charged with antirevolutionary conduct, Fisher could then seem guilty of moral weakness, too, which made him not only criminal but also foreign. The Americans' wish to unite their daily life with their vision of the future discredited all the Egyptian expedients to which they might succumb and left them to explain their delinquent conduct as best they could—with cynicism or guilt or self-righteousness, all vainly trying to palliate, pardon, or sanctify alien acts perpetrated by Americans.

The call to prove one's worth—in native courage, in love of freedom, in attainment of the promised future—lay at the heart of Continental Army service, but not always of the army's day-to-day behavior. The gap between the revolutionaries' ideals and their conduct was sometimes narrowest in the army and sometimes widest, because army service presented some of the most rigorous demands, which men often equaled and other times fled. In the war experience and especially in army service, revolutionaries faced a clearer, more rigorous test of their capacity to live for a vision. We can best understand their response to this test if we remember that the prevalence of failure or shortcomings does not necessarily demonstrate the revolutionaries' indifference to the vision.

We can see one version of the success and the failure of this wartime trial of strength in the experience of Continental Army chaplains. Five days before he was killed in the assault on Savannah, October 9, 1779, Major John Jones wrote to his wife, Mary, "If it is my fate to survive this action, I shall; if otherwise, the Lord's will must be done. Every soldier and soldier's wife should religiously believe in predestination."[21] Whether the date of a man's death or the state of his soul was predestined, many soldiers shared with Major Jones the conviction that the outcome of their services depended on God. Yet all observers agreed that profanity, drunkenness, neglect of the Sabbath, and disrespect for the clergy were widespread among Continentals. Christian revolutionaries deplored such conduct as a sign of irreligion. In many cases they were right. More often, the conduct may have shown the soldiers' lack of decorum. The snide remarks about chaplains and the inattention to their sermons manifested less a fixed hostility to clergymen than a low opinion of some who had entered the army. Soldiers complained that chaplains were uninspiring time-servers or laughable pedants. Religious soldiers were keen judges of the quality of sermons, and too seldom could they say, as Corporal Amos Farnsworth did about Reverend William Emerson, "This was preaching he had no not[e]s."[22] One officer went to hear Chaplain John Murray but was unpleasantly surprised to hear another preacher—one of "the old reading Trojans."[23] A prepared text could be forgiven, as in the case of Chaplain Obadiah Noble, when the worshipper could say, "He reads, but is very pathetic."[24]

The soldiers had a slang term for a chaplain: they called him "a pulpit drum."[25] Like their word for young doctors—"Pilcocke's"—it cut several ways.[26] Literally, drums were stacked as a platform for chaplains to stand on while preaching to soldiers who gathered in a circle around them. The sermons, like the drums, aimed to regulate soldiers' conduct and hearten them in battle. A chaplain like Ammi Robbins, who prided himself on preaching with "great freedom and plainness," could not have found the comparison altogether complimentary; but he also enjoyed reading, praying, and singing with the soldiers in the evenings.[27] Then the drum had a different sound: "Sometimes Tibbals, who strikes the drum admirably, gives it a touch at the right time when we are singing—it is beautiful harmony. A soft fife is also an addition."[28]

Soldiers responded to a flow of emotion. The most successful chaplains, such as Robbins, Israel Evans, Abiel Leonard, or John Hurt, the last of whom served as chaplain for ten years during and after the war, could not only call for military obedience, clean living, and chaste language, but could also try to move soldiers to make patriotism "a constant festival of human kindness."[29] When Dr. Lewis Beebe went to Crown Point to hear the "pulpit drum," he said that he "was entertained with a Sermon by the Revd. Mr. Robbins . . . delivered in the presence of two Regts it was a most animating and encouraging discourse, delivered with spirit and warmth; he gained the most strict attention of almost every hearer present, and was universally admired as an orator and divine."[30] Soldiers eager to feel love of America, pride in military service, and strength in combat responded to chaplains who could foster such ardor and gave short shrift to those who could not. Chaplain Ebenezer David prayed with the sick at Fort George, and after prayers some gathered around him to converse; "when much had been said by Interogation Answer and exhortation when I was about going away one says '*Oh how I doe love to hear Ministers talk*.' "[31]

The religious emotions of soldiers appeared most distinctly on special occasions—a unit's leaving home for the army, its preparation for battle, its times of personal trial, its communal celebrations. Devout, well-behaved soldiers and all chaplains complained, however, that most of the time too few men discussed religion and behaved seriously. Instead, profanity, drinking, and loose talk showed bravado not just toward the enemy but toward God. Like the junior officers, whom they no doubt partly imitated, soldiers cultivated a swaggering, cavalier manner as their defense against their hardships. Back with the army after several months at home, Chaplain David wrote, "As yet I have not been able to reassume my camp feelings which were wholly laid aside."[32] For most soldiers, "camp feelings" meant the kind of tough, heedless pose that chaplains often deplored and mistook for hardened sin. In visits to the sick, "the talk is very chaffy and light with the most of them."[33] At the height of the mortality among prisoners of war in New York City, a visitor found men in Bridewell Prison "preparing to lay down for the night . . . most of them, laughing and bantering each other with apparent pleasantry about which of them would be dead the next morning. One would say, 'I am much stouter than you and I will have your blanket.' 'No,' would be the reply, 'I am much heartier than you and stand the best chance of seeing you carried out feet foremost.' "[34] During the southern army's extreme suffering for lack of food in the summer of 1780, soldiers "used 'starvation' as a cant word, and vied with each other in burlesquing their situation."[35] In 1778, after a firing squad executed a deserter, "two Men wer digging a grave to bury the Corps," a private later recalled; "they took it up to lay it in, and the wind quackeled in the throat of the Corps and one of the Men said 'dam you hold your tongue now 'tis too late for you to say a Word.' "[36]

An orderly, decorous piety stood little chance of prevailing in the Continental Army. American soldiers saw themselves as righteous men fighting for a righteous cause, but not as an army of saints. Their ministers at home as well as their chaplains encouraged them to fight a double battle to redeem their souls from sin and their country from the invader. Like the congregation that shared a revival of piety or the continent that had to unite in order to achieve the promise of the future, the soldiers could claim a special infusion of God's benevolence which marked them to do great things for others' benefit and for their own glory. This double redemption would yield moral gain from physical sacrifice. The clear union of personal effort, corporate unity, national welfare, and universal significance provided the emotional impetus for sustained service. And the emotional gratifications of personal merit, of shared struggle, and of victory with independence were the main and often the only rewards soldiers received. At the end of 1780 a sergeant wrote in his journal, "Through the whole campaign, I have enjoyed an uninterrupted state of health . . . for which I desire to bless and praise God's holy name . . . and beg him to give me new resolution to devo[te] my spared life to his service . . . and if it shall be His holy will, see these United States free and independent and my friends and relations in peace and safety to rejoice with them, and above all, be brought to the full enjoyment of God in his Heavenly kingdom, for Christ's sake."[37] Private Elijah Fisher attended divine service with the commander in chief's guard on August 15, 1779: "We had a Sermon Preached at Head Quarters by Mr. Armstrong and he took his text in the one hundred and twenty-sixth psalm at the fifth varce you have these words—'they that sow in teers shall reep in joy.'"[38]

The evangelical aspiration that encouraged the army's wartime perseverance appeared most conspicuously in such moments of celebration or trial, but did not make the army an evangelical institution or camp life a revival. To be a good chaplain was even more difficult than to be a good company grade officer, and the army found the supply of good ones similarly short. More men sought the posts than the army needed. Some treated it as a sinecure; commanders complained that chaplains drew pay but remained away from the army. Some ministers did not want to break their ties with their home congregations, and some congregations were reluctant to renew leaves of absence, especially when the minister was popular at home. The conscientious chaplain had two main duties: "divine service"—two Sunday sermons, as well as prayers and addresses on special occasions—and private worship or consolation with soldiers, especially the sick and the dying. In their hospital visits, the chaplains did almost as much good for the soldiers as the doctors could and much more than the officers.

Chaplain Ebenezer David said, "I have ever found the Chaplains visits taken well by the sick."[39] The journals and memoirs of doctors, officers, and enlisted men record few visits by junior officers to their sick men. Captain Alexander Graydon probably spoke for many of them when he explained why he had avoided the imprisoned Continentals in New York City, who faced a choice between pestilence and enlistment in the British army. "I once, and once only, ventured to penetrate into these abodes of human misery and despair. But, to what purpose repeat my visit, when I had neither relief to administer nor comfort to bestow! What could I say to the unhappy victims who appealed to me for assistance, or sought my advice as to the alternative of death or apostacy? . . . I rather chose to turn my eye from a scene I could not meliorate; to put from me a calamity which mocked my power of alleviation."[40]

Many chaplains probably followed a similar course, but others visited the sick daily, joked or prayed with them, and listened to monologues like that of a "very sick youth from Massachusetts," who asked Ammi Robbins "to save him if possible; said he was not fit to die, says, 'I cannot die, do, sir, pray for me, will you not send for my mother, if she were here to nurse me I could get well; O my mother, how I wish I could see her, she was opposed to my enlisting, I am now very sorry, do let her know I am sorry.'" Robbins "endeavoured to point him to the only source of peace, prayed and left him; he cannot live long."[41] Chaplain Caleb Barnum was still preaching the justice and goodness of the revolutionary cause from his deathbed as fever killed him at Fort Ticonderoga in the summer of 1776. Hezekiah Smith explained to his wife his decision to stay in the chaplaincy: "The prospect of usefulness in the glorious cause of our country, joined with that of usefulness to souls, inclines me to yield. . . . The Lord . . . disposes me to be in the army, out of which I could not, at present, control myself."[42]

Chaplains also helped do generals' work in sermons and addresses. Commanders required soldiers to attend divine service; one punishment for absence was digging up stumps. Militia Colonel Benjamin Cleaveland, a former Continental Army officer, wanted prisoners of war as well as soldiers to attend services; so the loyalist Lieutenant Anthony Allaire heard "a Presbyterian sermon, truly adapted to their principles and the times; or, rather stuffed as full of Republicanism as their camp is of horse thieves."[43] A commander might suggest the text for a sermon and urge a chaplain to "dwell a little more on politics" if he was one of the few who failed to do so.[44] After Chaplain Benjamin Boardman had preached on Jehoshaphat's prayer for God's help against invaders, Colonel Samuel Wyllys thanked him and "said it was the best sermn he had ever heard upon the occation and troubles of the day."[45]

The Continental Army began with regimental chaplains and in 1778 converted to brigade chaplains, thus needing fewer ministers and giving them wider duties. Congress had voted to adopt a brigade chaplaincy in 1777, but Washington's opposition had delayed the plan. He preferred regimental chaplains because the duties of a brigade would be too great for one man and because religious diversity among regiments might create religious disputes if all the regiments in a brigade could have only one chaplain among them. Washington's objections to the plan in his letter of June 8, 1777, caused Congress to suspend the plan until 1778. Nevertheless, chaplains regularly spoke to full brigades and sometimes exchanged pulpits.

The surviving sermons strive to attain a very demanding ideal: to nourish and justify the hopes for America's future that made soldiers fight the British, to foster individual courage in the face of both suffering and combat, to celebrate the unity of courageous men in a just cause, to awaken soldiers' watchfulness for the signs of their own salvation, and to encourage the orderly conduct of a disciplined soldier and an upright Christian. When Chaplain Ammi Robbins preached on the escape of Lot from Sodom, one listener said that his preaching "was all life and engagedness."[46] Chaplain Israel Evans, preaching to the New York Line and Lafayette's Light Infantry, said, "Could my influence reach as far as my wishes are extended; could I appear before the inhabitants of the United States in all the irresistable majesty of ancient elocution; could I wield the thunder of Demosthenes, and arrest the lightning of Pericles; how should the nerves of opposition to our country be withered, and every American be fired into a patriot or a soldier."[47] When Evans spent the night at Reverend Ebenezer Parkman's house in Westborough, Massachusetts, the two men talked about Arnold's treason, and the next morning Evans left his host a copy of his most recent publication, *A Discourse, Delivered At Easton, On the 17th of October, 1779, to the Officers and Soldiers of the Western Army*, which had been printed "to be distributed among the Soldiers Gratis."[48] For the most part, Evans's goals as a chaplain, like those of other chaplains, were the kinds of inspiration that Americans expected their generals to achieve. And, just as revolutionaries at home felt dissatisfied with generals, so commanders and soldiers found chaplains wanting. Although Washington kept his own religious views private and rarely referred to God or to Christ, he set great store by religious exercises and able chaplains for the army. He too complained of chaplains' neglect of their duties and was rumored to have a low opinion of many of them.

When we compare the demands made on chaplains with those made on other officers and when we study the recorded services of individual chaplains, we can hardly conclude that they were singularly derelict. We can suspect that chaplains bore a large part of the Continental Army's displeasure when soldiers and officers found that war life was not as consistently inspiring, orderly, or tolerable as they wished. Despite the most blatant contradictory facts, ministers had to remain spokesmen for the promise. On Thanksgiving Day, 1777, Private Joseph Martin's unit, which had not been paid since August, heard a sermon they could not properly attend to because they wanted a "fine Thanksgiving dinner" but had received "*half* a *gill* of rice and a *tablespoonful* of vinegar!!" The preacher's text "upon the happy occasion" was John the Baptist's advice to soldiers, which ministers treated as an injunction to discipline—"Do violence to no man, neither accuse any falsely. . . . " For some reason the preacher left out the next clause; it would have been, Martin later said, "too apropos." But as soon as the service ended, a hundred soldiers shouted, "And be content with your wages."[49]

Many chaplains, like many officers, responded to this stress by neglecting their duty. Others, by word and example, led the revolutionaries' efforts to reconcile deeds with dreams. "I pray," Chaplain Hezekiah Smith wrote to his wife, "that my preaching may be attened with power."[50] The new recruits of 1780 were coming into "Continental Village" at Peekskill, New York. General John Nixon's brigade had been so scattered during the summer that religious services had stopped. Now they would resume. Like his eloquent sermons against profanity and on Arnold's treason, Smith's prayer represented the renewed hope for the army's achievement of ideal conduct, following yet another failure. This was the conscientious chaplain's most important and difficult task: making an ideal seem attainable to men who were falling short of its demands. After hearing a sermon by Smith in 1775, Lieutenant Benjamin Craft said, "He preached exceedingly well, and I wish I had a heart to profit by what I heard."[51]

Since the chaplains spoke for an ideal of discipline, piety, unselfishness, and courage that surpassed ordinary human achievement, their efforts could end only in failure. The army's most dedicated perseverance or bravest combat still did not match the strength for which the chaplains appealed in their evocations of the ideals of 1775. The more successfully they represented the revolutionary vision of righteous strength striving against the enemies of happiness, the more clearly the army's shortcomings could be seen. No one suggested that chaplains should stop appealing to revolutionary ideals and simply tell soldiers to eschew vice and obey orders. The need for proof of physical courage on behalf of a moral vision remained the chaplains' message and the soldiers' ideal. Beneath the striving, however, lay a profound fear of failure—a fear, in its simplest form, that the soldier would run, that the officer would err, that the chaplain would despair. Yet even without such complete failure, revolutionaries could never make their achievements provide the proof they sought. The fear of giving up the effort ran through the times of achievement as well. For revolutionaries to persevere, especially amid reverses, they would have to find ways to withstand the inescapable threat that they were not worthy to win.

Abiel Leonard, pastor of the First Congregational Church of Woodstock, Connecticut, and teacher of a private grammar school, was appointed chaplain of Israel Putnam's Third Connecticut Regiment in 1774. When the war began, he sold his parsonage, used his own money to hire a preacher to take his place, left his school, and went to Cambridge with his regiment. He was thirty-four years old and widely respected in New England for his eloquence. Two of his sermons had been published, and effort had been made to print others. He left behind his wife and children, including a child by his first wife. She had died fourteen months after their marriage.

Until the Battle of Bunker Hill, Leonard divided the work of religious services for the army with President Samuel Langdon of Harvard. During the siege of Boston he continued to serve several regiments and made daily trips between Prospect Hill and Cambridge Neck. Soldiers who heard him said that he "preached well" and "spoke excellently." Washington found him "active and industrious"—a "warm and steady friend to his Country" marked by "exemplary and praiseworthy" conduct, which included "great pains to animate the Soldiery and Impress them with a knowledge of the important rights we are contending for."

In 1775 Leonard published *A Prayer, Composed For the Benefit of the Soldiery, in the American Army*. Leonard and the soldiers told God that "from a sense of that duty I owe to my country and posterity I have voluntarily engaged in this service. And I desire now to make a solemn dedication of myself to thee in it through Jesus Christ; presenting myself to thy Divine Majesty to be disposed of by thee to thy glory and the good of America." They prayed, "by means of the present contest may the liberties of America be established upon a firmer foundation than ever; and she become the excellence of the whole earth, and the joy of many generations!"

Leonard's congregation in Woodstock wanted him to return to his pulpit, and Washington wrote letters in January and March 1776 to help persuade them to extend their minister's leave of absence. Washington and Putnam assured Leonard's congregation that "his usefulness in this army is great, and he is employed in the glorious work of attending to the morals of a brave people who are fighting for their liberties."

In 1762, before coming to Woodstock, Leonard had been seized with "Distraction" on his way to decline a call to the Scituate, Massachusetts, pulpit. According to his doctor, he had been "sometimes Dumb and inattentive, sometimes Raving. His Mother was sent for and was soon on the Rode." The doctor thought that these were "the symptoms of long Distraction." The following year Leonard had recovered and accepted the call to Woodstock. Since the beginning of the war, Leonard had visited Woodstock in August and September of 1775, but he had said that even with "the pleasure of an agreeable wife and pleasant children around me, yet I am at Cambridge sleeping and waking, impatient to know every manoevre."

Leonard was a central figure in the army's public celebrations and in the generals' appeals to the soldiers' patriotism. At six o'clock on the morning of July 18, 1775, the Connecticut regiments assembled on Prospect Hill to hear Congress's *Declaration of the Causes and Necessity of Taking Up Arms*, written mainly by Thomas Jefferson. Leonard read it aloud "with religious solemnity" and then made "an animated and pathetic address to the army . . . succeeded by a pertinent prayer." Putnam gave a signal; the troops "shouted their loud AMEN by three cheers"; the Indian allies gave "a war-whoop"; and a cannon was fired from the fort. Above the troops, the new flag of the Third Connecticut Regiment now flew—scarlet cloth with the motto in gold, "AN APPEAL TO HEAVEN." The newspapers commented, "The *Philistines* on Bunker's hill heard the shouts of the *Israelites*, and being very fearful, paraded themselves in battle array."

In December 1775, when the Connecticut troops were eager to go home, Leonard preached a sermon in the Old Congregational Church in Cambridge, on a text from the address of Joab to the choice men of Israel—a favorite text with revolutionary ministers—"Be of good courage, and let us play the men for our people, and for the cities of our God: and the Lord do that which seemeth him good." Leonard's sermon was "a very animating, spirited and learned discourse, to the soldiery, upon the necessity and importance of their engaging and continuing in the service of America, and of displaying true valour and courage in the defence of her rights and liberties, from the principles of love to GOD and their country." George Washington, who was in the audience, called Leonard's words "a Sensible and judicious discourse, holding forth the Necessity of courage and bravery and at the same time of Obedience and Subordination to those in Command."

A few hours after the liberation of Boston, on March 17, 1776, Leonard preached "an excellent sermon" at Cambridge to a distinguished audience, including Washington. In his text, "the Egyptians said, Let us flee from the face of Israel, for the Lord fighteth for them against the Egyptians."

At evening roll call on July 9, 1776, in New York City, each brigade of the army heard the Declaration of Independence read aloud. Leonard's brigade sang part of the eightieth psalm; he "made Prayers," and the soldiers gave three cheers. The newspapers reported that the Declaration was received "with loud huzzas, and the utmost demonstrations of joy."

By 1777, Leonard had become the preeminent chaplain in the Continental Army. Yet, despite his successes, the failure of the chaplaincy troubled him. In 1777 he spent much time thinking about the chaplaincy and working to improve it. He went to Philadelphia and preached before Congress. To some members he explained the need to pay chaplains well and "render them more respectable and usefull." To this end, he urged Congress to create the higher-ranking position of brigade chaplain, and on May 27, 1777, Congress voted to appoint brigade chaplains with the pay of colonels. Congress expected "clergymen of experience, and established public character for piety, virtue and learning" to use this "new and honorable Establishment" to suppress cursing and other vices, "to strengthen the Officers hands by publick and private exortations to obedience," to discourage desertion and encourage enlistments, and to recommend cleanliness. Brigade commanders should recommend only "pious Clergymen zealously attached to our glorious Cause, who will not begrudge the exertion of every nerve in the Service." Leonard was appointed a brigade chaplain, but his plan for the chaplaincy was defeated by Washington's objections. In the spring of 1777, Nathanael Greene and John Adams were praising Leonard's efforts. Greene wrote to Adams, "He engaged early in the army and has been indefatigable in the duties of his station. In a word he has done every thing in his power both in and out of his line of duty to promote the good of the service." Adams had heard Leonard preach in Woodstock on September 3, 1775, when his text had been "And the work of righteousness shall be peace; and the effect of righteousness quietness and assurance for ever." Adams told Greene, "There is no man for whom I have a better opinion." Moreover, Henry Knox wanted Leonard to continue as chaplain for the artillery. Yet, during the summer of 1777 Leonard "expressed much sorrow" that chaplains "stood in so little Respect and were able to do no more good in their Place."

In the spring and summer of 1777 Leonard was also in poor health. He had spent the winter at home and had not fully recovered from smallpox, which he had contracted by inoculation. It left him, according to an officer who knew him, "with a low hypocondriac habit of body." In May he returned to the army in New Jersey and visited Congress in Philadelphia. In July he was on furlough. According to tradition, he went to Woodstock because one of his children was ill. On his way back to the main army, which was marching south through New Jersey, Leonard spent about two weeks at Peekskill, New York, with his friend Colonel Jedidiah Huntington. They had frequent conversations on the chaplaincy. Leonard's "hypocondriac habit of body" was "much increased." He "was melancholy and his mind disordered."

On Sunday, July 27, he left Peekskill and crossed the Hudson "on his Way to Genl Washington's Camp." He went to a Sunday service and stayed in Kakiate, New York. Again according to tradition, "he was met on his journey back to camp by the tidings that he had been censured and superseded" for overstaying his furlough. That Sunday evening he went to bed at Judge Coe's tavern in Kakiate, and during the night he cut his throat with a razor.

Leonard lived eighteen more days. Dr. Albigence Waldo reported that "the cut is so near his chin that his tongue is wounded and he cannot speak, but writes . . . Expresses a great desire to get well." His friends hoped for his recovery, though "his wound is terrible"; "the Gash was deep." He was taken to Peekskill by a horse litter on August 3. A man who saw him that day said, "He has his reason yet is unable to speak." On the way home Leonard was moved as far as Danbury, Connecticut, where, on August 14, 1777, he died.

Reverend William Gordon wrote to Washington that Leonard's "fit of lunacy" showed "how soon may reason be unsealed! Let not the wise then glory in his wisdom." A chaplain at Peekskill said that "People here are pretty generally satisfied what disappointments lead him to so dreadful an act." An officer who saw Leonard at Peekskill before and after "the unhappy accident" told a friend that it "cannot be imputed to him, by any means, as a deliberate act." In addition to Leonard's poor health, "some disagreeables in his situation . . . brought on a kind of delirium."

After Leonard died, the many people who knew him would have shared the response of former Captain John Chester, who wrote, "Good Doctor Leonard is Dead and I heartily Sympathize with you and other friends on the Loss of so valuable a Man." Early in his ministry, Leonard had distressed strict Calvinists by preaching a cheerful theology that emphasized God's benevolence, but few ministers enjoyed equal public esteem, and none matched his importance in the army. Yet, when word came of Leonard's self-inflicted wound, a friend spoke of the emptiness of popular respect as a source of strength, while to a colleague Leonard seemed alone, unable to draw on God's strength for his own: Colonel Huntington said, "What is Man, even those who stand highest in the Esteem and Love of the World, vain, transitory and perishing"; Chaplain David said, "What are men when left to themselves. . . ."[52]

On the day Leonard died, John Stark's militia made their first contact with the enemy in the three-day Battle of Bennington, which gave the first major check to the invading army of Burgoyne. We are so familiar with the revolutionaries' success in impeding, immuring, and defeating Burgoyne's forces that we may forget how much the British and their German auxiliaries frightened Americans, especially people in the path of the invasion. As St. Clair's force retreated from Fort Ticonderoga, Continental soldiers deserted and headed home. Civilian refugees fled southward on wagon, horse, and foot; one of them later recalled that a few people had helped each other, "but, generally, a principle of selfishness prevented much interchange of friendly offices. Every one for himself was the constant cry."[53]

If we liken the fear of Burgoyne's army to the fear of failing to attain the promised revolutionary vision, we can say that this cry waited unvoiced within the revolution's celebration of communal virtue. Courage was an innate national trait; fear was a private weakness. Victory was a divine promise; defeat was a crime. Americans' communal declarations of ardor and celebrations of victory escaped the solitude of selfishness by repudiating it. But the escape was never permanent, and the man whose ardor flagged or who suffered defeat condemned himself to the solitude of the unworthy. Once trapped there, he stood in danger of the eternal slavery that his selfishness fostered and deserved. Joining the national effort to achieve the revolutionary vision could free one from this fate. Yet, one who sought freedom could never lose the fear of such a fate, because the revolution had no legitimate communal recourse for the weak. The reactions both to success and to reverses in the autumn of 1777 revealed the influence of this fear in the way Americans laid blame for defeat and demanded the victory they claimed to deserve.

Burgoyne's invasion alarmed New Englanders and New Yorkers, especially after St. Clair's retreat from Fort Ticonderoga, because they doubted their ability to stop him. But eventually the New England militia mobilized and, standing in reserve, helped Horatio Gates to stop and surround Burgoyne. The battles of Freeman's Farm and Bemis Heights were fought primarily by Continentals. Gates ordered the dispositions of the troops but was not present at either battle. Benedict Arnold's battlefield leadership at Bemis Heights, though he held no command, carried the victory beyond a turning of the British right flank to the capture of a redoubt that left Burgoyne exposed on all sides except the river. Burgoyne's withdrawal to a new position was useless: he was greatly outnumbered, and the militia harassed him continually. Ten days later, he submitted to a "convention" that promised that the British soldiers would be paroled back to England, never to fight in the war again. Gates made this promise because he feared that Sir Henry Clinton might soon relieve Burgoyne from the south. Congress was neither honorable nor foolish enough to keep it. Among the soldiers, a rumor said that Burgoyne had bribed Gates to get the convention.[54]

Like the sudden rescue from gloom at Trenton and Princeton, Gates's victory confirmed God's superintending Providence. Only in retrospect did revolutionaries decide that American losses, like the retreat from Ticonderoga, had been God's means for leading the British on to destruction.

> God's face seems cover'd with a veil,
> His purpose does conceal,
> We cannot see the myst'ry of
> This wheel amidst a wheel.
> But when his counsels come to light
> We see the plan was wise;
> These wings that seem'd misterious things,
> We see are full of eyes.[55]

This view of Providence underlay the American war spirit, rising and falling between gloom and euphoria. The revolutionaries did not submit their destiny to an all-wise God while they, humbly and in ignorance, accepted events as His answer. They insisted that His answer—that is, the decree of Providence—was already known: American victory. God was "bound by his faithfulness to stand by and support a righteous cause. The righteous Lord loveth righteousness."[56] In reverses, temporary fears that such certainty might be wrong made many revolutionaries look out for themselves, made others increase their efforts for the cause, and made most of them eager to find and blame the would-be saboteurs of God's plan. In the hour of success, the revolutionaries were ready to believe that the fulfillment of their providential destiny was at hand. God had shown that they were right; now victory was imminent. They assumed that, when America prospered, they understood the intent of Providence—only reverses were mysterious.

This notion of Providence also helped persuade Americans that their victories were the work of the whole people, not just the army or any other special group. Since defeat, according to the divine plan, was not possible, the United States did not owe its survival to any group of saviors; and since everyone had made sacrifices in adversity, everyone could claim credit for accomplishing God's intent. In personal misfortune, God's Providence might still help to reconcile the individual to the impenetrable odds of war. As a nation, the United States had nearly made the favor of Providence a national promise—brightening the country's successes, leaving moments of defeat clouded in darkness.

In a *Song made on the taking of General Burgoyne*—printed in broadside within weeks of the victory at Saratoga—one line ran, "Brave Gates will clear America before another year."[57] Most Americans would have thought that this was too slow. Both civilians and Continental soldiers had expected Washington to beat Howe's army during September and October. After the capture of Burgoyne, people readily spoke of the capture of Howe, too, and an end to the war. Even after Howe occupied Philadelphia, Americans hoped to hold their Delaware River forts, keep British shipping out, and force Howe to leave. In November 1777, Chaplain Ebenezer David heard "the people . . . cry fight fight and make an end of it."[58] Americans overestimated what Washington's army could do, partly because the Continental authorities and the newspapers spread exaggerated accounts of the army's numbers and well-being. These were meant both to keep Howe ignorant of American weaknesses and to keep up revolutionaries' spirits. Extravagant rumors of victory and defeat circulated during the late summer and autumn, and whatever truth they included about Washington's fluctuating strength and increasing difficulties of supply was obscured by a wishful eagerness to believe well-intentioned lies.

To understand the controversies that disturbed the revolutionaries during the winter of Valley Forge, we must realize how widespread was the anticipation of victory during the campaign of 1777. Hardly anyone spoke of the possibility of a long war. In the victory celebrations of 1783, several orators remarked that no one had foreseen an eight-year struggle. Sometimes those who did warn that the contest might last for years, as John Adams did, were also the most impatient for bold capital strokes that would end it at once.[59] The spirit of 1775 always remained the guide for most revolutionaries' understanding of the war. Although they knew that neither the public's contributions to the war nor the army's prowess came close to the *rage militaire*, which Americans had celebrated for barely a year, they continued to regard the later expedients—Fabian caution, conscription, confiscation—as regrettable temporary recourses, not the elements of a different method for winning the war. They continued to look for signs of a quick victory won by the innate strength and unique righteousness of God's chosen people. In the days between the battles of Brandywine and Germantown, Samuel Adams could see only two alternatives: "compleat Victory" or guilt. "Our troops are victorious in the North. The Enemies Troops are divided and scattered over a Country several Hundred Miles. Our Country is populous and fertile. If we do not beat them this Fall will not the faithful Historian record it as our own Fault? But let us depend, not upon the Arm of Flesh, but on the God of Armies. We shall be free if we deserve it. We must succeed in a Cause so manifestly just, if we are virtuous."[60]

Yet Washington's army did not succeed against Howe, and revolutionaries did not usually blame their own lack of virtue for the failure. On a smaller, much less publicized scale, the commander in chief suffered reproaches for his defeat like those heaped on St. Clair and other Continental Army generals. Late in 1777 and early in 1778 a number of revolutionaries began to question the abilities of the commander in chief. They certainly had plenty of grounds for criticism. His attempts to hold Long Island, the loss of the garrison of Fort Washington, the ill-informed conduct of the Battle of Brandywine, the intricately synchronized attack at Germantown that failed to mesh properly—few generals could make errors like these and have them overlooked; the British generals who opposed Washington got no such consideration in New York or in London. But unlike the comments on Howe in England, the criticism of Washington was private, not published or spoken formally. And although it mentioned specific mistakes, it dealt more fully with Washington's strategy and his failure to achieve clear victories like Gates's defeat of Burgoyne.

The most important critics were members of Congress who had long believed that independence could be won mainly by the strength of soldiers' zeal for the revolution, led by a general who could transform that zeal into victory. Thomas Mifflin, one of the principal critics, was widely famed for practicing this kind of command with citizen volunteers and militia. His animating addresses turned them out or kept them in the field. We have already seen the low opinion that a former member of Congress, Benjamin Rush, held of several generals. During this winter, he extended his censure of Washington from a discussion of Washington's excessive reliance on incompetents to a thorough conviction of his unfitness. James Lovell, John Adams, Samuel Adams, Jonathan Sergeant, and Abraham Clark privately wrote and talked about Washington's deficiencies.

The commander in chief, according to the criticism, was weak-willed. He deferred to young flatterers like Nathanael Greene and Alexander Hamilton; he avoided decisive battle unnecessarily. The general's poor judgment, not the army's weakness, kept the Americans from beating Howe. George Bryan and Benjamin Rush tried to convince Christopher Marshall that there was "a general murmur in the people . . . against the weak conduct of Gen. Washington. His slackness and remissness in the army are so conspicuous that a general langor must ensue, except that some heroic action takes place speedily."[61] Jonathan Sergeant wrote to James Lovell, "We want a general; thousands of lives and millions of property are yearly sacrificed to the insufficiency of our Commander-in-Chief. Two battles he has lost for us. . . . I fear we shall rather sink with him than throw him off our shoulders. And sink we must under his management."[62] Washington's army lacked discipline; the critics' remarks implied that they expected discipline to come mainly from the soldiers' admiration of the commander in chief, which he should secure by praising the prowess of his men and setting an example of courage and zeal. In trying to establish discipline, Washington relied too much on formalities—general orders implemented through hierarchical authority—and too little on direct bonds between commander and soldier to inspire achievement. Two weeks before Henry Laurens became president of the Continental Congress in November 1777, he recorded the talk he heard among the delegates:

> buz! says one
> 'I would if I had been Commr of that Army with such powers have procured all the necessaries . . . without such whining Complaints.'
> 'I would says 2d. have prevented the amazing desertions which have happened. it only wants proper attentions at fountain head.' 3d. 'It is very easy to prevent intercourse between the Army and the Enemy and as easy to gain Intelligence but we never mind who comes in and goes out of our Camp.'
> 'In short 4th, our Army is under no regulation nor discipline' etc etc etc.[63]

In addition to these military criticisms, anonymous rumors floated around, saying that Washington had accepted American independence with undue slowness.

This criticism had no visible purpose except to give emotional relief to the people making it. We have no reason to doubt the judgment of one member of Congress who said that a vote in Congress on the command would have unanimously reappointed Washington.[64] Unanimity was likely because the vote would have been public. The critics of Washington were distressed at the failure to win prompt victory against Howe and at the consequent prolonging of the war. They would have preferred to win the war without needing French troops in America, and they had begun to see that a longer war would extend official corruption, popular greed, and self-indulgence.

Such dependence and delinquency threatened the society these men wanted to build. The victory at Saratoga and the loss of Philadelphia gave with one hand and took with the other: the first promised American victory but the second promised a longer war that patriotic zeal alone might not be able to win. Some of the most active and ardent revolutionaries faced the prospect of a decrease in public effort and zeal—though not in public desire for independence—coupled with greater reliance on Washington and the Continental Army for the success of the revolution.

These revolutionaries were not directly hostile to Washington and the army. They just wanted a swift stroke that would shorten the war and forestall the further entrenchment of the army as an institution. They feared the use of the public's dependence on the army to exact concessions. Washington partly symbolized this dependence, and during the winter of 1777/1778, some critics could readily imagine that if only Washington had won as Gates had won, America could have been spared the inescapable but regrettable necessity of relying ever more fully on the abilities and efforts of one man and on those who surrounded him, rather than on the virtuous strength of the public. An anonymous paper, titled "Thoughts of a Freeman" and left in Congress's meeting place, warned that "the people of America have been guilty of idolatry, by making a man their god. . . . No good may be expected from the standing army, until Baal and his worshippers are banished from the camp."[65]

The criticism and resentment remained private partly because this dependence was nowhere clearer than in Congress itself. Far from thwarting or overruling Washington, in most cases, members acceded promptly to his specific requests and gave him what he asked for if it was within their power. Problems arose when Congress made military appointments, issued orders, and revised departments on its own initiative. Then Congress and Washington sometimes had to reconcile their preferences. But Washington scrupulously deferred to the supreme authority of Congress, while at the same time, the quickest way to get something done in Congress was to have

Washington recommend it. Consequently, hardly any of the revolutionaries, including those who were criticizing Washington, would have proposed that he be replaced as commander in chief. But some would privately resent that the revolution was not being won in the way they had hoped.

Washington must have seen, when facing artillery fire, that if the smoke from the vent lined up with the smoke from the muzzle, and they both lined up with him, he was the target. When General Thomas Conway became inspector general by appointment of Congress and Horatio Gates became president of the Board of War by appointment of Congress, and when the talk about Washington's weaknesses spread in Congress, the men near Washington—Greene, Lafayette, Hamilton, John Laurens—saw an attack on him. He agreed, and they were right. But they were wrong when they also saw a coordinated plot to discredit Washington in order to make Gates commander in chief. The critics of Washington shot off a lot of smoke but no projectile.

Conway was an Irishman who had come to America from the French army and had proven adept at drilling soldiers. His promotion to major general and inspector general was partly due to Congress's susceptibility to officers who were good at self-advertisement. Washington had a low opinion of Conway even before deciding that Conway was his personal enemy. This view was clinched in Washington's mind when he heard that Conway had written to Gates: "Heaven has been determined to save your country; or a weak General and bad Councellors would have ruined it."[66] Washington vented his bitterest sarcasm on the two—on Conway for remaining silent in council, then criticizing decisions; on Gates for his muddled letters to Washington, which denied criticizing him, then protested that private correspondence had been rifled, then defended discussion of deficiencies in the army. Benjamin Rush, John Adams, and others had known about Conway's criticisms before they were reported to Washington. Many officers, doubtless including Washington, had long known about the complaining comparisons of Washington's reverses and Gates's successes. At Valley

Forge, Lieutenant Nathaniel Chipman heard "that it is a common topic of conversation in Connecticut, and, indeed, through New England, that General Washington will not fight. 'Let Gates,' say they, 'take the command, and we shall see an end of the war.'"[67] When Congress put Conway and Gates in new positions and added Mifflin to the Board of War, the pattern of undermining the authority of the commander in chief seemed to become clear. In February 1778, after the *Boston Gazette* published an anonymous letter that praised Gates's ability to inspire quick military success by liberty-loving New Englanders, William Gordon—writing as "A naturalized AMERICAN" in the *Independent Chronicle*—warned that a "scheme" was "in agitation" to effect "a capital change in the military" and that the letter praising Gates was part of it.[68] Instead, it is likely that, while some members of Congress regarded these appointments, like the private criticism, as a veiled rebuke of Washington, most expected the two men to help achieve for the army the discipline that Washington had failed to instill. The appointments probably were, at least for some members, a studied censure of Washington's failure to win. But they were not steps toward removing Washington.[69]

In the fog of correspondence that surrounded the controversy, the only people who knew for sure that a cabal existed were the people who had the least information—Washington and his intimates among the officers. The letters of Washington's critics suggest that, although each man was unsure whether a cabal existed, each one knew that, if it did exist, he was not part of it.[70] One of the letters most harshly critical of Washington was written in January 1778, by Benjamin Rush, unsigned but in his own handwriting. He sent it to Patrick Henry, who sent it to Washington. Rush's letter to John Adams, contrasting Washington's abilities with Gates's, was reported almost word for word in a letter from William Gordon to Washington.[71] Before long, all the critics evidently learned that none of them had been left out of anything because nothing had existed to be left out of. Then they began to charge that a cabal existed at headquarters, among Washington's favorites, who sought to discredit anyone who opposed the favorites' influence by falsely accusing him of conspiracy against the commander in chief.

The cabal controversy seems to have been triggered mainly by the loss of Philadelphia, which humiliatingly confirmed the disappointment of the revolutionaries' hopes for a quick victory. They judged the loss by the expectations Thomas Paine evoked: "What a rich and happy country would America be, were she, by a vigorous exertion, to reduce Howe as she has reduced Burgoyne. Her currency would rise to millions beyond its present value. Every man would be rich, and every man would have it in his power to be happy. And why not do these things? What is there to hinder? America is her own mistress and can do what she pleases."[72] After Philadelphia fell, letters and newspapers soon adopted the argument (which the British later conceded and which historians have confirmed) that Howe gained no great advantage by taking the city, that the revolution did not depend on fixed posts, and that wintering in the city would distract the British. This analysis, though correct, did not satisfy all the people who adopted it, especially members of Congress. Richard Henry Lee typified the distress that underlay this seeming unconcern when he said in October that cities were only "spots in the great Map of North America—But it is far from being certain that Gen. Howe will retain Philadelphia two months."[73] A loyalist correctly said of his fellow Pennsylvanians, "tho' our people affect to consider the loss of this metropolis as nothing yet it strikes deep."[74] The Continental Army's wintering in a fixed camp outside the city struck some as the kind of leisurely self-protection that confirmed the charge that officers wanted a long and moderate war. Some people wanted Washington to try to take Philadelphia by assault; he polled his generals on the idea, presumably to buttress his decision with their recommendations against an assault. During the week before the army moved to Valley Forge, a committee of Congress recommended that Washington conduct a winter campaign; the generals persuaded the committee that it was not feasible. Pennsylvanians complained that the army ought to protect them more fully. Washington chose Valley Forge as a compromise between a winter station that would have been more convenient for the army but less threatening to the British and a winter campaign to mollify the complainers.

At the same time, the failures in the 1777 campaign and the loss of Philadelphia disturbed Washington and his staff as deeply as others. Although they did not talk about their mistakes, we know that they saw where they had erred because they tried not to err again. A good example is Nathanael Greene, one of the principal denouncers of a cabal. From the ruinous attempt to hold Fort Washington in 1776, he went on to become, in 1780 and 1781, a master of the war of maneuver. Although the men at headquarters could cite the disadvantages of numbers and the enemy's mobility as handicaps that had prevented Washington from capturing Howe as Gates had done to Burgoyne, Washington's general orders showed how keenly he felt the contrast. His call for his troops to emulate the northern army's victories dwelt, with a fervor uncharacteristic of Washington's public writings, on the mortification his army would suffer by being outdone.

Washington was better at learning from his mistakes than at publicly acknowledging them, especially when his actual mistakes took up only a small part of the criticism of him. Most of the criticism either asked for impossibilities—duplicating the defeat of Burgoyne—or criticized his successes—cautiously keeping the army intact by maneuver, rather than risking destruction by standing fast to hold territory. But this kind of success was hardly more agreeable to the generals than to the critics. Though they learned Fabian maneuver, it was not the kind of war they wanted to fight. They wanted to meet the enemy directly and smash him. Washington and the officers close to him knew that to date they had been neither the kind of generals Americans wanted—inspiring commanders who swept all before them—nor the kind of generals they themselves admired—masterminds of a well-trained mechanism. And, to rub it in, they had lost the capital. A year earlier, Washington had written, "You know the importance of Philadelphia, and the fatal consequences that must attend the loss of it."[75] Keenly aware of their own shortcomings in the campaign and now faced with their first widespread criticism, which was true enough to sting but misinformed enough to be rejected, Washington and the officers close to him reacted by concluding that they were the victims of a conspiracy.

During the autumn of 1777 and the winter and spring of 1778, Congress was exiled to York, Pennsylvania, where cramped quarters and high prices constantly reminded members how their fortunes had fallen. Some members' criticism of military commanders may have been embittered by Congress's own conspicuous failure to adequately reform the commissary general, clothier general, and quartermaster general establishments during 1777. William Gordon, in defending Washington in the newspapers and denouncing a scheme against him, described the plight of the soldiers: "Were they not without a head to the Quarter-Master's department, ever since July? Did not the unhappy removal of the Commissary-General . . . distress them in every movement, and in every shape for want of provisions?"[76] In January, at Valley Forge, a diary recorded, "The cry against Congress still continued as high as ever: men of no less rank than Colonels spoke of them with the greatest contempt and detestation."[77]

Members of Congress could minimize the troubles their own decisions had caused by emphasizing the weaknesses of commanders. Washington, on the other hand, did not usually speak of the power of individual generals—whether Schuyler, Gates, or himself—to solve the army's lasting problems of manpower and discipline. Instead, he stressed the importance of regular pay, clothing, and supply, all of which had faltered or failed late in 1777. Several of Washington's critics had themselves encouraged the suspicion of executive authority, which had bound the staff departments with unworkably minute regulations, divided responsibility, and squabbles over patronage. If Washington was correct in blaming the army's mishaps partly on the failures in these departments, his critics could hardly escape the implication that they had helped to drive themselves into exile by their shortcomings as administrators.

Congress had never claimed broad powers, and the Articles of Confederation retained voting by state and other checks that, after their ratification in 1781, impeded the exercise of administrative authority by Congress. However, during the first year of the war, the revolutionaries had prided themselves on united voluntary obedience to Congress's recommendations. Congress initiated policies that had widespread effects—for example, the invasion of Canada and the printing of paper money. And Congress was vigilant to maintain its dignity and its authority over those it had commissioned. Similarly, when Congress established staff departments in 1777, it sought to reduce the discretion of administrative officers by making subordinates subject to detailed congressional regulations and to chiefs and deputies who were constantly checked by Congress. Thus, despite Congress's limited constitutional powers, the members took upon themselves the responsibility for both representing national civil authority and personally supervising administrative activities undertaken on the basis of that authority. But many of the regulations proved impracticable, and Congress was too distracted by other concerns and by the sectional and factional struggle for office to supervise its appointees consistently in the interests of efficiency. The subordinates in the staff departments pursued a policy of expansion and expenditure, while the chiefs and their deputies often had little control over the subordinates and devoted much of their time to infighting, private business, or stopgap expedients.

Congress fell from the prestige and authority it had enjoyed in 1775, because of its own faulty decisions on matters clearly within its responsibility. Later, the states would go beyond their early tardiness and evade or ignore Congress's decisions, but in 1777, while congressional appointees still ran the war and Continental money still circulated, Congress tried to control its servants not by consistently supervising them but by limiting their discretion, by dividing their authority, and by curtailing their rewards. Instead of republican economy, it got appointees who could accomplish too little and employees whom it could not keep track of, much less control. Under such circumstances, only the kind of narrow emphasis on generals' abilities that Washington's critics had adopted could explain the army's defeats and the loss of Philadelphia without referring to the administrative failures. During the winter at Valley Forge, Congress left the selection of a new quartermaster general to Washington. He chose Nathanael Greene, one of the principal objects of criticism by those who condemned Washington for relying on favorites and one of the officers who was most certain that a congressional cabal against Washington had existed. As Greene's later friction with Congress showed, the delegates' forfeiture of authority and tacit acknowledgment of failure rankled.

The hostile mutual suspicions between Washington and his critics were not the prevailing outlook of the American Revolution. Such hostility emerged under the stress of heavy setbacks and strong fears. It showed the bitter side of righteousness backed into a corner by its own defeats. In March 1778, President Henry Laurens asked, "Why are we so Courtly and mincing? is there a name under Heaven that shall sanctify the peculator or screen the man whose neglect of Duty has brought thousands to Misery and Death? forbid it torpid patriotism of 1775—No! let the Offender be dragged forth, and the people told, this is the Man! God awaken us."[78] Finding the offenders—whether profiteers, generals, or delegates in Congress—meant sustaining the ideals of 1775. An offender, not a general loss of virtue, had prevented the promised victory. The war against the greatest power in the world was fought in the belief that virtue gave strength. If the cause could summon too little strength to win, might this mean that it had too little virtue to deserve to win? Or might the cause owe its failure to only a few weak men who sabotaged the virtuous efforts of others? When revolutionaries argued the latter possibility, they were free to conclude that the war had not shown Americans to be unworthy of independence. Their hope for the promised land could unite them while they sustained the virtuous strength of 1775. To preserve this united strength, the weak must be identified, "dragged forth," and isolated in their crime. By linking the proof of patriotism with the experience of spiritual awakening, the revolution placed its strongest hope for national survival on the strength of communal zeal. Judged by the ideals of 1775, or even by the demands for quick victory in 1777, Americans' strength had faltered. To isolate a few leading offenders provided one explanation. But if faltering had in fact spread much more widely, revolutionaries ran the risk of becoming atomized into defenseless individuals isolated by selfishness and deadness of heart. Against this danger the revolution seemed to have little recourse except a spirit of awakening expressed in revival of the *rage militaire* or a counterfeit spirit attained by pillorying offenders. As the Continental Army went into winter quarters at Valley Forge, most revolutionaries were still seeking to escape this danger by the army's prompt victory over the British.

CHAPTER V

Valley Forge

Valley Forge was the first winter encampment of the Continental Army since it had begun to recruit men routinely for three years or the duration. Valley Forge was also the first winter encampment of the Continental Army that accomplished substantial training. And Valley Forge was the first winter encampment at which the army suffered severe and general hardship due to currency depreciation, high prices, and poorly organized supply. These facts made the winter at Valley Forge memorable among Continentals long before it had acquired special meaning for most Americans. A year later, recalling the soldiers' construction of huts in December after "a long and unsuccessful campaign," Lieutenant Samuel Shaw said, "It will not make a disgraceful page in our 'new history.'"[1] The celebrations and orations in 1783 reviewed the army's victories and trials but seldom mentioned Valley Forge. The winter encampment of 1777/1778 did not gain popular renown until after the war. But in the army, even after the winter of 1779/1780, which had much harsher weather and greater supply problems, Valley Forge remained a symbol of the army's unique services to the revolution. It had been a test of national survival because it had been a test of the army's survival amid hardships caused in large part by fellow revolutionaries.

Valley Forge was a city of log huts twenty miles from Philadelphia. The neighborhoods were brigades. Soldiers lived twelve to a hut, and the officers of two companies lived together in single huts. These cabins, fourteen by sixteen feet, were built in December from trees felled nearby, and the same woods provided fuel for round-the-clock fires, the main source of warmth for men in the open with too few clothes. For the first three months, the main activities, apart from occasional alarms, were keeping warm and finding food and fuel. The usual food of the army had long been flour and beef. Men drew a pound of flour and a pound of raw or cured meat and cooked it themselves or took turns cooking for their mess. Flour alone, or some other form of ground grain, was often the only ration at Valley Forge. It was mixed with water and baked in coals, in pans, or on a stick. This was the "Fire Cake" that, as a diet for soldiers who knew the agricultural plenty of their country, became a constant reminder of their separation from "Ye who Eat Pumkin Pie and Roast Turkies."[2] One officer's memoir included a recipe for cooking spoiled pork and hog fodder.[3] When food gave out, men relieved their hunger, or at least their minds, by sticking their heads out in the cold and calling out to passers-by in an undertone, "No bread, no soldier."[4] Company grade officers underwent hardships like those of their men if they did not have money to provide extra clothes and rations for themselves. Field grade and general officers suffered much less, if at all.

In spite of the hardship, camp life did not consist solely of sitting around and brooding. In addition to the work necessary to keep the camp running and the forage parties that took food from farmers in the area, Valley Forge was an active place: civilians came to visit men in the army; soldiers came and went on furlough; new recruits arrived; and in March a new form of training began. A few officers' wives, including Lady Washington, as she was called, spent part of the winter in the camp.

The shortage of food was sporadic, and it varied among units. Some may have run short hardly at all.[5] The most severe problem was clothing. Although Continental regiments had designs for uniforms, they wore what they could get—odd pieces of uniforms, the ever-popular rifle shirt, all-purpose overalls, or rags and blankets. When we are invited to feel sorry for the officers who had to make overcoats out of blankets, we should remember that they wore these in the presence of men who had no blankets. The army's needs and the difficulty of importing from Europe made cloth and clothing scarce and expensive. The symbolically patriotic homespun did not appear in sufficient quantity to end the shortage. Despite the occasional charitable contributions of clothing to the army, civilians most often competed with soldiers for clothing. Money often determined which group won the competition, and the army frequently lost. Soldiers who sought money for food or liquor sold their clothing and even their muskets to civilians—in violation of both state laws and military orders. A newspaper writer asked, "How can it be, that any and every individual, can purchase shirts, stockings, shoes, etc. and the vulture-eyed agents, etc. be unable to purchase for the soldiery?"[6] The most likely answer was that the best profit lay in selling to civilians. Not only during the Valley Forge winter but throughout the war, greater comfort for civilians often meant greater discomfort for soldiers.

Few revolutionaries explained the distress of the army in this way. Due partly to Washington's efforts to keep the extent of his army's weakness a secret and partly to the public's longstanding preference for stories of strength rather than reverses, the hardship at Valley Forge came as a surprise to most people, while some evidently knew nothing about it during the winter. Among the most surprised were the state officials Washington asked for extraordinary aid. Governors were indignant at Continental officials' negligence, and people at home were outraged to learn that soldiers lacked shoes and clothing. The calls for aid drew substantial shipments of cattle and grain, as well as some clothing. These could not replace the regular workings of staff departments, as Congress later learned when it tried to rely on direct state shipments. But the help did alleviate conditions at Valley Forge.

The public's ignorance, surprise, and generosity in dealings with the army during the winter were early signs of the increasing separation between the viewpoints of the public and the army. While both groups could, in the short run, blame misconduct in staff departments for the army's crises, the recurrence of similar problems would bring the two groups' differing assumptions into ever-clearer conflict. Continentals were growing surer that civilian revolutionaries ignored the army's welfare while pursuing wealth and enjoying its fruits in the fast rise of prices and income. Most citizens followed the war news not as the story of institutional survival that it usually was, but as the story of victories and defeats. Willing to respond to unexpected emergencies, they took the continued functioning of the army for granted and tried to have as little to do with it as possible. The widespread assumption that the army routinely took care of itself underlay the difficulties Washington and others experienced in trying to convey their own sense of urgency about supply, pay, or recruiting. Soldiers continued to leave camp and plunder nearby citizens; yet officers' and officials' warnings that the army could not survive without regular supplies did not meet hostility from civilians so much as calm. The assumption that the army could sustain itself also reinforced the public's indignation at soldiers who tried to get as much bounty money as they could. The army's first prolonged shortage of food, beginning during the fall campaign and lasting through the Valley Forge winter, increased this misunderstanding between citizens and soldiers. The citizens remained either unaware of the difficulties or proud of their extra contributions, which, in any case, they believed ought not to have been necessary. Meanwhile, the soldiers began to take pride in surviving as an army despite the heedlessness of the public. The winter at Valley Forge, in spite of the recriminations and misunderstandings that filled it, was the last time that revolutionaries expected to be united in the zeal of 1775. In the two years after Valley Forge, most revolutionaries paid less and less attention to the war, while at the same time the army became ever more clearly a distinct organization with grievances against those who had called it into being. The Continentals did not become career soldiers, but they did begin to become professionals for as long as their stay in the army lasted. At the same time, a group of politicians whom historians have usually called nationalists, including many army officers, became increasingly convinced of the need for a strong continental government. Among themselves, they frankly attributed this conviction to their loss of confidence in the virtue and the patriotism of most of their fellow revolutionaries.

This division within the revolutionary cause had antecedents before Valley Forge and before the war, but it became fully apparent to the participants only during the years 1778 through 1780. During the Valley Forge winter, the ideal of united, voluntary, self-sacrificing, and therefore victorious effort remained intact while events foiled the expectation. Commanders, soldiers, Congress, citizens—all believed that they had done exemplary service to the ideal; but after capturing an enemy army, they found that they had lost their capital city and that their main army looked more like a fugitive than a victor. The winter recriminations arose from an awareness on the part of both sides—Continental officers and their civilian critics—that their own group had failed to equal the ideal of effective service. This awareness may have enhanced their oft-expressed eagerness to believe that they had equaled it or could yet equal it and that the ideal was still the valid guide to winning the revolution.

In the weeks before the Battle of Trenton, many revolutionaries had momentarily feared that defeat was imminent. No such gloom prevailed in the winter of 1777/1778. Revolutionaries were confident enough to believe that only the misconduct of some of their compatriots stood between them and victory. Soon, most Americans would believe that they had, in effect, already won the war, while a smaller group, including the army, would grow increasingly sure that only their effort carried on the revolution. The mutual accusations during the Valley Forge winter marked the last time in the war years that critics expected each other to achieve the united national effort that once had promised to win and preserve independence.

The recriminations that divided revolutionaries during the Valley Forge winter, like the soldiers' suspicions that their generals had betrayed them in 1776, arose in part from a spirit that faltered during reverses. The survival and victory of the army after 1777 owed much to the growth of a spirit of dedication among soldiers—a dedication that could withstand adversity. To sustain the soldiers' spirit and to increase the prospect for battlefield victory, the army turned to more systematic development of professional discipline. This discipline encouraged rather than denied the soldier's capacity for virtuous patriotism, but professionalism also provided a recourse when virtue did not suffice. The spirit of 1775 was buttressed by the spirit of military professionalism.

However, because of the distinctive character of American soldiers, the Continental Army remained quite different from European armies. To prevail within the American army, professionalism would have to be accommodated to the spirit of Continental privates. Their temperament combined paradoxical elements that seldom conformed to the European military goal of predictability. European officers who marveled at the American soldiers' lack of discipline in 1777 were even more amazed at the soldiers' docility amid hardships during the ensuing winter. A European army, observers agreed, would long since have mutinied or broken up when pay and food ran out.[7] At Valley Forge, where the threat of mutiny was overcome, the spirit of Continental soldiers foreshadowed their spirit during the bizarre major mutinies of 1780 and 1781. It was a mixture of patriotism, resentment, and fatalism. This last quality differentiated the enlisted men from many officers, who still expected to receive their due or resign. During this first winter of long-term enlistment and severe shortage, anyone could see that only a fool would remain a soldier for reasons of immediate material interest. The soldiers' complaints were genuine and justified, but might come out as jokes, such as tying straw to the tail of a quartermaster's horse and setting it on fire or, as Private Dennis Kennedy did, "threatening to desert as soon as he got shoes and cursing Congress."[8] Soldiers with such an outlook in effect admitted that they were stuck because they wanted to stay in the army even though their grievances were not remedied. This dedication had appeared during the campaign of 1777 in the soldiers' overweening confidence in their own prowess on the battlefield. In that campaign they had often ignored the evidence of their own shortcomings in expertise; now the same confidence helped the soldiers to overcome the strong inducements to mutiny or desert. The government and the public, which were not fulfilling their promises to the soldiers, had them at a disadvantage because the soldiers believed that they ought to serve for the welfare of their country and that they were as strong and as special as they had been told. When we read of the Continental Army's adoption of European military techniques, we should bear in mind the revolutionary spirit that helped to keep men in the ranks. We can watch General Nathanael Greene's respect for this spirit grow in his aphorisms: in 1777—"nothing but habit makes the soldier, and pride the officer"; in 1778—"Pride and sentiment support the officer; habit and enthusiasm the soldier"; in 1780—"There must be either pride or principle to make a soldier."[9]

The official returns showed that, on the average, eight or ten men deserted every day during the winter months. The number was probably higher, but no one knew for sure. Desertion was the enlisted man's version of the officer's resignation. Resignation might be discreditable, but it was legal. Desertion was not. However, the effect of both was similar: separating those who would fulfill the terms of their engagement, despite the surprises of camp life and default by the public, from those who would not. Although it was one of the worst military crimes, in practice it was an extension of the principle of voluntarism on which the Continental Army largely relied. Congress and the commanders tacitly admitted as much by refraining from the death penalty and by holding corporal punishment down to one hundred lashes. The high rate of desertion late in 1777 and early in 1778 gives us a clue to the minds of those who did not desert because it shows how easily they could have left the army.

For the soldiers who stayed, the most significant creation of the Valley Forge winter was a self-conscious professionalism. As we have seen, the soldiers' ability in combat had been growing in 1777, though erratically; their discipline remained faulty for years after Valley Forge. The principal legacy of the winter's experience and training was a unique attitude toward service in the army—an attitude based on a definition of being a soldier that satisfied men who wanted to be good ones, but only for as long as the war required. This definition took effect through a plan of discipline that systematized attitudes long developing among Continentals.

In order to understand the character of the Continental privates' professionalism, one must examine the demeanor cultivated by their superiors. The gentlemen-officers now set out to cap their status with public recognition of their worth and indispensability. The officers' demand for recognition often focused on the question of promotion. Officers insisted that the promotion of any of their peers or subordinates to a superior rank implied that those who had not been promoted were not fit for the rank they held. Since such public notice that the authorities thought them unfit would destroy all respect for them, their usefulness had ended and they would have to resign. In May 1776, when Nathanael Greene feared that he would not be promoted, he told Washington that if Congress's decision had "a direct tendency to degrade me in the public estimation," it "would sink me in my own esteem, and render me spiritless and uneasy in my situation, and consequently unfit for the service."[10] This reasoning was proclaimed much more often than it was followed, but most officers believed that promotion ought to have followed strict lines of seniority, with the exception of special promotions for singular battlefield merit. Even in such instances, officers argued that they would have performed as well as the meritorious officer if they had been where his chance for distinction had occurred; so he could not claim superior merit—only luck—and promoting him would falsely malign others. Experience showed, according to Henry Knox, that "rank is esteemed an unalienable right."[11]

Some of the less vocal officers, no doubt, and even a very few flamboyant ones, like Anthony Wayne, avoided this festering ambition and brooding resentment. However, most officers sought the distinction of high rank so avidly that they opposed all means by which someone else might surpass them. Thus, a corps increasingly proud of its ability to lead men in combat wound up insisting that the mark of this ability be distributed according to a principle that was the mainstay of the placeman: time in grade.

During the Valley Forge winter they modified this principle, with Washington's endorsement, by seeking the right to buy and sell commissions. In the British army, between the ranks of ensign and lieutenant colonel, a command might be, in effect, a personal possession. This practice enabled gentlemen to obtain commissions, and it helped to insure that men who became officers would have the independent means with which to support their status on a small salary. To American officers, it seems to have been a token of pride and a financial recourse in adversity. If inability to support themselves or their families forced them to resign their commissions, they wanted a return on the money they had invested thus far by having to support themselves on depreciated pay. The officers' notion of their due took them farther and farther from their fellow revolutionaries' desire for an army that relied on public spirit, not gain and privilege. The officers were beginning to claim vested rights to a status that, according to the ideals of 1775, ought not even to exist in a free country, except when war called for temporary exercise of authority from disinterested motives.

Although such principles as promotion by seniority and by purchase of commissions seemed straightforward, officers could not agree on the practical workings because the Continental Army had never become a national army in which state distinctions had no official place. Instead, the organization of the army along state lines complicated the question of seniority. Should an officer rise according to his time in grade compared to all other officers of the same rank or to all officers of the same rank in his state line? If the first, how could senior captains in a Massachusetts regiment become majors when Pennsylvania regiments needed majors while Massachusetts regiments did not? If the second, might not a captain in a small state line with little turnover remain in grade for years while officers once junior to him became majors and lieutenant colonels in their large, changing state lines?

But before addressing these questions, officers had to try to determine who was senior to whom in the first place. This determination of seniority within a given rank was called the "arrangement" of a state line; it occupied countless hours throughout the war, and it was rarely settled to universal satisfaction. Congress gave governors and generals blank commissions. Those issued were not collated or compiled into an Army List. When disputes arose, committees of arrangement and boards of officers drew up seniority lists that conflicted with each other. Colonel John Crane and Colonel John Lamb had the same date of rank in the Continental artillery. When a board of officers gave Crane seniority, Lamb wrote to Washington, "It is impossible for a soldier, who is tenacious of his honor, (the only jewel worth contending for) to suffer himself to be degraded by being superseded; and his just right torn from him, and given to another, without resenting the injury, in a becoming manner. I must frankly acknowledge, that my sensibilities are deeply wounded by this event."[12] The possibility of having to renegotiate officers' seniority once a state line had been tolerably arranged could distress Washington as did few other dangers. Did cavalry officers outrank infantry officers of the same grade or even a higher grade regardless of date of rank? Did Continental officers who had formerly served as militia officers have seniority over others with the same date of rank but no such experience? Did an officer who had been temporarily brevetted to a higher rank have seniority over another officer of the same rank after both of them officially received the higher rank on the same day? Did an officer who had resigned his commission and later returned to the army have seniority over another officer of the same grade who was first commissioned on the same day that the former officer received his second commission?

These questions would of course trouble the army no matter what system of promotion prevailed, but they show us one of the reasons why Congress and the commander in chief might shrink from adopting strict seniority as the criterion for promotion. Because an officer's "honor" must not be compromised, the most refined, even sophistical, calculations of seniority might make the difference between command and resignation. Early in 1777 John Trumbull refused a commission from Congress as deputy adjutant general, with date of rank September 12, 1776, because General Horatio Gates had first appointed him on June 28, 1776, and "A soldier's honor forbids the idea of giving up the least pretension to rank." When Trumbull's friends in Congress pointed out that Gates had not been authorized to commission him, Trumbull replied, "To sink under the command of men whose superior in rank I had been acknowledged, though perhaps not established, tasted indeed too loathsome of degradation."[13]

It is written, "Lift not up your horn on high: speak not with a stiff neck. For promotion cometh neither from the east, nor from the west, nor from the south. But God is the judge: he putteth down one, and setteth up another."[14] After a week of debates that one delegate called "perplexed, inconclusive and irksome," Congress adopted on February 19, 1777, what was later called the "famous incomprehensible Baltimore Resolution," which purported to regulate promotion by "the misterious trinity of *Seniority Merit and Quota*."[15] That is, Congress would consider time in grade, merit, and equity among the state lines in making rules for promotion. In fact, as Gouverneur Morris said, "it is no rule."[16] Congress thought that promotion by strict seniority was inconsistent with republican principles. Such autonomy would erode the supremacy of civil authority. Congress kept a free hand and passed the resolution so that a superseded officer could believe that his being passed over did not reflect on his competence. In practice, Congress left promotions below the rank of general to state recommendations, while reserving authority to alter them or to make its own choices. Seniority within the regiment to the rank of captain and seniority within the state line to the rank of colonel became the customary though not inflexible criterion. The opinion of senior officers still had influence, as did the self-advertisement and political connections of officers who lobbied state legislatures or Congress.

During the Valley Forge winter, Congress was irritated by the vanity of the officers but could not afford to ignore them. Since the summer of 1777, officers had been resigning, and more were threatening to follow them. These resignations had several causes. Some newly commissioned officers repeated the experience that others had first undergone in 1775 and 1776; they found that army life confined or threatened aspirations more than it fulfilled them. In addition, short issues of food and clothing became more frequent, then constant, during the months when resignations increased. Depreciation of the currency lowered the value of a pay scale once intended to support a gentleman, and the government's default on pay forced officers to spend their own money and then borrow. Some officers who might have been willing to withstand these hardships could not let their families suffer too as the cost of all goods rose. If husbands' concern did not move them to resign, wives urged them to do so.

Washington warned Congress that the army would be unable to function unless the resignations stopped. In March 1778, he told President Henry Laurens that since August 1777, "between two and three hundred officers have resigned their Commissions and many others with difficulty disswaded from it."[17] One officer heard in the last week of December 1777 that "his Excellency lately expressed his fears of being left Alone with the Soldiers only."[18] However, no such crisis had yet arrived, even at Valley Forge. Later in the war, when there were always more officers than places for them, Washington still worried that the number might fall too low. The resignations probably removed in many cases the very officers Washington and others had been complaining about: the gentlemen who had entered the army only to cut a figure, the grafters who had made their bundle on fraudulent recruiting and pay, the officers who, as one of them said to Lieutenant Samuel Richards, "could not and would not live so."[19] One could argue that despite the loss of some able officers, the resignations of 1777 and 1778 did more good for both the army and the resigners than their continued connection would have done.

In spite of strong reasons to leave the army, many officers stayed at Valley Forge or received winter furloughs and stayed in the service. They used the crisis created by the resignations of others to enhance their growing professional identity. The most important public recognition they demanded was a half-pay pension, to be paid after the war. When Colonel Theodorick Bland first proposed half pay in November 1777, Washington anticipated many of the objections and asked, "Would not this . . . give a great disgust to the people at large?"[20] By December, Washington had decided that only the promise of pensions could keep the army officered with competent men. He told President Henry Laurens, "I do most religiously believe the salvation of the cause depends upon it. . . . Untill Officers consider their Commissions in an honorable, and interested point of view, and are afraid to endanger them by negligence and inattention . . . no order, regularity, or care, either of the Men, or Public property, will prevail."[21] He supported half pay in emphatic letters like this one, but the plan met vehement opposition in Congress. The debate, according to the Connecticut delegation, was "the most painfull and disagreeable . . . that hath ever been agitated in Congress."[22] Among the delegates, the officers had allies who, we can infer, had little faith in popular zeal as a source of military effectiveness. These delegates from the middle and southern states accepted the argument that the army needed discipline and experience, which could not be maintained without its present hierarchy. This emphasis on professionalism, status, and coercion rather than popular zeal foreshadowed the effort to create a stronger national government as a surer basis for independence than public virtue could provide. Congress probably would never have voted half pay on its supposed merits. The delegates adopted it under threat of resignations that, they were told, would cripple or disband the army. Hoping for the defeat of half pay, James Lovell wrote, with underlined sarcasm, "There is really no argument for it but a fear of all our *best* officers leaving the army."[23] Congress voted a pension for seven years, beginning after the war. In August 1779, the delegates recommended that the states give officers half pay for life, and in October 1780, another time of crisis, Congress itself extended half pay to the life of the officer. The delegates reserved the right to substitute some other form of compensation at a later date.

In 1778 the opponents of pensions argued that this measure

was the very kind of artificially created privilege that the revolution sought to end. Half-pay pensioners in Britain were notorious as bribed supporters of tyranny buttressed by corruption. America had no place for "a set of haughty idle imperious Scandalizers of industrious Citizens and Farmers."[24] President Henry Laurens regarded the demand for half pay as an admission of "a total loss of virtue in the Army" and tried to console himself that "there are many Thousands whose hearts are warm with the reasoning which induced the original Compact and who have not bowed the Knee to Luxury nor to Mammon."[25] Many Americans were suffering in the war as much or more than the officers but stood to receive no such recompense. Half-pay officers would be drones in society, living idly on the labor of honest citizens, the butts of ridicule and hate. Besides, if the officers' need for money caused the resignations, how could half pay help? It would give them no money with which to get through the war years.

This last argument revealed the most about the immediate significance of pensions. Officers did say that the promise of future financial security would enable them to continue to support themselves with their own or borrowed money during the war without facing poverty at the time of discharge. But the opponents rightly detected that the pension as a symbol carried as much weight with officers as with those who denounced it. Captain Joseph Hodgkins said in February, "What the soldiers has sufferd the past year Desarves a Penshon During Life."[26] He did not say that soldiers or officers would need a lifetime pension but rather that they deserved one. Half pay would both reward the officers' oft-claimed superior contributions to independence and acknowledge at once the nation's dependence on their professional expertise. Enemy soldiers held the capital; the work of fighting them promised increasing hardships and decreasing pay; no liberty-loving populace had surrounded the redcoats or driven them into the sea; the conspicuous failures among the early batches of officers and the resignations in adversity showed that, if the present officers left, Congress could not replace them with equally suitable citizens in arms; the country needed the army, the army needed the officers, and half pay would make it impossible to pretend otherwise. The spirit of 1775 had continued to fall apart, and the officers rubbed Congress's face in the pieces. As much as Washington, Congress, and others had criticized the Continental officer corps, they rightly concluded that they had no choice. Experience and willingness to serve gave more hope for the survival of the army than did the prospect of trying to replace officers who resigned. But, as we shall see, after the winter at Valley Forge, Continental Army officers were marked men in the minds of many revolutionaries. Americans did not forget that the officers had used the public trust of command to extract private advantage from the revolution as a token of superior virtue.

The recognition the officers demanded would have secured their status as military professionals. Yet, the state of mind they perfected had much in common with the demand in revolutionary ideals for selfless patriots who deserved happiness. The officers' professionalism, like the ideals of 1775, was an absolute that brooked no compromise. Officers, like the Americans as a people, based their claim to distinction on their superior ability to deserve it. The characteristics of the professional demeanor to which officers aspired reveal much about the consequences of a revolutionary's attempt to embody an absolute ideal.

Two different prospects could arouse an officer's anxious concern about his standing with other officers and the public: fame and shame. Far from being extremes of notoriety that few men would expect to experience, to many officers both of these seemed latent in almost any situation, requiring their constant vigilance lest their motives and achievements be undervalued. Commanders encouraged this anxiety because they believed that an officer's personal responsibility keyed up the valor with which he led men. Officers expected to be mentioned by name in official reports, to distinguish themselves for promotion, to be remembered always by a grateful posterity through histories of the revolution. This search for fame did not bear the reproach that material self-seeking did. Rather, it was the proper accompaniment and reward of military virtue.

By the same token, an officer adjudged a coward could

expect, in addition to being cashiered, to have his name published in his home state newspaper and to hear other officers warned to shun him. He might even wind up being marched out of camp wearing a dress, with soldiers throwing dung at him. Such shame threatened him not only through formal punishment of military crimes but, pervasively, through opinion and rumor. Besides avoiding shameful acts, one had to prevent or correct the imputation of shame, which might come by false accusations or simply by insufficient appreciation of one's merit. When Lieutenant Colonel Isaac Sherman complained about General Anthony Wayne's official version of the assault on Stony Point, he told Wayne that an officer who had "fine and delicate feelings which ever distinguish the generous and manly soul" sought "the happiness of his country . . . the grateful applause of his fellow citizens," and the means of "transmitting his name in an amiable point of view to the world."[27] On this score, ambitious officers, especially young ones, carried to its highest pitch the revolutionaries' characteristic emphasis on the decisive importance of the present moment for the future welfare of America and for the revolutionaries' reputation and self-respect. They were ever watchful for the critical opportunity that would make them immortal heroes—always aware that all their former services might be forgotten if they faltered or suffered disrepute. As an embittered exile said of his countrymen, "Hosanna one hour, and crucify the next was the prevailing principle among the Americans!"[28]

This cast of mind encouraged in some officers a blend of touchiness and recklessness that was, in effect if not in intent, suicidal. We have seen how testy the new-made gentlemen could be about their status, and we will see them starting duels. In combat, some of them indulged the flight to fame despite its needless cost or risk to both their cause and their men. Admirers of John Laurens regretted that "he fell unnecessarily, in an unimportant skirmish" at the end of the war, due to "his rash exposure." John Marshall later said that Laurens, who was twenty-seven years old when he died, pursued military fame "with the ardour of a young soldier, whose courage seems to have partaken largely of that romantic spirit which youth and enthusiasm produce in a fearless mind."[29] Casimir Pulaski leading cavalry against fixed defenses at Savannah, Alexander Hamilton showing off by putting his men through the manual of arms in the open within range of the enemy at Yorktown—the extra dare, unnecessary for victory, even an impediment to victory, excited officers because it contained the hidden edge of their prowess. On one side lay mediocrity, on the other, death. The farther they pressed, the closer they came to making themselves immortal.

The officers' bravado had much in common with aspirations that moved most revolutionaries. The extravagant rhetoric of the revolution, which celebrated native courage, pure patriotic selflessness, and quick victorious freedom, should neither be taken as a literal rendering of the revolutionaries' minds nor be dismissed as an artificial stimulant. Like the young officers' audacity, it tested the boundaries of glory to which the revolution could aspire. Few patriots would have said that the rhetoric was false or that the revolution ought not to have tried to equal heaven's promise of universal freedom and happiness, sustained by communal virtue and revered by posterity. They would escape a static, hopeless life; they would fight corruption, arbitrary power, and the other tools of enslavement by sacrificing for the public welfare, by finding institutions and officials that could thwart tyranny. But they would often fail. Even success in such measures did not accomplish the full promise. And in the risky vanguard, where the gap between achievement and ambition might become so great as to destroy hope—that is, life—the revolutionaries relied on the enthusiasm of rhetoric to make the two seem closer or seem one. When conduct failed to match the public standard, one could pretend that the discrepancy did not exist. In the case of combat prowess, officers who played sick in their tents during battle or alarm later acted as though they had done nothing wrong.[30] More characteristically, an officer's duties seldom or never made his valor the center of wide attention, and he had to brag or resent the luck that gave a few men the chance for distinction. But some tried to bring the ideal and the deed together in action—to make their glory true—and in the attempt they went beyond concern for victory, beyond care for their men's lives, and even beyond the thought of future service in the revolution. They had to find their own height at once or fall. Some fell because they would not see the limit beyond which their ideal surpassed their powers. We can liken these few, as a loyalist likened all revolutionaries, to the wild geese who dashed themselves to pieces by flying against a lighthouse in the night—killed by a beacon that saved the lives of the earthbound.[31]

An officer summarized much of his concern for his reputation in the word "honor." The term referred not simply to his own conscience or self-esteem but also to public acknowledgment of his claim to respect. To have honor and to be honored were very close, if not the same. Officers believed that they could not continue to serve without honor, and this broad definition of the term required them to correct any imputation of dishonor, as well as to avoid dishonorable deeds. To excuse the inaccuracies in one officer's newspaper reply to public accusations, another officer explained to the same newspaper, "A Soldier's honor is his life; he felt himself touched to the quick, and his ardour allowed him not time for recollection."[32] In addition, officers were keen to detect attacks on their honor in other people's offhand remarks, criticisms, or even silence. Failing to mention an officer's name in the report of a battle, failing to give him an independent command, failing to promote him—any of these might so mortify him that he would construe the silence as a declaration that he was unfit for his post.

Honor was the most precious possession of a gentleman. It had no degrees—a gentleman could not lose a little honor. When Georgia officials instigated a court-martial of General Robert Howe, whom they blamed for losing Savannah, Howe told the court, "In a profession so chaste as that of arms, where honor is so feelingly alive that it must smart and agonize at the least shadow of aspersion, expression can give no proper colourings to my anxieties."[33] Honor was a mark of distinction that won deference to a gentleman's conspicuous superiority and thus enabled an officer to command men. Such notions were of long standing among Europeans, and the eighteenth-century vogue of sensibility seemed especially to encourage this form of expression among military men. The American officers' self-conscious imitation of European models might become doubly touchy because of the officers' difficulty in securing satisfactory recognition as gentlemen in the first place. These pretensions made the officers' growing professional self-consciousness look very sinister to many of their fellow revolutionaries. Not only did the officers claim to have indispensable military expertise and to deserve special pensions, but they also vaunted a distinction, an inviolable merit whose supposed strength lay in the idea that they alone had it.

We can compare the officers' self-absorbed, jealously watched honor with the wish of other revolutionaries to achieve a full personal freedom, unchecked by government or compromise. Although freedom from all constraint and from all complicity with sin was not part of the systematic political thought of the revolution, it was a state that some revolutionaries tried to achieve and that most of them probably wished the revolution could secure, while knowing better. The rhetoric of the revolution often appealed to the desire for such freedom, and even as an unattainable goal it provided much of the emotional impetus for virtuous libertarian resistance to tyranny. It was the ideal by which to weigh modern compromises. The extremes, to those who sought them, seemed like the proper fulfillment or extension of a desirable course of conduct. The keenest sense of honor made the best officer; the fullest sense of freedom made the best citizen. The citizen who kept himself free from army service was pursuing his private happiness at the expense of communal effort no less than the officer who worried more about his honor than about his ability to lead his men. Safeguarding freedom, like safeguarding honor, could make the individual more important than the cause.

During the winter at Valley Forge, we see this attitude in the spread of a new vogue among Continental officers—the duel. A man duelled in defense of honor, usually his own but sometimes that of another. After Washington and his staff had exposed, as they believed, the cabal against the commander in chief, General Thomas Conway's snide remarks about Washington caused John Cadwalader to challenge him. In the exchange of fire, Cadwalader wounded Conway in the mouth. More typically, officers duelled in response to insults, real or fancied. Dr. James Thacher was astonished at the "calmness and composure" of a lieutenant of dragoons who described the duel in which he had been wounded and had killed another officer. The day before, the two men had been "on the most intimate terms of friendship. . . . The duel originated in a trivial misunderstanding," but the victor showed no "sorrow or remorse of conscience for having sacrificed the life of a friend and valuable officer."[34] Failing to resent an insult undermined an officer's honor or even convicted him of cowardice in the eyes of others, though an officer evidently could, as Timothy Pickering did, refuse to duel at all yet still serve without suffering disabling shame. Thacher called it "this fashionable folly."[35] Chaplains, civilians, and some officers deplored the increased duelling; they used the oldest and least effective weapon against it—ridicule. They pointed out the number of times that shots were exchanged at close range and both missed. But if the duelling officers had possessed much sense of the ridiculous, they would have been very different men, and the issue probably would not have arisen. In fact, commanders seldom discouraged or punished duelling, even though the Articles of War prohibited issuing a challenge, fighting a duel, or permitting a duel.[36] As Patrick Henry explained to Washington on behalf of Lieutenant Elisha White, "He with many others supposes that Custom has in some sort controuled the Laws agt Duelling in Cases where provocation can be pleaded."[37]

Although the practice of duelling imitated the etiquette of European officers and the long-standing code of the gentleman, it did not flourish in 1775 and 1776, when American officers were first striving to become military gentlemen. In March 1779, a writer in the *New Jersey Gazette* complained that duelling had "of late become so much in vogue among the Gentlemen of our Army."[38] American officers who stayed through the Valley Forge winter sought to prove themselves more than military gentlemen; they were professionals who could command unqualified respect. Descriptions and criticisms of duelling mention not the example of Europeans but the pride and sentiment of the officers, whether the writers thought them honorable or foolish. In January 1779, the French minister to the United States wrote home, "The rage for duelling here has reached an incredible and scandalous point. . . . This license is regarded as the appanage of liberty."[39] We can infer that duelling increased because it settled questions of honor in a distinctive, gallant way for men newly self-conscious about their uniqueness and their proper public inviolability. Lieutenant Samuel Shaw said of his colleagues' duelling, "These new gentry expect a great deal of deference, their ideas are sublimed, and, fond of imitating their betters, they cannot abate an iota of this article."[40] The duel combined the officers' conceit, punctilio, and recklessness to show the world as well as themselves that they were a separate order of men.

At the same time, officers cultivated close friendships with each other. They were convinced that the intimacy in their life of keener patriotism, risk, and pride prepared them to understand each other's experiences and opinions better than anyone else could. They built both the friendships of men who had trusted each other and the studied bonds of men who believed that they were singularly fit for each other's company. During the Valley Forge winter one diarist wrote, "Nothing tends to the establishment of the firmest Friendship like Mutual Sufferings which produce mutual Intentions and endeavours for mutual Relief which in such cases are equally shar'd with pleasure and satisfaction—in the course of this, each heart is laid open to full view—the similar passions in each, approximate themselves by a certain impulsive sympathy, which terminates in lasting esteem."[41] These friendships probably helped to insulate officers from the critical opinions of both enlisted men and civilians. Officers could judge each other's conduct by the criteria that only they understood. Colonel Walter Stewart spent Christmas Eve, 1781, in Philadelphia, where he found that officers had become less popular than they once had been. He wrote to Anthony Wayne, "Be assured, the Army is the place for sociability, friendship, and happiness."[42] The opinion of a circle of friends might decide a man's self-respect or disgrace. The anxiety with which such cliques weighed questions of professional pride and personal honor heightened the threat of ostracism through shame, which was the main punishment for failure. Thus, officers blended belligerence and sentiment in a demeanor that sustained their service by defining a professional character to emulate.

The officers' single-minded determination to achieve their professional character had a price: their isolation, often from their civilian fellow revolutionaries, sometimes from their fellow officers. The officers' absolute ideal of professional status, like the ideals of other revolutionaries, could isolate the patriot from the welfare of his cause by fostering a self-centered drive to prove personal worthiness. When the patriot measured himself, standing alone, against the absolute ideal, he faced the threat of despair—no less in the form of false bravado, recklessness, and duels than in the form of fleeing the enemy. To avoid or overcome this threat, men would need resources in addition to claims of individual prowess. The professional discipline that grew among the enlisted men of the Continental Army was a form of group identity related to, yet distinct from, the officers' demeanor. The absolute ideal of personal worthiness would no longer be the only test of achievement on behalf of the revolution. The army developed an auxiliary standard: expertise in the technical skills of soldiering. This auxiliary standard found its fullest expression not so much in individual excellence as in group solidarity. And that solidarity rested not only on innate communal strength but also on the shared ability to surmount a lasting communal weakness.

This form of discipline helped guide the service of Continental officers as well as enlisted men, though many officers were slow to subordinate their own preoccupations to its demands. The prevailing ideal in the officer corps continued to make the individual military gentleman and his glory the center of concern. But many officers did become proficient at implementing the Continental Army's new standards of professional competence.

As soldiers of all ranks withstood hardship and became more

expert, they clearly began to enjoy military service for its own sake. Washington told a committee of Congress that the best cement to give the army "consistency and energy" was "to make the Officers *take pleasure* in their situation."[43] This pleasure differed from the *rage militaire* at the beginning of the war because it derived much of its strength from the satisfaction of survival and solidarity amid reverses. James McHenry told his father of living with "a single blanket—the hard floor—or the softer sod of the fields—early rising and almost perpetual duty. These habitudes however I prefer to those of idleness and inactivity—they are more consistent with the profession of a soldier and repetition has now made them agreeable."[44] The arguments on behalf of requests for pay and for better support, as well as Americans' fondness for praising their own services, encouraged soldiers to refer to the sacrifices they had made on behalf of comfortable civilians, not to the fact that they liked their duty in spite of—perhaps, in part, because of—its difficulty.

Very few Continentals said that they might like to remain professional soldiers in peacetime. Almost every revolutionary would have agreed that the professional soldier's desire for continued employment and activity helped make standing armies alien instruments of tyranny. Yet the professional enthusiasm that a few Continentals were developing did not seem to them any more hostile to liberty than their wartime service in defense of liberty. Neither they, nor the larger group of soldiers who just were pleased to have mastered some secrets of war-making, described their pleasure as a sign that they wanted to make a career in the army. Even so, they showed that they enjoyed the temporary career they had fallen into. In a discourse to soldiers in 1777, Hugh Henry Brackenridge—preacher, poet, and dramatist of the army's exploits—celebrated the growing "love of military duty" among Americans who had first gone to war reluctantly. At the beginning, "We were without the love, and without the skill of war." After two and one-half years, "In the love of war we are sufficiently advanced. It is happy, since we must fight the tyrant, that we love to fight him."[45] Such formal statements of esprit de corps appear less often than revealing offhand remarks that contradicted the soldiers' avowed abstract distrust of military professionals. When Lieutenant Colonel David Cobb told his commanding officer that he did not want to be transferred to another regiment in the reorganization of 1780, he explained, "It is from the agreeableness of connection that I continu'd in service."[46] Such remarks certainly contradicted the recurrent protestations of eagerness to leave the army and reluctant continuance in unpleasant duty only at the nation's call. Enjoyment grew upon men unawares, as they expended their wits and their endurance, as they developed a competence that was rare among their countrymen and that owed less to the will of the many than to the strength of a few.

On May 5, 1778, Friedrich Wilhelm August Heinrich Ferdinand, Baron von Steuben, was named inspector general of the Army of the United States. Before coming to America, he had revised his Christian names for euphonious effect. His grandfather had revised the family name for noble lineage. The prince of Hohenzollern-Hechingen had secured him the title of baron before they both fled bankruptcy incognito. In Paris, with the advice of Benjamin Franklin, Silas Deane, and Caron de Beaumarchais, he had promoted himself from former captain to former lieutenant general. On the left breast of his uniform he always wore the Star of the Order of Fidelity.[47]

For the two months before his appointment, Steuben—soon known to everyone as "the Baron"—had served at Valley Forge as a volunteer training officer. The best way for a foreign officer to get a paying job from Congress was to act as though he did not need it. Steuben's work in drilling men and his suggestions for administrative improvements won Washington's recommendation that he succeed Conway, who had resigned as inspector general, and Congress agreed. Through his personal effort on the parade ground, his book of *Regulations*, and his supervision of an inspectorate at all levels of command, Steuben introduced a new attitude toward discipline and a new degree of economy into the Continental Army. These began almost at once and continued to improve, with some setbacks, until the end of the war.

Just before Washington resigned his commission at the end of the war, he purposely waited to write his last letter as commander in chief to Steuben: "Altho' I have taken frequent Opportunities both in public and private, of Acknowledging your great Zeal Attention and Abilities in performing the duties of your Office: yet, I wish, to make use, of this last Moment of my public Life, to Signify in the strongest terms, my intire Approbation of your Conduct, and to express my Sense of the Obligations the public is under to you for your faithful and Meritorious Services."[48] When Washington added, "I am persuaded you will not be displeased, with this farewell token, of my Sincere Friendship and Esteem for you," he may have been indulging his dry wit along with honest sentiment, since Steuben was accumulating testimonials in his prolonged campaign to get paid. A year earlier, General Horatio Gates had written to Steuben, "Believe my Dear Baron, my great respect for you, will not end with the War; The Astonishment with which I beheld the Order, Regularity and Attention, which you have taught the American Army; and the obedience, exactness, and true spirit of Military Discipline, which you have infused into them, does you the highest honor."[49]

Steuben's blend of sympathetic insight and aloof rigor enabled him to see the strength of public spirit that kept soldiers in service and helped him to deflect or overcome their resistance to working together under orders. He wrote to Franklin in 1779, "We want, above all, the true meaning of the Words *Liberty, Independence*, etc. that the Child may not make use of them against his father, or the Soldier against his Officer."[50] Historians have usually said that Steuben introduced Prussian discipline into the Continental Army.[51] But if one means the kind of discipline that Frederick the Great described in his *Testament von 1768*, the statement is wrong. Frederick said of soldiers, "Since they greatly outnumber their superiors, they can be held in check only through fear. . . . Since officers must necessarily lead them into the greatest dangers, the soldiers (since they cannot be influenced by ambition) should fear their officers more than all the dangers to which they are exposed. Otherwise nobody will be in a position to lead them to attack against three hundred guns that are thundering against them. Good will can never induce the common soldier to stand up to such dangers: he will only do so through fear."[52]

These ideas were the military commonplaces of the eighteenth century. Long before Steuben came to America they were shared, though not in such absolute terms, by most Continental officers, from the commander in chief down. However, they were not shared by enlisted men, whose diaries and memoirs suggest that although they experienced many emotions in the presence of Continental officers, fear was not usually one of them. Washington and his officers did rely on the soldiers' patriotic commitment to American independence and liberty and to the welfare of their families as an impetus to remain in the army and fight. But to secure the necessary obedience, officers followed the philosophy of Frederick and of the British army by trying to make themselves haughty objects of the soldiers' awe.

Washington believed that the authority to give five hundred lashes instead of one hundred would have increased the success of this approach. That was unlikely. Steuben discerned the paradox that most Continental soldiers had discovered soon after entering the army: a soldier could not practice the free autonomy and communal self-determination promised by the revolution; but, without them as ideals, he had little reason to stay. Respect for the soldier's dignity as a citizen and a volunteer underlay the earliest American revolutionary writings about a form of army discipline that would improve on Britain's method. Similar attention to the soldier's willing attachment to both the cause and his superiors underlay Steuben's discipline. The Continental Army could not become disciplined unless its soldiers would agree not only to enlist but also to obey. The two did not necessarily go together.

The privates' defiance did not represent an alternative plan of united action against the enemy. Rather, it asserted personal autonomy, an independent will to do as they pleased. Even as

Continentals improved at cooperation in combat, their survival as an army was threatened by continued negligence in clothing and cleanliness, by the loss and misuse of muskets, and by desertion. Officers' authority and privates' stubbornness warred constantly. Soldiers believed in revolutionary ideals, often with literal expectations, and tried to implement them by staying in the army and disobeying orders. Continentals could cooperate enthusiastically, but they could not be sure that all of their comrades would freely choose to cooperate amid reverses. Not far beneath the surface of the enthusiastic bayonet charge lay the spirit of every man for himself. How could officers make their men's conduct more reliable? Timothy Pickering's *Easy Plan for Discipline* had advised officers to win the affection of their men, and as a militia officer, Pickering marched on foot, carrying a pack. He was not a military egalitarian; instead, he wanted to lead by example and with the fullest knowledge of his men's situation. The surest way to win Continentals' respect was to be more active and able than they were—that is, to endow formal authority with the moral authority of superior service. This would not always secure obedience, but it would secure respect and deprive disobedience of its color of revolutionary sanction. Steuben perceived this truth—unlike many American officers, who were either too impatient of tedium or too uncertain in status—and he made it the central feature of his discipline. His success owed less to the originality of his ideas than to his ability to inveigle Americans into working toward their own ideals of competence. Disobedience did not end as the army began to take better care of itself and to develop its expertise in the field, but the validity of military authority became clearer. At parade on the evening of November 26, 1777, Sergeant Thompson of the Delaware Regiment ordered Private William Howell to incline to the left and join his company. When Howell refused, Thompson shoved him in his proper place. Howell called the sergeant "a Chuckleheaded Son of a bitch."[53] By contrast, a soldier trained under the Steuben method sassed an officer by saying, "Damn your orders sir."[54]

The use of sergeants to train and drill soldiers was one of the first mistakes Steuben saw when he arrived at Valley Forge. He called it "the miserable British sergeant system."[55] It increased the officers' distance from their men; yet that distance led not to authority but to ignorance because its main origin, at least in the American army, was the officers' finicky distaste for the parade ground. Steuben caused the Americans to marvel by drilling enlisted men himself. Of course, no one could imagine that such behavior compromised his status as a gentleman, because he was, as he himself said, a former lieutenant general, an intimate of Frederick the Great, and a baron of the Holy Roman Empire.

Steuben expected American officers to follow his example, and he had more difficulty in getting them to the Valley Forge parade than in teaching his modified European maneuvers to the privates. Since even Washington ordered officers to drill men only as a "disagreeable necessity," we need hardly wonder that young gentlemen held off.[56] All through April and May of 1778, General Anthony Wayne and his brigade and regimental commanders kept warning against "the neglect and little attention paid to the repeated orders for Manovering the Troops by some of this Division."[57] Then the commanders repeated the orders that "the Officers will attend the Parade better than they have hitherto done."[58] In August the commander of the First Pennsylvania Regiment was still trying to convince the officers that "the better they are acquainted with Maneuvers, when they can go through every part of their duty with exactness, it will be much to their honour." Otherwise, they would continue to look like the unskilled officers the commander saw on the parade ground and on guard duty: "They are Looked upon as Negligent bad officers." In short, "there is no way of Gaining this Knowledge but by Closely attending their duty, Never being absent from parade, and Manouvering the Men in Rotation, which has been the Plan laid down for some time past."[59] Besides avoiding the parade ground, officers avoided camp when they could and went home or to nearby towns. In January, President Henry Laurens wrote to his son at headquarters, "By the continual passing of Officers from your Camp one would think you had all broke up for the holydays."[60]

Experience had shown that such delinquencies in training could gravely hinder the army in the field. The only element of drill uniform throughout the army when Steuben arrived was the manual of arms simplified from the British method. All unit maneuvers for marching, going into battle, and changing position varied according to the preference of the unit commanders. A letter from Valley Forge recalled the army's maneuvers in 1777: "It was almost impossible to advance or retire in the presence of an enemy without disordering the line and falling into confusion; that misfortune, I believe, will seldom happen again—for the troops are instructed in a new and so happy a method of marching that they soon will be able to advance with the utmost regularity, even without music and over the roughest grounds."[61] Steuben established a standard to which the whole army could refer. He did not try to introduce "the entire system of drill, evolutions, maneuvers, discipline, tactics, and Prussian formation into our army. I should have been pelted had I attempted it, and should inevitably have failed."[62] Instead, he devised a modified system of field maneuvers, whose main goal was simplicity and uniformity. As Steuben drafted each new lesson for maneuvering, his subordinate brigade inspectors disseminated the instructions within the army and showed how the movements worked with a model detachment of twenty men. Then the company grade officers were all supposed to instruct their men in the new lesson. Steuben began the large-scale movement of battalions even before the soldiers had perfected the necessary small-unit maneuvers. He later said, "I was forced to begin my task at the wrong end, and after executing great maneuvers with six or eight thousand men together, I have sent my generals and colonels to learn the manual exercise."[63] Battlefield experience had taught men the necessity of mastering large-scale maneuvers, such as forming a line of battle from a marching column and forming a marching column from a line of battle. By comparing their new instruction with their previous disorder, soldiers could see by experience why they needed to learn all stages of field exercise, from the manual of arms up to movements of divisions. Captain Ezra Selden said that Steuben kept the army "very busy" with his "new mode of Exercise. . . . He never informs what is to be Done in future; but gives Lessons and we Practice until he gives new Directions."[64]

As Steuben later explained to a Prussian officer, "The genius of this nation is not in the least to be compared with that of the Prussians, Austrians, or French. You say to your soldier, 'Do this' and he doeth it; but I am obliged to say 'This is the reason why you ought to do that,' and then he does it."[65]

Parade-ground exercises had other purposes, as Steuben showed in his personal drilling of a hundred-man model company, which illustrated the new plan to the rest of the army. Competence in military exercises supplemented the soldiers' long-standing pride in their own courage and prowess with pride in their proficiency in technical skills. At the beginning of the war, Americans had simultaneously claimed to have these skills and scoffed at the British army's reliance on such rote. Americans wanted to have the proficiency but did not want anyone to think that they needed it. Their prowess could not be defined by mechanical exercises. The outcome of this attitude was both simplification and neglect.

Steuben understood the American soldiers' aptness to learn and quickness to doubt the worth of what they were learning. On the parade ground he outdid them in both his mastery of military decorum and the extravagance of his individualism. In three languages the Baron broke standing orders and called down God's wrath on soldiers who had two gauche feet. When he ordered his aide to help curse them in English, they grinned at him and executed the maneuvers more skillfully. From Valley Forge, Chaplain David Griffith wrote in June, "The strictest attention is paid to discipline since the appointment of the new Inspector-General, the Baron Steuben (a Prussian), and I think the whole army is much improved in that particular. Every Brigade is out twice a day, and has been for many weeks past."[66] One soldier recalled, "I was kept constantly, when off duty, engaged in learning the Baron de Steuben's new Prussian exercise. It was a continual drill."[67] Technical skills differed from claims or tests of personal bravery and strength because skills could be proven. Among Americans, native courage—like patriotism or personal worthiness—required repeated confirmation, always subject to challenge by others and doubt by oneself. Proficiency, on the other hand, was both demonstrable and lasting. A successful discipline for the Continental Army could not ignore the soldier's underlying eagerness to prove his patriotism and courage, as would a discipline that merely insisted that he obey commands by rote out of fear of punishment. Nor could it rely just on the soldier's ardor, which might fold in battle and then reclaim its glory in rhetoric. Steuben wanted to instill ardor into exercises that offered the Continentals attainable excellence. He explained to one of his aides, "The business is to give our troops a relish for their trade, to make them feel a confidence in their own skill."[68] His instruction and example in the formalities of an old guild showed fighters how they could become master soldiers.

Once learned, these skills could become part of men's courage. In the assault on Number Ten redoubt at Yorktown, on October 14, 1781, Captain Stephen Olney, a veteran of Valley Forge, was right behind Lieutenant Colonel Alexander Hamilton. Under heavy fire, they were the first up from the ditch, through the palisades, and onto the parapet. Olney recalled, "When I found my men to the number of ten or twelve had arrived, I stepped . . . on to the parapet, and called out in a tone as if there was no danger, Captain Olney's company, form here!" Several British soldiers at once stabbed Olney with bayonets. Two of his men behind him fired, and the British soon surrendered to the general envelopment of the redoubt. Although Olney had to hold in part of his intestine with his hands while giving orders, he enjoyed another fifty years of life in which to recall the benefits of military drill.[69]

In addition to revising the maneuvers and the manual of arms, Steuben summarized his view of the responsibilities attached to each rank in his *Regulations for the Order and Discipline of the Troops of the United States*. It eventually went through seventy editions and became known as the Blue Book; the Baron called it "a rhapsody."[70] In fact, a recurring word in the *Regulations* was "love." The officer's attention to the sick, the company commander's "kindness and humanity," the lieutenant's inspections by repeated visiting, the noncommissioned officer's circumspect preservation of his authority—all were designed "to gain the love of his men" not by informality or familiarity but by diligence. Steuben repeatedly warned against harshness and ill-treatment. Punishment would be necessary—the only kind he specifically mentioned was "confining the offender"—but the instant obedience that Steuben expected subordinates to give would come mainly from their respect for their superiors' competence and concern.[71] A witness at one of Steuben's inspections in 1779 said, "He appears to be about fifty years of age, and is venerable and dignified in his deportment, rich and elegant in his dress, having a splendid medal of gold and diamonds designating the order of *fidelity*, suspended at his breast. . . . He is distinguished for his profound knowledge of tactics, his ability to reform and discipline an army—for his affectionate attachment to a good and faithful soldier, and his utter aversion to every appearance of insubordination and neglect of duty."[72]

Even before Steuben's arrival, many civilians and some officers had believed that the force of opinion—"love and confidence," in Steuben's words—moved men more effectively than coercion.[73] The *Pennsylvania Packet* published a letter from an experienced officer to a subaltern written during the Valley Forge winter, advising the new officer that "The love of the soldier is the happiness of an officer. . . . An haughty overbearing temper, may indeed inspire them with fear, but never with affection."[74] Six months before he became the army's adjutant general at Valley Forge, Colonel Alexander Scammell explained his method of commanding soldiers: "I shall endeavor to do all that I can for them, and if possible make them pay me ready and implicit Obedience through Love and Affection rather than through Fear and Dread."[75] For such opinion to instill the respect that Steuben and these officers counted on, the soldiers first had to accept the goal of military proficiency. Continentals were already accustomed to judging their officers' ability. The mastery of drill and maneuver made proficiency a well-understood, widely accepted basis for respect. Pride in a demonstrable professional skill could give men's opinion force in support of obedience and competence, while the personal pride of patriotism alone did not point to any particular line of conduct and sometimes became simply an adjunct to private vanity. First, in Steuben's sequence, came the skills of the parade ground, then attention to dress, cleanliness, equipment, health, camp sanitation, orderliness on the march, grievances among the men, and all the other elements of mutual respect and hierarchical obedience. These provided a code by which soldiers could judge their officers and expect to be judged by both their officers and their fellow soldiers. To accomplish work that men knew by widely shared standards to be excellent and that clearly served the common benefit could win the love of those whom such work aided. And, thereby, love could win allegiance to merit.

We can see Steuben employing this force of opinion on the parade ground: the *Regulations* called for "patience" and "mildness" in training recruits, "punishing only those who are wilfully negligent";[76] a poem written at Valley Forge described one form of punishment:

> For if the soldier fails t'exert
> His utmost pomp and pride of heart—
> He's from the column set aside
> Till learn'd in military pride.[77]

A year after Valley Forge, Dr. James Thacher watched one of Steuben's inspections: "The Baron . . . took into his hand the muskets and accoutrements of every soldier, examining them with particular accuracy and precision, applauding or condemning, according to the condition in which he found them. He required that the musket and bayonet should exhibit the brightest polish; not a spot of rust, or defect in any part could elude his vigilance."[78] A company commander recalled an inspection later in the war. The Baron "had not proceeded far before he said to a soldier, 'For why is your gun so dirty?' The soldier begins to answer. He says, 'Hold your tongue.' He calls upon the captain, says: 'Captain, there be no discipline in your company. A man speak for himself.' After he had gone a few steps further, he observes a man in the rear rank step back and seat himself. He turns to the captain and says, 'There be no discipline in your company. I do recommend to you to get a parcel of chairs made for your men, and one great big one for yourself.' "[79] On another such occasion, one soldier's diary recorded, "This morning exercise Baron Steuben Commanded, somewhat fatiguing, but through Divine goodness was enabled to go through it acceptably."[80]

In Americans' public service, the word "love" had other meanings than a bond of loyalty between superiors and subordinates. Although Steuben did not discuss the subject in his *Regulations*, he understood that love of country was the main motive for soldiers' staying with the army.[81] His plan of discipline did not ignore Americans' love of liberty or their vision of personal independence and communal happiness. These remained the impetus to war but not the guides to conduct within the army. Instead, the army became an internally disciplined group apart, more self-consciously virtuous than the society at large. The professional loyalty and pride of achievement that Steuben encouraged provided a tangible partial expression of the unity in unselfish service to which revolutionaries aspired. Lieutenant Colonel Jean Baptiste Ternant, one of Steuben's deputies, showed that he had learned the Baron's purposes and methods as he went along the line of a company during an inspection. As each man's name was called, the soldier presented arms and stated the length of his enlistment. With men serving limited enlistments, Ternant did nothing but strictly examine their arms and accoutrements; "but to every soldier who exclaimed when called upon by name, '*for the war*!' he respectfully bowed, and raising his hat, said, 'you, Sir, are a gentleman I perceive, I am happy to make an acquaintance with you.' "[82]

Few of the soldiers who practiced Steuben's plan of discipline wanted, as Steuben did, to make it a career. Motives other than a desire for lifelong employment in the army guided their growth in military competence. In addition to a bounty of money and land and the prospect of occasional pay, they could know that they were meeting the demands of the revolution. The desire to prove their native courage, to exemplify sacrifice for future liberty, and to demonstrate the superior strength of freemen remained the source of Continentals' ardor. At Valley Forge and afterwards, professionalism could grow all the stronger because soldiers became increasingly convinced that the public had left them to win independence at their own expense. Far from suppressing revolutionary ideals, the Continental Army took advantage of soldiers' readiness to work for self-defense and for their vision of America's future. The army gave this readiness one form of institutional practice. In the process, the ideal of personal freedom was sharply curtailed, for the duration of service, to a mutual respect among the ranks for the proper discharge of duties. The goal of united benevolence became, in practice, the public service of a unique group, implemented by its pride in expertise. In the summer of 1779, the colonels of the Third, Fifth, and Sixth Massachusetts regiments assured General William Heath that he commanded troops who "from raw, undisciplin'd civilians, accustomed to the ease, pleasure and comforts of a tranquil domestic life, have by experience learn'd to endure both the fatigues and hardiness of a soldier, and to acquire the American fortitude, which is ever able to confront the most obstinate veterans of Great Britain."[83]

The "American fortitude" shown by the Massachusetts Continentals was more than the native courage of 1775. This fortitude they had to "acquire." As we have seen, the Continentals' ardor might lapse or waver under the tedious rigors of camp life or the sudden reverses of combat. The most serious challenge to its effectiveness at critical times was fear. Frederick the Great said that soldiers should fear their officers more than the enemy, but the Continental Army never achieved this level of systematic intimidation, even though Washington's general orders before battle sometimes backed up appeals to patriotism with warnings that those who ran would be shot on the spot. Unlike Frederick, the revolutionaries did not allow that fear was relative. In fact, Americans only reluctantly admitted that being overcome by fear was possible—usually among ignominious cowards. Robert Cooper's sermon *Courage in a Good*

Cause, preached to Pennsylvanians at the height of the *rage militaire* in 1775, had summarized the American's choice: "To draw back, if you were even before the cannon's mouth, would fix both awful guilt and indelible disgrace upon you. . . . If then you would escape deep guilt before God, and lasting contempt among men, forward you must go, wheresoever the drum shall beat, and the trumpet sound for battle. You have, in a word, no alternative, but either to venture your lives bravely, or attempt to save them ignominiously; to run the hazard of dying like heroes, or be certain of living like cowards."[84] Yet, fear was a form of selfishness even less voluntary or controllable than the pursuit of property. It was an alien mark of sinfulness that Americans tried in vain to obliterate. When it overcame soldiers —after a short time in camp at Cambridge or at Germantown among veterans—the ideals of 1775 told them only that if they could not defeat it by the force of patriotism they were contemptible wretches.

Even when such an admonition brought men to the battlefield, it gave too little help to those who saw what Private Elisha Stevens saw on September 11, 1777: "The Battel was at Brandy wine it Began in the morning and Held til tonight with out much Seasation of arms Cannons Roaring muskets Cracking Drums Beating Bumbs Flying all Round. men a dying woundeds Horred Grones which would Greave the Heardist of Hearts to See Such a Dollful Sight as this to See our Fellow Creators Slain in Such a manner as this."[85] Faced with such a prospect in another battle, one man said that the preparation, commotion, and tension before the fighting "made my thoughts flutter and divide."[86]

The attempt to eliminate fear by deploring it and ignoring it might have gained independence if citizen-soldiers could have fought and won the short, violent war that many revolutionaries wanted. However, too few Americans wanted to risk this experiment personally after 1775. The Continental Army's success could not depend simply on denouncing fear or on bragging about fearlessness or on intimidation worse than the enemy's. The army used all of these, but its discipline relied on a man's willingness and trained ability to impersonate a professional soldier even when his ideal of personal freedom or his dread of the enemy urged him to escape.

After breakfast on the morning of November 14, 1776, John Adlum, a seventeen-year-old private, was looking around Fort Washington when he met a forty-year-old Yankee soldier. "He walked with me for two or three hours and explained to me the nature of our independence and the policy of its having been declared when it was." Then the Yankee explained how few balls out of all those shot ever hit anybody, and he gave his opinion on fear: "There is something in human nature that makes death appear formidable and will in a degree shrink from it. I have heard men say they did not know what fear was. I do not believe them." But "a man may act coolly and deliberately as if he had no fear."[87]

Those two words—"as if"—contained the foundation of Steuben's method of discipline. The fact that the Continentals were still in the army at Valley Forge, poorly disciplined yet withstanding great hardships without quitting, showed that the army could neither fully indulge the soldiers' love of freedom nor smash it for the purposes of discipline. Even if the officers had found the coercive means to rule by force, the soldiers probably would have gone home, and few would have taken their places. Instead, while revolutionary ideals remained strong in soldiers, they had to act, by choice, as if their ideal were military expertise. Similarly, once adopted, such expertise was their recourse in times of fear. In the middle of a funeral sermon on General Francis Nash, who was mortally wounded at Germantown, the chaplain almost forgot his subject as he exhorted the North Carolina Brigade, "Remember the mistake of that day, and never do you commit it. What I mean is—never, in pursuit of a flying enemy, never separate or break your ranks. . . . But though I recommend bravery, and applaud you for it, yet beware of rashness. Regularity, and a strict attention to orders is the life of every action, and the duty of every one concerned in it. In retreat—but I hope never to see you retreat again—in retreat (and the bravest have often retreated) good order is equally essential. . . . If you cannot maintain your ground, why fly in disorder? 'Tis unworthy of a soldier and a christian. Fear is a very thin shield, and betrays more than it defends."[88] Explicit, attainable rules and techniques could enable a scared man to act as if he had native courage, even though he was relying, in part, on what Americans called "mechanical courage."[89]

This cast of mind was far from revolutionary ideals but close to revolutionaries' conduct. Would a revolutionary have agreed that he only acted as if he were virtuous? Would a Christian have consented to live only as if he were saved? Could an American have believed that independence promised to let him live only as if he were free? The revolutionaries could not rest content with provisional worthiness any more than they could settle for expedient calculations of effect without the assurance of deserving motives. For the security of posterity, the revolutionaries would prove that their country was uniquely blessed. Lasting proof eluded them, but they still sought it. They would escape the constant contention with appearances and expedients. They would once and for all tear aside the veil that seemed to keep them from happiness. In practice, of course, most revolutionaries did not pursue the immediate millennial fulfillment of their ideals through attaining perfect virtue, perfect freedom, or perfect assurance of salvation. Like Continental soldiers' trained courage, they settled for lives short of their ideal.

The main difference between Continentals and their fellow revolutionaries was that Continentals knowingly adopted a discipline that judged and guided conduct by standards other than the state of the heart. Most revolutionaries, having fallen short of the ideals of 1775, lived according to their various compromises; but they preferred to believe that they were achieving or would soon achieve or ought to be achieving the fullness of their ideals. The Continentals shared this hope for their own future—perhaps more strongly than most—but they had to knowingly suspend it as the rule for their daily lives. Their fellow revolutionaries evaluated conduct by the ideals of 1775—sometimes cloaking selfishness with claims of freedom, sometimes condemning self-sacrifice because it fell short of perfect virtue. The vision of perfect freedom maintained its strong appeal, and the expedient partial surrenders were made with public reluctance and private guilt. In the army, on the other hand, the temporary surrender of personal freedom became a source of communal and personal pride as Continentals developed an expertise with known, attainable standards of excellence—an expertise they believed to be the main defense of American public freedom and the main expression of revolutionary virtue. Most Americans, we can suspect, knew that the visions of perfection that gave such emotional strength to the revolution lay beyond their immediate attainment in practice. But this knowledge or intimation remained largely private and unspoken during the war years. Each individual might know that he made compromises, but this knowledge did not mean that the public ideals of the whole people should be debased by explicit expediency. The American's unspoken compromise—living as if he were worthy of the revolution—could isolate him as he contrasted his private shortcomings with absolute communal ideals. The soldier's systematic compromise—fighting as if he had no fear of defeat—could join him more closely to other soldiers who publicly acknowledged their reliance on discipline to surmount weakness. The survival of American independence entailed not only the preservation of revolutionary ideals and the reluctant use of the coercive powers of government, but also the growth of a military discipline that proudly replaced individual freedom with the professionalism of an army.

Years before Steuben had come to America, Timothy Pickering's plan of militia discipline had deplored "barbarous scourgings" and "*fear* . . . the grand principle of despotism" as bases for discipline. Among Americans it was essential "*that the men be clearly informed of the* REASON *of every action and movement—or the* USES *to which they can be applied*."[90] Understanding the reason and uses would, like Steuben's drill, entice men into discipline. The flaw in Pickering's plan appeared in its title: "*An Easy Plan*." Early in his book Pickering evoked the prophecy of Micah, expressing an American's wish that "he might never see a soldier while he lives: that our swords might be beaten into ploughshares, and our spears into pruning-hooks: and that, void of fear, every man might sit quietly under his own vine and his own fig-tree; enjoying and rejoicing in Heaven's indulgent bounties." He assumed that, in spite of this longing, "enlightened" minds could choose "a just and necessary subordination and obedience . . . *only* to *defend* their *laws*, *liberties* and *country*."[91] He argued that in choosing discipline and in understanding its elements, soldiers' reason could remedy their lack of experience.

These arguments proved correct but insufficient. The experience, the habit, even some of "the trappings (as well as tricks) of the parade," all of which Pickering minimized in the word "easy," were in fact essential protection for the enlightened mind when fear swept over it in camp or in battle.[92] Only a competence in soldiering and a pride in that competence partly for its own sake, in addition to a reasoned patriotic choice, could keep the freedom-loving citizen present and fit for duty for as long as the revolution needed him, or even for as long as he had agreed to stay. Steuben commented on the qualifications of a good soldier, "Some of these are no easy lesson to a mind filled with ideas of equality and freedom; and in many instances are only to be learned with industry and pains."[93] When Steuben sought "above all, the true meaning of the Words *Liberty, Independence*, etc.," he was not trying to abolish all "ideas of equality and freedom" but to identify some of the communal responsibilities intrinsic to any bonds—family, army, church, or state—short of complete personal autonomy. If words and ideas like liberty, independence, freedom, and equality could be used not only to repudiate a tyrant but also to liberate a revolutionary from all constraining obligations of any relationship, an American would be left to face his enemy's tyranny and his own weakness with no resource but an enlightened mind. Since Americans had chosen to retain and create institutions, including an army, as guarantors of independence, they could define their proper obligations to those institutions only by attaining the true meaning of their revolutionary words—a meaning that would both preserve the ideal and justify the necessary communal constraints.

In the summer of 1781 Private Josiah Atkins lamented his absence from home by asking, "Am not I oppressed, as being obliged to leave my own state of peace and happiness, friends and relations, wife and Child, shop and tools, and customers, against my mind and expectation, and come these hundreds of miles distance in the capacity of a soldier carrying the cruel and unwelcome instruments of war[?]" But these emotions had not stopped him from "learning the military art," and in his account of Anthony Wayne's attack on Cornwallis's army at Green Spring, Virginia, on July 6, Atkins showed that he well filled "the capacity of a soldier": "Our officers and soldiers, like brave heroes, begun the attack with (at first) but an *handful of men*. . . . How great was thy mercy, O Lord, in our deliverance! The like was hardly ever heard of! Six hundred men have attacked and stood, the fire, sword, and bayonet, of the force of an army of 5,000, yea, of the whole army under Lord Cornwallis. When we were often broke, often formed; several times almost surrounded; and yet . . . came off again in heart! . . . I cannot forget this memorable action! So few as 1000 men should attack the whole British force and lose no more even when we were several times cut off and scattered to and fro! . . . and being weary before the attack began. The fatigues of that day I cant describe. . . . Our general gave us great applause for our fortitude and good conduct in this action. He assured us that he himself was eye-witness to our regiments attacking the whole British army with spirit."[94]

The soldiers' choice of a hierarchical, partly mechanical regimen for three years or the duration of the war had the support of a set of values—Steuben's plan of discipline—distinct from revolutionary aspirations yet shared and applauded by revolutionaries in the army. Their voluntary adoption of a code that, in its immediate effects, contradicted their own ideal life of the future was tolerable because the soldiers could enjoy both pride in their code and hope for future fulfillment of the revolution's promises. They could more surely count on behaving as if they had native courage, and they could live as if they need have no fear that anything but the enemy stood in the way of their future freedom.

Steuben was eager to see colonels instructing privates; his *Regulations* ordered officers to know the character, the whereabouts, and the conduct of their men. Attentiveness to the privates' well-being and grievances would strengthen the officers' authority. Although some officers had long taken this approach and others were learning to do so, many resisted it because it seemed to compromise their standing as gentlemen. As we have seen, such officers believed that their authority depended partly on their aloof freedom from pedestrian concerns, and they had become more dedicated to maintaining that aloofness than to sustaining the spirits of their men. Yet an officer could exert more authority through his men's imitation of his attentiveness to duty than by trying to out-swagger them. The Continental Army had tried to insist that officers be flamboyant while privates remain docile. As it turned out, the privates had such a high opinion of their own prowess that an officer had to be exceptionally overweening to outdo them, and they seem never to have respected a system of discipline that allowed an officer to be ostentatious without being diligent while expecting a private to be diligent yet humble.

By contrast, Steuben told officers to spend time with the sick and wounded, to visit men at all hours of the day, to see for themselves what food soldiers were eating. At inspections the Baron "inquired . . . into the conduct of the officers towards their men, censuring every fault and applauding every meritorious action. Next he required . . . a list of the sick, with a particular statement of their accommodations and mode of treatment, and even visited some of the sick in their cabins."[95] In the summer of 1780, Steuben ordered a detachment of sappers and miners off of Constitution Island, where they had been left to build fortifications, sustained only by brackish water, salt shad, and bread. Steuben said, "You may as well knock those men on the head, as keep them there." One of the privates recalled, "He had more sense than our officers."[96] The regimental commander, Steuben said, should not permit his officers to ride horses, since sharing fatigue strengthened bonds of loyalty. In April 1779, Washington ordered that no officer was to ride unless duty required it: "Sensible of the force of good examples on the minds of the soldiery, it ought to be the pride of an officer to share the fatigue as well as danger to which his men are exposed."[97] The company commanders, according to the *Regulations*, should know their men by name and character; the company grade officers should exercise their authority not with hauteur and anger but with active concern and mildness. Mildness did not refer to the degree of discipline, since Steuben demanded implicit obedience, but to the demeanor of the officer. Even if the officer were going to correct soldiers' disobedience, he stood to gain more respect by calm self-control than by the rage that Continental officers indulged so indiscriminately. Steuben's Valley Forge instructions told officers to "explain with mildness what the soldiers are to do; they are not to use them ill, neither by abusive words or otherwise, but to point out their Faults patiently. There will be no other punishment for the soldier, who neglects his duty or is inattentive, than to make him exercise an whole hour after the others have done."[98]

Steuben neither overlooked nor disapproved the American officers' eagerness to act as gentlemen. But he did not take their aspirations as literally as they often did. Who knew better than the Baron how much pretense went into making a new gentleman in America? Far from contradicting the belief that an officer should play the gentleman, he used it more than most. At the same time, he insisted that social pretensions serve the ends of the commission, not the other way around. Although Steuben did not make officers as diligent as his *Regulations* ordered, his example of flamboyance and painstaking care won respect and imitation from many junior officers. In 1781 Lieutenant Ebenezer Denny described the two hours of evolutions routinely executed each morning, which ended as the "old soldiers" who were "well disciplined" marched in review, "saluting the Baron and field officer of the day, as they pass." To Denny, Steuben was "our great military oracle."[99] At the end of the war, the officers of the New Jersey Line wrote to Steuben, "The esteem you have ever borne for our army—the unremitted labour which you have exercised for the establishment of our honor and good character, as well as your affectionate anxiety and participation in our sufferings, have endeared you to us in a superlative degree. . . . We conceive it to be our duty (and we feel unusual pleasure in doing it) to give you these individual assurances of gratitude and love."[100]

Steuben won wide popularity in the army because he combined an extravagant individual style—admired by Americans of all ranks because they wanted one of their own—with a thorough mastery of his duties. He was known for being the first on the parade ground before dawn, for swift censure of negligence, and for public apology after making a mistake. Unlike many senior officers, Steuben, who hated to eat alone, did not scorn company grade officers but invited them to his dinners. Several gave food a high place in their memories of the Baron. After the war, he was still entertaining veterans in New York City; he "lectured his old and new friends on military tactics and discipline and told stories of the wars."[101] However, he had a small budget. He had to apologize for not having the correct wine in which to boil the boar's head. From its inception the drama of the Baron's career was being followed in Paris by Caron de Beaumarchais, who had helped to create it with a recommendation and a personal loan. In December of 1778 Beaumarchais wrote, "I hear that he is the inspector general of all the American troops. Bravo!"[102]

Eighteenth-century armies, even in America, were not known for their use of camouflage, but Steuben's discipline served the mind of the Continental soldier as camouflage served the body. Many lives, a worthy cause, and a man's own skin could depend on painstaking, rigorously enforced concealment by camouflage, which hid showy marks of identity. But a man wearing leaves was not a tree, any more than disciplined Continentals were the automatons that prevailing military theory and Whig libertarian theory said they must be. Rather, the soldiers adopted "camp feelings" that shielded their love of freedom, their vision of the future, and their pride of individual strength.[103] Gradually, they no longer made these aspirations their immediate guides to conduct in daily encounters with the severe tests of camp and combat. Like other plans of discipline, Steuben's manual of arms first taught soldiers how to stand still and be quiet—no small accomplishment for an American of that era. From that point it defined the drill, the duties, and the techniques by which men could effectively persevere in their chosen form of service to the revolution. These fixed responsibilities and attainable standards provided specific criteria by which men could be judged. They tested works and left the test of grace in the hands of its Creator.

Steuben showed his own tendency to lose self-control when, in 1779, the Board of War found it hard to get the *Regulations* printed fast enough. On July 4, 1779, General Anthony Wayne was writing to Washington, "Will your Excellency be so Obliging as to direct Baron Stubens to furnish each Officer belonging to the Light Corps with the Military Regulations there are but two or three in the Whole Corps."[104] Philadelphia was short of printers, binders, printing plates, and paper, but Steuben blew up at Timothy Pickering and Richard Peters, the members of the Board. Afterward, his letter to Peters adopted the distinction that was central to both his character and the demeanor that his discipline encouraged: "Altho' I give to the D——l the Honorable Board of War, I still always Except my dear friends Messrs Peters and Pickering; I beg, my dear sir, you will make a similar distinction between the Inspector General and Baron Steuben—You may d——[n] the first as much as you please, but pray, preserve your friendship to the Latter."[105] The distinction between the inspector general and Baron Steuben was reflected in the distinction between the private and the citizen. The Continental soldier remained both, and with the regimented techniques of the private he sought to secure the happiness promised to an American citizen.

The love that enabled Steuben's discipline to succeed went beyond the soldiers' love for diligent officers and sergeants commended in Steuben's *Regulations*; it included the soldiers' love of America and of the vision of future harmony and happiness that underlay many revolutionaries' wartime exertion. At the end of the war Steuben wrote, "A desire of fame was my ruling motive for visiting America; but when I saw so many brave, so many good men encountering every species of distress for the cause of their country, the course of my ambition was changed, and my only wish was to be linked in the chain of friendship with those supporters of their country, and to render that country which had given birth to so many patriots, every service in my power."[106] Steuben understood the importance of this patriotism in Continental soldiers' perseverance. He kept such dedication at the heart of the plan of discipline he taught. From the soldiers' words and conduct, we can infer that their training and their willingness to adopt professional military standards drew on their revolutionary ideals for strength while protecting the ardor of those ideals from constant incentives to rage or flight. The ardor remained strong because its camouflage was not an alloy, but, as soldiers hoped, a means to its future uneclipsed fulfillment. We hear this state of mind in a soldier's song:

> No Foreign Slaves shall give us Laws, No Brittish Tyrant Reign
> Tis Independence made us Free and Freedom We'll Maintain
> We'll Charge the Foe from post to post attact their works and Lines
> And by some well Laid Stratagem We'll make them all Burgoins
> Each hearty Lad shall take his Lass all Beaming Like a Star
> And in her softer arms Forget the Dangers of the war
> And when the war is Over We'll set them Down at Ease
> We'll plow and sow We'll Reape and Moe and Live Just as we please.[107]

Continental soldiers never became models of discipline on any plan. The army did not fully master Steuben's drill and maneuvers until 1782; even then insubordination continued, and some soldiers dealt with hardship by stealing or deserting. But as the army developed discipline, the soldiers preserved minor yet conspicuous signs that their conformity was voluntary and purposeful, that it alone did not define their character. For example, orderly sergeants made their own additions to orders of the day which they were supposed only to copy. Colonel James Chambers of the First Pennsylvania Regiment threatened severe punishment for the "perfect nonsense Insarted in some of the ordly Books by the serjeants."[108] The orderly book of the Second New York Regiment contained patriotic war songs and love songs.[109] An orderly book in the Virginia Division contained poetic comments on "Woman Lovely Woman" and profane comments on the division commander, General William Woodford.[110] But the most common of the soldiers' signs of independence were hair and hats.

The rapid spread of fashionable display during the war encouraged a studied attention to one's hair. Robert Treat Paine, a signer of the Declaration of Independence, left Congress in December of 1776 and went back to Boston. Six months later, William Whipple, another signer, dined with Paine on his way home to New Hampshire and remarked that Paine "is much alter'd in his dress since he left Philadelphia which was in December last, he then had short straight hair, but now a Prodigious fore top, Ear Curls, and an immense quantity of hair tyed in a Club behind, on the whole his head is dressed in the true Macharoni stile."[111] Even before independence had been declared, Continental Army officers were forbidding soldiers to wear "side locks"; through the rest of the war commanders pursued a constant and evidently unsuccessful campaign to get all soldiers to cut their hair short.[112] General Wayne called long hair unmilitary.[113] Doctor Rush called it unsanitary.[114] Colonel Pinckney called it effeminate.[115] Why would a soldier prize it? They could have found one answer in the diary of a sixteen-year-old girl whose home quartered General William Smallwood's staff. She described Captain Alexander Furnival, who was twenty-five years old: "He has, excepting one or two, the handsomest face I ever saw, a very fine person; fine light hair and a great deal of it, adds to the beauty of his face."[116] Even though soldiers knew that long hair made colds more likely when they got wet on the march and made it harder to get the nits out so as not to be lousy, many of them kept it long and loose. Lieutenant Colonel Francis Marion wanted men's hair not to hang over their collars; he warned his regiment that "they will not be allowed to appear with their hair down their backs and over their foreheads, and down their chins at the sides, which make them appear more like wild savages than soldiers."[117] Commanders repeated such warnings in vain. The commanders seem to have believed that the reason for the long hair was stubborn individualism, and they were probably right.

On parade day the men became uniform—all hair tied in back and powdered white. At other times, the contest continued.

Early in the war, hats had served as a mark of patriotism. Plymouth minutemen wore an "extraordinary sort of caps"; liberty-loving soldiers and civilians wore cockades.[118] No doubt such men agreed with Abigail Adams that "every man who wears a cockade appears of double the importance he used to."[119] Some hats had bucktails, and men who wore hunting shirts sported both bucktails and cockades. Officers tried to make privates' hats an important mark of discipline. On special occasions, such as a march through Philadelphia or a celebration of the Fourth of July, Washington sought symmetry and regularity amid festivity by ordering all soldiers "to adorn their Hats with *Green-Boughs*."[120] Hats could give the look of uniformity to a regiment even when the issue of clothing had been short and haphazard. At Valley Forge, Anthony Wayne ordered, "The Officers will compel the men to wear their Hatts in one way; in the most soldier-like position."[121] He expected to be able to issue a hat to every man so that all would look alike. Later in the war, he furnished the Pennsylvania Line not only with hats but with ostrich plumes for them. A Virginian who saw the soldiers marching said, "They put me in mind of the army marching on Dunsinane, when mistaken by Macbeth for Birnam Wood: for the feathers appear before you can well discover the shoulders to which the head that supports them is annexed."[122] Officers, on the other hand, showed off their status with hats in the height of style, which differentiated them from the men. In May 1781, Captain Samuel Shaw recommended that an officer pay ten dollars for a pair of boots but spend fifteen dollars on a beaver hat.[123] Even the commander in chief expressed his character in ordering a new hat: "I do not wish by any means to be in the extreme of the fashion either in the size, or manner of Cocking it."[124] Many privates resisted the officers' attempts to enforce a neat, uniform appearance in each regiment. Men failed to cock their hats and instead wore the brims down. Men took the bands off of hats to shape them differently. In the Second Rhode Island Regiment in July 1779, the sergeants' ripping their hat bindings off and the colonel's forcing them to put the bindings back on preceded a brief mutiny in the regiment.

Like long hair, floppy hats flaunted the sign that official conformity would not overwhelm the soldier. They preserved the kind of pride seen in the first conspicuous hats and cockades, and they helped the soldier show off in a manner akin to the officer's gaudiness. They did not usually betoken hostility to the army or thoroughgoing defiance of officers' authority. Veteran soldiers who had shown pride in discipline insisted on wearing them. These marks of style were not so much signs of rebellion as small but constantly visible reminders that the Continentals intended to be independent men as well as soldiers. Like the Baron's eight-pointed Star of the Order of Fidelity, these badges did not make the man, but they announced him. Although they breached the camouflage of discipline, they revealed the spirit that gave the Continentals' system of discipline its strength. Shortly before Birnam Wood comes to Dunsinane, we hear a report on the army of the enemy, the tyrant Macbeth:

> Those he commands move only in command,
> Nothing in love.[125]

The inspector general's department under Steuben brought important administrative gains as well as field discipline to the line of the army. Steuben wanted a field command. Failing that, he tried to make the Inspectorate an empire that would have the authority not only to teach and to report on discipline but also to enforce it. Commanders rightly protested that this proposal infringed on their own authority. At the beginning of his service, Steuben was unpopular with many senior officers, but Washington, who understood the difference between Baron Steuben and the inspector general, praised the former and curtailed the latter. Steuben still complained that Congress had left the inspectors with too little distinction by failing to give them enough extra pay.[126]

Continental officers, state officials, Richard Peters, and Dr. James Tilton agreed that the Inspectorate under Steuben saved

The Inner War

1. Du Simitier, *Benedict Arnold.*
A portrait made between his march to Quebec
and his defection to the British
(pages 23–24, 255–294).

2. John Trumbull, *Jedidiah Huntington*.
Faith Huntington's husband, sketched by her brother
(pages 54–58).

3. John Trumbull, *Self-Portrait*.
A self-portrait of the young officer as an artist
(pages 54–58).

4. *The Burning of Charlestown,* June 17, 1775. The first sight of war for Faith Huntington and many others (pages 54–58).

5. Charles Willson Peale, *Henry Lee*.
Light-Horse Harry Lee—successful partisan and strict disciplinarian (pages 80–82).

6. John Stewart's Silver Medal for the Assault on Stony Point.
The medal that Crazy Jack Stewart did not live to see
(pages 95–96).

7. Charles Willson Peale, *Richard Montgomery* (pages 120–126).

The Soldiers

8. "The Soldiers in the Field doing duty,"
from *The Downfall of Justice* (1777).
First Soldier: "Keep up courage, my boys,
we will soon bring those villains to terms."
Second Soldier: "These d——d Extortioners are the
worst enemies to the country."
Third Soldier: "I serve my country for sixteen pence
a day, pinched with cold."

9. *The Banner of Washington's Life Guard.*

10. A. Dupre, *The Battle of Cowpens.*
In this kind of combat, Continental soldiers' discipline proved valuable.

11. Baron Ludwig von Closen's
Sketch of American Army Uniforms.

n Américaine

lemen, Artillerie

12. James Peale, Detail of Continental Soldiers from *George Washington*.

13. Charles Willson Peale, Detail of Continental Soldier from *Washington at Trenton*.

14. Charles Willson Peale, *Baron Friedrich Wilhelm von Steuben*.

15. Charles Willson Peale, *Jean Baptiste, Chevalier de Ternant.* As Deputy Inspector General, Ternant introduced Steuben's method of discipline to the Continental Army in the South.

16. Charles Willson Peale, *General William North.* Steuben's aide-de-camp and lifelong friend.

The Officers

Most of these officers are mentioned in the text.
Their portraits help us to study the character of the younger,
less well known military gentlemen.

17. John Trumbull, *Colonel Howard.*

18. Charles Willson Peale, *John Laurens.*

19. A. Rosenthal after Charles Willson Peale,
Walter Stewart.

20. A. Rosenthal after Charles Willson Peale, *Samuel Blachley Webb*.

21. *An Unknown Officer*, artist unknown.

22. H. B. Hall, *Tench Tilghman*.

23. Charles Willson Peale, *Self-Portrait*.

24. Charles Willson Peale, *An Unknown Officer of the Maryland Line.*

25. Gustav Behne, *John Peter Gabriel Muhlenberg*.

26. Charles Willson Peale, *John Eager Howard.*

The Public Views the War

27. *America Triumphant and Britannia in Distress* (1782). Americans celebrate victory and anticipate their enjoyment of prosperity and liberty. They expect to see, before the British leave New York, "the Trator Arnold, taken with remorse for selling his country, and Judas like hanging himself."

28. Charles Willson Peale, *A Representation of the Figures exhibite and paraded through the Streets of Philadelphia* (1780). Philadelphians commit Benedict Arnold's effigy to the flames for treason.

29. John Trumbull, *The Death of General Montgomery in the Attack on Quebec, Canada*.

30. Charles Willson Peale, *Benjamin Rush*.
Pennsylvania politician, signer of the Declaration of Independence, army surgeon, hospital administrator, pamphleteer, and polymath of the republic's early years, Doctor Benjamin Rush also studied the wartime mental disorder that he called Revolutiana.

large numbers of lives and a great deal of money by its equipment musters. Peters said, "His Regulations and Perseverance produced Order and Economy out of Chaos and Waste."[127] Companies had to keep records of the clothing and weapons each man had, and the men were held accountable for this equipment at inspections. Before Steuben's Inspectorate was established, the Board of War routinely expected the army to waste five thousand muskets and ten thousand bayonets a year. This loss decreased annually; hardly any were lost in 1783. Steuben wanted a soldier to "regard his arms and accoutrements with all the solicitude of friendship."[128] The conservation of clothing, especially keeping soldiers from selling it, was one of the most important parts of the health care that helped decrease the high rates of sickness and death. Dr. Tilton said that Steuben's supervision "contributed more to the health and comfort of the troops, than did the utmost efforts of all the medical staff."[129]

The inspectors reported strength, equipment, and the state of discipline to commanders. These reports became the basis for praise and reprimand in general orders. Negligence could be identified for punishment or for the public shame that officers sought to avoid. Conversely, a commander could receive the much-desired public acclaim. An officer who wrote a twelve-page memoir of his eight years in the Continental Army spent a page and a half describing one inspection by Steuben and the ensuing review by Washington that caused the light-infantry company of the Eighth Massachusetts Regiment to be mentioned in general orders. "The general inspector, Baron Steuben, came on upon the right and as I was paying him the salute, remarks 'Captain, I am glad to see you at the head of so fine a company.' He passed in front of the officers and received their salutes, then marched back in rear of the regiment to the right. Tells me to order my company to search arms. At the word, the soldiers open pans and draw ramrods, let them down the barrels with a little force; they rebound pretty well. The baron lifts up both hands and exclaims, 'My God! is it all silver?' He then looks round to the officers, who were standing about, and says, 'Come here, officers; all you officers come here and help me to admire this company.' The officers drew near. He made some handsome remarks in favor of the company. He then turns to me and says, 'You need not take off your packs, you need not show me your book, I will not inspect your company, I will admire it.'"[130]

Washington gave much weight to the inspectors' reports, and in dealing with officers he did not confine his comments to general orders. We can see how seriously he took his officers' attentiveness when we read the surviving record of what evidently was one of his rare explosions of temper. In May 1777, the commander of the Third Virginia Regiment, Colonel Thomas Marshall, warned his officers in the orders of the day, "His Excellency General Washington threaten'd to arrest the Command'r of a Regiment Yesterday for suffering fish and Bones and other Nastiness to lie about his Camp."[131] The Inspectorate gave Washington and his subordinate commanders more systematic information about the condition of all their regiments. The generals could then reward dutifulness and reprimand neglect. Through records, inspections, and public evaluations of regiments, the Inspectorate helped make the uniform standard of discipline an important test of merit and pride.

One of the elements of Steuben's discipline that succeeded most quickly was his tightened control of the march. Ever since Knox's hauling of artillery to Boston and Arnold's march to Quebec, the Continental Army had shown to greatest advantage in movement, when action kept spirits and health up, brooding and discontent down. On the night of January 2, 1777, the army moved to make its surprise attack on Princeton. Sergeant Joseph White recalled that "Capt. Benjamin Frothingham, came to me and said, you and I must march together; we marched some ways, I being exceeding sleepy, I pitched forward several times, and recovered myself. Said he, you are the first person I ever see, sleep while marching."[132] In 1779, Ensign Daniel Gookin marveled at his own men: "To see with what patience the soldiers endured the fatigues of this march wadeing rivers, climbing mountains and a number of other things too tedious to mention, afford a pleasing prospect that in time we shall have soldiers equal to any in the world."[133]

This spirit achieved its fullest expression in the southern campaign under Greene. Between April 1780 and April 1782, the Delaware Regiment marched 5,006 miles.

The greatest problem on the march was straggling, which slowed movement, delayed readiness for action, and enabled soldiers to break away and steal from inhabitants as the army passed. Tighter columns, patrols, fatigue details for wood and water, equalizing the rate of march by drum signals all kept the column moving more smoothly and cut down on straggling. Although marauding by some soldiers for both food and valuables never completely stopped, the Continental Army's movements contrasted greatly with those of the militia, especially in Pennsylvania and the southern states, which routinely laid waste the countryside in its path, whether inhabitants were friends or foes.

The Continentals took pride in their own stamina, and this was fortunate for them, since few pleasures awaited them at the end of their journey. With Greene in South Carolina, through days of mud up to the knee and pine swamps "about two miles long and half leg deep,"[134] past flooded rice fields where thousands of wild ducks paused, a lucky officer might reach the temporary state capital of Jacksonborough and be assigned to Governor Rutledge's honor guard: "I spent the afternoon very agreeably, drinking wine and smoking segars."[135] The privates' relief usually had to be even simpler than the officers': "We marched . . . to old fort Schuyler where we built fires and lay on the Grass."[136]

Among the black soldiers in the Continental Army were former slaves who served longer than most white soldiers for less pay. We can infer that their prewar experience had shown them that survival, not to mention victory, required more than native courage. Before enlisting they must have learned self-preservation under circumstances in which the desire for freedom could not alone teach a person how to confront bondage. We can especially note the Rhode Island freedmen's health and discipline on the march through Connecticut in January 1781, when a traveler saw them. "At the ferry-crossing I met with a detachment of the Rhode Island regiment. . . . The majority of the enlisted men were Negroes or mulattoes; but they are strong, robust men, and those I saw made a very good appearance."[137] Descriptions of black soldiers used words like "sturdy" and "able-bodied."[138] Former slaves succeeded as soldiers first because freedom was the reward for their service and second because they knew as well as and sometimes better than their fellow Continentals how to survive the service that won freedom.

Throughout the war, from Cambridge to Yorktown, the Continental Army was one of America's great spectacles, which people went out of their way to see, whether it was camped or marching or in battle. Relatives visited soldiers, even at Valley Forge, and women turned out in windows and doorways to see the army pass. The stories of these brief, frequent encounters show both the army's popularity and the distinctiveness that quickly set it apart from the public. Americans wanted to see the soldiers marching, and people's remote curiosity about this different order of men communicated itself to the soldiers. "As we advanced in the country the richer the inhabitants were; quantities of young women still gathering at the Houses on the Road to see the Glorious Life of a Soldier, ragged, dirty and fainting with thirst and Drinking water out of every puddle he comes by till at length he takes up, where he eats with as good a stomach as a dog whatever the Commissary allows them."[139]

Thousands of sightseers gathered at Yorktown and were so bold in their curiosity that they interfered with siege operations. Even though Washington complained about them, he had, in a way, asked for them by advertising the army on the way south from New York. The high point had been the carefully planned march—in effect, a parade—through downtown Philadelphia. This served a double purpose: it encouraged the public's confidence in the army's strength and imminent victory, and it enhanced the soldiers' pride in their special calling to defend the public. Encounters like these exemplified and reinforced the conviction that the army was no longer a band of citizens in arms who might be replaced tomorrow by the citizens who watched them today. Soldiers knew that they were professionals for the time being, and the public should support them because it needed them.

Nine days after the victory at Stony Point, the Light Dragoons rode into Philadelphia at 10:30 Sunday morning, July 25, 1779. Captain Henry Archer reported to Anthony Wayne, "I came into the City with Colours flying, Trumpet sounding, and heart elated, drew crouds to the doors and windows and made not a little parade I assure you—these Sir were Baron Stubens instructions and I pursued them litterally, tho' I could not help thinking it had a little of the appearance of a puppet shew." Archer had spent three days in Philadelphia when he wrote this letter, and he added a P.S.: "I have had the happiness of treating some of the male Butterflies with the most humiliating contempt."[140]

Both privates and officers shared this vanity but were less happy in their public encounters with some women spectators. A small detachment looking for deserters in New Jersey "saw a pretty young lady standing in the door of a house, just by the roadside." The leader asked her how far it was to Maidenhead. She answered, "Five miles." Another soldier said to her "'that he thought the commodity scarce in the market, since he had to go so far to seek it.' 'Don't trouble yourself,' said she, 'about that, there is no danger of its being more scarce on your account.' The fellow leered. . . ."[141] In the watching women, soldiers saw boldness and curiosity without all the proper marks of gratitude. A soldier on another march could explain such conduct to his own satisfaction: "I imagine it would make the Devil laugh to see the pretended innocent behavior of the young Women, if perhaps you should take hold of them and offer to kiss them. It really made me laugh also to see them, how fond they were to be taken notice of and yet pretend to be angry, I dislike all Women that wish for what they pretend to hate."[142] But Continentals sometimes found a greeting more to their liking: "The troops halted yesterday an hour to play a number of tunes on the drum and fife, for some country girls, a dancing same evening."[143]

Visitors to camp and watchers of the march were probably

the most widespread form of direct contact between revolutionaries and their army. These civilians evidently wished the army well, but their presence dramatized the army's difference from the society at large. When the French and Spanish ministers visited the Continental Army at Morristown in April 1780, Washington put on a show for the distinguished foreigners, the governor of New Jersey, and the citizens. According to a newspaper account, "On the 24th a considerable division of the army exhibited a number of military manoeuvres, and various evolutions; the dispositions were made by Baron de Stubens, under the direction of the Commander in Chief: The Minister of France could not forbear to express his admiration at the precision of their movements, and the exactness of their fires, which were performed before a large concourse of people of all orders. . . . Every body remarked the good disposition of the army, the spirit that pervaded it, and the alacrity with which the military of every rank appeared to offer themselves for the defense of the honourable and glorious cause they had espoused."[144] People went out of their way to watch the army partly because they knew that they were dependent on the success of the marching, the discipline, the numbers, and the perseverance that made the army a spectator's sight. For the time being, the army's distinctness was a mark of its credit. Later the former spectators would expect the former soldiers to overlook the implied dependence.

Soldiers who had rarely left their own localities before the war changed under the influence of their army travels. Their experience of other states and the ways of the world made them bolder in demanding respect, especially wages. Far from making freemen submissive, army service could give them the grounds to demand their rights. Elijah Fisher, a former private and a veteran of five years' service, got in an argument with his employer over terms of work, pay, and board: "he Called me A Dirtey mean Low spirited———because I asked him how much he Charged me for the two Nights and one super. I told him I had ben about the world and in jentleman's Compeny and Naver heard that Carecter of myself before and I had (I would be Judge by any one that know what good behaver was) behaved myself hansom to him I thought, tho' he had not to me in this affore."[145] On the march, soldiers noted natural beauty, productive soil, and local habits with keen interest. According to David Ramsay, the army's marches "gave birth to many geographical inquiries and discoveries, which otherwise would not have been made."[146] Some soldiers grew more opposed to the enslavement of blacks by seeing it on a larger, crueler scale in the South.[147]

Opponents of half-pay pensions charged that after the war the returning officers would have "imbibed ideas different from what they had when they entered the field" and would use their "considerable influence" at home to "infuse" the ideas "into those they converse with."[148] We can infer from other critics of half pay that the "new ideas" referred especially to demands for stronger continental government and greater respect for the gentlemen who had sustained the continent's independence. The officers' spokesman argued, "If from low stations in life they have risen to high ones in the army, is it not a proof they have merited it by their virtue? . . . Men by a more free intercourse with the world, enlarge their understanding, and acquire a more liberal way of thinking, besides more experience, have more opportunities of comparing the customs, manners, and laws of one country with those of another. Can these acquirements be prejudicial to any state? certainly they cannot: but rather the contrary."[149]

Continentals' increased self-respect, based on wider experience in service to the revolution, were part of what David Ramsay called the "expansion of the human mind" during the revolution. Many "self-made industrious men" who, in ordinary times, would have made a respectable local reputation, found their abilities fit for wider scope. "It seemed as if the war not only required but created talents." The mingling of citizens of different states in the army, as in Congress, brought frequent collisions, but wore off asperities. Ramsay's conception of the expanding human mind in America included all forms of endeavor—literature, science, political thought, government, more interstate marriages.[150] His Independence Day oration in 1778 celebrated the future growth of arts and science in

America, as well as the degree of professional discipline the Continental Army had already attained. "The attention of thousands is now called forth from their ordinary employments to subjects connected with the sovereignty and happiness of a great continent. . . . No one can foresee what great events may be brought into existence, by the exertions of so many minds expanded by close attention to subjects of such vast importance."[151] This wider horizon for activity or just for imagination —this heightened intensity of experience—was central to the legacy that the revolutionaries gave to their posterity. At the end of the war, Chaplain Israel Evans told a brigade of Continentals, "Posterity, through all the long periods of time and futurity, shall open the mighty volume of the American independence, and applaud the unexampled bravery and fortitude of the armies of the United States. . . . Nations shall be taught lessons of heroism and grow great by our example. . . . Millions yet to exist, will wish to have lived in this age, and to have seen what you have beheld."[152] Though anyone could share it, during the war no large group of Americans lived Ramsay's promise on a continental scale so fully as the army did.

Even an active civilian could feel this wartime opportunity that he could not fully enjoy at home. George Williams exemplified Ramsay's new men of affairs who, having "by their own exertions" established "personal independence, were most generally trusted, and most successfully employed in establishing that of their country."[153] A merchant and shipmaster from Salem, Massachusetts, a member of the Committee of Safety, then during the war a representative in the legislature and member of the state Board of War, Williams was forty-six years old in 1777 and just beginning to face the recurring problems of getting clothes to the army. He wrote to his friend Colonel Timothy Pickering, the Adjutant General, "I wish I was free from the publick Business and on my horse to see the world."[154]

The army's growing capacity to flourish amid hardship and to face the enemy more effectively helped make the Continentals the center of wartime resistance to British power. The army experienced a unique depth of sacrifice and intensity of service to the revolution. Americans at home acknowledged this uniqueness by the interest and anxiety with which they followed accounts of combat and expressed their curiosity as spectators. In the uniqueness of the army's revolutionary experience and in other revolutionaries' reliance on the army lay a potential claim to superior revolutionary merit. We can infer that this potential claim helped cause the opponents of officers' pensions to attribute "considerable influence" to veterans and foresee in officers the ability to "infuse" ideas into civilians. If military men laid a dangerous postwar claim to special stature, their assertion would rely not on the easily discredited technique of keeping their arms and forming a standing army, but on their proven distinction in the cause. Civilians rightly feared such a claim, perhaps because their dependence on the army entailed a strain of envy of the army's more conspicuous communal heroism.

On August 10 and 11, 1779, the four hundred men of Colonel Henry Jackson's Additional Continental Regiment made a forced march from Rhode Island to Boston. They covered the forty miles in twenty-four hours and "were broken down with fatigue." They marched through a severe rain all night and reached Boston Neck as the sun was rising. Near the entrance of the neck was a tavern, whose sign was a picture of the earth as a globe with a man's head and shoulders sticking out of it, his arms extended, and the rest of his body enclosed in the globe. On a label from his mouth was written, "Oh! how shall I get through this world?" The soldiers read this, and one of them said to the sign, "[En]list, d——n you, [en]list, and you will soon get through this world! Our regiment will all be through it in an hour or two, if we don't halt by the way."[155]

To judge by the frequency of mentions and the warmth of expression in soldiers' accounts, the Continentals remembered their hours of recreation as a special part of the army's unique experiences. Sometimes it was solitary—officers read novels and plays; Major John Singer Dexter tried in vain to supplement his reading by borrowing a book from a private—"I have seen the Soldier who owns the letters of Eloisa and Abelard and no arguments or offers of Satisfaction could prevail on him to part with them."[156] Men of all ranks played musical instruments; the violin or flute appeared in moments of sadness; fifers played for pleasure as well as the march. Whenever nearby citizens personally welcomed the army, soldiers were glad to entertain or to be entertained, especially if women were present. There was never enough dancing to suit the army. In the absence of parties, a man in town could set out "to find him some white stockin'd woman."[157] Sometimes citizens had planned ahead for his arrival. "We passed in the morning by a house really Crowded with young Women, into which I went, where I found several officers with each a Girl in his arms. Willingly after I entered (which bashfulness kept me from at first) I took a Girl . . . which was rather homely and who, I thought, *began* to cry, so as soon as I could get off conveniently, I quit."[158]

Soldiers of all ranks usually had to make their own recreation in camp. Washington often tried in vain to stop the gambling that officers and privates enjoyed; soldiers liked to swim and play ball games; fifer and drummer boys played war; officers, including the commander in chief, played cricket; Washington sometimes went outside with his aides and threw a ball around. Much to the disgust of Samuel Adams and other repositories of revolutionary morals, officers both patronized the theater and imitated the British by acting in amateur productions in camp. Congress eventually made attendance at plays or participation in them grounds for dismissal of any employee of the United States government.

Soldiers liked to sing. A British prisoner spending the night in a tavern in Easton, Pennsylvania, in 1779 complained about "the noise of the American soldiers who vociferate their songs so loud that the whole house rings with War and Washington, a favourite ballad."[159] According to an army doctor at Valley Forge, the barefoot soldier "labours thro' the Mud and Cold with a Song in his mouth extolling War & Washington."[160] Love songs and hymns were also popular, but no documents surpass the patriotic songs as straightforward expressions of the soldiers' revolutionary ideals.

Officers set great store by the dinners they had for each other, even when this meant sharing only Derby cheeses sent from Connecticut to Valley Forge by a major's mother. When the dinner was a proper one, etiquette guided an elaborate series of toasts, both patriotic ones and individual ones for wives and girlfriends. In fact, the most popular form of recreation throughout the army was drinking. Though commanders tried to discourage soldiers from getting more liquor than the gill which was issued, the sutlers were usually at hand, and soldiers often managed to buy. Drinking among officers was almost official policy, since on special occasions, such as St. Patrick's Day in the Pennsylvania Line, officers drew a quart each when privates drew a gill. On July 3, 1777, General Lachlan McIntosh gave orders for a review in Savannah the next day "to Celebrate the Anniversary of the most Extraordinary and glorious Revolution in the History of mankind, the Declaration of Independency of the United States of America; the Commissary is ordered to provide a quarter Cask Rum, a Beef, a Hog and a Weather to Barbecue upon the Occasion."[161] If officers had civilian connections, they might get "excellent Jamaica Grog and super-excellent French Brandy in its purity."[162] Small wonder that we find repeated journal entries like this one: "I felt very unwell, this whole day, from last night's carouse."[163]

This drinking, like most other forms of recreation in the army, was communal. Sometimes it seemed like a way to escape squalor and fear, but in most cases this escape was not solitary. Rather, the much-prized fraternal entertainments bolstered the Continentals' conviction that they shared a unique life that outsiders, even those who worked for the army's benefit, could not know. After General Daniel Morgan reported his victory at Cowpens, Colonel Otho Holland Williams wrote him from the main southern army, "We have had a *feu de joie*, drunk all your healths, swore you were the finest fellows on earth, and love you, if possible, more than ever." He enclosed Nathanael Greene's announcement of the victory to the army in a general order that "was written immediately after we received the news, and during the operation of some cherry bounce."[164] The conviction of uniqueness penetrated the army, especially after the first winter of three-year enlistments, more by experience than by principle. The slowly mastered discipline, the hard marches past curious onlookers, the lively play took men farther from their earlier hometown lives than they had at first intended or realized. Officers, of course, always wanted to be a distinct class of gentlemen; but this aspiration, like the soldiers' early intent to sweep all before them, expressed primarily an individual confidence in one's ability to fully embody an ideal of patriotic strength. Such aspirations grew out of a communal enthusiasm that, in adversity, threw a person back on his own individual resources. The army, on the other hand, provided a number of techniques for perseverance that had no place in revolutionary ideals. The new professionals did not think of themselves as betrayers of those ideals or even, in most cases, as men who had in any way compromised them, except by temporarily necessary routines. Yet they had created a refuge of prescribed standards of conduct and a record of unique experiences that, in the process of enabling them to serve the revolution, had broken the national unity of mind that revolutionaries prized so much.

Shortly after the arrival of spring at Valley Forge, the army learned that France had recognized the United States by a treaty of alliance. The *Pennsylvania Gazette* published a postscript with the news on May 2, 1778, and on May 5, Washington's general orders "set apart a day for gratefully acknowledging the Divine goodness, and celebrating the important event which we owe to His benign interposition." The day was Wednesday, May 6. At 9 A.M. the troops assembled by brigades to hear the chaplains read a summary of the treaty. General and Mrs. Washington and other general officers and their wives attended at the New Jersey Brigade, where they heard Chaplain Andrew Hunter give a prayer and a sermon, which was "most eloquent" and "very touching."

At the same hour, among all the brigades at Valley Forge,

chaplains were present to "offer up a Thanksgiving, and deliver a discourse suitable to the occasion." To the First and Second Virginia Brigades, Chaplain John Hurt was saying, "Let us then consider the present duty as a point on which the fate of nations is suspended; and let us, therefore, redouble our diligence, and endeavour to acquire the highest perfection in our several duties; for the more we do for ourselves, the more reason have we to expect the smiles of Providence." He believed that victory was probably near: "Oppression thenceforward shall be banished the land—Peace shall till the desolated soil, and commerce unfurl her s[a]ils to every quarter of the sea-encircled globe. . . . Who is there that does not rejoice that his lot has fallen at this important period; that he has contributed his assistance, and will be enrolled hereafter in the pages of history among the gallant defenders of liberty? Who is there who would exchange the pleasures of such reflections for all the ill-gotten pelf of the miser, or the dastardly security of the coward? You, my fellow-soldiers, are the hope of your country; to your arms she looks for defence, and for your health and success her prayers are incessantly offered." He closed with a poem:

Thus shall we see, and triumph in the fight,
While malice frets, and fumes, and gnaws her chains,
AMERICA shall blast her fiercest foes!
Out-brave the dismal shocks of bloody war!
And in unrival'd pomp resplendid rise,
And shine sole empress of the Western World!

At 10:30 a cannon was fired in the Artillery Park. This was the signal for the troops to be under arms. The brigade inspectors inspected the soldiers' dress and arms, formed the men in battalions, and announced to the brigade commanders that the battalions were formed. An observer noticed "the cleanliness of their dress—the brilliancy and good order of their arms." An officer said that the "army made a most brilliant appearance." Each major general took command of the first brigade in his division, while the other brigades were conducted by their own commanders in separate columns. The commandants designated field grade officers to command the battalions, and these officers ordered the battalions to load and ground their arms.

At 11:30, a second cannon was fired to signal the beginning of the march to the alarm posts on the lines. Major General Stirling commanded on the right, the marquis de Lafayette on the left, and the baron De Kalb the second line. The brigades wheeled to the right by platoons and marched in order of battle to positions pointed out by the brigade inspectors. "But this arrangement can convey no adequate idea of their movements to their several posts . . . of the air of our soldiers." One of Washington's aides reported, "The line was formed with admirable rapidity and precision. . . . The martial appearance of the troops, gave sensible pleasure to every one present."

Once the brigades were in place, Washington and the general officers made a circuit round the lines to review the whole army at its posts. They went from right to left down the front line, then turned and went back from left to right along the rear. A person watching the soldiers could see "the remarkable animation with which they performed the necessary salute as the general passed along. Indeed, during the whole of the review, the utmost military decorum was preserved, while at the same time one might observe the hearts of the soldiery struggling to express their feelings in a way more agreeable to nature." One soldier wrote in his diary, "We had Rejoicing on the account of the French declaring for us Independent." Several days earlier the soldiers had begun "to congratulate each other on the prospect of an approaching peace."

When the review was over, Washington, his aides, and his guard took post on high ground to the right in the rear. A flag on the redoubt was dropped, and the third cannon signaled the beginning of the *feu de joie*. Washington's guard fired their muskets. Then thirteen cannon—six-pounders on a height in the northwest corner of camp—were fired one by one. After the thirteenth, a running fire of musketry began on the right of the First Virginia Brigade and continued around the lines through the whole front line of the army. The second line took it up on the left and continued it back around to the starting place. A fourth cannon shot signaled the whole army to huzza, "Long live the King of France." The battalions reloaded, and again the thirteen cannon began a second running fire twice around the camp, with the huzza, "And long live the friendly European Powers." Another reloading, another thirteen cannon, another *feu de joie*, and then came the last huzza, "To the American States."

Lieutenant Colonel John Laurens said, it "was executed to perfection"; the running fire had a "beautiful effect." A letter in the *New York Journal* said, "The gradual progression of the sound from the discharge of cannon and musketry, swelling and rebounding from the neighboring hills, and gently sweeping along the Schuylkill, with the intermingled huzzas . . . composed a military music more agreeable to a soldier's ear than the most finished piece of your favorite Handel." Laurens assured his father, "the plan, as formed by Baron de Steuben, succeeded in every particular, which is in a great measure attributed to his unwearied attention, and to the visible progress which the troops have already made, under his discipline."

The brigades marched back to their parade grounds and were dismissed. One officer noted, "no accident happend during this day." In the afternoon, Washington treated all the officers to a cold collation. An arbor had been constructed with tents in front of the Artillery Park, and tables were spread with "a profusion of fat meat, strong wine, and other liquors." The officers walked to the entertainment thirteen abreast, with arms locked. They were joined by ladies of the neighborhood. Washington ate with them, and they highly praised Louis XVI and drank many patriotic toasts, accompanied by three cheers. Everyone spent the afternoon in "mirth and jolity." "The General himself wore a countenance of uncommon delight and complacence." He received, Laurens said, "such proofs of the love and attachment of his officers as must have given him the most exquisite feelings." Another officer said, "I never was present where there was such unfeigned and perfect joy, as was discovered in every countenance." All of the soldiers got an allowance of brandy, and all men in confinement were released "that they might taste the Pleasur of the Day."

At five o'clock, Washington took leave of the officers. While he rode away, they all applauded him and shouted, "*Long live General Washington*!" The officers were still shouting huzzas and throwing their hats in the air when Washington and his staff were a quarter of a mile away. "His Excellency turned round with his retinue, and huzzaed several times." As Washington rode around the camp, the noncommissioned officers and privates of each brigade took up the applause and the cry. In the evening, everyone returned to quarters. The next day a letter written at Valley Forge said, "I have long since discovered, that pleasures of the most agreeable kind, may be found even in the bustle of a camp. What do you think, my dear friend, does the soldier feel, on reviewing the dangers he has passed—in planning or executing the overthrow of tyranny—or celebrating the exploits of heroes."[165]

CHAPTER VI
Treason

The central figure in the army's survival and in the American victory was not Baron Steuben, but George Washington. If anyone could have doubted this after the victory at Trenton, the ruin of General Charles Lee made Washington's preeminence official. When Washington publicly reprimanded Lee for his conduct during the Battle of Monmouth, Lee wrote insulting letters to the commander in chief. As a result, Lee was court-martialed for his conduct in the battle and for insubordination. His spirited defense in his court-martial and his later personal attacks on Washington while Congress was reviewing the court's verdict of guilty succeeded in forcing the court and Congress to choose between Washington and Lee. They chose Washington.[1]

The overwhelming praise of Washington during the war touched on some of the revolutionaries' strongest aspirations and doubts. Americans depended on his virtue, and some of them warned against such dependence. They exalted his character but not his authority. In the celebration of Washington's greatness we can see two faces of the revolutionaries' enthusiastic hope for America's future. He represented America's capacity to attain lasting virtue. But the very fact that revolutionaries were celebrating a representative—a symbol—boded ill for the widespread popular attainment of a comparable virtue.

Though Washington consciously set out to attain ideal virtue in public behavior, he did not create or control the purple cloud of rhetoric that appeared instantly in 1775 and surrounded his name throughout the war. Unlike Charles Lee or Ethan Allen or Thomas Paine, he did not advertise his patriotism with his own writings. A person who read nothing about Washington except Washington's own deliberate, balanced prose might well be surprised to learn that such extravagant emotion had surrounded him as commander in chief. Washington's fellow revolutionaries created the godlike Washington, and he won their permanent gratitude by publicly doing nothing to contradict and much to confirm this ideal. The praise of Washington's battlefield command assured revolutionaries that he answered their desire for an inspirational general, but his prowess in battle, while important, remained secondary to his virtuous character.

The rhetoric surrounding Washington suggests that Americans did not want a new king or benevolent ruler so much as a high priest of the revolution, an exemplar of the qualities that would achieve the continent's promised future. For this reason Alan Heimert rightly has compared Washington's position to that of George Whitefield, who could, by his God-given personal influence, bring to the troubled the assurance that they had grace.[2] Washington did not need to preach; he only needed to be as virtuous as people said he was. He was a Gideon, a second Matthias, an American Nehemiah, an American Joshua, a Moses.[3] His patriotism showed the spirit in which the revolution was made. By looking at the praise and gratitude Washington received, revolutionaries could see how they would appear in history. At the end of the war Congress said to Washington, "You have, by the love and confidence of your fellow-citizens, enabled them to display their martial genius, and transmit their fame to posterity."[4] In the tributes, several themes stand out: although Washington was rich, he served the public welfare rather than staying at home to enjoy his independent means; although he brought great talents to the discharge of difficult tasks, he accepted no salary and charged no commissions; and although he commanded the army, he neither indulged personal arrogance nor amassed power. In emphasizing certain of George Washington's virtues, revolutionaries revealed the temptations that they particularly feared and that they hoped posterity would believe they, as well as Washington, had overcome.

Anyone who has read nine years of the sermons, the testimonials, and the verse about Washington—especially the verse—might agree with Washington's critics that the praise ran to excess. Washington's fame was unique. Soon after his appointment as commander in chief, the newspapers began to report that babies were being named after him.[5] Celebrations of his birthday began during the war, at least as early as 1779, and when Washington appeared in cities, he received not only ceremonial greetings and addresses but also the spontaneous acclaim of crowds.[6] In Philadelphia, where Washington was met with jubilation on his way south toward Yorktown in 1781, a loyalist Quaker saw him "several times walking the Street, attended by a concourse of Men, Women and Boys, who Huzza'd him, and broke some of my father's Windows."[7] To Washington's critics, the rhetoric and the popularity from which it grew suggested that public admiration had surrendered too much of the independent judgment that could alone preserve self-government. This argument implied that the public had to be saved from itself by its friends who saw the error that it was making. What was this error? It was treating Washington as "the Father of the People," "the Father of His Country," "the common father of all."[8] All of these phrases and the attitude they expressed originated during the war. The critics of Washington feared that such loyalty would confer an authority outside the law that would enable Washington to rule others by his will alone, enforced by the army. This fear was doubly groundless: Washington would never have tried such rule, and if he had, the public would quickly and easily have defied it.

Washington's status as father came less from his authority, legal or reverential, than from his constancy. Washington's clocklike ideal was almost as far from the army's actual workings as the millennium was from wartime America. Yet he continued to work steadily, as if he were naturally patient, writing letters to officers, governors, legislators, and Congress. These letters explained, in his measured, unhighlighted prose, that the additional efforts he was obliged to request might enable him to extemporize a while longer, in spite of the likelihood that the army would completely break up in the near future for lack of supplies or recruits. People who dealt with Washington in person said that his face-to-face appeals for help deeply moved those present.[9] He may have had this effect because he discussed his own setbacks and the army's needs and his strong feelings about the latest crisis, all in the calm, restrained manner he cultivated. The contrast between his steady demeanor and the urgency of his message, in writing or in person, not only gave his words greater weight but also conveyed the implicit promise that Washington would still be discharging his duties in spite of the dissolution caused by the insufficient effort of others. Sometimes he strongly condemned the spread of greed among revolutionaries, which made them work for themselves and not the cause. But unlike Robert Morris while he was superintendent of finance, Washington did not write official letters full of artful sarcasm about the negligence of others, contrasted with descriptions of his own merits. And we know from Washington's letters during the supposed cabal in 1777 and 1778 that he could write that way when he wanted to.

The father of his country was the man who would not burn out in sudden, brief enthusiasms, who would not give up his ideal because of difficulties or fears, who would not demand rewards and power equal to his worth, who would allow the public to share his distinction without shaming them by telling them how far short of him they fell. In September 1776, Major Lewis Morris, Jr., wrote to his father, a signer of the Declaration of Independence, that after independence had been secured, "those losses which every Man has sustained will make his Perseverance and Patriotism shine forth with more conspicuous Luster, and like a Cincinnatus or Camillus will be caressed by his country and called the Father of his People."[10] Constantly concerned with their own stature in the eyes of posterity, the revolutionaries saw their own strengths represented in Washington. This outlook was proclaimed in one of the most popular songs of the revolution, "War and Washington." In it, Americans said to Britain,

The lustre of your former deeds,
whole ages of renown,
Lost in a moment, or transferr'd
to US and WASHINGTON! . . .
'Tis heav'n-born FREEDOM fires us
all, and strengthens each brave son,
From him who humbly guides the
plough, to godlike WASHINGTON.[11]

They would all be, like Washington, fathers of their country. At the same time, they could rely on him to embody their ideals of public service more fully than they did themselves.

Anyone could see that the revolutionaries' own conduct did not conform to their image of Washington. They loved passionate eloquence and bravado; they never tired of describing their own patriotism; to compensate for their sacrifices, they made considerable profit from the war when they could; during the retreat across New Jersey in 1776 and after the loss of Fort Ticonderoga in 1777, they were swept by sudden fears that resistance might collapse. Wartime behavior in America was often less conscientious, less purposeful, and less stable than Washington's work as commander in chief. Yet his countrymen preferred to praise his persevering virtue as representative of the revolution. Thus, their celebration of Washington's greatness could, by implication, claim for them a share of his eminence. If his glory embodied the achievements of a whole people, his countrymen could, by praising him, vicariously join in his achievements, his virtue, and his steadfastness, even while they failed to match his constant self-restraint. The rhetoric about godlike Washington did not seek to exalt the commander in chief by contrasting him with his weak and wayward countrymen. It therefore did not betoken their submission to the superior wisdom of a leader they could never hope to emulate. Washington understood this fact better than his critics did. Although he did not talk about his unique distinction, he showed—for example, in his consistent deference to civilian supremacy and in his readiness to disavow the Society of the Cincinnati at the end of the war—that he knew how fully American independence and his own effectiveness depended on the revolutionaries' own work toward their ideals. Americans might rely on the talents of a great man, but they would never make that reliance grounds for subordination. As long as Washington exemplified his countrymen's ideals, they would allow him to work hard in a post of unique honor. If he had tried to subvert those ideals, his ruin would have rivaled Benedict Arnold's.

Americans often talked about the kind of inspiring leader they wanted. In practice, they did not want a powerful commander at all—that is, a man to whom they would delegate coercive authority. Rather, they wanted someone whose eloquence or example could make them want to do what they knew they ought to do. The reluctance with which Americans went to war, in contrast to the enthusiasm with which they demanded independence, made such a figure very important to the success of the revolution. He sustained the call to necessary service, and he sustained the service when the call went unanswered or answered by too little. If one talked enough about the magnificence of the leader's service, who could say that one lagged in dedication to the cause? This was the danger in Washington's wartime stature as the father of his people. His contemporaries might vindicate their revolution with his reputation in lieu of earning their own reputations by comparable effort.

On March 5, 1779, William Tudor gave the annual oration to commemorate the Boston Massacre. He spoke at noon in the Old Brick Meeting House; his audience included "the Council, and a great number of all ranks of people." Tudor was a former student and clerk in John Adams's law office and had been judge advocate of the Continental Army until his resignation a year earlier. He spoke for almost forty minutes, and his address, as was customary on Massacre Day, warned against the dangers of a standing army. He briefly summarized the familiar argument that luxury "first unfits men for patriotic energies," then corruption puts to sleep "that virtuous jealousy of public men and public measures, which was wont to scrutinize not only actions but motives."

Tudor then quickly turned to a new danger: "a people ruled by a despot, who from a private station, rose to uncontrolled dominion, at a time when they were sternly virtuous. And this mode of introducing bondage is ever to be apprehended at the close of a successful struggle for liberty, when a triumphant army, elated with victories, and headed by a popular General may become more formidable than the tyrant that has been expelled. . . . Witness the aspiring CROMWELL!" In the case of Rome, "BRUTUS and his virtuous associates" assassinated Caesar too late to save the republic; "a standing army, and a perpetual dictator, were and ever will prove too hard for the patriotic few. Learn hence, my countrymen, that a State may sink so low in slavery that even virtue itself cannot retrieve her. From these examples, prudence dictates—*resist beginnings*. A free and wise people will never suffer any citizen to become too popular—much less too powerful. A man may be formidable to the constitution even by his virtues." Although Tudor said that he was "little solicitous of rhetorical applause," his father noted that "when finished there was a general claping of hands to show their Approbation."[12]

Nine months later, John Sullivan, the day after his resignation as major general, wrote to warn Washington that "the Faction Raised against you in 1777 . . . is not yet Destroyed. . . . Their Plan is, to take Every method of proving the Danger arising from a Commander, who Enjoys the full and unlimited Confidence of his army, and Alarm the People with the Prospects of Imaginary Evil. . . . This Plan was adopted the Last winter, and if you will take the Trouble of reading Mr Tudors Oration, Delivered at Boston in March Last, you will find Every Line Calculated to answer this purpose. The words are Tudor's, but the Thoughts are Borrowed. I heard them thrown out Long before they were by him laid before the publick. . . . The next Step is to persuade Congress That the military power of America should be placed in three or four Different hands Each having a Seperate Quarter of the Continent assigned him, Each Commander to answer to Congress only for his Conduct; This they Say will prevent an Aspiring Commander from Enslaving the Country, and put it in the power of Congress, with the assistance of the other Commanders, to punish the attempt."[13]

A few private comments by members of Congress who applied Tudor's argument specifically to Washington and a few warnings to Washington like Sullivan's seem to be the only evidence to indicate the existence of a plan like the one Sullivan described.[14] We can doubt that the people applauding Tudor endorsed Tudor's suspicion of Washington; Jonathan Mason's Massacre oration one year later in 1780 held up Washington as the preeminent example of American patriotism.[15] One can readily believe that the idea of a divided command was floated in conversation with hardly any expectation that it would be tried or even that those who mentioned it would try to secure its adoption.

After the Valley Forge winter, criticism of Washington as commander in chief changed its emphasis. Although in 1777 and 1778 Washington's critics had sometimes warned against making him so great that he could endanger the public liberties, the most common censure said he was weak-willed, indecisive, a loser. Slow to endorse independence, his accusers charged, he had been even slower to discipline the army because he remained distant and did not inspire his men. Within a year, Washington had become, in the eyes of his detractors, a potential dictator whose virtues attracted public gratitude and commanded the loyalty of a victorious army that might tyrannize a virtuous but defenseless populace. This changed line of argument showed that the recent critics of Washington had also seen the changes in the Continental Army; the critics feared that Washington would be tempted by "the enthusiasm of the army."[16] The army was far from a fit engine of tyranny, but it had shown that it would hold together and improve its skill under Washington's command. Discipline was proving successful, and a few revolutionaries were quick to warn that disciplined virtue was dangerous.

The critics of Washington's eminence shared some of their vocabulary with spokesmen for the loyalists. In the warnings against an American dictator, the ghost of Cromwell played a double part. Several revolutionaries said that Cromwell had the proper prescription for army discipline: "Pay well, and hang well."[17] The Americans did neither, but the prospect of a Continental Cromwell disturbed some revolutionaries and many loyalists. The revolutionaries feared that the loyalty and obedience that helped to win independence could, under the influence of their successful leader, betray the revolution by giving power to one man. The loyalists argued that a rebellion that relied, as the Americans did, on a spirit of popular enthusiasm would certainly become a dictatorship because it could tolerate no disagreement. A prisoner confined in the Philadelphia jail by order of Congress left graffiti on the wall that said, in part, "The days of *Cromwell*, puritanic rage/Return'd to curse our more unhappy age."[18]

The figure of Cromwell came closest to reconciling the contradiction within the loyalists' view of their opponents. The loyalists usually said, without any admission of inconsistency, that the rebels were oppressive zealots who persecuted dissent and that most Americans were loyalists who had been deluded or tyrannized by a small faction of rebels. Behind these purported statements of fact probably lay the assumption that most Americans, when in their right minds, would become loyalists or were loyalists at heart but that zealotry itself was a form of delusion or tyranny over the mind. Once freed from the sway of such excess by the restoration of British rule, Americans would not persist in rebellion but would gratefully return to their senses. Cromwellian England best exemplified this aberrant union of popular enthusiasm and popular subjection to dictatorship. While some revolutionaries worried that a tyrant might subvert the revolution by his popularity, loyalists argued that the revolution was inherently tyrannical. The continent could escape such a fate only by the rebels' defeat.

Why did revolutionary critics of Washington raise the specter of Cromwell? Why did the criticism of Washington change fronts? The warnings probably arose from a fear that the loyalists were partly right—not when they expected Americans to give up revolutionary zeal, but when they said that enthusiasm subverted independent judgment and brought people under the sway of a leader who could command zealous loyalty. For the men who most actively warned that the Continental Army might engineer political oppression were often the same men who, in 1776 and 1777, had wanted the Continental Army to sweep all before it under the influence of the revolutionary ardor with which it followed its inspiring commander. When the army survived Valley Forge, when the British withdrew from the capital, and when victory seemed near, vigilant men could conclude that the revolution might create a monster, just as loyalists had said, unless this threat were forestalled. These men feared that the army and the public might follow Washington beyond victory to slavery.

In fact, the Continental Army had not created an armed host of righteousness on the new model that these critics both wanted and feared. Revolutionary zeal and attachment to Washington were indeed the main motives for cohesion in the army, but, as we have seen, survival and victory after 1776 increasingly depended on the willing adoption of modified European techniques for camp and battlefield operation. This professionalism was a source of pride in both proficiency and service to the cause; however, it did not pretend to embody the ideal revolutionary life or express the freedom to which revolutionaries aspired. No one could have convinced Continental soldiers that the Steuben plan of discipline was the liberation for which they had been fighting and that they ought therefore to make it the instrument for ruling an independent America. By the same token, the improvement of discipline did not confer authority on commanders through their embodiment of the virtue of the cause. The soldier served the revolution because his patriotism attached him to his country; when he obeyed his superior officers, he did so because the country had given them authority, and because they were dutiful in their discharge of the obligations that discipline placed on them. The soldier was not likely to follow his commanders from victory to tyranny, because he did not suppose that his commanders' authority or his own obedience had any grounds for existence after victory. In fact, one of the principal accomplishments of professionalism among soldiers was their increase in proficiency despite the negligence of officers.

Not everyone in the army preserved this distinction between temporary military authority and revolutionary zeal. Those officers who felt that their virtue and valor made them the vanguard of the revolution demanded more than the automatic obedience of their subordinates; they also sought respect and deference from their inferiors in patriotism among the public at large. Most Americans who warned against the subversion of the revolution by the army directed their criticism toward these officers, not toward Washington. The loyalist James Chalmers, in his reply to *Common Sense*, had warned that "a democratical government would soon give way to a military system imposed on the colonies, by some Cromwell of our armies." Washington, "our virtuous citizen," was not such a man; "the person whose turbulent ambition, and extensive talents would enable him to erect a tyranny, is perhaps at present a subaltern." Cromwell knew that soldiers would prefer a life of dissipation in the army instead of "their ploughs, looms, etc. He also knew that nine tenths of his officers, being a sort of Demi-Gentry, (if I may so express myself) had still a stronger aversion to resign[ing] their fastidious profession (unhappily for mankind) more pleasing than their former peaceable dep[o]rtments."[19]

In the five-year debate over officers' pensions, which was heightened at the end of the war by the controversy over the Society of the Cincinnati, people who opposed the officers' pretensions elaborated that loyalist warning at length. But these critics found that the officers were not content to become half-pay placemen or professional authoritarians outside of productive society; the American military demi-gentry claimed to be the truest revolutionary patriots. These officers best exemplified the dangers in making revolutionary zeal the guide to military conduct. Instead of making them unselfish servants of the cause, their zeal had sanctified their claim to social, military, and patriotic superiority.

Some of these officers, especially during the controversies over pay and pensions, got into the habit of saying what "the army" wanted and what "the army" would do. They were, in fact, talking about what they wanted and what they would do. Some of them believed that they spoke for the army. Others hoped to make Congress and the states believe so. In this, they succeeded remarkably. Critics of the officers argued that the officers, by claiming to be indispensable to the army, were perverting public service to gain private advantage in pensions and in a false show of superior merit. Moreover, these critics feared that the officers could control the army for such base ends. The main military effort to influence civil government came, late in the war, from Continental Army officers. Many revolutionaries seemed ready to believe that these efforts grew out of the army's survival and success. The officers, these civilians assumed, spoke for a military interest that would inevitably try to entrench itself through its armed might. The idea that privates could become proud long-term soldiers and yet remain would-be freemen, rather than would-be careerists, got much support from the public in discussions of the army's strength and victories. But this idea seemed to be forgotten when public suspicion and fear of officers extended to "the army." Recruits' bounty bargaining and soldiers' complaints about lack of pay must have helped convince people that the army was becoming a fixed faction.

In addition, the civilians were at a disadvantage because much of what the officers said was right: Congress had promised pay that it had not paid; the army had taken more risks, undergone more hardships, and come closer to the ideal of public service during the war than most civilians had. Why should citizens not assume that the soldiers' consciousness of virtue, of grievances, and of strength would turn the army against the people? Privates did share the officers' awareness of those three attributes. Unlike the officers, however, they did not unite the three to arrogate righteousness to the army and thereby claim primacy in the revolution. Soldiers could distinguish between pay and soldiering, between soldiering and personal virtue, between virtue and the right to rule. These distinctions kept the army functioning and helped keep it subordinate to civil authority.

In retrospect, the revolutionaries' suspicions of the army may seem at least premature. How could officers enslave America when they had not yet expelled the British? But revolutionaries did not know and were eager not to think that five more years of war awaited them after the Valley Forge winter. The survival of the army during the Valley Forge winter, the withdrawal of the British from Philadelphia to New York in June 1778, and the announcement of the American alliance with France in May convinced many revolutionaries that the war was almost over. In Lancaster, Pennsylvania's capital in exile, people danced the "Burgoyne's Surrender," and bettors who thought the war would last longer than six more months could get five-to-one odds. Even after such bettors won at the beginning of 1779, they probably could have gotten favorable odds if they had been foolish enough to lay a new bet that the war would last much longer. American officers, British officers, loyalists, foreign observers, and revolutionaries at home said that Americans were "tired of the war."[20] Continental Army recruiting lagged because men wanted more money for their service or wanted to avoid service and because state authorities felt less urgency to fill the army when victory seemed near. In October 1778, Lieutenant William Thompson reported to his regimental commander that the Pennsylvania Executive Council refused to appropriate money for recruiting the state's undermanned Continental Line: "They again hinted that the war would be shortly finished, and there was no need for throwing the State to farther Expences."[21]

Although the states used conscription more widely than in 1777, it remained primarily a technique for determining who would hire a substitute rather than for allotting military service. The means of evading conscription reached new heights of refinement every year of the war. Men charged with providing a recruit sent a man to camp but failed to pay his full bounty. Then they connived at or even encouraged his desertion, thus both filling their draft quota and saving themselves the expense of a full bounty. The most popular method of evasion seems to have been signing up men who were physically unfit or otherwise exempt. The quota was filled, but the ringer was sent home when he reported to camp. Some state laws defining acceptable recruits grew longer as the years passed, thus providing a syllabus of citizens' hoaxes. Here is Virginia's for 1780: "A soldier between eighteen and fifty years of age, of able body, sound mind, at least five feet four inches high, and not being a deserter from the enemy, or from any corps of regular troops in the service of this or the United States. . . ." In 1781 the legislature added the provision, "not subject to fits."[22]

In practice, Americans had given up the pretense that the war would be fought by citizens of all kinds. There was a class of men from whom soldiers were usually drawn. With careful collation of enlistment rolls and civil records, scholars are drawing composite pictures of this class—men in their late teens and early twenties, usually unmarried, poor.[23] But it remains highly probable that more men who fit the composite description did not enlist than did. Demographic and economic characteristics alone were not motives sufficient to fill the army. Able-bodied young men who sought their own material well-being above all else had alternatives better than service in the Continental Army. Privateering, farm labor, brief service as a militia substitute all offered more money, food, and physical comfort than regular army duty did. At the most basic level of self-interest, even dependence on charity or wandering beggary gave a better chance of survival than the ever-present threat of death by combat or disease in the army. The distinguishing feature of the recruits was their willingness.

The army's perseverance was distinctive among revolutionaries because for two years, from spring 1778 to spring 1780, most Americans tried to disregard the armed conflict in the belief that British withdrawal from the continent and recognition of American independence were imminent. In 1778 the British ministry sent commissioners to America to negotiate a reconciliation that would have been, in effect, an American surrender. Revolutionaries, with the help of an extensive newspaper campaign against the commission, decided that such an overture showed Britain to be near giving up.[24] These two years deepened and permanently fixed some revolutionary leaders' mistrust of their fellow Americans. These leaders have since been called nationalists because they believed that a strong central government in the hands of able, active men could rescue independence from the effects of popular selfishness and neglect. They favored the increase of governmental, especially executive, power at the expense of responsiveness to the popular will, and they increasingly distrusted the popular will as a source of tangible support for the revolution. They did not believe that Americans had turned loyalist, only that revolutionaries had turned greedy. Americans had not undertaken their revolution on the premise that they were depraved and selfish. Rather, they expected to forestall the encroachment of such conduct by separation from British sources of corruption. They expected to succeed because the public, despite its weaknesses, was virtuous.

The public's loss of interest in the war for independence between 1778 and 1780 took the nationalists beyond their earlier warnings about waning public virtue to a fixed skepticism—in some cases, a bitter cynicism—about popular willingness to support independence with effort and money. A few men—like Thomas Burke, member of Congress and governor of North Carolina—underwent a full transformation from defender of popular guidance of the war effort and vigilant opponent of governmental power, to supporter of strong government.[25] More often, nationalists like Washington, Hamilton, Greene, Robert Morris, and Gouverneur Morris had from the beginning preferred to rely on central government to control the national resources for war. They had not favored governmental institutions so highly responsive to the popular will as those the revolutionaries first adopted. But these men had not joined the revolution in 1776 with the thorough conviction that the public would do more to sabotage independence than to secure it. By 1780, the nationalists believed that the public, when left to its own wishes, would do just that. The danger that they later saw in highly responsive, weak government and the reliance that they placed on centralized power derived much conviction from their experience during the two years in which the war seemed over while it went on.

The difficulties of recruiting, the evasion of military service, the lapse of popular war effort showed a faltering of public virtue. Revolutionaries had undertaken war on the premise that virtue gave an entire people the strength to sustain independence because they would voluntarily sacrifice private ease for public safety. Willingness to sacrifice through serving in the military or through providing regular pay and supplies for the army had fallen sharply by the summer of 1778. Perhaps the revolutionaries' persistent expectation of victory arose partly from a fear that the failure of public virtue might doom their cause if the war went on.

We find many grounds for such a fear in Americans' conduct from 1778 to 1780. People were weary of the war, but they were not weary. In these years the United States enjoyed what one historian calls "an enormous economic boom."[26] As long as Continental currency had value, the American army supplied itself by spending money—an ever-accelerating flow of paper dollars that swelled in volume until they became worthless. Congress continued to print paper money, but the states did not tax enough to draw the earlier issues out of circulation. According to a newspaper writer in 1779, "It was said by many people at the commencement of the war, 'we will fight for our liberties, and let posterity pay for them.'"[27] The steady depreciation encouraged people not only to spend the money fast before it sank further, but also to charge more for goods and labor in order to hedge against future losses, a practice that hastened the depreciation. During 1779 the quartermaster general's and commissary general's departments spent a total of $109,169,000 currency.[28] E. James Ferguson estimates that during the whole war the Continental and state governments, the British army, and, after 1780, the French army spent the equivalent of $214 to $215 million specie in America. In his journal, a French army commissary officer wrote of the Americans, "They love money."[29] Most of the money went first to the farmers who supplied the armies, the towns, and the cities with food. People complained that the government's purchases drove up all prices and further depreciated the money; meanwhile, those with something to sell made money from the expenditures. The deputy quartermaster general in New Jersey reported in November 1779, "Our People cry out against the Q.M. for raising the prices and none more willing to get the highest than themselves."[30] His report in June contained the best brief summary of the career of Continental dollars: "Bad as the money is its wanted."[31]

So as not to get stuck with bad money while it got worse, people spent it. Despite the rise of necessary expenditures, many Americans had money left over for luxuries, primarily imported ones, obtained by privateering, risky trade with Europe, and traffic with the enemy. A European laughed at an advertisement in Philadelphia: "Tobacco, as good as the best imported."[32] Native vices tasted sweeter if they seemed foreign. Americans wanted British goods so much that a merchant who imported clothing from France relabeled it British. From Paris, Benjamin Franklin complained in 1779, "When the difficulties are so great to find remittances to pay for the arms and ammunition necessary for our defense, I am astonished and vexed to find, upon inquiry, that much the greatest part of the Congress interest bills come to pay for tea, and a great part of the remainder is ordered to be laid out in gewgaws and superfluities."[33] The Americans had credit in France and the Netherlands, where they could buy both Continental products and British goods through the Dutch. European subsidies and loans helped the United States fight the British and helped Americans spend money on European manufactured goods.[34] Edmund Pendleton believed that some of the dealers were British agents, but his countrymen seemed oblivious to the danger of subversion: "Such is the Spirit to trade, that if Belzebub was to appear with a Cargoe—the people would deal with him."[35]

We cannot know with precision how widely these imports were shared. There can be little doubt that they spread rapidly during these years, and the few Americans who made fortunes from privateering or importing or trading across British lines could not have done so unless many less wealthy revolutionaries had been able and anxious to buy. In "a nearly universal black market," profits on imported goods ran up to 600 percent.[36] Before the war, nonimportation, the call to wear homespun, and the rejection of tea had mobilized resistance to British tyranny.[37] Such repudiation of luxuries had both applied economic pressure on Britain and demonstrated Americans' commitment to virtuous frugality. No tyrant could exploit a dependence on luxuries in order to enslave Americans. Now, as they told themselves that the struggle with Britain would soon end, they seemed to be losing the virtue on which independence was supposed to rest. New Hampshire's delegate in Congress, Josiah Bartlett, knowing that the Americans' cause was as just as the Israelites', regretted that "we are a crooked and perverse generation, longing for the fineries and follies of those Egyptian task masters from whom we have so lately freed ourselves."[38] Perhaps thinking of such warnings, one of Washington's aides said, "All cry out that nothing but Oeconomy can save us, and yet no one allows that he or she is extravagant."[39]

An extensive trade with the enemy in New York City grew in all three directions, to New Jersey, New York, and Connecticut. During the Valley Forge winter, Pennsylvanians took food to Philadelphia for hard money. But the trade through British lines around New York was for manufactured goods. By 1780 importation at New York City had reached its prewar volume, thus serving a much larger market than the region controlled by the British army.[40] State authorities and the Continental Army tried in vain to block the trade that made this importation profitable. It persisted throughout the war, and after the American victory at Yorktown, nothing could stop its rapid growth. According to an article in the *New Jersey Journal*, people in New Jersey objected to paying taxes for the support of the war in 1782 because "our hard money is continually going in great quantities to our enemies: the country is drained of its cash"; if the army and the government could not prevent the people from sending money to the enemy to buy British goods, then the people ought not to support the army and the government with taxes.[41] In 1778 Governor William Livingston had said that good wine would remain rare in America until the United States declared war on Portugal.[42]

Some pamphlets and newspapers warned that the trade with the enemy was a conspiracy by the British and their secret tools among revolutionaries to recoup by corruption what they had lost by arms. Before the war, the spread of unrepublican self-indulgence had encouraged revolutionaries to suspect a British plot to enslave Americans by enervating them with vice.[43] But the War for Independence hastened rather than curbed the development of a complex economy, of social differentiation, of aspirations and pretensions by people newly active in expanding commerce. The economic activity of wartime quickly distracted Americans from the war itself, long before independence had been won.

We can guess that the energetic social activity and personal indulgence not only sought to keep shaky money moving but also enabled people to enjoy independence and prosperity, free from the demands of a war whose victorious outcome they saw no reason to delay. British imperial administration and mercantilist economic policy would have made rich careers for a few British and American servants of the crown while encouraging America to remain an economically backward subsidiary to the wealth of the empire. If the revolutionaries had wanted to prolong their years as unambitious farmers and fishermen, with a leaven of mechanics and a few merchants, they could have made no better choice than continued British rule. High on the list of freedoms threatened by British policy was the freedom to aspire toward new lands, new enterprise, new happiness—continental and individual. The revolutionaries explained this threat as an attempt to enslave them through corruption, to tax them with one hand and bribe them into docile obedience with the other. In fact, Americans feared that the British government would cheat them out of their aspirations and that only a few favorites would enjoy the kind of wealth and power many people wanted. The spreading luxury and corruption, which revolutionaries blamed on British conspiracy, were instead the tempting fruits of American freedom. Before the war, American revolutionary thought took credit for the liberation of these hopes, while imputing the selfishness to British design. If gratifying the love of office, of profit, and of finery was bribery, Congress and its dollars and the War for Independence bribed a far greater number of willing

Americans than the king and his ministers ever dreamed of rewarding. The British may have been the main enemies of American freedom; the Americans were the main enemies of American virtue.

Some Americans' determination to profit from the war went beyond the opportunities provided by supply and demand. In 1778, when holding recruiting officers accountable for the expenditure of bounty money had failed to end graft, Congress resolved that "it is essential to the liberties of the United States that due attention should be paid to the expenditure of their public monies, to enable them to support the war, and avoid that system of corruption and tyranny which prevails in the government of their unnatural enemies."[44] Yet a popular saying current during the war advised, "Grease well and speed well."[45] After reading the complaints from all sides, both from the public and the Continental Line, one might conclude that the administration of the Continental Army staff departments was thoroughly corrupt. Quartermasters and commissaries embezzled public funds and sold government supplies for their own profit. Some quartermasters paid more than the going rate for transport because they owned the vessels or wagons they were hiring for government use. Purchasing agents bought supplies nominally with their own money and then, in their capacity as owners, sold the supplies to themselves in their capacity as government buyers, of course at a profit from public money. Or they used government money for private speculation and then balanced their accounts by returning the original amount after it had depreciated to a fraction of its former value. By August 22, 1780, Congress had decided that the maximum penalty for embezzlement, misappropriation, or negligence in the staff departments should be death.[46]

Soldiers probably suffered much more directly from the graft of contractors or suppliers, though these men were sometimes government officials too. Americans repeatedly sold defective food, clothing, gunpowder, and other supplies to their own army. Wagoners drained the brine from barrels of pickled meat to lighten their loads, then charged at the full weight for shipping spoiled meat; meat-packers drained the brine and replaced it with water, which kept up the weight but ruined the meat; barrels of flour arrived at camp with the flour in the middle scooped out; cobblers used odd scraps to make shoes that looked good when new but quickly fell apart; the army received bundles of blankets that, when opened, revealed that each blanket was only a fraction of the proper size; gunsmiths cheated the government when hired to repair arms; large quantities of gunpowder were "bad and not to be depended on."[47]

Graft continued among both Continental officers and enlisted men, though the Inspectorate and the departure of many short-termers by 1778 probably decreased it substantially. Recruiting remained the officers' best source of public money—Continental bounties—for private use. Some officers still cheated their men on pay; officers also took bribes to discharge soldiers. Captain Bartholomew Von Heer, commander of the provost company, or military police, extorted bribes from sutlers in return for licenses to trade in camp. Soldiers took bribes from civilians who passed the army's lines to trade with the enemy. Soldiers drew more rations than they were entitled to and sold the surplus. Most often, enlisted men sold Continental property. Congress tried to stop this practice by having muskets and other property marked and livestock branded.

We should not picture the army and its suppliers as men devoted mainly to fraud and theft any more than we should picture revolutionary society as lost in idle luxury. Rather, we see that inextricably involved in the winning of the revolution were the practices that the revolution sought to expel from American society. A vivid and precise vocabulary described these practices: "smart money" was a recruiter's illegal take; "horse-beef" was soldiers' rations of dubious origin; "custom-house oaths" were perjury; "mushroom gentlemen" were the newly prosperous revolutionaries; "jockeying" was getting rid of paper money before it lost value.[48] As Washington's aide Tench Tilghman said in 1779, "We Americans are a sharp people."[49] This sharpness, which was so clear in common speech, found its way into revolutionary ideology only as an implacable enemy—primarily alien but potentially native—and hardly found its way into the revolutionary vision of the future at all. If American independence depended on public virtue, how could one resolve the conflict between the demanding ideals and the sharp practices that betrayed them? Revolutionaries could denounce engrossers and extortioners, both rich farmers and rich merchants, but the rich were not the only ones who indulged fraud and greed. Selfishness itself, apart from the volume of its proceeds, drove out virtue and left a man unable to defend himself. Speaking of the builders of defective boats in 1775, Private George Morison described a dilemma that persisted for many revolutionaries when self-seeking later grew more widespread and more successful: "Did they not know that their doings were crimes—that they were cheating their country, and exposing its defenders to additional sufferings and to death? . . . These men could enjoy the sweets of domestic ease, talk about liberty and the rights of mankind, possibly without even a recollection of their parricidal guilt, which in minds subject to any reflection, would excite the most poignant remorse."[50]

Perhaps the widespread failure to enlist, to stay in the army, to supply the army, and to avoid corrupting vices could seem less parricidal because the war seemed almost over. But the British did not leave in 1778, nor in 1779, nor in 1780. Instead, in 1780 they returned to the offensive. What hope could American independence and virtue rely on when they faced not imminent victory but the danger of defeat? If surrender to the British on the battlefield should complete the ruin of public virtue, how could American minds escape "reflection" and "the most poignant remorse"?

Americans' wartime derelictions did not mean that many people were losing their desire for independence; nor had revolutionaries lost their hope for the success of revolutionary ideals. Indeed, we can judge from their response to the defeats and surprises of 1780 that they wanted all the more strongly an independent republic secured by patriotic virtue. The reverses of 1780 revealed in Americans' attachment to independence a desperation that went beyond hostility to British rule. The character of independence still mattered as much as the achievement of it. Unless the winning of the war proved the virtuous strength of the whole people, independence might soon be lost through the revolutionaries' inability to sustain it. Or, if the United States survived, it would become like other countries whose populace lapsed in virtue—a nation managed by its corruption, with no hope for the blessed future once promised to America. These concerns prevailed as widely in America as profiteering, self-indulgence, and graft. Thus, when reverses began, the revolutionaries' alarm expressed more than a fear that they might lose the war; it revealed a determination to prove that wartime lapses had not killed public virtue and lost the promised land.

The heightened desperation in the revolutionaries' fight for independence may help us to understand the violence of the civil war within the war against Britain. The battle between loyalist and revolutionary forces at King's Mountain on October 7, 1780, showed in its bitterness how deep ran the revolutionaries' hostility toward native-born betrayers of America.[51] And this organized combat of militia and provincial forces was not the worst. In New York and New Jersey between 1777 and 1782 and in North and South Carolina and Georgia between 1780 and 1782, revolutionaries and loyalists waged an intermittent, vicious vendetta war. South Carolina suffered the most from its internal divisions. A South Carolina loyalist said that "the whole province resembled a piece of patch work, the inhabitants of every settlement, when united in sentiment being in arms for the side they liked best and making continual inroads into one anothers settlements."[52] These people were usually civilians or irregular forces who carried out successive reprisal killings. One South Carolina legislator had twenty-five notches in the barrel of his pistol.[53] Old family and local hostilities became part of the bitterness, and the cruelty bore no resemblance to the polite formalities that were supposed to be part of eighteenth-century warfare. In January 1781, after he had taken command in the South, Nathanael Greene wrote back to headquarters, "The Whigs and Tories persecute each other, with little less than savage fury. There is nothing but murders and devastations in every quarter."[54] Greene's aide spoke even more vividly: "Such scenes of desolation, bloodshed and deliberate murder I never was a witness to before! . . . The two opposite principles of whiggism and toryism have set the people of this country to cutting each other's throats, and scarce a day passes but some poor deluded tory is put to death at his door. For want of civil government the bands of society are totally disunited, and the people, by copying the manners of the British, have become perfectly savage."[55]

These killings literally enacted loyalists' and revolutionaries' rhetorical denunciations of each other as agents of evil. Such violence showed the hatred that could not stop short of the victory of one side by the subjugation or eradication of the other. After the British had taken Charleston, many South Carolinians had sworn loyalty to the king. But when the British tried to force these people to fight for the king, the South Carolinians revealed their true loyalties and resisted the British army. The fervor of their piecemeal resistance, their murderous suppression of loyalism, and their refusal to allow others the kind of cautious disengagement they had wanted the British to allow them suggest that the South Carolinians' commitment to independence long preceded the arrival of the British army. Some men's temporary collaboration with the enemy, like the lapsing of other revolutionaries' public virtue, temptingly offered surcease from war's sacrifice but suddenly left them more vulnerably exposed to an enemy grown more threatening. At least for a moment, perhaps, each collaborator stood alone with the fear that his traffic with the British had left him in isolation to face the redoubled assault of the enemy he should have fought from the start. Faced with such isolation and weakness, it is little wonder that, under the influence of long-standing familial and regional ties, revolutionaries quickly and persistently sought strength through communal resistance. Giving no quarter, they enforced with blood the conformity in which lay their best security against invasion, treason, and secret apostasy. Four days before Greene's letter to headquarters, a British officer in the field near Camden wrote, "The People of this Part of America, are infinitely more violent in their Resentments, and prejudices against England, and their determin'd Resolution more fixed to be separated from Us for ever and continue for ever our Enemies, than any other part of this Continent I have yet seen. The violence of the Passions of these People, are beyond every curb of Religion, and Humanity, they are unbounded, and every Hour exhibits, dreadfull, wanton Mischiefs, Murders, and Violences of every kind, unheard of before."[56] Although this conflict involved only a fraction of the American populace, it shows how deeply the passion for independence ran in revolutionaries who were spared this severe a test.

The South Carolinians who temporarily acceded to British conquest were not the only Americans who wavered in the face of force. Some people continued to live in the devastated areas between the lines, where they survived by fearful apathy. In this no-man's-land, revolutionary and loyalist irregulars used robbery and brutality to advance their cause and themselves. It may often have been hard to tell them from the bandits who plundered and murdered indiscriminately.[57] The people who neither fled nor fought in the midst of this rapine adopted a defensive expediency best described by Timothy Dwight's memory of Westchester County, New York, in the autumn of 1777. Furniture stolen or broken, houses damaged or decayed, fences burnt or thrown down, cattle gone, fields and roads in weeds—amid all this, people "feared every body whom they saw; and loved nobody. . . . To every question they gave such an answer, as would please the enquirer; or, if they despaired of pleasing, such an one, as would not provoke him. Fear was, apparently, the only passion, by which they were animated. The power of volition seemed to have deserted them. They were not civil, but obsequious; not obliging, but subservient. They yielded with a kind of apathy, and very quietly, what you asked, and what they supposed it impossible for them to retain. . . . Both their countenances, and their motions, had lost every trace of animation and of feeling. Their features were smoothed, not into serenity, but apathy; and instead of being settled in the attitude of quiet thinking, strongly indicated, that all thought, beyond what was merely instinctive, had fled their minds forever."[58] Similarly, in 1782, Nathanael Greene's aide, Major William Pierce, reported that in the Carolinas, the "people of both these Southern States have passed through a variety of changes and a choice of difficulties and misfortunes. . . . The principles of men get warped in searching after a circumspect mode of conduct to avoid the censure of the contending parties." However, Pierce could now say that "the people throughout the whole country appear to be our friends."[59]

Americans often switched from accommodation to partisan violence, from apathy to rage, especially in response to the British army's movements. Perhaps both quiescence and ardor were responses to fear. We can compare these responses to the widespread lapse of the war effort from 1778 to 1780, a different manifestation of apathy. Faced with an occupying army or with the unchecked cruelty in a zone neither royal nor republican, some Americans hoped to escape the threats of partisans and the dangers of partisanship by giving no offense. Similarly, after three years of high mortality in the army and unprecedented wartime dangers and demands, many revolutionaries sought refuge from the war in their belief that its end was near. Like the trimmers who were selfish enough to save themselves, the revolutionaries who were tired of the war looked out for themselves by profiting from it. Accommodation to the powerful, seeking to be left alone, protecting or amassing property—these suggest a fear of struggle. But the threat of subjugation aroused an even deeper fear: that one would lose the ability to struggle. Apathy, expediency, and selfishness could endanger survival even more than foreign enemies did because the fatal consequences of such weakness were inevitable and widespread. The rhetorical and physical violence with which revolutionaries changed from apathy to engagement indicates earlier and stronger origins for their fervor than simply British military provocations like the invasions of New Jersey and South Carolina. Perhaps only the fear of deserving a tyrant could exceed the fear of fighting one.

To best understand the change from quiescence to belligerence, we should not confuse apathy with neutrality. An American who wanted armies to leave him alone while he enjoyed the fruits of independence differed sharply from a person who did not care whether Britain or America won the war. The entire British effort to tighten imperial administration—through taxation, parliamentary regulation, more power for royal officials, or military force—attacked Americans' desire to be left alone. As a loyalist wrote in South Carolina's *Royal Gazette* after the British occupation of Charleston, "I can scarce refrain from smiling at the simplicity of the common saying of many of our people in this province to the British troops, 'if you will not meddle with us, we will not meddle with you,'—Can they suppose . . . that Britain will tamely give up her colonies, purchased at the expence of so much blood and treasure."[60] Even when the revolutionaries could not draw large numbers of men and large amounts of supplies from the countryside, they could move through it freely and, in most cases, control any loyalists. But the British, even when they did not meet effective resistance, could not exert effective control. Americans' wish to be left alone made most of the continent hostile to the British, even when that hostility did not move people to bear arms.

Some scholars have suggested that the continent contained large numbers of neutrals during the war.[61] The revolutionaries claimed, however, that the supposed neutrals were selfish equivocators who had secret sympathies. The Americans most often mistaken for neutrals were probably revolutionaries who wanted the fruits of independence without the violence of war. Governor William Livingston denounced "the sculking Neutral, who, leaving to others the Heat and Burden of the Day, means in the final Result to reap the Fruits of that Victory for which he will not contend."[62] The danger that alarmed revolutionaries was not large numbers of indifferent Americans but Americans moved by the desire for gain without risk in a war whose outcome had long seemed certain. The prospect of losing the war because too few people wanted independence worried the revolutionaries far less than the prospect of harboring among the victors those who had awaited victory in order to exploit it. The revolutionaries did not fear neutrality so much as they feared expediency. Expediency and apathy threatened the survival of independence through internal weakness—the inaction of Americans who wanted freedom but not war, gain but not sacrifice. The neutral who took no part in the war matched his principles of detachment with his uncommitted conduct. The apathetic revolutionary who took no part in the war evaded the demands of revolutionary principles but did not repudiate them. In 1780, when the consequences of apathy began to threaten the survival of revolutionary virtue, Americans' fervent reaction suggests that neutrals had been far fewer than backsliders.

Between May and October of 1780 the popular expectation of imminent victory received three sharp blows: the surrender of Charleston, South Carolina, to the British on May 12; the rout of Horatio Gates's southern army at Camden, South Carolina, on August 16; and the defection of General Benedict Arnold to the British on September 25. The loss of Charleston sent more Americans into captivity than any other defeat of the war—2,571 Continentals and about 800 militia and citizens. Three months later, Americans suffered their bloodiest battlefield defeat of the war at Camden, where 1,050 men were killed or wounded. Gates had arrived with 3,050 Continentals and militia. After the battle, only about 700 reported for duty at the rendezvous.

Congress had given Gates the southern command against the known wishes of Washington, partly because of Gates's reputation for inspiring the populace to support the Continentals, as he had done in capturing Burgoyne. On the day of battle at Camden, Gates put his North Carolina and Virginia militia in the center and on the left. They alone outnumbered the whole British force. But they ran without firing a shot, and that night Gates found himself sixty miles from the battlefield. Three months later, some Virginia militiamen explained their conduct. After describing their lack of training and their fatigue, they concluded, "Panic-Struck by the Noise and Terror of a Battle which was entirely New to most of us; We . . . were so unhappy as to abandon the Field of Battle."[63]

Similarly, although General Benjamin Lincoln probably could not have taken his force out of Charleston before the siege without being defeated in the field, his decision to defend the city also relied on South Carolinians' promises to fight to the end. The civilians of Charleston were among the first to favor surrender. Mercy Otis Warren later explained, "The conduct of the citizens of Charleston cannot be accounted for, but from the momentary panic to which the human mind is liable, when sudden danger presses, before it has time to collect its own fortitude, and to act with decision and dignity, consistent with previous principles."[64] Soon many South Carolinians swore loyalty to the king and took British documents of "protection," expecting to be left alone in return for not opposing occupation.[65] Thus, the two defeats not only wiped out a large part of the Continental Army but also showed how little the populace could count on its own firmness in battle in the face of a British offensive. Were Americans losing the ability to defend themselves? What influence could so undermine native courage? Revolutionaries knew that native courage accompanied public virtue and that both were most often lost through surrender to corruption.

Finally, Benedict Arnold had almost succeeded in selling the most important fort in America, West Point, to the British by betraying his own command there. Americans thought, too, that he had tried to help the British capture George Washington. Despite their pride in getting the enemy into the woods or controlling all the territory outside of British lines, the revolutionaries still reacted most strongly to the loss of set battles and fixed posts, such as Fort Washington, Fort Ticonderoga, and Philadelphia. West Point had long seemed to be the impregnable security for communication between New England and the rest of the continent. We can hardly appreciate the depth of their shock when Americans realized how close they had come to losing the fort and the commander in chief by betrayal. In 1780 Washington's army had suffered a more severe winter with greater supply problems than at Valley Forge and had continued to go hungry in the summer and fall. Relying on the states to provide supplies had left the army weaker than ever. The threat of disbandment remained constant, and Washington could not undertake an autumn campaign in 1780. Arnold's plot dramatized the army's weakness. The losses and the near-loss challenged the expectation of imminent victory and called into question the assumptions about American strength on which such an expectation had partly rested.

The newspapers of the war years contained comparatively little discussion of the war through much of 1778, all of 1779, and the early months of 1780. Then, in June 1780, and in the following months, an outpouring of articles filled the columns, calling revolutionaries to renew their lapsed effort to support the army and expel the British. Both in newspapers and in private correspondence people said that the loss of Charleston might do more good than harm if it awoke Americans to win their independence, which remained far from secure. The idea of awakening recurred often because many writers described the public spirit of the previous two years as sunk in a long sleep. Seeing through their mistaken security and selfishness, Americans would regenerate their army with new recruits and reenlistments, as well as with pay and supplies and the help of militia. These could best come from a popular willingness to place the war effort ahead of personal security for life and property—that is, from public virtue.

These appeals did not revive the *rage militaire* of 1775, but they did represent a widespread wish for such a revival. Knowing that the most common and most important decisions of the later war years dealt not with allegiance to independence but with the character of independence, the revolutionaries feared not so much losing the war as losing the virtue that gave the war its purpose. They partly expressed this fear in a recurring nostalgia for the spirit of 1775. Almost everyone who talked about the beginning of the war contrasted Americans' early ardor and unselfishness with the meanness of later years. General Jedidiah Huntington, in May 1780, anticipated the French army's disgust at the Americans' ill-supplied army and greedy populace: "Is it not a possible Thing to revive the Feelings which pervaded every Breast in the Commencement of the War, when every Man considered the Fate of his Country as depending on his own Exertions."[66]

The call for a revival of public support for the war in 1780 and the later celebrations of Yorktown and of peace tried to reclaim the conviction that the revolution owed its success to Americans' unified virtuous efforts. But these attempts first to overcome, then to forget, the weaknesses and divisions during the war—even if successful—could not fully recover the spirit of 1775, because that spirit had assumed that Americans were fighting to escape or defeat such wartime selfishness. The spirit of 1775 was not just supposed to revive from time to time or to share American character with vices that might sometimes prevail. Rather, the spirit of 1775 was supposed to be the American character. From Chester County, Pennsylvania, "I.C." wrote in April 1779, denouncing the pride, greed, and luxury that had arisen in the last four years: "O ye heroes of America, was it to obtain an unlimited restraint to such licentiousness that ye drew your swords, and rushed to victory with such military prowess! . . . Or have we bid farewell to common sense itself, as well as the character under that name, that we are willing to sacrifice all that is precious . . . only to have it in our power to gratify a few moments of the most precarious pleasures of sense; or at best to hoard up a heap of yellow dust. . . . O that God would raise up, and send on the American stage, some Addison, Tillotson or Whitefield; or rather, someone in the spirit and power of an Elijah, to turn the hearts of the children to the fathers, and the disobedient to the righteousness of the just, and thus prepare us a people for the Lord our God."[67]

The true spirit of 1775 was one of anticipation rather than accomplishment. The revolutionaries had believed that they were passionately united in willingness to sacrifice, in innate strength, in aspiration to achieve permanent continental happiness. When they looked back to 1775, they could remember not so much what they had done as how they had felt. They rightly believed that this feeling of anticipation gave the crucial impetus to revolutionary effort throughout the war. They did not want to stop seeing this spirit as a constant source of American success and instead see it as an unattainable ideal or as a set of values that needed the corrupt aid of worldly devices in order to survive. Consequently, while the revolutionaries were persevering in their war and enjoying their independence with many departures from their ideal of public virtue, they cherished their original picture of themselves. In the revival of newspaper appeals after the fall of Charleston, one writer warned, "In times of public danger like the present, I hold every species of inaction of the nature of treason."[68] Inaction had prevailed before the crises of 1780, just as fear had spread during the advance of Burgoyne in 1777. If fear and inaction were treason, who were the traitors?

During the Revolutionary War, Doctor Benjamin Rush observed a variant of the mental illness that he knew as hypochondriac madness or "tristimania." The popular names for this variant were "tory rot" and "protection fever." But these names were misleading. Rush called the special disorder "Revolutiana." It did not affect active loyalists; rather, it was "confined exclusively to those friends of Great Britain, and to those timid Americans, who took no public part in the war." The sufferer's derangement was induced "by the real or supposed distresses of his country." The characteristic mental symptom of tristimania was "distress," manifested in delusions such as these: the victim believed that he had "consumption, cancer, stone, and above all . . . impotence, and the venereal disease"; he believed that he was an animal, that he had an animal in his body, or that he had inherited the soul of an animal; he believed that he had no soul; he believed that he would drown the world with his urine; he believed that he was made of glass; he believed that he was dead. Rush observed that "all the erroneous opinions persons affected with this form of derangement entertain of themselves are of a degrading nature. . . . But the most awful symptom of this disease remains yet to be mentioned, and that is DESPAIR." According to Rush, "many of them died" of protection fever—in some cases during exile or confinement, in some cases by "seeking relief from spirituous liquors"—but "the disease . . . passed away with the events of the American revolution." In peacetime it was hard to remember anyone who had not been an active partisan. When Rip Van Winkle came down out of the Catskills after sleeping through the Revolutionary War, his daughter did not recognize him. She thought that long ago her father had shot himself or had been carried away by Indians.

Rush knew only two remedies for protection fever. The first was "to avoid reading news-papers, and conversing upon political subjects, and thereby to acquire a total ignorance of public events." If the sufferer objected to that remedy, "he should be advised to take a part in the disputes which divide his fellow citizens." The revolution, Rush said, was like the breath of garlic eaters. Anyone who did not want to be offended by it had to eat and stink with the rest. By "imbibing a portion of party spirit, we become insensible of the vices and follies of our associates in politics, and thus diminish . . . this source of hypochondriacal derangement."[69]

Of course, Rush's observations of mental illness did not describe all revolutionaries, since most took some active part in the contest. However, the expressions of reawakened zeal in 1780, which denounced the preceding two years of sleep and which climaxed in the public's reaction to the treason of Benedict Arnold, revealed the disquiet caused by the corruption within the revolution. By pillorying Arnold, Americans seemed to be trying to prove that such corruption did not exist or that it could be extirpated. In their choice of words and rituals for the denunciation of the worst American traitor, they drew on their concern about their own betrayal of their highest revolutionary ideals. If we can liken their distress over the widespread shortcomings among revolutionaries to suffering from protection fever, we can say that in the revival of war rhetoric in 1780 and especially in the reaction to Arnold's treason, the revolutionaries tried Rush's second remedy on themselves.

The victims of protection fever were not neutrals; they had clear sympathies, but they did not want to be linked with the wartime distresses that the active people on their side were helping to cause. So they tried to remain detached, but their illness gave them the delusion that, in spite of their detachment from the evils of war, their bodies or their souls harbored some malignancy or fragility that became an obsession. Active revolutionaries often proclaimed that they were escaping the selfishness that would have enslaved them if they had collaborated with British corruption. When widespread self-seeking began to look irreversible—capped by unprecedented military defeats and the treason of the most successful battlefield general on the American side—the revolutionaries focused on the corruption of one man whose ruin would signify the defeat of corruption within the revolution. These accusations palliated, for a while, the awareness that some of Arnold's traits ran deep in the American Revolution.

The reaction to Arnold's treason revealed that in his crimes, as in his achievements, he shared many attributes with his countrymen. Even while they tried to disavow him with their denunciation, his selfish guilt continued to rankle in their minds. If the hero Arnold could betray the cause and come so near to ruining it, what security did America have? Light-Horse Harry Lee told Anthony Wayne, "I cannot rid my soul of the curses. . . . Have any other detection, have more conspirators come out[?]"[70] To study Arnold's character was to see the frightening ease with which virtue could be perverted.

Arnold's character—which thousands thought they knew so well when they heard him called a hero, and again when they heard him called a viper—remains hard to grasp.[71] He sought extremes: the highest rank, the hardest march, the hottest combat, the most luxurious social display, the coolest secret calculation, the most decisive act of the war, the highest possible price. Whatever satisfaction those extremes seemed to promise always eluded him. Arnold received high praise for his energetic and animating command at Fort Ticonderoga, in Canada, on Lake Champlain, and at the battles of Saratoga. Washington singled him out for a personal gift of epaulettes and sword knots as a token of esteem and offered him command of a wing of the army in 1780. Newspaper articles written under the pen name of "Monsieur De Lisle" late in 1777 and early in 1778 told Americans that Arnold "is said to possess what we call, in our country, the 'rage militair.'"[72]

But two problems dogged Arnold: money and promotion. Charges of plunder and graft followed him from Canada and reached a peak after his command of liberated Philadelphia in 1778. At the instigation of Pennsylvania state authorities, he was court-martialed in 1779 on several charges and convicted of using wagons in public service to transport his own merchandise. He was sentenced to a reprimand, which Washington made as close to a compliment for Arnold's other services as he could. In fact, Arnold had used his authority over city commerce to profit his own secret investments in British manufactured goods. Contemporaries suspected as much because of his lavish expenditures, but they could not prove it. He earned the enmity of Pennsylvanians by his arrogant exercise of military authority, his aristocratic social display, and his preference for the company of rich Philadelphians who had collaborated with the enemy during the British occupation of the city. He married one of them. His wartime extravagance mirrored his career as a merchant before the war, when he had built one of the biggest houses in New Haven, Connecticut. Now, as ever, Arnold's tastes outran his graft, and he needed more money. He pursued military status with comparable ardor. He had begun his wartime career in a dispute over rank with Ethan Allen. At Saratoga, he quarreled with Gates, who gave him no command. Arnold then went into battle on his own and was shot in the same leg that had been wounded at Quebec. Due partly to the apportionment of general officer appointments among the states and partly to some delegates' aversion to Arnold's ambition, Congress, in February 1777, had promoted five junior brigadier generals over his head to major general. Only after his service against a British raid on Danbury, Connecticut, was Arnold promoted to major general, and only after Saratoga was his seniority over the other five generals restored. As the British learned when they got him, no rank or income could match Arnold's claims.

One kind of phrase recurred in Arnold's vocabulary—"Conscious of the rectitude of my intentions"; "conscious of my own innocency and integrity."[73] He gave himself his head in everything he undertook and treated all opposition, whether an overdue challenge to his graft or a snub of his military prowess, as an attack on his integrity. In practice, his integrity amounted to nothing more than his indulgence of his will. After defecting to the British, he did not deign to pretend that he had changed his mind about the political ideas at stake in the war. When he began to praise the British constitution and deplore the Americans' French alliance, he claimed to be consistent with his former praise of American liberty, for which he had fought against Britain. The righteous side was the side he favored. However, such favor had a price. Arnold secretly negotiated with Sir Henry Clinton over a sixteen-month period before he got the right price and the right command to betray. In the meantime, he sent pieces of intelligence as gestures of good faith. Finally, he agreed to surrender West Point for £20,000. After the Americans captured Clinton's emissary, Major John André, and Arnold fled to New York City, the British still paid him £6,000, plus £525 expenses and pensions for himself and his family. His wife had earned hers by aiding his treason. Carl Van Doren has summarized the deal: "No other American officer made as much money out of the war as Arnold did."[74]

By any standard—moral, political, or psychological—Arnold's behavior was selfish and destructive. The British gave him rank and money but no command comparable to the one he had tried to sell to them. One would expect the Americans to have been at least as bitter as the British were prudent. Understandably, shock, denunciation, and the desire to punish followed this treason. But Americans saw more than a criminal in Arnold—they saw a freak. He was not just a deserter or an assassin on a grand scale; he was an aberration in nature. Yet they did not find ready consolation in his uniqueness. "Somehow or other," General Henry Knox's aide wrote, "I cannot get Arnold out of my head."[75] Arnold's rotten heart made him more vivid and harder to dismiss. Nathanael Greene said of him, "How black, how despised, loved by none, and hated by all. Once his Country's Idol, now her horror."[76] There were many simple explanations of the man: Arnold was greedy; Arnold was ambitious; Arnold had been vicious since birth; Arnold had sold himself to Satan; Arnold was mad. But the clarity of the explanations did not lead Americans from horror to insight and then to fuller reliance on their own refusal to sell out. Instead, when they spoke of Arnold, such certainty only intensified their horror. An open letter in the *Pennsylvania Packet* gave up trying to show him as he was and said to Arnold, "I took up my pen with an intent to shew a reflective glass, wherein you might at one view behold your actions; but soon found such a horrid ugly deformity in the out lines of your picture, that I was frightened at the sight, so the mirrour dropped and broke to pieces! each of which discovered you to be a gigantick overgrown monster, of such a variety of shapes, all over ulcerated, that it is in vain to attempt to describe them."[77] People seldom proposed specific plans to capture Arnold or kill him; nor did they write him off as only a pitiful homeless malcontent. They did not try hard to devise new ways to thwart potential traitors. There could be only one Arnold, and when his countrymen talked about him, that is what they said—over and over, in exhaustive detail and fervent imagery —there could be only one Arnold.

Eight days after Arnold's flight, the adjutant general of the Continental Army, Colonel Alexander Scammell, wrote, "Treason! Treason! Treason! black as hell! That a man so high on the list of fame should be guilty as Arnold, must be attributed not only to original sin, but actual transgressions. . . . We were all astonishment, each peeping at his next neighbor to see if any treason was hanging about him: nay, we even descended to a critical examination of ourselves. This surprise soon settled down into a fixed detestation and abhorrence of Arnold, which can receive no addition."[78] The next day a British intelligence report said that the Americans' reaction to the treason revealed "their distrust of themselves."[79] Among his countrymen, Benedict Arnold reached the limits of ignominy in 1783 when Silas Deane cut him dead socially in London.[80] To be cast out by an outcast was the just fate of a fallen American. Among others, opinion differed. The British made Arnold a brigadier general. When Lafayette heard this, he said, "There is no accounting for taste. . . ."[81]

Washington and Jefferson each approved an attempt to capture Arnold—once while he was in New York City and once while he was leading an invasion of Virginia. Jefferson drafted an authorization to kill Arnold as a last resort but then changed his mind.[82] Americans said that if they caught Arnold, they would hang him, then cut off the leg that had been wounded in the service of America, bury the leg with full military honors, and hang the rest of the body on a gibbet.[83] A public demonstration acted out this distinction with Arnold's effigy. The revolutionaries frequently said that the failure of Arnold's plot showed God's providential protection of General Washington and the United States; Americans seemed to hope that the defeat of Arnold's conspiracy would enable them to amputate from the righteous cause all that he stood for.

A year after the treason, the *New Jersey Journal* recalled that "the streets of every city and village in the United States, for many months, rung with the crimes of General Arnold."[84] In New Milford, Connecticut, hundreds of inhabitants paraded figures of Arnold and Satan through the illuminated town to the sound of firecrackers. The effigy was hanged, cut down, and buried. In Norwich, Connecticut, a crowd destroyed the tombstone of Arnold's father. To celebrate the victory at Yorktown, people in Newburgh, New York, burned Arnold in effigy. Within days of his flight to the British, Philadelphians paraded a two-faced effigy of Arnold, on which the head constantly turned, while behind him stood the devil, offering a bag of gold and holding a pitchfork to prod him into hell. At the end of the route, the effigy was burned—though, as a Quaker woman noticed, the newspapers said that the fire had consumed Arnold.[85] A five-year-old boy in Philadelphia—a refugee from Charleston—knew and remembered Arnold's crime by seeing on the cover of an almanac the picture of a double-faced Arnold shadowed by the devil with tempting gold and threatening dart.[86]

Arnold represented the worst crimes against virtue. Revolutionaries who had held him high among patriots now decided that his entire career showed a fixed, desperate hunger for riches. Even while undertaking large crimes of extortion and treason for huge sums, he would also cheat soldiers of their pay and embezzle petty amounts of army stores. Now Americans could see the truth and tell Arnold that

Thy public life was but a specious show
A cloke to secret wickedness and shame. . . .
Hence thou hast lurk'd beneath the fair disguise
Of *freedom's* champion, *mammon's* sordid slave. . . . [87]

A newspaper published Beelzebub's letter of instruction to Arnold. His "INFERNAL MAJESTY" commanded, "We expect that you will . . . put an end, by a capital stroke, to all the pretensions of that people, and we flatter ourselves that after their subjection they will be in a few years as corrupted, as wicked, as cruel as their mother country."[88] How else but by his double face could so many of Arnold's countrymen have spoken him so fair while he was so systematically corrupt? Fortunately, America was too virtuous to satisfy his lust for opulence. His was a greed that Britain and Satan had created and that only they could reward.

Nor had Arnold's combat services shown him to be a virtuous leader. One version said that he had never been brave but was a coward at heart; another said that Americans could allow him bravery because even bandits and assassins had a sort of bravery; another said that he had bravery but not courage—that is, animal spirits but not moral character. The valor of General Richard Montgomery, ending in death at Quebec, would live eternally, while Arnold's weakness would make him infamous to posterity. Revolutionaries agreed that Arnold's supposed valor had really been an unreliable giddiness, brought on by drunkenness or mental unbalance. Such violence revealed innate depravity, not native courage.

Beginning within days of his flight to the British, Arnold's countrymen began to make their most frequent and most eloquent comment about him: he must be feeling an agonized remorse. He would, they prayed, despair and die. Like Judas, he would hang himself. Or he would bear the mark of Cain. And an American mark of Cain on Arnold, unlike God's mark on Cain, meant that the first person who saw the traitor would kill him.[89] The revolutionaries gave their evil effigy of Arnold the capacity for remorse. In this quality it differed most from the man himself. There is no evidence that Arnold felt repentance for his treason, and much evidence that he felt none. He was, in Carl Van Doren's words, "the Iago of traitors."[90] Yet the surest and worst punishment revolutionaries could imagine for Arnold—the torture they knew he could not escape—was a life of guilt. After a career of pretending to be uniquely courageous while he was weak, of professing virtuous patriotism while he cheated his countrymen, of proclaiming innocence and integrity while he negotiated surrender to mammon, what fate could await him but the lifelong horror of realizing that he had betrayed God's cause?[91]

Private Samuel Downing was in the New Hampshire Regiment at Tappan, New York, when Arnold defected. In 1863, when Downing was one hundred years old, an interviewer asked him about Arnold. The old man's memory had changed the facts, but the revolutionaries in 1780 would have approved of the reaction to Arnold's treason that Downing gave to posterity: "he ought to have been true. We had true men then; 'twasn't as it is now. Everybody was true: the tories we'd killed or driven to Canada."[92]

CHAPTER VII
Division

The revolutionaries' ability to convince themselves that the public virtue of 1775 could survive among the populace exceeded their ability to convince the Continental Army. The year 1780 worsened the relations between the soldiers and their society, fostering a hostility that was relieved neither by adversity nor by victory. Despite sporadic voluntary efforts, like the temporary relief of shortages at Valley Forge or the women's charity drive in 1780, Continentals knew that the public's negligence lay at the heart of the army's hardship. Soldiers saw the agricultural plenty of a country that yet yielded them little pay and a marginal supply of food. They blamed not just the army's quartermasters and commissaries, but also the populace that had deserted the defenders of the cause.

A clear theme of material self-interest ran through this friction between soldiers and civilians. Soldiers sought bounties, pay, food, clothing, and support for their families. Officers also sought pensions. Civilians sought to avoid expense and to make money from the war more often than contribute money to it. Each group could increase its proceeds only at the expense of the other. Closely intertwined within this conflict of interests were conflicting claims to public virtue. No less than the guilt of greed and the guilt of bargaining for military service, the reproaches over faltering virtue underlay the increasing hostility between the army and citizens at home.

The year 1780 began with mutinies in the Continental Line and bequeathed worse ones to the first month of 1781. Using promises and force, Continental or state authorities ended all of these mutinies without remedying the soldiers' main grievances. The conditions in which soldiers' families lived became a constant source of discontent in the army and contributed to the soldiers' distress, which often threatened and sometimes ended in mutiny. A substantial minority of soldiers—in some states, perhaps one-fifth—were married, and their inability to support their families troubled them more than their own sufferings.[1] When currency depreciation accelerated, most states enacted special provisions for soldiers' families, usually requiring local authorities to provide food for them at the old price, with tax money paying the difference between the going price and the families' fixed price. Some plans called for direct gifts of food in the absence of soldiers' pay, the accounts between soldiers and the state to be balanced when pay was settled. But a strong current of public resistance impaired or defeated the intent of these laws. Massachusetts required soldiers to spend all of their bounty money at the going price for food before their families were entitled to special prices. Some local officials did not implement the law at all. A letter to the editor of the *Connecticut Courant* asked, "How is it that the poor soldier's wives in many of our towns go from door to door, begging a supply of the necessaries of life at the stipulated prices, and are turned away, notwithstanding the solemn agreements of the towns to supply such?"[2]

Wives' letters urging their husbands to come home described the suffering. Such pleas caused some married men to desert, others to refuse to reenlist, and all to hold a grudge against the niggardly government and citizens of their home state. By the end of 1776, when soldiers' wives were already facing extortionate prices, Eliphalet Wright warned, "As affairs are now going on, the common soldiers have nothing to expect, but that if America maintain her independency, they must become slaves to the rich."[3] Soldiers who disobeyed orders in order to compensate for the public's neglect of the army did so in vain. In 1779 Sergeant Samuel Glover was executed for leading a mutiny in the North Carolina Line in which he, on behalf of "His Brother soldiers"—unpaid for fifteen months—"demanded their pay, and refused to obey the Command of his superior Officer, and would not march till they had justice done them." His widow told the General Assembly of North Carolina that "the poor soldiers" were "possessed of the same attachment and affection to their Families as those in command." Because men knew that their families would suffer without subsistence, "a General Clamor arose among the common soldiery," and Glover "fell an unhappy victim to the hard but perhaps necessary Law of his Country." Ann Glover wanted the state to give her and her children an annual income. She apologized to the Assembly for her husband's conduct, but she begged leave to "ask you what must the Feeling of the Man be who fought at Brandywine, at Germantown, and at Stony Point and did his duty, and when on another March in defence of his Country, with Poverty staring him full in the face, he was denied his Pay?" The great majority of soldiers who continued to serve without pay and without mutiny would have agreed with Ann Glover's ungrammatical but forceful statement: "Allegiance to our Country and obedience to those in authority, but the spirit of a man will shrink from his Duty when his Services are not paid and Injustice oppresses him and his Family."[4]

Although some states had already voted adjustments of soldiers' depreciated pay and back pay still due, the most important negotiations and settlements occurred in 1780. This was both the year of the worst depreciation and the year in which the enlistments of most Continentals expired. Among other surrenders of responsibility, Congress charged each state to pay its own Continental Line. Most states reached agreements with their soldiers, but the settlements intensified rather than allayed the conflict between soldiers and civilians. Legislators and officers accused each other of bad faith in the negotiations. The soldiers could legally threaten to disband by not reenlisting, a tactic that officials regarded as extortion. Some states first tried to deduct the enlistment bounties from the amount of back pay owed to soldiers and then relented under pressure; they achieved neither goodwill nor economy.

Soldiers felt cheated by the method of payment, even when it was the full amount, legally tendered. States usually paid by establishing a table of depreciation that set the monthly value of the sinking money. This table showed the factor by which the pay should be multiplied in order to keep the compensation constant at its original value. After subtracting from the settlement any pay that soldiers had already received, the states computed the sum due to each man. This calculation obviously lowered the men's pay because further depreciation had lowered the value of the payments that were to compensate for earlier, lesser depreciation. Even then, states did not usually pay in currency but in interest-bearing certificates—in effect, promissory notes—redeemable after the end of the war. In theory, the soldiers could hold the certificates to maturity and receive the full sum, plus interest. In fact, the soldiers could not afford this involuntary investment of their wages because they needed money at once. Therefore, they sold the certificates at a large discount to investors who could pay a fraction of the face value in cash. These speculators stood to realize profits of several hundred percent when the certificates were paid off. After the war, ex-soldiers in Massachusetts wound up paying taxes to redeem those certificates for the speculators, thereby paying twice for the privilege of receiving a small part of their army pay in cash.

State governments resorted to this method because they could not get enough currency from their citizens by taxation. The states' eagerness to settle with their soldiers for the lowest possible sum may suggest to us—and certainly suggested to the soldiers—that the public was unwilling to pay taxes in order to pay the army. Consequently, the soldiers' resentment focused not just on the speculators—a group that included Continental Army officers and state officials—but also on the civilian public. In August 1780, General Alexander McDougall told a committee of Congress that the war had ceased to be a vindication of republicanism and had become a war "for Empire and Liberty to a people whose object is Property. . . . The army expects some of that property which the citizen seeks, and which the army protects for him."[5] This grievance against civilians underlay the mutinies against the authority of army officers, even when other grievances against the officers were also motivating the soldiers. In Ann Glover's recitation of the battles in which her husband had fought, as well as through the conduct of soldiers in other mutinies, we can see the pride of veterans who were asserting not their hatred of army service on behalf of the revolution but their claim to respect and reward for their public virtue.

The winter of 1779/1780 was extremely cold—the worst since the famous winter of 1740/1741. The ground and the rivers froze deep, the snow piled high, and the temperature stayed low night and day for days running. The British could drive horse-drawn sleds from Manhattan to Staten Island. The Continentals wintered at Morristown, New Jersey, where they suffered more than at Valley Forge. The long-standing problems of supply were compounded by impassable roads. Washington was probably more surprised to see the army stay together than he would have been to see the soldiers disband.

In fact, three mutinies occurred during the first six months of 1780—one on January 1 in the Massachusetts Line at West Point, one on May 25 in the Connecticut Line at Morristown, and one in June in the New York Line at Fort Schuyler. At West Point, one hundred Massachusetts Continentals decided that their three-year enlistments ought to end on January 1, 1780, even though most of them had enlisted several months after January 1, 1777. They were brought back to West Point; some were punished, and the rest were pardoned.

Early in May, a committee of Congress visiting the camp near Morristown described the prolonged food shortage, worsened by state laws that prohibited the army from buying food because army purchases raised the prices civilians had to pay. Once the army had exhausted a state's quota of specific supplies, the commissaries had no recourse if other states remained delinquent. Even when distant states had supplies, the quartermasters had no money or forage for transport. To quiet the men, officers gave their meat rations to the soldiers and lived on bread and water, but "a spirit of discontent" threatened "some violent convulsion." British agents got handbills into camp, calling Americans "to fly from slavery and fraud" and "join your real friends who scorn to impose upon you, and who will receive you with open arms; kindly forgiving all your errors." Washington said that the address "had a considerable effect," but he agreed with the privates' claim that "they were truly patriotic, they loved their country, and they had already suffered everything short of death in its cause."[6] In addition to the fear of starvation, these soldiers complained of no pay for five months and no extra compensation for the depreciation of the money. When the Eighth and Fourth Connecticut regiments formed under arms thirty minutes after evening roll call on May 25—after "growling like sore headed dogs" all day—they intended to march for home, not the enemy, and would have "plundered for their sustenance on their way."[7] Before leaving camp they planned "to tear their Commissary to atoms."[8] The Pennsylvania Division was "instantly alarmed, got under arms," and backed Colonel Return Jonathan Meigs when he faced the mutineers.[9] Private Joseph Martin later said that the Pennsylvania troops surrounded the mutineers without knowing what they were doing and, upon learning of a mutiny, wanted to join it.[10] Martin was wrong: the mutineers could not even get the support of the other Connecticut troops, and a Pennsylvania officer noticed their "fear of having to deal with the Pennsylvania troops."[11] After Meigs's confrontation with a sergeant, the mutiny was over. The men dispersed to their huts and laid down their arms.

However, the soldiers did not become docile. Still hungry, they gathered in groups on the parade ground and spent the evening, according to Martin, "venting our spleen at our country and government, then at our officers, and then at ourselves for our imbecility in staying there and starving in detail for an ungrateful people who did not care what became of us, so they could enjoy themselves while we were keeping a cruel enemy from them."[12] Two Pennsylvania officers, Colonel Thomas Craig and Colonel Walter Stewart, came to talk to them. Stewart was popular with privates, and the Connecticut soldiers repeated their complaints about food and pay to him, adding, "We were unwilling to desert the cause of our country when in distress; that we knew her cause involved our own, but what signified our perishing in the act of saving her, when that very act would inevitably destroy us, and she must finally perish with us."[13] Stewart told the soldiers that officers would hear their complaints but were sharing their sufferings. He appealed to the soldiers' pride: "You know not how much you injure your own characters by such conduct. You Connecticut troops have won immortal honor to yourselves the winter past, by your perseverance, patience, and bravery, and now you are shaking it off at your heels."[14]

The most notable element of the mutiny was the ease with which it was overcome. Stewart, Craig, and Meigs reminded the soldiers "of their past good conduct . . . of the Objects for which they were contending."[15] And even though the mutineers replied that "their sufferings were too great; that they wanted present relief, and some present substantial recompence for their service," a supply of food—with continued intermittent shortages—was enough to keep them on duty.[16] Eventually, soldiers received some paper settlement of pay and depreciation. The mutineers were at a disadvantage because they believed in the cause and wanted to remain soldiers. Although they had grudges against officers and commissaries, they were trying to mutiny not so much against military authority as against the public, whom both they and their officers blamed for their distress. By going home, they would have gotten food, and they would have left the public to suffer the consequences of its heedlessness. As Private Martin recalled their dilemma, "What was to be done? Here was the army starved and naked, and there their country sitting still and expecting the army to do notable things while fainting from sheer starvation. All things considered, the army was not to be blamed."[17] Rather than demonstrating a fixed determination to leave the army, the soldiers revealed during the course of the mutiny a wish to stay with the army and to use its importance to the cause as a form of military pressure on civilian authority. But there was very little authority for them to exert pressure on. The soldiers wound up having to choose between complete rejection of the army and continued service with their complaints ill met. They stayed.

During the winter, Continentals did not always stay in camp and suffer, even while remaining in the army. They sometimes went out and stole from inhabitants. Some New Jersey farmers, knowing a good thing when they saw it, brought food to camp and sold it at extortionate prices. When Washington ordered a systematic forage of the surrounding counties and discreetly hinted at the consequences of not feeding the army, the magistrates and citizens cooperated generously by sending supplies to camp. This enabled Washington to obtain needed food directly from the civil authorities rather than taking it arbitrarily wherever he found it.

Ezekiel Cornell, former Continental Army officer and Rhode Island delegate in Congress, reported to his constituents from Morristown that Washington still worried that the soldiers would disband: "I want words to express the feeling manner in which he represented his distresses and his fears of the country being subjugated by the power of Britain. . . . Nothing can save us from destruction but a spirited exertion in the several states. . . . But when I take a view of the civil policy of the several states in the union, I almost despair of being able to make any vigorous exertions until there is a power vested in some man, or number of men obligatory and binding on all the states in the union."[18] In the last years of the war, the discontent of the army became a catalyst for political divisions among revolutionaries.

Seven months after the Connecticut soldiers' protest, men in the Pennsylvania Line began the most serious mutiny of the war. Besides the grievances they shared with other Continentals, Pennsylvania soldiers had complaints of their own. In 1777 the soldiers of the Pennsylvania Line had enlisted "for three years or during the war." Despite warnings that this ambiguity would cause misunderstanding, the terms of their enlistment were not defined until 1779. Anticipating the expiration of three years in 1780, soldiers began to argue that the wording had meant whichever came first. However, Washington and the Pennsylvania authorities treated the enlistments as a commitment for the duration of the war. Washington knew that the soldiers' interpretation was the customary and correct one, and he asked for a return differentiating "between those for *during the war* and those for *three years or during the war*." But, as Hamilton explained to Greene, "The General would have the matter kept out of the men's sight as much as possible; because it is expedient to interpret the alternative in favour of the public, even if it should be found adviseable to give the soldiers a *douceur*."[19]

The army adopted the expedient solution. In return for one hundred dollars, the soldiers agreed that they were signed for the duration of the war. However, Washington's verbal chicanery was multiplied severalfold by the time it reached the privates. The Pennsylvania officers used both force and fraud to sign soldiers the way the general wanted. A deserter told the British that "the Colonel of each Corps . . . gave—100 dollars to such as would reinlist for the War as a Present from the Congress, but those who refused were sent to the Guard House and whipped."[20] General Arthur St. Clair, senior officer of the Pennsylvania Line, had said in February that the soldiers were three-year men. By July he was glad to report that they were enlisted for the duration.[21] Both this disagreement over the terms of enlistment and the bad faith with which it was settled underlay the uprising in January 1781.

The winter of 1780/1781 had very mild weather, and the Continental soldiers fared better around Morristown than they had the year before. While the officers of the Pennsylvania Line were celebrating New Year's Day, and their commander, General Anthony Wayne, was turning thirty-six years old, several hundred soldiers under the leadership of sergeants seized artillery and persuaded or forced about fifteen hundred soldiers to march out of camp. They stopped in Princeton, New Jersey. In addition to the grievances that almost all soldiers had through most of the war, the Pennsylvania Line felt victimized by the settlement of their terms of enlistment in 1779. When Pennsylvania state authorities started paying gold bounties for new recruits and for reenlistments while the long-termers did not even receive their regular pay, many soldiers decided that their terms were up, whether they had enlisted for three years or had accepted the "douceur" in 1779 and signed for the duration. Most of the mutineers wanted to stay in the army and were eager to reenlist after the mutiny had been settled in their favor. They sought in mutiny the bounty money they believed they had been cheated out of when the three-year-or-duration issue had been resolved in 1779.[22]

The mutiny was ended not by Continental Army officers but by the state government under President Joseph Reed, who negotiated with a board of sergeants. Reed agreed to discharge all men who had enlisted for three years and to accept each man's word about his term of enlistment, rather than wait for the muster rolls to arrive. Of course, many soldiers lied, and the subsequent discharges temporarily disbanded the Pennsylvania Line. Several observers of the mutiny remarked that the soldiers held no grudge against their officers.[23] Perhaps this conclusion came from the men's expressions of esteem for Wayne and Colonel Walter Stewart or from the mutineers' failure to seize or execute officers indiscriminately. In fact, this conclusion was wishful thinking, for hostility between officers and enlisted men triggered the Pennsylvania Line's mutiny.

That mutiny revealed some of the consequences of a loss of unity among revolutionaries. The army had prided itself on attaining a solidarity in virtuous service that was a crucial guarantor of the security of the revolution. However, its solidarity faltered under the strain of the army's redoubled hardship: officers brutalized men, hoping to cow them and prevent revolt; men mutinied and assaulted their officers; soldiers faced each other as some mutinied while others did not, as mutineers forced reluctant men to join the uprising, as regiments from other states suppressed their fellow soldiers' protests. At the same time that the mutiny of the Pennsylvania and New Jersey lines revealed the violence with which divided revolutionaries could turn on each other, it also demonstrated the Continental Army's achievement in surviving despite such hostility.

The officers of the Pennsylvania Line imitated Mad Anthony Wayne's gaudiness, arrogance, and harshness without imitating his constant attention to the soldiers' physical welfare and professional pride. A strong current of hostility had run between officers and men for years. In its report on the January mutiny, the committee of Congress that had been appointed to consult with Reed wrote and then crossed out these words: "The inferior officers of the army should be directed in their treatment of the soldiers never to separate severity from justice and to temper severity with mercy."[24] After meeting the mutineers, Reed had written to the committee, "I am surprised to find that they entertained strong aversion to many of their former officers. . . ."[25] The soldiers told Reed and other civilians "tales . . . of severities and unobserved promises."[26] Many of the mutineers who, on paper, had reenlisted in 1779 for the duration of the war probably did not think of themselves as liars when they got their discharges in January 1781 by saying that they had been three-year men in 1779 when their officers had used force and threats to get the reenlistments or had falsely recorded men as having enlisted for the duration. To the mutineers, the enlistments had expired in 1780.

Several officers who had tried to stop the mutiny in its first moments by a show of individual force had been killed or wounded or shot at, and others had been hunted out for revenge by the soldiers. Wayne reported to Washington that "a very considerable number of the field and other officers are much injured by strokes from muskets, bayonets and stones."[27] All of the officers were galled just by the men's lack of respect for their authority. Reed forgave the officers' anger at the state negotiators because, for the officers, "it is a sore trial. . . . The men certainly had not those attachments which the officers supposed, and their fears being now at an end, they give loose to many [in]decencies."[28] The men had drawn extra liquor for New Year's, and this probably removed some of their usual restraint; but neither their affronts to the officers nor the mutiny came from drunken impulsiveness alone.

We must recall the officers' inflated notion of their personal indispensability to the army and to the revolution in order to realize how much the mutiny shocked them. Reed said, "They appear so deeply to resent the conduct of the troops to them personally."[29] Officers knew that uprisings could occur any time, but they evidently assumed that in a crisis they could do as Wayne had done at Fort Ticonderoga when some soldiers started to march home without leave early in 1777: demand to speak to the leader, point a pistol at his breast, send the soldiers back to camp, lock up the leader, and, if an officer defended the men's right to protest, place him under arrest, too. In contrast, the mutineers of 1781, even when they did not assault or insult an officer, marched off and left him without a command, even without his enlisted servant. They delighted in showing an officer the flimsiness of his status. The commander of the Third Pennsylvania Regiment, Colonel Thomas Craig—whom we remember from the Christmas riot over the cobbler's bench in 1776—was so enraged by the mutineers' defiance that he burned his commission.[30]

Once the mutineers started negotiating with Reed, the whole crisis was out of the officers' hands, and they could only watch helplessly as their state government allowed their commands to dissolve. Already hostile to the state officials, officers later damned Reed bitterly for betraying them. Between the discharge of the mutineers and the reenlistment of many of them in the following months, the officers were quartered in the homes of loyalists and Quakers in Philadelphia. We can easily imagine the open or subtle mockery of their plight that they had to take from their involuntary hosts. Some of the citizens of Philadelphia gave a dinner for the officers at the City Tavern. Colonel Thomas Craig got drunk and stuck his sword through a waiter, killing him.[31]

Neither the Pennsylvania mutiny nor the briefer, quickly suppressed mutiny in the New Jersey line attracted all of the soldiers in either state line, and New England soldiers readily marched against their comrades to quell the New Jersey mutiny. Enlisted men used the term "brother soldier" and, by 1781, had developed strong bonds in their grievances against officers, Congress, and the states for default of promises. But the historian who would analyze mutinies can find so many long-standing grounds for revolt that he must ask not so much, Why did the mutinies occur? but rather, Why were most of the mutinies so easily ended? and Why did more mutinies not occur?

The great majority of soldiers wanted to continue to serve the revolution. They were willing to stay for less than the state and Continental governments had promised them, partly in the hope that the deficiencies would be repaid some day, but mostly due to pride in their own ability and service. In return for this willingness, they exercised a right to complain, which the officers did not acknowledge but usually acquiesced in. When inequities or hardships beyond the unofficial, tacit level of toleration provoked an uprising, the soldiers knew that mutineers were in the wrong even when, as individuals who had a contract with the state, they had justice on their side. Revolt tended to shatter the soldiers' brotherhood, as we see in the men's repeated surrender of ringleaders to punishment or in the Pennsylvania Line's eagerness to get discharges and reenlistment bounties or in the Massachusetts and Connecticut mutineers' intent to go home. The men enjoyed solidarity as soldiers, not as mutineers. When threats to their survival or injuries to their notion of fairness became so great that they had to put self-interest first, this decision divided them—not only mutineers from non-mutineers, but mutineers from each other.

Continental soldiers came to the army individually and left it individually. Their vision of their future foresaw a private share of a national happiness. The desire to prove individual and national prowess as a means of securing this happiness prompted the service of men who could have risked less and made more in almost any other activity. Their service illustrates the strength of the revolutionary appeal to individuals to be worthy of the nation's destiny. The outcome of the mutinies illustrates the inadequacy of an appeal solely to material interest or to long-range solidarity in material interest. Harsh and unjust officers could not wreck the army, because soldiers' perseverance relied on their own ideal, not on automatic respect for commanders. And mutineers could not wreck the army, because the solidarity of materialism lacked the sanction of revolutionary ideals. Monetary claims on one's countrymen, like other forms of self-interest, were real and pressing, but they were not heroic. Mutiny could not attract most soldiers and did not succeed partly because it had no ideal. Soldiers could criticize civilians by contrasting the virtue of the military with the greed of the public. This claim to virtue formed the basis for America's promised future, and no purely materialistic principle of solidarity, including mutiny, could attract comparable allegiance.

The January mutinies capped an ignominious year in which almost every facet of the American war effort had faltered or failed: Continental money was worthless; requisitions of state supplies fell short; graft and profiteering flourished; Washington's army could not take the field in the North; Lincoln's army was captured and Gates's army was defeated and dispersed in the South. The rising influence of the nationalists in Congress owed much to these reverses suffered by voluntarism and public virtue.

Before 1781, only three men could be identified throughout the United States by one word each: the General, the Marquis, and the Baron. In that year came a fourth: the Financier. Robert Morris accepted the new post of superintendent of finance in May 1781, after three months of negotiating with Congress to secure complete authority over his subordinates and the right to continue his private business while in office. The appointment of Morris was part of the last and greatest wartime recourse to centralized administrative authority.[32] The collapse of paper money and the failure of the system of state supplies had discredited the advocates of diffused authority. Congress had also established a War Department in February 1781, and General Benjamin Lincoln was named secretary at war. Morris was at the center of Continental administration. He said that he would not take responsibility for supplying the army during the campaign of 1781, but almost at once nearly everyone from Washington on down to express messengers turned to him for money. In his diary, he wrote, "It seems as if every Person connected in Public Service entertain an Opinion that I am full of Money."[33] He used French loans, his personal credit, and financial sleight of hand to procure stopgap sums for food, clothing, and pay. He also set out to change the philosophy by which the war effort was financed.

To Morris and other advocates of centralization, Congress's and the states' previous policies—fiat money, swelling in volume and sinking in value; price controls and export restrictions; quotas in kind, transported from farm to army—all arose from a vain hope that people could be persuaded or beguiled into effective support of the war effort by concealing its cost. When the cost became clear and support faltered, people hoped to escape paying the price of their folly by obtaining foreign loans. Morris wanted to cure them of "relying on the empty Bubbles of Hope, instead of the Solid Foundations of Revenue."[34] All transactions would be in hard money; no debt would be contracted without provision for its payment; Congress would ask the states to approve a tax on imports that would give the central government a source of income independent from one-time state grants; the government would borrow money from Americans and Europeans; the states would pay taxes according to quotas established by Congress; uncontrolled prices and unlimited exportation would increase agricultural production, and such an increase—when sellers could rely on specie payment from the government—would enable the Continent to buy supplies for the army without the former promiscuous expenditure of Continental and state paper money. Morris thought of 1781 as "the Period of weakness between the convulsive Labors of Enthusiasm and the sound and regular Operations of Order and Government."[35]

Morris won unanimous appointment as superintendent of finance not because most Americans agreed with him or admired him but because they needed him. The administrative techniques and financial connections that made him valuable to the cause did not rely on public virtue but on interest and coercion. Morris hired Thomas Paine to write essays that would "prepare the minds of the people for such restraints and such taxes and imposts as are absolutely necessary for their own welfare."[36] During the two years of Morris's service, he did not succeed in imposing the restraints, taxes, and imposts that would base American independence on the solid foundations of revenue. These had to await the tenure of President George Washington and Secretary of the Treasury Alexander Hamilton. Morris's manipulation of resources other than the contributions of the American populace—mainly foreign loans and his own notes—did finance the last years of the war, although the direct transfer of supplies from the public to the army continued in the South. And all sorts of previously separated activities—food, uniforms, pay, forage, transport, even the Hospital Department—came within Morris's administrative work. He did not supervise all of these activities, but the men responsible for doing so turned to him for money, and he suggested changes in their operations in order to save money. Morris was not popular, and he seemed not to care. His letters to Congress and to the states often described the efficiency, economy, logicality, and necessity of his measures and then sarcastically contrasted his reasonableness with the illusions, pretense, ignorance, or negligence of those to whom he was writing. He spoke from experience when he said, "Men are less ashamed to do wrong than vexed to be told of it."[37]

Americans depended on Morris, but they did not like him. Their reliance on his administrative expertise and his commercial and financial connections included none of the exaltation that made Washington so popular. Centralized administration in the years 1781 to 1783 was for most Americans an expedient stopgap, not a change in their long-standing hostility to government. People's dealings with Morris revealed much of their attitude toward centralized administration. State officials and members of Congress criticized him for arrogance, dictatorial demeanor, and corruption of the public trust. At the same time, almost everyone expected Morris to rescue the army by cutting back waste and negligence and by producing solid money from a treasury into which states paid hardly any taxes. Americans seemed to assume Morris could master administrative difficulties because he was authoritarian and corrupt. Had not revolutionaries long known that such was the nature of governmental power? Joseph Reed called Morris "a pecuniary dictator."[38] From Washington's virtue his countrymen expected exemplary perseverance; without demanding reward, he withstood difficulties—often of their making—and inspired them to believe that they shared his strength. From Morris's vice his countrymen expected marvels in eliminating difficulties, for which they would have to pay him until they could get along without him. Thus, if these are correct inferences about revolutionaries' attitudes, the American cause could use Morris without conceding that public virtue had lapsed beyond recovery. In the reaction to Arnold's treason, for example, the revolutionaries had fervently dramatized their insistence that the weak, greedy traitor had betrayed America while the courageous, virtuous populace had secured the republic against such corruption. No leader—not even Washington, much less Morris—could base a successful claim to long-term power on the public's betrayal of the ideals of 1775. By asserting in his private and public statements the permanent failure of public virtue, and by exploiting the resultant dependence on his talents and connections, Morris assured that the revolutionaries, in choosing their leaders, would get rid of the nationalists, as well as the army, when the war was over.

Morris and his close allies were not the only revolutionaries who had concluded that public virtue was a vain hope. Continental Army officers went beyond the enlisted men's resentment of public indifference and denounced their civilian countrymen as unfit to sustain republican government. The officers' criticisms had even more significance than the privates' mutinies. A disgusted soldier would go home, but disgusted officers found friends in the army and in political office who wanted to use their positions to increase the authority of government, especially Continental government. In their plan, the security of independence would rest less and less on the failing or vanished virtue of the people and more and more on the proven virtue and talents of able leaders.

During the war, a number of officers became active political opponents of state leaders and constitutions that they considered too weak in supporting the army. They believed that decentralized governments closely responsive to the public will had indulged the pursuit of personal freedom until the public's desire to be free from the obligations of war had endangered independence. Alexander Hamilton said that the folly and passiveness of his countrymen gave him "pigmy-feelings."[39] To overcome similar fears of neglect, contempt, and impotence, officers became more belligerent toward their countrymen.

General Alexander McDougall warned Governor George Clinton that the army could not supply itself "unless the civil authority and Congress will do their Duty." Soldiers would not allow themselves "to be made Scape Goats of, to bear the Iniquities of the Country, to support them in Ease and Liberty, and to lay a foundation for Riches and opulence for America" while the public left the army unsupported.[40] McDougall and others began to assume and nearly to assert that the officers of the army were the saviors of the country, who deserved social distinction outside the army and could best judge the necessary strengthening of state and Continental governments.

In supporting the governmental curtailment of personal freedom, these officers were not simply expressing a private political opinion that they shared due to their common experiences. Rather, they specifically named the officer corps as the repository of correct revolutionary thought and behavior. On April 6, 1780, the Continental Army officers in Philadelphia met at the New Tavern and adopted a manifesto, which was signed by Anthony Wayne, Walter Stewart, John Stewart, and Henry Lee. They were "anxious to give energy so far as our consequence may have force to the future operations of Government." To this end they announced their intention "to curb the spirit of insolence and audacity, manifested by the deluded and disaffected." They were not referring just to loyalists but to "a spirit of resistance, which we cannot but apprehend receives encouragement from the lenity of Governments, founded on principles of universal liberty and benevolence." To break this resistance, "we do declare to our country, that we will not associate or hold communication with any person or persons, who have exhibited by their conduct an enemical disposition or even luke warmness, to the independence of America; nor with any person who may give countenance or encouragement to them. . . . We do also declare, that we will hold any Gentleman bearing a Military Commission, who may attempt to contravene the object of this declaration, in the smallest degree, as a proper subject of contempt, and that we will with alacrity seize every opportunity of evidencing to the World, our abhorrence of a conduct so *derogatory* to the *dignity* of the *Army*."[41]

The Pennsylvania Constitution, with its annual elections, one-house legislature, and diffused executive power, was one of those most clearly "founded on principles of universal liberty and benevolence"; it attracted the opposition of line officers and quartermasters. During Greene's term as quartermaster general, his two deputies supported the party in Pennsylvania that sought to revise the constitution in order to strengthen government and to decrease its responsiveness to the electorate. The deputies used the patronage of the quartermaster general's department to support organizers of opposition to the party favoring the unicameral Constitution of 1776. Wayne and his fellow Pennsylvania officers who opposed their state government believed that its "lenity" allowed citizens to avoid war taxes because legislators feared to enact them. Even though Pennsylvania kept its Continental Line more fully manned than most states and voted its officers half-pay pensions for life before Congress did so, partly due to the work of the officers' strong government allies, the officers remained confirmed opponents of lenient government that could not overawe "a spirit of resistance" among the people.

Early in 1779, officers of the Pennsylvania Line, imitating officers of the New Jersey Line, formed a committee to seek pay, supply, and pensions from the state government. The political opponents of the Constitution of 1776 used their exertions on behalf of the army as one of their main appeals for political support. President Joseph Reed tried in vain to convert the officers from hostility to political neutrality. He told Anthony Wayne that "a popular Government must in the nature of things be most generally agreeable to the People of this State" because "property is too casually distributed in this State ever to permit that Aristocratick influence which some wish and which I admit to be the most natural to the Sentiments of Gentlemen used to the discipline and subordination of an army."[42] In the first week of September 1780, Reed heard "that some officers of considerable rank have pressed the General to assume dictatorial authority."[43] Nathanael Greene assured Reed that he had Hamilton's word that no such proposal had occurred.[44]

Hamilton was undoubtedly right, but the rumors of sentiment for dictatorship may have arisen from the officers' increased emphasis on the need for strong government. In the same week of September, Hamilton wrote a long letter to James Duane outlining his proposals for correcting the "excess of the spirit of liberty" that had left Congress with too little power. Hamilton wanted the army—"an essential cement of the union"—under the sole authority of Congress, not the states, most of which relied too much on a "popular spirit"; he wanted Congress to delegate executive control to central departmental administrators; he wanted Congress to establish its continental authority and secure the army's strength and funding by taxing the public more rigorously; he wanted to secure the support of moneyed men by a bank based on paper credit that private interest would uphold.[45] Most of the main elements of Hamilton's policy as secretary of the Treasury ten years later first emerged at the low point of public effort for independence, when army officers were concluding that they were the best patriots and perhaps the last ones.

Officers in all the state lines showed ever clearer signs that they felt separated from civilian society and hostile toward it. Their three main grievances were interrelated: civilians selfishly enjoyed prosperity, heedless of how precariously independence survived; civilians defaulted on even the minimal needs for the survival of soldiers and their families; having committed these crimes, civilians refused to admit their guilt by acknowledging their dependence on the superior patriotism of the army.

Officers' private letters contained repeated, bitter denunciations of the entire revolutionary populace. Colonel Henry Jackson said that "from morn to night, and from night to morn you will hear some of the best officers and soldiers (that any nation could ever boast of) execrating the very country they are risking their lives, limbs, and health to support for their inattention and neglect of them."[46] Lieutenant Colonel Ebenezer Huntington wrote home on July 7, 1780, "The Rascally Stupidity which now prevails in the Country at large is beyond all description. . . . Why do you Suffer the Enemy to have a foot hold on the

Continent? You can prevent it, send your Men to the field, believe you are Americans[,] Not suffer yourselves to be dupd into the thought that the french will relieve you and fight your Battles. . . . It is a Reflection too much for a Soldier. You don't deserve to be freemen unless you can obtain it yourselves. . . . I despise my Countrymen, I wish I could say I was not born in America. I once gloried in it but am now ashamed of it. . . . I have wrote in a Passion, Indeed I am scarce ever free from it. I am in Rags, have lain in the Rain on the Ground for 48 hours past, and only a Junk of fresh Beef and that without Salt to dine on this day, recd no pay since last December, Constitution complaining, and all this for my Cowardly Countrymen who flinch at the very time when their Exertions are wanted, and hold their Purse Strings as tho' they would Damn the World, rather than part with a Dollar to their Army."[47]

The officers believed that they alone had maintained the *rage militaire* of 1775, which they associated with the true revolutionary spirit of virtuous effort. Their early revolutionary ideals made their later hostility more bitter. Before 1776 was over, Lieutenant Samuel Shaw wrote, "When I left the town of Boston with a view of joining our army, my enthusiasm was such as to induce me to think I should find as much public virtue among our people as is recorded of ancient Sparta or Rome. Numberless instances might be brought to show how miserably I was disappointed."[48] The public had sunk into vice from which it could be rescued only by strong government in the hands of the remaining virtuous revolutionaries. Only a few officers hinted that the United States might need some form of military rule or unrepublican government.[49] Rather, their separation from civilian society and their pride in the officer corps encouraged the first step in identifying the class of public-spirited men who could save independence. The officers' consciousness of gentlemanly social status, of unrivaled patriotic services, and of refined feelings of personal honor made them more certain that they were part of this class. And only through the predominance of this class could they hope to receive the rewards for their service—respect and pensions—that they knew the country owed them.[50]

Although in many cases the army had given them whatever pretensions they had to being gentlemen, most officers believed that they were doing the army a favor by serving. In compensation for their hardships and expenses, they expected lifelong distinction as gentlemen leaders of the revolution. Captain Alexander Graydon, who resigned his commission in 1778 because he did not get the promotion he wanted, wrote to President Joseph Reed in October 1780 requesting exemption from routine Pennsylvania militia musters. He said that he still supported the cause and abhorred the enemy, "but after having held the Rank of a Captain in the Continental Army, he confesses that his feelings would have been wounded by being obliged to perform the Duty of a private Centinel in common with a set of men (the Peasantry of the Country,) with whom from their Education and manner of Life he cou'd not associate. For notwithstanding the Principles of Equality upon which this and all free Governments are founded, he presumes it will be admitted that in every society there will be some Distinctions and Gradations of Rank arising from Education and other accidental Circumstances."[51] Such security against losing hard-won distinction underlay both the half-pay pensions and the Society of the Cincinnati. By the end of the war, this feeling of solidarity could encourage some officers' desire to use the army against civilian authority to obtain such security.

At the same time that officers developed the conviction that their virtue could save their country in spite of its people, their words revealed a growing fear of isolation, not as an officer corps, but as individuals. During the war, their complaints and denunciations often overrode this concern, which emerged more clearly in 1783. Yet even before the crisis of disbanding the army, they began to realize that their interpretation of the revolution had little support among their countrymen. When newspapers, officials, and preachers called Americans to wake from the long lethargy that led to the reverses of 1780, most people, contrary to the officers' view, spoke as if such revived spirit could wipe away the derelictions of the past. No matter how much these spokesmen praised the perseverance of the army, they refused to admit that the public had irretrievably betrayed the revolutionary ideal of virtue.

The officers became convinced that the public did not understand the nature of the army's wartime experiences. When Lieutenant Colonel Samuel Webb, a prisoner of war, expected to be exchanged and to return to his regiment, Nathanael Greene wrote him, "We shall be happy to see you at Camp, where you will find the true military spirit, justice and generosity. The great body of the People you know are contracted, selfish and illiberal; and therefore not calculated to harmonize with a noble nature like yours."[52] The slowly improved proficiency in combat, the indescribable hardship, the recurrent threat of disbandment, the risky prevention of mutiny—people could not appreciate such service, any more than they could know the mind of a gentleman whose honor has been insulted, because they had never experienced such feelings of distinctiveness. Now the officers began to realize that most of the people who had praised sacrifice would believe that all revolutionaries had made comparable sacrifices; the future celebration of victory might seem to thank the army but would in fact praise the public for accomplishments that the public had nothing to do with and could never understand. Only brother soldiers could know how they had won independence. Many of the first Continental officers had suffered attacks of loneliness and nostalgia—homesickness—when they came to camp. Now the last officers stood in danger of being lonely at home and homesick for the army.

Although we cannot attribute a uniform outlook to all Continental Army officers, we can reconstruct from the ideals and conduct of many officers a composite description. To understand these officers' sense of isolation from the civilian public, we should remember their initial strong patriotic enthusiasm. The officers believed that they had begun their service in the heroic vanguard of a whole people. During the war years, the officers had embodied the cause, while the people had abandoned both officers and cause. Thus, the giddy popular mind endangered the survival of republicanism, while the officers at the head of the army were the main defenders of the republic. Like other revolutionaries and in heightened form, officers sought to demonstrate a virtuous strength that would win glory for both the man and his country. As public contribution to the war declined, this expectation of glory for military virtue became more important to the officers who persevered in the army. They believed that they were giving up the chance to make fortunes outside the army. Their sacrifices and debts, when set against the public's neglect, were badges of virtue. Such sweeping doubts about the survival of public virtue might have invited skepticism about America's ability to win and maintain independence. But the officers' assertion of their own professional prowess and patriotic virtue grew stronger as their esteem for their countrymen sank. Thus, they did not automatically equate the ruin of public virtue with the collapse of the American cause. In shifting their confidence from the many to the few, however, they further distinguished patriotism from majoritarianism. The survival of liberty would depend on entrusting more of the country's power to patriots, whose ability and virtue could offset the prevailing popular weaknesses.

American officers contrasted the Continental Army's fidelity to the ideals of 1775 with the public's waywardness. This assertion of superior patriotism expressed both the officers' professional pride and their claim that they embodied the authentic heritage of the revolution. This claim derived much of its conviction for the officers from their experience of the revolution as a test of personal worthiness. Few of the officers expected a military career. The inevitable loss of their special professional status alarmed them, but their hope for the survival of American independence centered more on their personal virtue than on their professional achievement. The active political role that some officers took in attempting to strengthen state and Continental governments suggests that they relied on the future influence of their patriotism, not of their military commissions. Dedicated to the proof and security of their own virtue, the officers substituted faith in governmental coercion for faith in popular voluntarism, thus basing their hope for America's future on their own strength. But despite the erosion of their confidence in public virtue and majoritarian politics, their political attitudes owed more to the American revolutionary cast of mind than to any form of international military professionalism. The Continental Army officers would not be the last Americans to see themselves as a righteous remnant who could save the country from its sins.

The role of Continental Army officers in the movement for the United States Constitution and in the Federalist party is well known. George Washington, Henry Knox, Alexander Hamilton, Timothy Pickering, Henry Lee, John Marshall, and Charles C. Pinckney are only a partial list. However, these officers' political opinions were shared by men outside the army, while other officers left no indication that they favored stronger government. Students of Confederation-period politics and the adoption of the Constitution find former Continental Army officers on either side of political questions and do not ascribe to army service alone a crucial role in shaping political action.[53] Thus, scholars have not statistically linked former Continental Army officers with proponents of the Constitution or with Federalist partisans of the early national period. However, if instead of counting the advocates of stronger central government, we analyze their view of American politics, we find many similarities with the outlook of the aggrieved officers in wartime.[54] The officers' isolation, their loss of hope for public virtue, and their righteous self-assertion foreshadowed the defensive militance of the Federalist party. The most vocal spokesmen for the officer corps adumbrated the psychology and the ideology by which partisans of stronger government purported to save the revolution despite the shortcomings of their fellow revolutionaries. The wartime experience of the military underlay the first formulation of the claim that a few patriots could wield special authority as saviors of the republic.

The Continental Army officers' patriotic professionalism may exemplify the recurring pattern in American history in which a group or faction of patriots claimed to be the sole true embodiment of the ideals of the American Revolution. Americans who saw widespread failure to conform to the ideals of the revolution could not acknowledge that such vice doomed the republic because they would thereby have condemned themselves to hopelessness. To retain confidence in their own virtuous strength, they felt the need either to drive out the traitors or to establish a hierarchy of patriotism, in which the weak relied on and deferred to their stronger countrymen. Both of these resolutions of the problem of lapses and division conveniently turned attention away from the comparison of the revolutionaries' conduct with their ideal and toward the comparison of some revolutionaries with others. In the face of universal failure to attain an absolute ideal, a corps of true patriots could sustain confidence in their own righteous strength and their hope for the future by contrasting their own virtue with the crimes of those whose revolutionary effort had failed in a different way. By this act of denunciation the faltering patriot could look less closely at his ideals of 1775, which condemned his compromises, and more closely at his delinquent countrymen. Thus, his zeal became the true embodiment of the revolution.

Continental Army officers were first practitioners, then victims, of this outlook, as the Federalists were later. The officers could claim primacy as patriots who had borne arms against the enemy, shielding a thankless populace. The Federalists could see themselves as saviors of the republic who had created and implemented a republican government that had secured independence despite selfish localism and foreign influence. But, in both cases, such isolation and arrogation of preeminence helped the critics of officers and Federalists to portray them as monarchical conspirators. The timely suppression of such alien designs proved the virtue, strength, and zeal of the populace that repudiated them.[55]

The increasing divergence of officers' and civilians' views of the war was reflected in their attitudes toward the militia and the manning of the army. In the war's last years, revolutionaries showed more and more reluctance to serve in the army and growing disdain for those who did serve. Yet the capture of Lord Cornwallis's army at Yorktown became a great national achievement. Although the Continental Army was receiving less support, fewer men, and declining respect from civilians, the defeat of the British was celebrated as a popular triumph as well as a military victory. This paradox was partly exemplified by the service of the militia during the war's closing years in the South.

Most of the combat during the last two years of the war was in the South. Congress, having appointed Gates to the southern command against Washington's wishes, left the choice of Gates's successor, after the defeat at Camden, to the commander in chief. Washington chose Nathanael Greene. Greene had a small force of Continentals—about one thousand until after Yorktown—and varying reinforcements of militia. He aimed to prevent Cornwallis and the British from securing undisputed control of the southern countryside. To that end, he had to keep his force intact as an encouragement for southern citizens to refuse submission to the British. After the surrender of Charleston and the Continental Army of the Southern Department in May 1780, many South Carolinians, like people in New Jersey four years earlier, had taken loyalty oaths to the British, hoping that such "protections" would cause the British to leave them alone. Instead, Sir Henry Clinton summoned all oath-takers to join the fight against the rebels or to face arrest. This choice brought out the widespread aversion to British rule and stimulated resistance, which took new hope for success with the return of the Continental Army to the South. The British never succeeded in controlling much beyond their fixed positions and their line of march. Expecting a populace of loyalists grateful for rescue and eager to reestablish royal government, Cornwallis was greeted for the most part with curiosity at best—not with guides, supplies, or intelligence about the enemy. These went to the Continentals, along with the fluctuating but effective participation of citizens in irregular units under men like Francis Marion and Thomas Sumter. Cornwallis, rightly regarding Greene's army as the core of popular resistance, set out to destroy it. The army's ability to move fast and to survive hard fighting—though not to win battles, except at Cowpens—kept the British from succeeding. The British kept losing men without gaining territory or support. A few months after he took command in the South,

Greene explained to Sumter the importance of the Continental Army in this accomplishment: "Partisan strokes in war are like the garnish of a table. They give splendor to the army, and reputation to the officer, but they afford no substantial national security. . . . You may strike a hundred strokes and reap little benefit from them unless you have a good army to take advantage of your success. The enemy will never relinquish their plan nor the people be firm in your favor, until they behold a better barrier in this field than a volunteer militia, who are one day out and the next at home."[56]

In the southern campaigns, the militia was an adjunct to the Continental Army. Without the army, the militia could not have maintained organized military opposition to the British, and southern resistance to conquest probably would have become a bloodier extension of the Carolina vendetta killings. General William Moultrie said that "the militia are brave men, and will fight if you let them come to action in their own way."[57] Most Continental officers disputed the first statement; those, like Daniel Morgan, who used militia successfully in the South learned that the militia could help in battle if the men believed that they were fighting in their own way, secure from having to stand up to a charge by a disciplined enemy. A French officer observed that the Virginia militia could do brave deeds when they had an advantageous position or when they had an avenue of retreat or "when the persuasive eloquence of their commander has aroused in them an enthusiastic ardor of which immediate advantage must be taken."[58] But such popular enthusiasm had already proven unreliable and insufficient to sustain resistance. The revolution had come to depend also on a disciplined army. Daniel Morgan, who flattered, cajoled, and inspired his men before their victory at Cowpens, did not believe that his techniques were an alternative to discipline. He relied on Continentals to face the enemy at Cowpens, and a few weeks later he advised Greene on militia tactics: "Put the militia in the centre, with some picked troops in their rear, with orders to shoot down the first man that runs."[59] Scholars who have studied the service of the militia demonstrate its usefulness as an auxiliary to the army's effort to prevent British control of territory and population.[60] Greene repeatedly complained about the militia not because he expected it to equal the Continentals' steadiness in battle or long-term perseverance on the march but because the southern populace treated the militia more as an alternative than as an auxiliary. The militia's service showed that popular enthusiasm had not ceased to be effective, but it had ceased to be the sufficient military recourse for Virginians' dislike of regular army service. Everyone recognized the need for Continentals, but citizens preferred to serve —if they had to serve—in the militia, and state authorities settled for militia reinforcements rather than more energetic recruiting and conscription.

The repeated militia mobilizations and the role of the local militia organization in maintaining revolutionary authority demonstrated the importance of its members' commitment to the American cause. As divisions among revolutionaries grew more pronounced, however, the popular preference for militia service rather than regular army duty became not simply an alternative or an auxiliary to the Continental Army but sometimes an expression of hostility to a professional military regimen. When Virginia ordered a draft in April 1781 in Rockbridge County for eighteen-month terms in the Continental Army, Samuel McDowell warned Governor Jefferson that "it must Ruin a number of those whose lot is to march," because they had missed putting in fall crops during militia service and would miss putting in spring crops if they joined Greene; "therefore their familys and Stocks must Suffer, as they (Mostly) have not any Person behind them when they are gone from home to work their small farms."[61] In response to this plea, Jefferson suspended the draft for the county, but his letter did not arrive until after the day of the draft. On that day, about one hundred men came to the county seat to stop officials from laying out draft districts. The men got into the courthouse, tore up the officials' papers, seized the table, and carried it off. But they gave a different reason for opposing the draft than the one McDowell had first offered on their behalf. They said "that they would Serve as Militia for those months and make up the Eighteen months that way, but would not be Drafted for Eighteen Months and be regulars."[62]

Faced with this attitude, Greene was less interested in discussing the merits or proper use of militia as auxiliaries than in warning that constant recourse to militia endangered the survival of the army whose efforts the militia was supposed to help. Virginia counties that had militia in the field were exempt from the draft. Thus, an emergency—such as an invasion or a failure to recruit Continentals, both of which brought out the militia—reduced rather than increased the state's ability to strengthen the Continental Army by conscription. Greene urged Governor Thomas Nelson to draft men as Continentals because a year's "severe service" was necessary for competence in the field. "Regulars alone can insure your safety. Men will not yield to the hardships of a camp, nor submit to the severity of discipline, without a certain line of duty prescribed as something professional."[63]

Virginians knew what Greene was talking about and wanted none of it. The defiance of the draft in Rockbridge had followed similar resistance in neighboring Augusta County, where "they complained they were Imposed upon and Said they were Cheerfully willing to Spend their hearts blood in Defence of the Cuntery. Yet they would Suffer Death before they would be Drafted 18 months from their famelies and made Regular Soldiers of."[64] The distaste for Continental service, which led to undermanned regiments, short-term drafts, and frequent militia calls, increased the disruption that the war caused in places like Augusta and Rockbridge. Unable to produce enough long-term volunteers, the public was unwilling to coerce long-term conscripts and thereby divide the cost of support for soldiers and soldiers' families among the community. People preferred to accept the more frequent, less useful, but briefer disruption of many men's lives rather than take the chance that they might be one of the few who had to go to the army and stay. Word of Virginians' hostility to a professional military regimen, even to that of their fellow revolutionaries, reached the generals who commanded the enemy's invasion. Five weeks after the disruptions of the draft, a British intelligence report told Cornwallis and Clinton that "the militia of Virginia were very averse to turning out and most of the young men had retired to the mountains. Some had even resisted with arms those who attempted to force them."[65]

Militiamen repeatedly refused to serve beyond the time for which they had been called up and even insisted on marching for home weeks enough in advance to be at home and not with the army when their terms expired. Sometimes they scattered and headed home early. Militiamen decided to stay or go to suit themselves, not according to the need for their services or the threat to their homes. Militiamen would fight—under conditions to their liking, for an agreed number of months—but they would not submit to the discipline of Continentals. They often cut a path of plunder wherever they went; they took an army supply shipment if they got to it first; they wasted public stores. Greene said, "These are some of the happy effects of defending the country with militia, from which good Lord deliver us! O, that we had in the field, as Henry V. said, some few of the many thousands that are idle at home!"[66] Greene believed that Southerners' willingness to stop short of full effort by sending the militia undercut the safety of the South to serve the ease of individuals.

Nor could other states fill their Continental lines. The states' settlement of soldiers' pay in 1780 helped to persuade men to reenlist in 1781. The settlements mollified the soldiers' sense of grievance more by promises than by substantial money payments. As in earlier years, large bounties brought some old soldiers and more new recruits into the Continental Army. By 1781, the fiction of an army of typical citizens temporarily under arms seemed forgotten, not just overlooked. People referred to "that class of men who are proper subjects for Soldiers," to "the Class of Men who are willing to become Soldiers," to men who have a "preference of the soldier's life to that of Labour" and "Men who make Arms a *profession*."[67] The public now set out deliberately to find and recruit young men who were willing to become regular soldiers.

The draft for nine months—that is, until the next recruiting period—continued to be the states' last resort. Each year officers had become more hostile to it because it brought only short-term soldiers. One officer called them "nine months' abortions."[68] Bounties to persuade men to serve short terms went to little better purpose "than to hire the populace to visit the army."[69] The draft met some open defiance, but more often evasion. One of Nathanael Greene's hosts on the trip home in August 1783, Colonel Thomas Blount of North Carolina, was, Greene said, "marvelous," by which Greene meant that the colonel told tall stories. But Blount caught his region's attitude toward service in the Continental Army when he told Greene that "so great was the aversion to military service in this neighborhood that out of fifty-eight persons fifty-six were found to have artificial hernia."[70] Some states tried to refill their Continental lines by offering a draft exemption to any man who turned in a deserter. An official in Halifax County, Virginia, reported, "It will make a man take his Brother or Even his Father, or a father his Son—for says he if I dont take him, somebody else will."[71] Some states decided that before requiring their married, employed, law-abiding citizens to go into the army, they would conscript militia delinquents, bachelors, and vagrants. In practice, such laws sometimes enabled people to falsely accuse a neighbor. Sending conscripts who fit the specifications of the law showed what the public thought of the army. Joshua Beall, the county lieutenant of Prince George's County, Maryland, told the governor that he had drafted Basil Shaw in lieu of a man who was married, had children, had seen service, and was industrious. Shaw "is a very idle Lasey fellow, who is rather a burden, than a help to his family, for which reason I chose him to go into service."[72] Convicts were pardoned in return for their voluntary enlistment. North Carolina decided that any militiaman who ran away in battle, as the North Carolina militia did at Camden and Guilford Courthouse, would be drafted as Continental soldiers for the duration of the war.

Perhaps these official expedients and popular evasions better reveal the widespread reluctance either to enlist or to submit to the draft than do the rare occasions of outright defiance. The army had become a place for wartime professionals and luckless civilians. Its victories showed the strength of the nation, but service in it no longer embodied virtues to which very many Americans even pretended to aspire. This profound division between soldiers and civilians was only partly concealed by the jubilation that came with the successful end of the war. Behind the proud praise of American achievement lay the knowledge that revolutionaries had taken divergent paths to victory. The mutual suspicions and grievances running between the army and the populace gravely impaired Americans' confidence that they were united in active defense of liberty. They asserted rival claims to wartime primacy in preserving the republic from both foreign enemies and domestic derelictions. In its later versions, the legacy of the revolution would sometimes discreetly conceal, sometimes stridently recall, but never fully overcome the bitter memory that amid the adversity of war many of the victors had become strangers.

Americans' celebration of the victory at Yorktown exemplifies the contrast between the employment of military professionalism and the praise of national prowess and communal patriotism. The army was often avoided, forgotten, even scorned; yet military success proved the nation's righteousness and might. George Washington never lost sight of the tenuousness of the military combinations that made the capture of Cornwallis's army possible. But after the victory, most people seemed to treat it as a providential yet inevitable confirmation of Americans' virtuous strength. Washington could look back and see how precarious victory had been. His countrymen could look forward and see the imminent fulfillment of their promised future. At last at Yorktown, Washington could see the success of an intricate, interlocking plan that united the efforts of scattered land and sea forces of the allies to capture an entire British army. Cornwallis had intended to chase Greene to the ground. Failing that, he continued north to Virginia and tried to trap Lafayette's small army. Instead, the American army, the French expeditionary force, and the French fleet descended on him. The last of these was the greatest surprise and the decisive one. Washington set out to put his mark on the victory. He broke the first ground for the siege works; he touched off the first gun.[73] Perhaps at the British surrender he thought of a quotation he had recorded the year before: "The hour of victory, we are informed by Lord North is the time for negotiation."[74] During the months of slack American war effort a year before Yorktown, Washington had grown more certain that neither the course nor the outcome of the war were under his control. He knew how fragile were the resources on which the Continental Army survived and how tenuous was the combination of British misjudgment and allied cooperation on which victory depended.

Washington's assessment of the painstaking military steps to victory did not receive comparable emphasis in civilians' versions of America's triumph. The popular celebrations of Yorktown repeated those for the defeat of Burgoyne in the expressions of pride in national strength favored by the blessings of Providence. The recent public lethargy, which had received so much attention a year earlier, seemed almost forgotten. The joy was so great that, according to David Ramsay, "well authenticated testimony asserts that the nerves of some were so agitated, as to produce convulsions."[75] A person who read only the accounts and praises of American victory might have concluded that the *rage militaire* of 1775 had finally achieved its inevitable triumph. In his oration, Nathan Fiske could not help enjoying the mortification of the British ministry and king, as well as Cornwallis's "humiliating subjugation . . . to American Rebels, as he scornfully stigmatized us. . . . What a radiance will this struggle for Liberty, which has produced such exertions of genius and prowess, throw around America! 'Tis enough to make us proud of our country, and to glory in the name of Americans; yea, even to make it criminal to be destitute of this pride."[76]

On November 27, Philadelphians went to the corner of Lombard Street and Third Street to see Charles Willson Peale's illuminated transparencies that pictorially interpreted victory. His Temple of Independence rested on a first cause—the Stamp Act, the Tea Act, and the Coercive Acts—and on a foundation, the battles of the war; "The Voice Of The People" supported the illustrious senators and the brave soldiery on thirteen columns; above the statues of Justice, Hope, and Industry were the statues of fallen heroes, capped by agriculture, arts, and commerce. The other transparencies honored Washington and Rochambeau and displayed a life-size genius of America, clothed in white, girdled in virtue, crowned with perseverance, holding a banner of equal rights and a globe of universality, trampling on Discord.[77] The people of Philadelphia had already celebrated the victory on the evening of October 24. Every house in the city had lights in the windows, except the homes of Quakers. Gangs went around breaking the windows and smashing the furniture of houses whose owners refused to illuminate.[78]

The united celebrations of victory, though heartfelt, concealed deeper division among revolutionaries than the recriminations during the autumn of 1777 and the Valley Forge winter. In 1777 both Washington's friends and his critics, as well as Congress and its critics, had believed that the United States would win independence with an army supported morally and materially by a zealous public. The defeat of Burgoyne proved what such a combination could do, and Washington would have loved to do the same to Howe, just as his critics said he ought to have done. But who had defeated Cornwallis? By 1781 the record of public neglect left little doubt among soldiers or the advocates of stronger central government that only the virtuous perseverance of a few had won the war in spite of the selfishness of most revolutionaries. By contrast, the popular expressions of joy at Cornwallis's surrender left little doubt that the army's victory represented the public's successful resistance to tyranny. A frequent promise to soldiers said that after their fighting they would enjoy the special gratitude of their fellow revolutionaries. Soldiers would receive in their own lifetimes the veneration that all revolutionaries expected from posterity. They did receive thanks but not the prompt and lasting distinction they had been promised. Veterans of the Revolutionary War did not acquire unique admiration until the nineteenth century. The public reaction to the Yorktown victory foreshadowed the celebrations of peace in 1783; Americans decided that they owed their independence less to their army than to the national virtue and courage that the soldiers partially and temporarily embodied.

The popular attitude had changed because the relationship between the army and the public had changed. If soldiers had come from a populace eager to serve in and to support the army consistently, popular gratitude to veterans could have served the same purpose at the end of the war as in the original promise—a compliment to the soldier's sacrifice, courage, and prowess from revolutionaries who knew that they shared these virtues. By 1783, Americans' respect for the Continental Army's victories had been alloyed by repugnance toward its professional regimen and fear that this strength would be turned against the civil governments that had left the army unpaid. The public debt was a tangible symbol of the revolutionaries' failure to fight the war as a united populace. Many Americans, through their state and Continental governments, owed money to the comparatively few Americans who had fought with greatest perseverance. The monetary debt could in fact measure the debt of deference owed by lesser patriots to superior ones. By this reasoning it was fitting, if not sinister, that the public debt became one of the nationalists' main arguments for the consolidation of governmental power. More than a financial obligation, the debt exemplified the failure of public virtue, because citizens had hired men to do their fighting and had paid too few taxes to balance accounts. The kind of strong government that could collect taxes and finance the public debt was also the kind of government whose coercive powers could force citizens to discharge the obligations they lacked the virtue to discharge voluntarily. But this logic required Americans to acknowledge the irremediable failure of public virtue as the basis for independence. In their reaction to victory at Yorktown and in the subsequent disbandment of the army after the treaty of peace, the revolutionaries repudiated their symbolic indebtedness and tried to reclaim their patriotic prowess.

CHAPTER VIII

The Legacy

In 1782 the Continental Army reached the peak of its military professionalism. The regiments on the Hudson were fully uniformed and had developed both professional pride and parade-ground drill to their highest point during the war. Despite some continued breaches of discipline, especially the plunder of civilians for food, the Continentals had become a respectable army. Reviews for Secretary at War Benjamin Lincoln and Count Rochambeau confirmed by special demonstrations the discipline for which Washington and others had been complimenting the army. Publicly and privately French officers admired the proficiency the American army had attained; they complimented Baron Steuben for his successful introduction of the smooth, silent movements.[1] Washington introduced chevrons for the sleeves of soldiers' uniforms to mark the term of years they had served without a breach of discipline—one chevron for three years, two chevrons for six years. Rather than service stripes, these were a good-conduct award, and not all soldiers who received them managed to keep them until discharge. Washington also created the purple heart, which was a cloth badge, not a medal, and which was not an award for sustaining a wound but an all-purpose decoration for "any singularly meritorious action."[2] Both of these went only to enlisted men.

Washington's general orders gave more recognition to veterans of several years' service and began to cite "the Annals of the Army."[3] The Continentals now had a tradition of persevering service and of victory that gave the army confidence in its own strength and enabled soldiers to measure their professional pride by their own and their fellow soldiers' former conduct. By 1783 many of the soldiers on the Hudson had been recruited in the last two years, though some recruits may have returned to the army after earlier service. New recruits could emulate the model of military expertise by referring to the annals of the service into which they had enlisted.[4] Washington thanked Baron Steuben for the success of his training and congratulated the soldiers on their "spirit of emulation, bordering on enthusiasm."[5] In November 1782, General Robert Howe wrote to Steuben, "Your children, for so I call our army, have been laboring day and night to build their huts. . . . I cannot conclude this letter without conveying to you what I am sure your attachment to the army will render pleasing to you, that they universally think and speak of you with love, pleasure, gratitude, and applause."[6] They had succeeded at what Washington called "the pleasing and honorable Task of becoming Masters of their Profession."[7] On Friday, April 12, 1782, Washington was so pleased with the appearance of the Connecticut brigades that he told his aide to call the roll of the entire line—1,427 names—while he listened and the soldiers showed off.[8]

After the soldiers built their timber-and-stone huts at New Windsor, New York, for the winter of 1782/1783, they constructed, under the supervision of General Horatio Gates, a large building on a hill. Its central hall was 110 feet long and 30 feet wide, with an arched vault and an orchestra space at one end. The wings held rooms for offices, quartermaster's and commissary's stores, and courts-martial. The building had a cupola topped with a flagstaff. Chaplain Israel Evans inaugurated the building on February 6, 1783, with an oration before the officers, the commander in chief, and the wives of Washington, Knox, and Edward Hand. Evans had first proposed the erection of the building, and he gave it a name: the Temple of Virtue.

At the end of the war, Washington and his advisors unsuccessfully proposed the formation of a peacetime national militia and small regular army. Systematic military instruction would perpetuate and disseminate wartime skills without employing a large standing army and without trusting once again the proven inadequacies of popular voluntarism and the state militias. These proposals, despite their praise of freemen embodied in militia, based national defense on professionalism, not voluntarism.[9] They had little public support and were not adopted by Congress. Americans refused to conclude that the war showed independence to rest on professionalism as well as voluntarism. By this refusal the revolutionaries implicitly rejected the officers' claims that the country would owe its future survival to the army. How better could revolutionaries assert that the public had won independence than by making the public its sole guardians? America could use an army but need not depend on one.

In 1782 Americans again became convinced, this time with more reason, that the war was over. The widespread discussion of imminent peace had an effect like the confidence of 1778: an increased reluctance to levy or pay taxes. The trade in manufactured goods across British lines reached its greatest extent during these last months, while Congress depended on loans for its fragile solvency—or, rather, its concealed insolvency. According to Thomas Paine, "The common cry has been, WHY DON'T CONGRESS BORROW—WHY DON'T CONGRESS BORROW[?]"[10] The war ended for most Americans more than a year before the Treaty of Paris, and the support of an army lost almost all its urgency. The Continental government could hardly sustain an army in wartime, much less establish one for the coming years of peace.

The growing public repudiation of indebtedness to the Continental Army alarmed the officers who sought distinction and financial security from their wartime service. When Congress had first voted postwar half pay for officers, opponents had warned that if the chance came, they would repeal the pensions and substitute some compensation that carried no such invidious distinction. In 1780, after Arnold's defection, the officers got a promise of half pay for life, but by 1782 the public's dislike of this pension had become clear to the officers. The chances of collecting the pension looked unpromising, and the officers had begun to worry more about their return to civilian life. Beginning in October 1782, Washington's customary pleas for support had become grave warnings about the officers' resentment. If Congress tried to reduce the size of the officer corps, Washington wrote, "a train of Evils will follow, of a very serious and distressing Nature." He saw "men goaded by a thousand stings of reflexion on the past, and of anticipation on the future, about to be turned into the World, soured by penury and what they call the ingratitude of the Public, involved in debts, without one farthing of Money to carry them home, after having spent the flower of their days and many of them their patrimonies in establishing the freedom and Independence of their Country, and suffered every thing human Nature is capable of enduring on this side of death."[11] According to actuarial calculations, the average officer could expect to collect half pay for twelve years between discharge and death. The officers decided to ask Congress to commute their life half pay to a fixed term of full pay after discharge. A delegation headed by General Alexander McDougall went to Congress to represent the officers' wishes. A committee of Congress conferred with the delegation and settled on five years of full pay.

At the same time, the advocates of stronger Continental government wanted Congress to adopt an amendment to the Articles of Confederation giving the central government authority to levy an impost. To add urgency, they stressed the demands of "the army," by which they meant the officers. The nationalists hoped that those revolutionaries who disliked a Continental tax would accept one in order to discharge the army without dangerous contention over long-deferred pay. The opponents of pensions and an impost said that commutation was a device for fixing an unneeded tax on the public by creating an inequitable and dangerous demand on Congress by placemen. In this way, debate over the powers of Continental government centered on the officers' deserts and on the pension advocates' ever-present lobbying threat that the officers' discontent could cause trouble for civilians.

Richard Kohn has convincingly reconstructed the collaboration between a few nationalists in Philadelphia and some officers at headquarters.[12] The nationalists encouraged the officers to threaten civil authority in order to alarm members of Congress who disliked pensions and the impost. These threats appeared in two anonymous manifestos written by Major John Armstrong, Jr., in the quarters of General Horatio Gates and circulated in the camp. They ran through the usual litany of the officers' superior patriotism and the nation's debt to the leaders of the army. The only thing new in these documents was the timing of their circulation and Armstrong's proposal that the officers threaten to take the army west if war continued, leaving Congress and the populace undefended, or, if peace came, to retain their arms until the amount due to each officer was ascertained and reliable provision was made for its future payment.[13] When we compare descriptions from camp of the soldiers' mood with the stories circulating at Philadelphia, we can see that the threat of the army's defiance of Congress was largely created in Philadelphia. Kohn reasonably infers from the timing of correspondence that the nationalists —through Alexander Hamilton, then a delegate in Congress— forewarned Washington of the discontent they were purposely encouraging. Washington, the nationalists calculated, would control the officers in time to prevent open defiance of civil authority, but the threat of such defiance would scare Congress into accepting commutation and the impost. Sure enough, Congress adopted the nationalists' measures, although the impost was substantially weakened.

To the nationalists, the officers were not so much allies as tools. For the officers to play their part convincingly, they had to believe that they could in fact execute their vague threats to defy civil authority, and the reluctant delegates in Congress had to believe it, too. According to a later account, Robert Morris was asked how the army could get supplies if it defied an order to disband. Morris replied, "*I will feed them*."[14] If he said this, he probably wanted the officers to believe it but shared no such illusion himself. Perhaps he could have fed them, but the shrewd men, including Hamilton, knew that the test would never come, because the enlisted men would not follow their officers.

The privates wanted their pay, but they had no interest in

helping the officers get pensions. Though the threatening officers seemed not to realize it, it was too late for them to expect their men to share a sense of common interest with the officers. Even more than pay, the privates at Newburgh wanted to go home. Six weeks after his address came out, Armstrong wrote to Gates, "The soldiery are anxious to disperse—no ties, no promises, will hold them longer—and with them will every loitering hope of ours break also."[15] Most men probably had assumed at the time of enlistment that they could count on little from the Congress besides the bounty. Congress need only discharge the Continentals, and the righteous officers would be left by themselves. Washington was able to quiet the Newburgh protests easily, perhaps because most officers, though they enjoyed waxing indignant, knew that their soldiers—given a choice between serving the officers' interests and going home—would choose home any day. When General Henry Knox drafted a reply to the anonymous address, he spared no details in portraying the abandoned officers: "Will the three years Men who came out upon large bounties and their wages secured by a private contract at *home*, tarry a moment after they are told by Congress they may go. . . . And when the Soldiery forsake you, what will be your situation? *despised* and *insulted*, by an *enraged* populace, *exposed* to the *revenging* hand of *justice*—You will then flee to *Caves* and *Dens* to hide yourselves from the *face* of *day*, and of Man."[16]

The officers knew it, but they did not want to admit it. Thus, Washington became the central figure in overcoming the threat to defy Congress. The first anonymous address called for a meeting of officers; Washington intended to make the meeting his; so he called one. He would give the officers a chance to disavow gracefully the anonymous threats, not because the soldiers would leave them powerless, but because the commander in chief had appealed to them. Washington had a strong moral position from which to make such an appeal, for he had repeatedly and forcefully represented the officers' hardships and requests to Congress and had supported the officers with his influence. But to ensure the success of his appeal, Washington met privately with a number of officers in the days before the general meeting and consolidated support for disavowing the anonymous addresses.

When the officers gathered in the Temple of Virtue, they keenly felt their injured merit; they had reason to know that they could do nothing more than they had already done; and they had among them men who were determined to prevent open defiance of civil authority. Washington asked the officers to reject rash counsels that would mar their reputation for self-sacrifice. Then he read a letter from a delegate in Congress, Joseph Jones, which Washington represented as a promise that Congress would pay the officers. Washington deftly reminded them of his own preeminent reputation for disinterestedness by excusing himself while he put on his new eyeglasses to read Jones's letter, saying "that he had grown gray in their service, and now found himself growing blind."[17] This seemingly off-hand remark touched the officers' strong affection for Washington and emphasized what everyone present knew: that he had withstood more tests of perseverance and hard work than any other officer. Yet he stayed loyal to Congress even though it had often compounded his difficulties.

After Washington left the meeting, there was only thirty minutes of debate. Knox then put forward, and the officers adopted, his resolution expressing loyalty to the commander in chief and disavowing the threats of the anonymous addresses. Washington had not won all the officers over to his stoical resignation to the will of Providence. But, as Knox saw, the officers did not want to change from first among patriots to mutineers. They had always wanted to embody superior patriotism. The anonymous addresses had played on the officers' revolutionary ideals by telling them that they had taken America from "impending servitude to acknowledged independence." Congress's and the public's scorn for their rights showed that they now faced tyranny in another garb: "the plain coat of republicanism." The address strengthened this appeal by warning them that they would soon lose their most prized source of wartime strength and preeminence "when those very swords, the instruments and companions of your glory, shall be taken from your sides, and no remaining mark of military distinction left but your wants, infirmities and scars."[18] Armstrong's words drew on the officers' military pride, which they could assert against civilians who failed to reward merit. More than five years earlier, during the first push for half pay, an officer had warned "the Extortioners and Withholders among the Farmers" that "it most evidently is in the power of the army to do themselves justice, and avenge the wrongs which they and their families have suffered by your avarice and extortion. . . . The officers will never entertain the remotest intention of seeking this kind of redress, if your injuries are not so accumulated and irritating, that it would betray a want of military honor and spirit to overlook them unredressed."[19] In December 1782, when the delegation of officers was leaving camp for Philadelphia, Captain Samuel Shaw had told a friend, "*Point d'argent, point de Suisse*, is the prevailing sentiment. . . . It is devoutly to be wished that this application may have the desired effect. If it does not——"[20]

Although they resented ingratitude, they feared isolation even more. Not only would it leave them powerless, but it would also repudiate them as leaders of the revolution. They could have done nothing but ruin their own reputations by a futile attack on the authority of the government they had helped to establish. The officers who stopped short of defiance probably knew this as well as those who organized the repudiation of the anonymous addresses. Washington's appeal allowed the hot-tempered officers to believe that if only their respect for him had not restrained them in a susceptible moment, they would have shown the country how a patriotic gentleman officer demands his due from ungrateful stay-at-homes.

The nationalists' plan to scare reluctant members of Congress into voting for the impost and commutation succeeded not because a military coup was possible, or even because army officers might have defied civilian authority, but because the members feared that Continental soldiers might join the officers in disobeying Congress until they were paid. Jesse Root, a Connecticut delegate, knew that his constituents "could not bear to see men strutting about their streets in the port of masters who had a right to demand of the people a part of their annual labour and toil to support them in idleness." But Root wanted Congress to pay the promised pensions even though the promise had been wrong. More than six months before the Newburgh crisis, he had attempted, the secretary of Congress recorded, "to alarm the fears of Congress" by warning that if Congress neglected or trifled with the officers, "they will either quit the service immediately, or refuse to lay down their arms when the war is over until they have some better security."[21] We can infer that the civilians who feared the officers' vague threats fell victim to their own stereotype of a standing army and to their awareness that Americans had used the army without rewarding or even maintaining it as promised. According to James Madison, the report of the officers' discontent—made graver by difficulties in the peace negotiations and by the resignation of Robert Morris—"oppressed the minds of Congs. with an anxiety and distress which had been scarcely felt in any period of the revolution."[22] As an alternative to the nationalists' proposal, Congress could have faced down the officers, told them to go home and try to collect their lifetime half pay from a bankrupt central government or unwilling states, and told the soldiers to go home with little or nothing. If the delegates had tried this alternative, they probably would have succeeded, but they could not believe it.

The nationalists sought to add the officers and, by implication, the enlisted men to the coalition of public creditors whose demands could induce Americans to strengthen the Continental government. The nationalists' strength always lay less in widespread support for strong government than in public obligation to the nationalists for services to the revolution. The war had shown that independence could not be won without an army and a government. Nationalists had provided money, administrative ability, and persevering service where other revolutionaries had often failed. Robert Morris exploited this dependence and the sense of obligation it induced by resigning as superintendent of finance when the pressure to adopt the impost and commutation was greatest. Morris probably hoped to dramatize the country's dependence on his talents; if Americans realized that they needed him, they would accede to his wishes. Instead, in the coming months fewer and fewer revolutionaries would express a need for the nationalists as leaders, and the army would quickly disband. But during the Newburgh crisis, members of Congress imputed to the nationalists that sinister combination of administrative efficiency, coercive power, and unscrupulousness that the revolution had used, in part, for victory but that constantly threatened to devour the virtuous. When the virtue and strength of the populace had faltered during the war, revolutionaries had relied on the army and the nationalists to persevere. Now that the army and the nationalists seemed to be turning against the populace, how could revolutionaries escape the wrath of their own creatures?

The nationalists confidently arrogated power because they stood to gain by it and because they believed that public virtue had become too weak to sustain American independence. Gouverneur Morris expressed this view with characteristic vigor on January 1, 1783, the day that the delegation of officers from camp arrived in Philadelphia: "The Army have Swords in their Hands. . . . I am glad to see Things in their present Train. Depend on it good will arise from the Situation to which we are hastening. . . . Altho I think it probable that much Convulsion will ensue Yet it must terminate in giving to Government that Power without which Government is but a Name. Government in America is not possessed of it but the People are well prepared. Wearied with the War, their Acquiescence may be depended on with absolute Certainty and you and I my Friend know by Experience that when a few Men of Sense and Spirit get together and declare that they are the Authority such few as are of a different Opinion may easily be convinced of their Mistake by that powerful Argument the Halter."[23]

Gouverneur Morris, Robert Morris, Alexander Hamilton, and their allies in the officer corps went further than other nationalists in forsaking the ideal of public virtue as the nation's security. By contrast, George Washington, though he grew pessimistic about the survival of public virtue, never doubted that both republican government and American independence would have to rest on popular approval. The more extreme nationalists more quickly dismissed the populace from political calculations once it had proven incapable of sustained self-sacrifice. According to these men, the people could be eased into "Acquiescence" by exploitation of their self-interest—the same shortsighted selfishness that had caused them to lose the ideal of revolutionary virtue. Only the true patriots whose honor and public spirit had always matched the *rage militaire* of 1775 could sustain American independence. For these nationalists, the success of the revolution could not be separated from their service and their authority. They believed that they alone had upheld the ideals of 1775 and that the derelictions of other Americans endangered the survival of the republic. Only the men who had won the war could preserve the victory. Military virtues, social hierarchy, and strong government had become not the antitheses of revolutionary ideals but the necessary instruments for the nation's survival—instruments whose merits had been proven by the nationalists alone in the tests of war.[24]

A similar outlook developed in more extreme form among Federalists in the late 1790s. John R. Howe has discussed the contribution of republican ideology to a violent, extremist political style.[25] By viewing political conduct as part of a grand confrontation between liberty and tyranny, virtue and corruption, partisans could see the survival of republicanism at stake in any controversy. Treason, conspiracy, true patriotism, or the preservation of national ideals and independence became the most convincing interpretations of disagreement among revolutionaries. We can see an earlier form of the fervor of the 1790s in some Continental Army officers' conviction that they alone embodied the revolutionary spirit that civilians had betrayed. The officers' military glory seemed to them to express, not threaten, the revolution. The emphasis their ideals placed on climactic crises that tested personal worthiness may have stimulated the violent political self-expression that led some Americans to exalt themselves and to denounce their fellow revolutionaries.

The disbandment of the army, which quickly followed the Newburgh crisis, separated the officers from the soldiers, that is, from "the army," and left the officers subject to the reproach of the citizens whom they had denounced. As civilians began to save the revolution from the pretensions of a military elite, the officers received the kind of righteous opprobrium that they had previously meted out so freely. We can better appreciate the officers' isolation when we contrast their attitude toward pay and discharge with that of enlisted men.

The postwar prosperity that the soldiers hoped for did not begin with their receiving back pay or even current pay. Washington tried to get Robert Morris to obtain three months' pay to give the soldiers at discharge, believing that the money would help reconcile soldiers to going home without a final settlement. He wanted to spare them the embarrassment of arriving in their hometowns broke. Congress could not delay the disbanding of the army until the soldiers' accounts were settled, because each day of the army's service put the government further in debt and made payment more remote. Morris tried one of his intricate account-juggling schemes through Havana, Cadiz, and The Hague, but it did not pay off in time. President Elias Boudinot said that by "an inevitable accident" the notes arrived in camp six days after most soldiers had left.[26] Then Congress and Morris blamed each other for the government's default on the promise of three months' pay. Many, probably most, of the soldiers who received Morris's notes sold them quickly for less than their face value in order to get cash. Some Continental Army officers who had the private capital or who entered into partnerships with other speculators set up note-buying operations in camp and in the soldiers' home states. Later Morris was accused of sabotaging confidence in his own notes so as to buy them up cheap and make all the more profit when the government redeemed them. He denied it. A brief mutiny by a few hundred unpaid Pennsylvania soldiers embarrassed Congress in Philadelphia but secured nothing for the soldiers.[27]

The ease with which Continentals were discharged, their pay and bounty bought for a song, showed how little danger they had posed to civil government and how far from a peacetime standing army they had remained. As news of the peace treaty reached the army in April, soldiers who had enlisted for the duration of the war began to suspect that officials were delaying a formal announcement of peace in order to extend the soldiers' service. Some men defied or insulted officers who tried to hold them to military duty. Although Continentals had learned European techniques of warfare and had developed professional pride in military competence, they had not become a European-style army. They looked forward to better futures than a military one. Colonel Daniel Morgan's promise in 1777—"that the War should not end till the Soldiery were provided out [of] the Estates made by it and of such as had too much Property to their Share"—was unkept.[28] In 1778 the loyalist William Franklin had said of Continentals, "To keep them quiet they are assured by their officers that as soon as the war is over they should not lay down their arms till they had made themselves ample amends for the losses they sustained by the depreciation of the currency etc."[29] But unlike the protesting officers at Newburgh, the soldiers did not even attempt these threats, despite the inequity of their unpaid disbandment. The soldiers were eager to return to civilian life. Judging from their wartime complaints about civilian luxury during army suffering, they probably expected to prosper. Even though the economy had become less active since the boom days of 1780 and 1781, the Continental's old adage that any change had to be for the better must have seemed especially true for discharge. Lieutenant Colonel Stephen Bayard reported from Fort Pitt, "The soldiers have said, as soon as peace was concluded, they would immediately go home, as they then consider themselves free men."[30]

Many officers could not give up their professionalism so quickly. The eagerness of civilians and soldiers for peace left the officers deeper in an isolation that had been growing for at least five years. It became critical in 1783 because the officers were about to lose their commands, their friends, and their sense of their own unique indispensability to the survival of their country. In short, they would have to return to the society from which they had come. The officers' concern about their discharge indicates that comparatively few of them felt secure as gentlemen on their own account, with or without a commission. Nathanael Greene anticipated that one of the officers' special financial burdens after their discharge would be a "military distinction or character to maintain."[31] Their army service had made them feel like gentlemen, and with good reason they feared that maintaining this distinction outside the army would be difficult, probably impossible without external aid. In vain the general officers and regimental commanders petitioned Washington to delay the disbanding until accounts were settled.

One of the main arguments for officers' pensions said that army life had made the officers unfit for ordinary civilian work. Sometimes this unfitness referred to their absence from their professions or the war's interference with their learning one. But more often the unfitness was temperamental. That is, the officers supposedly felt an aversion to the drudgery needed to earn a living: "In an army people contract habits of Indolence, an attachment to company, a disinclination as well as incapacity for business." After some years in the service, men "will loose sight of their former employments and will unhinge their minds from . . . attentive concern for business."[32] Five years' full pay would enable them to overcome this handicap without sinking into poverty. The officers considered this unfitness an inevitable outgrowth of the pride and display that their station in the army had required. Officers "can not return to their former employments," General Arthur St. Clair explained, "their habits are too much changed."[33] Such refinement seemed essential to their public service: the public ought to see it as a part of the officers' patriotism and provide for it as a disability, comparable to the debts the officers had accumulated by serving without adequate pay. An officer leaving the First Virginia State Regiment expressed the problem of many Continental officers: "I may now go where I please, but where to go or what to do I am at a loss. The pay etc. that the Country gives us is not sufficient to live genteely on, and poor me, unfortunately have spent all I had in the Army, so that it's out of my power to commence Trade, which I was brought up to. To work I never did, and to go a begging I can never consent to."[34]

Although the officers, with much justice, said that their army lives had been full of deprivation and sacrifice, they also had come to enjoy the purposefulness, status, and camaraderie. Any form of peacetime enterprise, even with a secure income, would seem ignominious and dull. One officer later said that after the war it took him a year to feel like a farmer again.[35] As we have seen, many of the officers had not developed an administrative competence or a routine of duties whose stability would lend itself to other work. The spirit of the officer corps, which they were loath to lose, grew more out of hardship, combat, recreation, rhetoric, and the shared desire to be gentlemen than out of constant work in supervising their units. Because Continental officers had not maintained a private detachment from the fascination of gentlemanliness and had too seldom tempered their elation by attending to the sustained drudgery of professional duties, they had come to identify their own characters and their standing in the country with a status that was about to end. A few ex-officers killed themselves not long after their discharge. One of them wrote in his suicide note, "I march off as gaily and almost as eagerly as when my friend Genl Wayne Sent me to attack Lord Cornwalles."[36] Other officers' defense of pensions and descriptions of the disbanding of the army suggested great anxiety about their ability to be civilians as successfully as they had been officers.

The officers' demand for recompense and for aid in returning to civilian life brought them new trouble besides adjusting to their discharge. In response to the vote to pay commutation, a flood of public abuse—as if long swelling but dammed until now—poured over Continental Army officers. The most bitter came from New England, and the longest debate took place in Connecticut, but similar hostility affected the whole continent, as the criticism of the Society of the Cincinnati also made clear. All of the arguments against half pay that were aired in Congress in 1778 now filled newspaper columns, spiced with invective. The people had not known about half pay until two or three years after it was voted, the newspapers said. If the army had dissolved for lack of officers, another could have been raised. If officers were unhappy without pensions, they should have resigned. In fact, while officers had been civilians before being commissioned, the war had obstructed their business, "and a generous country gave them employ."[37] Officers had left "their merchandize, their shops, or their ploughs"; let them return.[38] In the army the officers had ten times the opportunities for profiteering from the war that civilians had, and there were ten times as many profiteers among officers; so the officer corps obviously had made one hundred times as much from the war as citizens had made. "Some officers left home in low indigent circumstances. . . . All who return, return in affluence."[39] Had not civilians suffered by British raids, by service in "the militia called forth to face death and danger in the field of battle," by "the patience, the perseverance of the country," by heavy taxes, by a large debt?[40] "I am willing that the soldier should stand on as good a footing as the citizen, but not better."[41] "Why would they wish to mingle with their fellow citizens with that badge of distinction, which would tarnish all the glory of their former exploits?"[42] Not only had formerly obscure officers made money from the war, they even came home looking healthier: "their countenances are fairer and fatter than before the war."[43] The metaphors got mixed as the officers, already fattened in luxury, wrested bread from the mouths of repining infants, yet remained ravenous harpies with whetted beaks and piercing eyes, ready to prey on the public revenue.[44] Why should taxes support a parcel of Narcissuses in their sins of Sodom?[45]

The officers prated about their losses, but everyone could see men who had been nobodies before the war and now expected to live off the earnings of hard-pressed citizens and then claim superior patriotism in the bargain. In vain, the officers' spokesmen computed that five years' full pay would cost an assessment of a penny on the pound for each taxpayer and argued that commutation was pay for services rendered, not a pensioned sinecure. A spokesman for half pay recalled the war years when "all were fleeing from the service of their country" and wives, parents, or near relations were urging soldiers to "look out for themselves with their neighbours at home."[46] Another proponent reminded his readers that life half pay had been voted in October 1780, "when one army was took in Charleston and another was beat in Carolina—and Arnold made a plot to give up all the other forces, and all the paper money was stone dead."[47] The supporters of commutation used the nationalists' argument that the public's loss of virtue had left the revolution dependent on the army, to whom the public now owed a debt. The denunciation of the officers represented a widespread rejection of this argument and a reassertion of public virtue in contrast with officers' corruption. The opponents of commutation reminded the public that the revolution had begun in order to eradicate placemen, whose idle haughtiness made them tools of tyranny. Half pay did not repay service or losses, because recently commissioned officers received the same amount in pensions as longtime veterans. In the course of the debate, suddenly, the enlisted men—former extortioners who had wrested extravagant bounties from the people—became the objects of compassion. Why should the officers expect pensions when the soldiers got nothing? The soldiers had done the fighting, and, if any men got half pay, they should be the ones. In fact, the militia had equal or better claims. At great cost to their livelihoods, these freemen had turned out repeatedly to defend their families and farms. They too should get pensions. This reasoning evidently assumed that distributing sinecures equally to everybody would make them safely republican.

Of course, the opponents of commutation intended that no one should get a pension. They tried to apply the voting rules of the Articles of Confederation retroactively to the Congress that had voted half pay for life. They falsely said that too few state delegations in Congress had approved half pay. They argued that Congress had no authority to grant half pay. They objected to the officers' use of threats at Newburgh to intimidate Congress. When the officers' spokesmen replied that none of the legal objections had arisen while the officers' services were needed, the opponents said, in effect, that the objections were arising now. They saw the grant of pensions and the request for an impost as parts of an interlocking plot to introduce tyranny with placemen and to support placemen with centralized taxation. Yet in 1782 Connecticut, home of the loudest opponents of pensions, had allowed officers who were already qualified for half pay to resign before the end of the war so that new officers could be commissioned and made eligible for pensions. When criticized in Congress for this practice, the Connecticut delegates replied that other states were doing it, so why should Connecticut lose its share? In 1783 a convention assembled in Middletown, Connecticut, to denounce commutation and the officers. The unpopularity of Governor Jonathan Trumbull's defense of the pensions contributed to his retirement from public office. Toward the end, the newspaper debate thinned out into silliness, and it became hard to tell the satirists from the extremists: "N.B. As I am an advocate for the People, I am the Voice of God."[48]

Even more clearly than the first debate during the Valley Forge winter, this controversy over pensions revealed the deeply divided interpretations of the war. General Arthur St. Clair spoke for many officers when he said that the opponents of half pay could not be sincere; they "make use of it only to cover their dislike to rewarding the men who have made them free."[49] In attacks and rebuttals the spokesmen of the two sides repeatedly questioned the sincerity, the intelligence, and sometimes the sanity of those who disagreed with them. Each group represented itself as the defender of the revolution against the crimes of the other. The opposition was always perpetrating falsehood or suffering delusion. The officers and their supporters saw the public's debt to the army so clearly that their opponents' refusal to acknowledge it connoted a loss of political decorum. When a spokesman for pensions summarized his opponents' outlook, their defiance of Congress seemed to demand "a liberty of doing what we please, and of obeying any law we approve and opposing any law we dislike."[50] To men who saw themselves defending sanctity of contract, obedience to law, and the independence of America, "these convulsions" were licentious and would yield to "a general conviction of the necessity of a supreme power and a more peaceable acquiescence in their decrees."[51] The defenders of the revolution would guard America not so much from a differing version of the way independence had been won as from political delusion that incapacitated its victims' civic responsibility.

Then, suddenly, the whole controversy disappeared from

public debate. By the spring of 1784, opponents of commutation had not reversed it or persuaded the officers to renounce it. They just quit talking about it. Several reasons may explain the collapse of vocal opposition. People gradually learned that commutation had been lawfully voted and that it would not cost very much. While most people in New England, and probably throughout the country, opposed half pay, the opposition could not create the aura of united revolutionary indignation to which they were accustomed when denouncing the sycophantic agents of tyranny. Even Samuel Adams upheld Congress's right to grant pensions in order to obtain "a disciplined Army." Commutation, in his opinion, had been "perhaps too much altercated" in Connecticut and Massachusetts.[52] The supporters of commutation wrote satires of the critics' overreaction. These evidently were effective; letters to the editor complained that such frivolity ought not to enter a momentous debate.[53] The surviving hostility toward the officers focused on criticism of the Society of the Cincinnati.

In the eyes of the critics, the officers' worst crime was not so much their attempt to get on the public payroll—a time-honored American ambition—as their claim to social distinction based on superior revolutionary merit. Once it seemed clear that the officers would not achieve this distinction, concern over pensions fell off sharply. The public wanted the officers, like the privates, to return to civilian life inconspicuously, not only laying aside their military character for the safety of republicanism but also forgoing invidious claims to have done more for independence than civilians had done. Officers could share the celebration of national victory, just as they could receive the applause of spectators at the liberation of Charleston and New York, but they should not presume to take it personally and claim a superior patriotism symbolized by a pension. Former Captain James Morris, who lived near Litchfield, Connecticut, recalled the spread of the news of commutation: "I became obnoxious to the mass of people. . . . When I had any severe sickness they hoped I would die. One noisy old man said he hoped I would die and that they would take my skin for a drum head to drum other officers out of town."[54]

The opponents of commutation wanted more than the preservation of social equality against the officers' claim to be supported like gentlemen; the opponents also wanted to prove that officers had not surpassed civilians in service to the revolution. To the army as a whole the public expressed gratitude. For the soldier who flaunted his personal claim to gratitude, civilians felt envy and suspicion. To some officers, the critics' irresponsibility proved how ineffectually such citizens would sustain independence. Lieutenant Colonel Ebenezer Huntington, disgusted by "a people who criminate us for making them free," decided to store his uniform to be ready for "a revolution, which will happen in Eighteen Months, unless government is supported." The licentiousness of the officers' critics convinced him that "even tyranny is better than Anarchy."[55] Anthony Wayne agreed with William Irvine that the people "have been put in possession of *extreme* of liberty at too cheap a rate. . . . There are too many of our Citizens that would not hesitate, to *wipe* off the large debt due to the army, with a *Sponge*." In the face of such widespread opposition, he damned the critics with the word "faction," meaning that they were not true patriots. "The revolution of America . . . will fill the brightest page of history to the end of time; and the conduct of her Officers and Soldiers will be handed down to the latest ages as a model of Virtue, perseverance and bravery;—the smallness of their numbers, and the unparalle[le]d hardships . . . and dangers that they have encountered, in the defence of this Country . . . places them in a point of view, hurtful to the eyes of the leaders of *faction* and *party*, who possessed neither the virtue or fortitude to meet the Enemy in the field, and seeing the involuntary deference *yet* paid by the bulk of the people to their protectors and Deliverers,—envy that green eyed mo[n]ster, will stimulate them to seize with avidity every pretext, to depreciate the merits of those who have filled the breach and bled at every pore. . . . The Hottentots hold that after killing a good man, the *Assassin* possesses his soul—if the leaders of faction have adopted this Idea I could almost forgive them for their own are D——n bad."[56] Here we see Wayne's rendition of the civilians' effort to reclaim from the army the glory of winning the Revolutionary War. By discrediting the officers for their pensions and their aristocratic pretensions, civilians could demonstrate that the public and not the army had secured independence.

The winter at Valley Forge and, by implication, the whole war had been reinterpreted when a writer could argue that "the army . . . was preserved from impending destruction, at the expence and by the vigilance of the towns."[57] Americans reclaimed the war from the army to whom they had tried to entrust it, and they showed how the people had won the war together. The future security of American independence would rest not on a military establishment but on public virtue. To believe that public virtue had the strength to sustain independence, Americans wanted to believe that public virtue had won it. This belief underlay the reinterpretation of the war, in which civilians could portray themselves as the rescuers of the army at Valley Forge rather than the main cause of the army's hardship.

The demobilization of the soldiers exemplified the effort to make the army as unobtrusive as possible. The soldiers who had enlisted for the duration of the war left the army first. In the first two weeks of June, regiments marched out of camp toward Massachusetts, Maryland, New Hampshire, and New Jersey, where they were disbanded. They received a furlough that was, in fact, a discharge. More men were discharged by December, until the whole army was disbanded. The soldiers were dispersed before they were released because their commanders feared that poverty and resentment would cause the soldiers to abuse citizens.

The departures from camp dramatized the wartime attachments that had grown among soldiers and had separated them from civilians. Hardly anyone doubted that the parting was inevitable and final, and few wanted to delay it. But the army had given its soldiers bonds of memory, endurance, and skill that would have little public place in their future lives. The wartime dedication to army life they had shown—often grudgingly or jokingly, even during mutinies and complaints—now was expressed in their attachment to men whom they would not see again. One of them recalled, "The soldiers . . . were as strict a band of brotherhood as Masons and, I believe, as faithful to each other." There were some "misanthropists," but for the most part, "we were young men and had warm hearts. I question if there was a corps in the army that parted with more regret than ours did, the New Englanders in particular."[58] General Robert Howe's farewell orders tried to console the soldiers, "who if they meet with no other reward, will retire with a heart felt consciousness of having amply filled the measure of their duty, and of having deserved, though they should not obtain, the rewards, applause and gratitude of their country." Howe knew that, "as a patriot," he ought to welcome the disbandment of the army; "yet to his feelings as a man, it is an awful point of time. . . . In the course of service, sympathies have been excited, affections impressed, and friendships established in his mind, which time, absence, or accident, shall never wipe away. . . . As his sensibility upon this occasion is too big for utterance, he will fly, if possible, from the painful recollection, and haste to do what he shall always take pleasure in, that is, to hope the officers and men . . . may be as happy as he wishes them, and they will be ever happy indeed."[59] The pride in a unique form of service, which other revolutionaries could never know, infused these farewells as it would later infuse the memoirs of men who remembered the war years.

In the midst of this emotion, both officers and privates had to worry about paying their way home. Secretary at War Lincoln arrived at New Windsor before the disbandment. He was supposed to have brought Morris's notes for three months' pay; instead, he tried to borrow a few dollars from Baron Steuben for some officers who needed travel money. Steuben replied that "my finances were a miniature copy of those of the new empire."[60] Six weeks earlier, the Baron had proposed to Washington that the discharge of the army climax in an elaborate, disciplined ceremony. Instead, the regiments had left camp one by one, without formalities, under the euphemism of a furlough. As the officers were parting, Steuben went around trying to cheer them up. When it was over he wrote, "This disbandment of the army . . . was so thoroughly comic that you would have laughed yourself sick had you seen it."[61]

Some soldiers got home by begging. Maryland Continentals

had begged their way north through the Carolinas and Virginia in 1782. In April 1783 a prisoner of war released in New York went about the city and said to people, "Your servent gentlefolks, I wish you much Joy with the nuse of peace, I hope it will be a long and lasting one," and asked for a handout; "some of them would pity us and would give something, some half a Dollar, some a quarter, some less, some nothing but frowns."[62]

The officers' partings drew on the long-standing, self-conscious distinctiveness of the officer corps and on the officers' fondness for displays of emotion. They had cultivated close friendships and then, as friends and gentlemen, had borne the central responsibility for directing the war and keeping the army together. The dissolution of this band of brothers awoke keen feelings as units scattered in the spring. By the time Washington bid his formal farewell to the remaining officers in New York City in December, all those present must have known how little sympathy they could expect from a suspicious public. On December 4, in the long room of Fraunces's Tavern, Washington said to the officers, "With a heart full of love and gratitude, I now take leave of you. I most devoutly wish that your latter days may be as prosperous and happy as your former ones have been glorious and honorable." After he asked each man to shake hands with him, the commander in chief, 209 pounds, and General Henry Knox, 280 pounds, embraced. One by one, each officer came forward to take leave of His Excellency. Many, including Washington, wept; and all savored the "delicious melancholy" of the occasion.[63]

The Society of the Cincinnati took its strength from bonds like these. Henry Knox—who, at his bookstore, had shared military reading and discussion with Nathanael Greene before the war—planned the organization for veteran officers in 1776. Like Cincinnatus they would go back to their farms, but they would cherish their military glory by meeting from time to time, electing officers, and wearing an eagle badge on a ribbon. They would establish a fund to save former officers from poverty, and their society would be perpetual because membership would be hereditary, succeeding to the eldest son. The society was formally created in camp on May 10, 1783. Washington became president-general. Knox's plan appealed to a common desire among officers to perpetuate their military bonds. Jethro Sumner wrote to William Heath from North Carolina, "Before any intimation had reached us of what had been done at Hudsons River the Officers of this line had it in contemplation to form themselves into a society, less extensive, but with views similar to those of the Cincinati."[64]

Public hostility to the society found a popular spokesman in "Cassius," that is, Aedanus Burke of South Carolina, whose pamphlet attacking the organization was published in Charleston, Philadelphia, New York, Hartford, and Newport. Attackers and defenders of the society agreed that Burke's pamphlet tapped a widespread suspicion of the Cincinnati. "The epigraph of Burke's pamphlet," Jefferson later wrote, "was 'Blow ye the trumpet in Zion.' It's effect corresponded with it's epigraph."[65] Burke's arguments found widespread support in public and private criticism of the society and its members: the group's first general meeting in Philadelphia in 1784 spent much of its time discussing ways to deflect criticism.

According to the attacks, the Society of the Cincinnati was a conspiracy by a group of crypto-aristocrats who intended to supplant republican institutions with a nobility. Badges of status and hereditary succession were obvious attempts to corrupt American virtue with European social distinctions. Burke did not believe that Knox had devised the organization: the mastermind was Baron Steuben. The Baron intended to recreate the hierarchies that tyrannized the European lands from which he had come. Thomas Jefferson told Washington that the officers' well-meant affection might unintentionally create an organization hostile to "the natural equality of man" and conducive to foreign influence, privilege, military distinction, "habits of subordination," and the subversion of liberty.[66] Privately Jefferson believed that Steuben and Knox were "the leading agents" among officers "trained to monarchy by military habits" who proposed to Washington that he "assume himself the crown" with the support of the army. When, according to Jefferson, Washington indignantly refused, "the same individuals" created the Cincinnati "to be engrafted into the future frame of government." Jefferson thought that the society had been about to dissolve itself under the pressure of opposition in 1784 but that its life had been prolonged by the popularity of membership among officers of the French army.[67] Jefferson's fears reflected the concerns of the Cincinnati's many opponents. The officers' claim to superior patriotism and their effort to keep that superiority visible had to mean that they expected both economic and political privilege. In showing their reluctance to become ordinary citizens, the officers were revealing their determination to rule.

Steuben and Knox laughed at the public outcry. Knox wrote to Steuben, "Your society, monsieur baron, has occasioned great jealousies among the good people of New England, who say it is an altogether outlandish creature, formed by foreign influence. . . . You see how much you have to answer for by the introduction of your European distinctions. . . . Burke's allusion has fixed it, and you must support the credit of having created a new and hereditary nobility."[68] Steuben replied, "A ça, Monsieur le Cincinnatus! your pernicious designs are then unveiled —you wish to introduce dukes and peers into our republic? No, my Lord; no, your Grace, that will not do; there is a Cassius more far-sighted than this German baron; of whom you have made a cat's paw to draw the chestnuts out of the fire. . . . But listen! I will prove to Cassius that this dangerous plan had its birth in the brain of two Yankees; *i.e.*, Knox and Huntington: therefore

> 'Blow ye the Trumpet in Zion.'

We know very well these Bostonians and the people of the Holy Land, who beneath a Presbyterian and modest air conceal the most ambitious designs. . . . then,

> 'Blow ye the Trumpet in Zion.'

See the pamphlet of Cassius—read it—tremble! . . . I love you too well, you American dogs, to speak all the evil of you that you merit."[69]

Both the Cincinnati's organization and the provisions of the society's constitution were native to America, although we can assume that Knox took the idea of the society from European chivalric orders. Of course, the officers wanted to remain gentlemen, a status as old in America as the first colonists from Europe. The provision for hereditary membership probably entailed less emulation of foreign aristocracy than perpetuation of the revolutionaries' constant concern for posterity. The Cincinnati did wish, as their critics charged, to keep alive the wartime distinction of military service. They believed, as wartime appeals had said, that military service was the highest form of revolutionary achievement and that every succeeding generation would gratefully preserve the memory of the army's valor. Just as revolutionaries expected their posterity to remember them as the fathers of their country, the officers could ensure that the distinction of a hereditary society would keep alive the distinction of the founders. The eagle badge would claim deference in the form of respect due to patriotism. Members of the society became supporters of and officials in strengthened governments, including the federal government under the United States Constitution. The society neither intended nor attempted to introduce itself and hereditary officeholding into the institutions of government.

According to the Cincinnati's opponents, the military aristocrats further intended to spread alien opulence and luxury in America, partly supported by pensions wrested from taxpayers. The society seemed to revive the subversion of republicanism that revolutionaries had attacked in the form of Parliament and privileged officers of the crown. The Continental officers' desire to preserve the economic status they believed their services had earned and to perpetuate an elite of patriotism gave their countrymen the chance to reassert vigilance on behalf of liberty. The opponents of the society kept mentioning two of its attributes that stimulated both their suspicion and their envy—the superior fame that the officers' services had won and the badge that symbolized it. In twenty pages of her *History*, Mercy Otis Warren dwelt with horrified fascination on baubles, scepters, diadems, crowns, military knighthood, military nobles, the eagle and the ribbon, stars, garters, more crowns, more diadems, more scepters, the splendor of courts and the regalia of kings.[70] The opponents tacitly accepted the argument of the officers that superior patriotic service deserved superior distinction in government and society. But rather than envy the officers' distinction, Americans would deny its validity. By attacking the Cincinnati, citizens could reclaim primacy in the revolutionary effort, discredit the officers' pretensions to have saved liberty, and renew the belief that luxury and ambition for distinction were monarchical, military, foreign.

Washington recognized the strength of the opposition to the Society of the Cincinnati. At the general meeting in 1784, he gave "a very long speech, and with much warmth and agitation, he . . . reiterated his determination to vacate his place in the Society, if it could not be accommodated to the feeling and pleasure of the several States." He was ready to propose "one great sacrifice more to the world"—that is, the officers' giving up their society—but he did not want to disappoint the foreign members.[71] Finally the general meeting proposed abolition of hereditary membership, but the state units did not ratify this amendment. The society remained hereditary, and Washington remained president-general.

Although criticism of the Cincinnati continued, the public outrage soon abated. By tacit consent, the delegates to the general meeting agreed that the eagle badge and ribbon would be worn in public only on days of convention and at funerals. Jefferson said, "They laid them up in their bureaus with the medals of American independence, with those of the trophies they had taken and the battles they had won. But through all the United states no officer is seen to offend the public eye with the display of this badge."[72] Here we see the strongest threat that the society had posed and the main reason that opposition dwindled. Americans did not want to forget the War of Independence; they wanted to believe that all of them had won it. If the officers would imitate the privates and refrain from flouting this belief, their organization could be tolerated. By defeating the officers' demand for deference, the opponents of pensions and of the Cincinnati—neither of which was ended—accomplished a miniature revolution. Citizens had overthrown the beginnings of aristocracy, showing that they were the true defenders of liberty.

In the last months of the Continental Army's existence, there were renewed warnings against a standing army. While Americans considered hierarchical regimentation necessary for an army, they disliked its existence, even though they were not personally subject to it. Revolutionaries who were hostile to the military drew on the same assumptions about politics and human nature that had underlain their resistance to Britain. These assumptions said in effect that a righteous person could survive only in a righteous world. Powerful government would overcome liberty; people who lived in the presence of corruption would become corrupt; military discipline would make soldiers prefer dictatorship. By this reasoning, freedom and a standing army could not both survive in the United States. As soon as Americans discovered a life of luxurious ease, conspicuous status, and unthinking obedience, they would succumb to it; then, by attracting support with bribery and corruption, or by seizing power with force, they would destroy the freedom of others. The critics of the Continental Army, relying partly on the officers' self-advertisement, began to suggest that the army matched this description, especially in the two years after the victory at Yorktown. The pretensions of many officers to superior social status and patriotism, compounded by the efforts of a few officers to defy civil supremacy, gave revolutionaries at home the evidence with which to reassert the consistency of their ideals. An official of Washington County, Virginia, reported to the state authorities in 1782, "Some how there is a general disgust taken place for what bears the name of a Regular."[73] Having won independence with the help of military ambition, coercion, and professionalism, revolutionaries now could again assert that American liberty would survive only if these alien tools of tyranny were eradicated. Americans wanted to exclude such vices from public life and thereby prevent their countrymen from surrendering to them.

Baron Steuben ended his appeal for a small regular army and a trained militia with these words: "I foresee, however, it will be subject to one very popular objection, 'It is in fact a

Standing Army.' Yes Fellow Citizens I admit it—it is a Standing Army, but composed of your brethren and your sons. Can you require or conceive a better security. Are they not your natural guardians? And shall it be supposed a cockade and feather, the *Vox et preteria nihil*, of the military character can alienate either their affections or their interest? Be assured you reflect upon yourselves by nourishing the suspicion, and wound the feelings of men who are at least entitled to your gratitude and esteem."[74] Steuben was briefly stating his belief that acquiring professional discipline—the cockade and feather—did not alter the character or loyalty of the citizen and that believing otherwise revealed a deep uncertainty about the strength of that character and loyalty in the first place. If Steuben expected Americans to disprove such uncertainty by adopting his military establishment in 1784, he was disappointed. Instead, they tried to prove their dedication to liberty by abolishing the army—except for a small corps of Indian-fighters—and by attacking former officers, who, according to the attackers, embodied all of the nation's susceptibility to military vices. The war years had created in America a group of men who advocated a permanent military establishment. For these men, the war experience had discredited the idea that all citizens could take the field as effective soldiers. American independence and security could more safely rest on the expertise of trained men than on the virtue of the citizenry. This reasoning, like the proposals for strong national government, received little popular support at the end of the war. The successful revolutionaries celebrated the winning of independence, not its precariousness, and in doing so they praised both civilians and soldiers as victorious patriots, not as employers and professionals. The preeminent popular message of 1783 was the triumph of public virtue, not its failure.

To deny the victory, the prevalence, or the sufficiency of public virtue was to challenge the success of the revolution and the existence of a unique American character. Only if the revolutionaries as a people had won the war did they have a hope to escape the vices that had enslaved the rest of the world. The Awakening cast of mind, which sought assurance of worth through zeal, underlay the revolutionaries' adoption of an ideology that explained the world in opposing, mutually exclusive dualities: liberty or power, virtue or corruption, freedom or slavery, courage or fear, salvation or damnation, happiness or despair. For the people as a whole, failure to sustain the necessary strength would not be a matter of degree, entailing easy resort to expedient alternatives. Failure would mean weakness, which would doom the revolution and the society.

The anxiety that pervaded the revolutionary mind gave Americans great energy in pursuing their ideals. But by making failure inadmissible, anxiety could also foster exaggerated claims of success. One such claim—the perseverance of public virtue as the main guarantor of independence—helped turn Americans against the officers' arrogance. Similarly, the officers' vaunted glory rested partly on their claim that they, almost alone, had won independence and that an army and a government, in the absence of public virtue, could maintain it. The officers' assertion of preeminence originated less in monarchical, militaristic, European sympathies than in the workings of a moral absolutism that lay at the heart of the American Revolution. The officers and their critics prefigured later parties and movements that sought to mobilize the righteous and expel or subordinate the alien. Politics premised on fallible people's capacity to fulfill absolute ideals would give much scope to delusions of achievement. Such achievement could substitute the pillorying of betrayers of the revolution for the unattainable proof of individual and national worthiness. The popular interpretation of victory in the Revolutionary War rejected the officers' pretensions, abolished the army, and in doing so restored the citizens to their original and vital stature as the pillars of America's future glory.

Americans celebrated peace by eating. There were orations, toasts, and salutes of various kinds in different towns, but almost every community that held a public celebration had a spread of hot dishes, meats, and drink. Some towns roasted an ox, and Southerners barbecued. The message of the formal speeches matched the mood of the communities' potluck. John

Murray of Newburyport, Massachusetts, speaking from the pulpit above George Whitefield's tomb, told his listeners how they felt: "Joy dances in every eye. Pleasure beams in every countenance; and every bosom beats high with the emotions peculiarly fitted to hail the auspicious day that declares the clouds of horror fled, to return no more for ever. . . . Thy vine and thy fig tree are thine."[75] The United States was about to enter the prosperous, happy future that the revolutionaries had promised. True, no one had expected the war to last so long or cost so much, but in the face of surprises and reverses, the revolutionaries had persevered until the inevitable triumph. The army, and especially the commander in chief, received praise for their service; cannons were fired, and militia paraded, but there was little of the celebration of military ardor and discipline with which the revolutionaries had begun the war eight years earlier. The *rage militaire* had long since ended, and for years Americans had wanted and expected the war to end. They no longer expressed their patriotism primarily by glorifying military strength. Veterans did not take conspicuous places at the celebrations, except for officers who sometimes shared prominence with state leaders. If former Continental soldiers were present, they blended with the citizenry and ate well. In Ipswich, Massachusetts, Levi Frisbie assured the people gathered in an "exceedingly crowded" meetinghouse that "every zealous and active friend to his Country's cause, of whatever rank or denomination, and whether employed at home or abroad, in the Cabinet or the Field, should receive from his grateful Countrymen, that portion of honor and applause due to virtue and merit." After the oration, the people gathered around two very long tables on the town green and partook of "cold hams, bacon, tongues, fowls, veal, etc."[76]

Major Benjamin Tallmadge carved a roasted ox for the citizens of Brookhaven, New York, where his father was minister. He said that "all was harmony and joy, for all seemed to be of one mind."[77] The peace celebrations strove for a union and a joy that revolutionaries wanted but that they could no longer expect with the confidence of 1775 or even with the anxiety of 1778. If the British had recognized American independence in

August of 1776, the national jubilee would have outstripped anything the revolutionaries later did to denounce Arnold or to celebrate Yorktown. Quick victory would have confirmed God's plan for His people who were preserving liberty and true religion for an enslaved world. Quick victory would have proven the strength of virtuous resistance to tyranny without requiring Americans to resort to some of the coercive techniques of fighting and governing used by the enemy. Americans could say and believe that victory in 1783 no less confirmed the spirit of 1775, but they could not feel it so spontaneously as they had felt their first zeal. Their conviction that they had proven a national strength and earned a glorious national future relied less on unquestioned assumptions and more on fervent proclamations. One who believed that the war had vindicated the ideals of resistance and of independence relied less on certainty and more on rhetoric. Americans' confidence was alloyed, like that of a militia officer in letters to his wife during 1781. When the capture of Cornwallis was certain, St. George Tucker wrote, "Amidst the late gloom the dawn of happiness now appears and the smiling prospect of Peace begins to be discovered. Can you assign a reason my dear Fanny why my style in several of my late letters so often breaks out into bombast? I wish I could avoid what I so cordially condemn: but I find that I am imperceptibly led from the exaltation of mind which I have for a fortnight experienced to burst into a turgid manner of writing which I condemn no less in myself than in others."[78]

All but a few of the celebrators in 1783 had been living, in many respects, nearly peacetime lives for two years, or, in most cases, five years or more. They welcomed the final treaty, but only in the hasty summaries of orators could the victory seem to flow directly from their united, virtuous striving. Despite the wartime descriptions of spreading luxury and corruption, the peace orations and after-dinner toasts reclaimed the revolutionaries' virtue by telling them that they had not yet been corrupted and by warning them to avoid such a fate. Most revolutionaries had been working to achieve the prosperity and happiness Britain had intended to deny them. Their love of freedom was, if changed at all, stronger than in 1775. But it was less risky. The version of the coming happiness that Americans gathered to celebrate promised much less sacrifice and hardship than prosperity and ease. On the festive day, instead of musters, parades, prayers, tears, and fast days, people got fireworks, a prayer of thanksgiving, a speech of self-praise, and a good meal.

Probably most of the celebrators knew or were related to men who died in the Continental Army or the militia during the eight years of war. Many could remember the cost of war when the armies had been near them or when soldiers had brought disease among them. The peace orations did not overlook the costs of the war, and the celebrations did not make light of them. But revolutionaries could remember many things about the war besides its costs and its promises—things that found little place in the discussion of victory but that may have helped to keep 1783 from being a spontaneously joyous confirmation of the ardor of 1775.

Americans knew that the revolution had included conduct they had hoped to avoid. This meant not only the sectional, factional, and personal rivalries, the graft of public officials and contractors, the greed of farmers and dealers in manufactured goods, the flourishing trade with the enemy, and the desperate devices to escape military service; it also meant the techniques that had helped to win independence: conscription of citizens, confiscation of property, creation of a regular army with rigorously disciplined soldiers and ambitious officers, reliance on the mysterious and probably corrupt financial and administrative resources of the Financier. Perhaps independence could have been won without these techniques, but it had not been. The survival of American liberty—Americans' self-preservation—could never be wholly separated from force, bloodshed, cheating, and selfishness wrought by revolutionaries on each other. In fact, Americans had shown at least as much ingenuity in extemporizing these techniques of survival as they had shown in planning the constitutions and laws that limited or prohibited such techniques. The revolutionaries had held onto their millennial vision of the future, but had done whatever seemed necessary to get through the war.

Yet, even though this was true and even though hardly anyone could help but know it, this was not the way the revolutionaries wanted to portray themselves. To posterity, they would be the generation that, in the face of threats from an all-conquering empire, had dared to live according to their principles and so had made posterity free. Newspapers in 1780 printed an imaginary American Revolution Centennial poem of 1875, so that revolutionaries could read their descendants' view of the war:

> When Freedom call'd they said '*We come, we come*!'
> Then buckled on their armour, steel'd their hearts,
> And through thickest ranks of British murderers
> (By Heaven inspired) they cut their glorious way. . . .
> '*Fair Liberty or Death*', they nobly cry'd,
> 'Is our unalterable aim, and creed,'—
> Not all the storms of time, or chance, or fate,
> E'er could shake the fixed purpose of their souls:
> A brother's blood fresh streaming from his wounds,
> Nor the expiring hero's dying groans,
> Nor pestilence that swept, with awful stroke,
> Thousands of manly youth to realms unknown;
> Nor tears from the lov'd partners of their souls,
> The infant's melting call, nor virgins sigh,
> Check'd their ardour, or made their virtue pause. . . .
> What arms of steel, what manly souls they were!
> Sublime o'er narrow views they pierced the veil
> Of distant years, lov'd us, although unborn,
> And purchased, with their arms and purest blood,
> The bright inheritance we now enjoy.[79]

In their histories—even when their histories, like their postwar politics, criticized fellow revolutionaries—they would equal or surpass the heroes of antiquity who had fought similar struggles. In 1781 Governor John Hancock urged the Massachusetts House of Representatives to imitate Pennsylvania's measures "for preserving the Materials necessary to a particular and clear History of the American Revolution." All states should contribute to such a work, "which if just and faithful, must do immortal Honor to the Citizens, of these States, and to those who have been distinguished by their Confidence in Council and in Arms—an History that must yield uncommon Entertainment to the inquisitive and curious, and at the same time afford the most usefull and important Lessons not only to our own posterity, but to all succeeding Generations."[80] Charles Thomson, the longtime secretary of Congress, probably knew more about the administration and politics of the Revolutionary War than any other American, but he refused to publish a history of the revolution: "I could not tell the truth without giving great offense. Let the world admire our patriots and heroes. Their supposed talents and virtues (where they were so) by commanding imitation will serve the cause of patriotism and of our country." According to another version of his refusal, he concluded by saying, "I shall not undeceive future generations." Before he died, Thomson burned his papers.[81]

Above all, posterity would remember that the revolutionaries had sustained the spirit of 1775 and the goal of 1776 against even greater challenges than anyone had foreseen. The revolutionaries' victory had a clear lesson for the future: "And if you are not happy, Oh! Americans, it must be your own fault; you have no charges to bring against God, for his want of goodness and care towards you!"[82] When Chaplain Israel Evans spoke these words on December 11, 1783, he may have been recalling the widely praised farewell Washington had written to the states in June. Washington's hopes for the future had ended with the warning, "At this auspicious period, the United States came into existence as a Nation, and if their Citizens should not be completely free and happy, the fault will be intirely their own."[83] Republics and the virtue on which they rested usually had short lives. Few peoples had sustained the voluntary sacrifice and communal strength needed to preserve self-government. American revolutionaries wanted history to show that they had not lost their country's chance for lasting liberty. If future generations forfeited the legacy of the revolution, the children who had grown weak and had failed would have to blame themselves, because the founding generation had left the country's strength, virtue, and liberty intact. Perhaps in bequeathing to posterity not only a legacy of ideals and sacrifices but also a version of history, the revolutionaries assured themselves that they had not betrayed the ideals of 1775. They could then know that they had not simply founded another country like the many corrupt and enslaved nations around them, but had proven that at least one generation of Americans could attain virtue and could be happy. The heavy responsibility implied in the warnings of Evans and Washington would then fall not on the revolutionaries for their wartime failures and compromises but on the children who heard the revolutionaries' version of the War for Independence.

If the revolutionaries could read the 150 years of praise of their valor, virtue, and wisdom since the deaths of John Adams and Thomas Jefferson, they would not be surprised, since they planned it and started it. In doing so, they entailed on their heirs an ideal of virtue and achievement that those heirs could never equal. The revolutionaries hardly expected posterity to equal it—they privately knew that they themselves had not—but they expected their successors to strive for it and to be grateful to their stronger ancestors. Victory in the Revolutionary War would make the future America a repository of the "spirit of wisdom, liberty, patriotism and bravery" because God gave these to "the *patriots* and *heroes*; and even *the whole body of the people* of the present generation."[84] But, as we have seen, an important source of that success did not appear in the revolutionaries' self-portrait: their use of coercion, corruption, and self-interest to survive and to prosper from the war and, in part, to win it. When later generations found themselves caught in similar toils, they would contrast modern conduct with the spirit of the revolution. What secret made the revolutionaries' struggles heroic and ours imitative?

The revolutionaries constantly invoked their ideals to redefine their experience and make it as heroic as it ought to have been. At the same time, they did not forget that they ought to be living those ideals. In the triumphs, in the crises, even in the times of negligence, Americans' minds infused events with universal moral significance. The war years had a special intensity for everyone not only because of the risks in the experience but also because of its meaning. Lucy Knox, who had left her loyalist parents to stay with her husband, a young Continental artillery officer, "often remarked that she *lived* more in one year at this period of excitement, than in a dozen of ordinary life."[85] When revolutionary virtue and heroism seemed to be at stake in any development, not even defeats, backsliding, or expedients could be "ordinary." Simply to survive among the victors was to share the war's test of worthiness and its promise of reward. In his thanksgiving discourse after the peace, Joseph Buckminster said, "Days that *try men's souls*, improve those minds that abide the trial."[86]

The war was long partly because of revolutionaries' frequent failure to contribute by physical force or material interest to the winning of American independence. Yet the whole war remained memorable to all of the victors because the prevailing measure of the significance of their contributions weighed not so much their physical or material sacrifice as their idealism. Americans did not feel like summer soldiers or sunshine patriots; they believed that their souls had been tried because they had cared about the outcome of the war on which the freedom of posterity and the transformation of the world depended. They had cherished their ideals, and their ideals had won. A war that had been much longer than anyone expected seemed short when judged by its promise for the future. In 1783 Ezra Stiles knew that his vision of a free, prosperous, cultured, and devout America would come true because "We live in an age of wonders: we have lived an age in a few years: we have seen more wonders accomplished in *eight* years, than are usually unfolded in a century."[87] If Americans had not widely shared this ability to see beyond material facts and to reinterpret events in order to make an ideal seem true, they probably would not have sought independence and surely would not have won it when they did. That ability gave them a reason to strive and a proof of the value of victory that no expedient calculation of advantage could have equaled.

The revolution had such comprehensive, demanding ideals

that no one could match them, and few could pursue them unswervingly. But the many derelictions of wartime behavior seemed to pale beside the one essential achievement—the ideals would survive. The revolutionaries' certainty of their superiority in the eyes of posterity suggests that they did not expect the ideals ever again to be in danger of extinction. Faced with the threat of despair and permanent slavery, the revolutionary generation had secured a refuge for the imminent fulfillment of their vision. To have shared such a victory was all the more momentous because of the rigor of such absolute ideals, which were especially difficult to sustain. If the revolution demanded perfect self-sacrifice for the future good of mankind and if one endorsed that demand and if the revolution triumphed and if one lived to share the triumph, one achieved a stature that could not be duplicated once the revolution was over. Those who later could only compare absolute ideals and modern conduct, always finding conduct deficient, would never know the thrill of persevering through the one crisis when the ideals themselves seemed in danger of extinction.

Nathaniel Niles had described this feeling in 1775:

> Life, for my Country and the Cause of Freedom,
> Is but a Trifle for a Worm to part with;
> And if preserved in so great a Contest,
> Life is redoubled.[88]

The momentousness of the contest obliterates any signs of expediency or degress of merit. To die in the cause is heroic and to survive among the victors is heroic. Everyone is a veteran of the war for freedom. The attempt to live constantly according to the demands of the *rage militaire* of 1775 quickly narrowed to a small group of people. Yet victory, which relied on the partial, fallible, intermittent efforts of the many, enabled a whole generation to claim that their strength had been proven by the standard of 1775 and to bequeath the standard and the example to posterity.

Acknowledgments

This book is a shortened and revised version of my doctoral dissertation, "The Continental Army in the American Mind: 1775–1783," completed at the University of California, Berkeley, in 1977. The research was done in the University Library at Berkeley, and I benefitted from the efficient help of the staff in the Inter-Library Loan and the Newspaper and Microcopy departments. The dissertation committee consisted of Robert Middlekauff, Chairman, Thomas G. Barnes, and Norman Jacobson. Each of them read an early version of the manuscript and gave me valuable advice.

Before completing the revision I received close critical readings and useful suggestions from David Bertelson, J. K. Bozman, E. Wayne Carp, Joseph Franaszek, Christian G. Fritz, John Ollila, W. J. Rorabaugh, John Shy, and Frank S. Smith. Their support for the project also contributed to its completion in ways other than the pages of notes they gave me.

Four scholars who have not read all of the manuscript also helped me at critical points. Edmund L. Drago has fostered and improved my work since I was an undergraduate; he and the History Department of the College of Charleston in Charleston, South Carolina, hospitably gave me a chance to try out a version of Chapter 6. Winthrop D. Jordan gave me insightful reactions to some early chapters. Sheldon Rothblatt, in his graduate seminar and historical methods course, encouraged an open-minded, venturous approach to the techniques of writing history. James A. Sandos not only read the early chapters but also, during twelve years of friendship, persevered in a prolonged conversation about the writing of history and the concerns underlying this book.

Four friends of mine who saw little if any of the manuscript nevertheless saw the author often while he was working on it. Michael Edwards, Stephen Maizlish, Philip Partain, and John Schubert did not escape the side effects of my involvement in this book, and I know that the book contains the beneficial effects of their presence.

Mrs. Clara B. Simmons, through her good taste and her love of learning, contributed materially to both the congenial surroundings in which I lived for six years and the financial solvency I enjoyed during that time.

The transition from a dissertation to a book benefitted from my appointment as a Fellow at the Institute of Early American History and Culture from 1977 to 1979. I had uninterrupted time for work on the manuscript, and I profited from the editorial efforts of Norman S. Fiering and Joy Dickinson Barnes. My colleague Drew R. McCoy extended welcome sympathy and aid. Thad W. Tate, besides being its Director, was the Institute's greatest single asset.

One way or another I have been trying to heed the instruction, example, and advice of Robert Middlekauff for fifteen years. His judicious combination of encouragement and discretion greatly influenced my decision to persevere in scholarly work and will continue to affect any efforts I may undertake in the future.

Appendix, Notes, Index

Appendix

A Note on Statistics and Continental Soldiers' Motivation

In recent years several studies of Continental Army soldiers have drawn upon enlistment rolls, tax records, and similar sources to describe more precisely the social composition of some military units.[1] These studies agree that most soldiers were under twenty-three years old and owned little or no property—conclusions that statistically confirm what Americans said during the Revolutionary War: the Continental Army consisted largely of young, poor men. Going beyond descriptive summaries of their evidence, several authors have also discussed the motivation of Continental soldiers. From their statistical findings, in part, they draw inferences about soldiers' motives for serving in the army. The authors appear to believe that when they have shown the soldiers' poverty, they have also established that men enlisted under the influence of economic need or ambition and not of revolutionary ideals. The most thorough study, by Mark E. Lender, likens the Continental Army to European armies of the eighteenth century.[2] These authors evidently agree with Edward C. Papenfuse and Gregory A. Stiverson that "many, and perhaps most, of Smallwood's recruits enlisted in the army not because of a sense of duty or patriotism, but because Maryland society offered them few other opportunities for employment."[3] Perhaps the most categorical statement comes from John R. Sellers: "I am not impressed by the patriotic fervor of the privates. I think that they acted overwhelmingly out of self-interest. I do not believe that they really fought with a true understanding of independence."[4]

Readers of my book will see the ways in which its interpretation of Continental soldiers differs from the conclusions of these other studies. There is no need to repeat here the discussion in my text or the sources cited in the doctoral dissertation on which this book is based.[5] I can, however, suggest some ways in which these attempts to infer motivation from statistics fail to convince me.

First, the authors set up a misleading dichotomy between self-interest and revolutionary ideals as motives for army service. Having shown that Maryland recruits were poor, Papenfuse and Stiverson go on to argue that "a sense of duty or patriotism" did not influence "many, and perhaps most" of them. Yet none of the authors in question explain the reasoning or the evidence on which they base such an assumption that poverty and revolutionary ideals were mutually exclusive. In fact, to accept this dichotomy would lead one to conclude that the only people capable of serving ideals or making sacrifices were those who had substantial property. Similarly, these scholars suggest that the recruitment of foreign-born soldiers—usually from England or Ireland—contradicts the idea of a revolutionary army moved by patriotism. This reasoning seems to imply that a recent immigrant could respond to no motive except self-interest. We can readily believe that soldiers' service was motivated by the offer of bounties, pay, and land; we need not also assume that no other motives were at work. Lender, in his dissertation and in his Bicentennial pamphlet, and Papenfuse and Stiverson, in their research note, quote Ralph Waldo Emerson's "Concord Hymn" to epitomize the version of the Continental soldier that their findings disprove.[6] The tone of all these studies implies that we are reading tough-minded exposures of harsh, unpleasant truths. However, the authors' recurrent assumption that soldiers must have served either revolutionary ideals or self-interest exclusively is at least as schematic and improbable as the nineteenth-century rhetoric that these scholars have discredited.

Even before we consider the likelihood that men were moved by both self-interest and self-sacrifice, we can see several ways in which the influence of offers of money and land fails to explain adequately the Continental soldiers' conduct. An argument for economic motivation should not only cite the soldiers' peacetime poverty and the army's offer of bounty, pay, food, clothes, and land; it should also explain why soldiers continued to serve when bounty money was gone, pay was rare and depreciated, and food and clothing often were in lower and shoddier supply than almost anywhere in civilian life. When portraying the New Jersey Continentals as deserters and mutineers, Lender says that they "were poorly paid, wretchedly fed and supplied." On the other hand, when portraying the New Jersey Continentals as "like the European armies," he says that they "fought because they thought the army offered a better life than the civilian world. . . . For some, it meant a better financial position because of bounties and army clothing, food, and pay."[7] As Lender's own statements suggest, the facts of Continental soldiers' wartime experiences reveal the difficulty of arguing that their army service always coincided with their material self-interest.

Nor can we assume, in the absence of further evidence, that poverty as measured by tax assessments was equivalent to unemployment.[8] Farm labor was in great, though seasonal, demand during the war years; privateering attracted many men; others opened new lands in Vermont and Kentucky. Even supposing that an unemployed man sought money above all, brief service as a militia substitute frequently offered equal or greater reward for much shorter, less rigorous military service.

Thus, young, poor men faced a more complex situation than choosing between civilian hardship or military betterment. Presumably there were many more young, poor men in Maryland in 1782 than the 308 recruits who joined Smallwood and fell under the scrutiny of Papenfuse and Stiverson. Maryland society offered the same choice to these other men; yet they found in civilian life opportunities preferable to the hardship and disease that Smallwood's recruits sustained. Throughout the war, far fewer men joined the Continental Army than the recruiters sought. And it remains highly probable that the great majority of young, poor men who fit the scholars' composite social portrait of recruits remained outside the Continental Army. In other words, a socioeconomic description of soldiers, although accurate, cannot adequately explain their motivation, especially when the majority of those subject to the same socioeconomic motives did not become Continental soldiers. To understand Continental Army service, we must explain why some young, poor men chose to enlist and stay in the army while others enlisted but did not stay and still others never enlisted at all.

In evaluating the socioeconomic studies of the Continental Line, we must also note those places where the scholars' information fails to support their contentions. Both Lender and Robert A. Gross liken the Continentals to European armies. Lender says that Continentals came from "the 'dregs of society'" and that the army was "similar to the 'standing armies' of Whig fears."[9] However, when we look at Lender's tables, we find that more than 40 percent of the soldiers owned some land, as measured by tax assessments.[10] This fact does not contradict Lender's general portrait of the soldiers' poverty, but it casts grave doubt on the idea that the Continental Army resembled European armies in its socioeconomic composition. When we turn to the soldiers' attitude toward army service, the analogy between the armies has even less validity. As Lender acknowledges, American soldiers were eager for discharge when the war ended.[11] They evidently did not regard themselves as career soldiers, nor did they prefer military life or its opportunities to a civilian career once peace came. By contrast, the British "dregs" remained professional soldiers.

Papenfuse and Stiverson, Lender, and Sellers all note that Continental soldiers did not fare well economically after the war.[12] Without being explicit, the authors seem to suggest that this information further identifies the soldiers as ne'er-do-well "dregs" who drifted from poverty to army to poverty, prisoners of their economic status. However, the soldiers' willingness to serve in the army, combined with their eagerness to leave it at war's end, shows that they clearly differentiated wartime military duty from peacetime civilian careers. They preferred the latter, and their subsequent economic failures do not imply that they found army life equal to or greater than civilian life in its attractions, material or professional. Whatever their economic status, they evidently had not developed the outlook of European soldiers. Evidence of Continentals' or veterans' poverty does not identify them as a unique group in American society or explain their motivation and conduct or establish a significant similarity to European professional soldiers.

The person who had read only these studies might find it hard to understand how the Continental Army, even with French help, won the war. Lender several times mentions the fighting ability of the New Jersey Brigade.[13] Sellers's doctoral dissertation is a narrative of the Virginia Line's first five years.[14] On what motivation and outlook was this persevering, successful service based? The Continental Army repeatedly failed to provide the material rewards—food, clothes, pay—it had promised to the soldiers; the American officers' use of a modified form of the harsh, corporal discipline current in European armies never consistently managed to intimidate American soldiers. There were three major mutinies and a series of minor ones in the Continental Army throughout the war, while there were no mutinies in the British army's wartime regiments in America. Moreover, as Lender and other scholars demonstrate, desertion from the Continental Army was relatively easy and at certain times frequent;

deserters were seldom caught once they escaped the army.[15] The recurrence of adversity and the ease of desertion suggest that some motives other than physical force and material self-interest influenced those Continentals who chose to remain soldiers and became good ones, yet left the army as soon as their discharge was due.

Why, for example, did the "dregs" of America enlist in the American army rather than in the British army, which would have provided more reliably for their physical well-being? Why did most Continentals fail to accept British offers of money for desertion and mutiny? Why did American deserters who, we are told, must have had "few other opportunities" and must have been "the bottom of society" like the British soldiers, desert to their home regions or to Vermont and Kentucky much more often than to the British? In short, with so few Americans willing to fight as regulars and with such degraded, unself-sacrificing American regulars, why could the British not buy off the American soldiers and win the war with money?

Lender alone tries to define motives for the soldiers' service other than self-interest. However, he uses twentieth-century definitions of revolution and studies of modern soldiers to draw an unconvincing distinction between Continentals' "nationalism" or "love of country" and their idealism, the existence of which he doubts.[16] The matter of idealism brings us to the most prevalent and least defensible attribute of these studies. None of the authors ascribes service in the army to motives of self-sacrifice. Gross, although he refrains from drawing explicit conclusions about soldiers' motivation, presents this one-sided description most emphatically: "Most of the ordinary Continental privates from Concord were . . . men with little or nothing to lose by going off to war for three years or more."[17] Gross, like the other scholars, presumably refers to material possessions. A moment's reflection suggests the inadequacy of a materialistic criterion for weighing motives of self-sacrifice, since men "going off to war" stood to lose, above all, their lives. The most recent and most conservative analysis of military mortality in the Revolutionary War finds this war to be second only to the Civil War in its proportion of deaths to population.[18] Short of death, Continental soldiers sustained extremes of adversity that entailed almost all forms of loss and sacrifice possible for men who had no estates to lose. To account for their perseverance by their calculations of material advantage strains credulity.

Perhaps we see this question most clearly in the situation of American prisoners of war held by the British.[19] Whether by policy or by neglect, the conditions under which American prisoners were confined were wretched and lethal. Using the horror of these conditions and the likelihood that men who stayed in prison would die, the British tried to induce Americans to enlist in the British army. An unknown number accepted the inducement.[20] But, rather than serve the king, thousands of American soldiers and sailors chose almost certain death. A recent estimate sets the number of American prisoners who died in British captivity at 8,500.[21] No materialistic explanation of Continental soldiers' motives can adequately account for the diverse and recurrent instances of self-sacrifice in their conduct. Considered as people rather than as socioeconomic entities, soldiers had as much to lose as anyone had; they chose to risk it and, in many instances, to lose it. The student of the American Revolution must go beyond statistics to find out why.[22]

Notes

The notes in this book serve only to identify the sources of quotations and to refer to secondary authorities on a few points of detail. Readers interested in tracing the research by which I reached my conclusions should consult the doctoral dissertation on which this book is based. It is available from University Microfilms International and contains more than five hundred pages of notes, as well as a bibliography. Students of the American Revolution know that even such a volume of research and annotation is only an introduction to the sources for the study of the war years. None of the primary sources that I have used is new to scholars. These sources fall into three general categories: newspapers, pamphlets, sermons, and books published between 1775 and 1783; published public records of the thirteen states and the Continental Congress; and published journals, correspondence, and memoirs covering the war years. A list of these sources appears in the bibliography of my dissertation.

EPIGRAPH

1. Entry of Sept. 1781, "Extracts from the Letter-Books of Lieutenant Enos Reeves, of the Pennsylvania Line," *Pennsylvania Magazine of History and Biography*, XXI (1897), 235. On McLean, see F. B. Heitman, *Historical Register of Officers of the Continental Army* (Washington, D.C., 1893), 280; entry of Sept. 20, 1781, William Feltman, "Diary of the Pennsylvania Line," Samuel Hazard *et al.*, eds., *Pennsylvania Archives* (Philadelphia and Harrisburg, Pa., 1852–1935), 2d Ser., XI, 690.

Prologue
The Call to War, 1775–1783

1. "Rules and Orders regulating the Army of Observation," Rhode Island, *At the General Assembly of the Governor and Company of the English Colony of Rhode-Island, and Providence Plantations. June 1775* (Providence, R.I., [1775]), 35.

2. Peter Thacher, *An Oration Delivered at Watertown, March 5, 1776 . . .* (Watertown, Mass., 1776), 14.

3. [Hugh Henry Brackenridge], *The Battle of Bunkers-Hill . . .* (Philadelphia, 1776), 29; Thomas Paine, "The American Crisis," No. V, in Philip S. Foner, ed., *The Complete Writings of Thomas Paine* (New York, 1945), I, 123. For another view of the revolutionaries' attitude toward the founders of the colonies, see Catherine L. Albanese, *Sons of the Fathers: The Civil Religion of the American Revolution* (Philadelphia, 1976), chap. 1. See also Wesley Frank Craven, *The Legend of the Founding Fathers* (Ithaca, N.Y., 1956).

4. See below, chap. 8.

5. *New-Jersey Journal* (Chatham), Mar. 29, 1780. For a fuller discussion of this subject, see chap. 4.

6. Joseph W. Barnwell, anno., "Bernard Elliott's Recruiting Journal, 1775," *South Carolina Historical and Genealogical Magazine*, XVII (1916), 97.

7. Nathan Strong, *The Agency and Providence of God acknowledged . . .* (Hartford, Conn., 1780), 16.

8. William Wirt Henry, *Patrick Henry: Life, Correspondence and Speeches* (New York, 1891), I, 265–266; Ethan Allen, *A Narrative of Colonel Ethan Allen's Captivity . . .* (New York, 1961 [orig. publ. Philadelphia, 1779]). For a list of the eight editions in 1779 and 1780, see p. 132 of the 1961 edition.

9. Hugh Henry Brackenridge, *Six Political Discourses Founded on The Scripture* (Lancaster, Pa., [1778]), 14.

10. *New-York Gazette: and the Weekly Mercury*, Apr. 15, 1776.

11. Bernard Bailyn, *The Ideological Origins of the American Revolution* (Cambridge, Mass., 1967); Gordon S. Wood, *The Creation of the American Republic, 1776–1787* (Chapel Hill, N.C., 1969), chap. 1.

12. John Witherspoon, *The Dominion of Providence over the Passions of Men . . .* (Philadelphia, 1776), 40.

13. [John Trumbull], *M'Fingal. A Modern Epic Poem, In Four Cantos* (Hartford, Conn., 1782), 28.

14. [James Chalmers], *Plain Truth; Addressed to the Inhabitants of America, containing, Remarks on a Late Pamphlet entitled Common Sense* (Philadelphia, 1776), 114.

15. Paine, "American Crisis," No. I, Foner, ed., *Writings of Paine*, I, 55.

16. Entry of Sept. 23, 1777, John W. Jordan, ed., "Bethlehem during the Revolution. Extracts from the Diaries in the Moravian Archives at Bethlehem, Pennsylvania," *PMHB*, XIII (1889–1890), 72; I Cor. 16:22.

17. Anthony Wayne to Mary Wayne, June 7, 1777, Charles J. Stillé, *Major-General Anthony Wayne and the Pennsylvania Line in the Continental Army* (Philadelphia, 1893), 67; Samuel Cooper to his wife and children, July 18, 1775, Charles H. McKee, "Letters of a Soldier of the American Revolution," *Connecticut Magazine*, X (1906), 25.

18. Almon W. Lauber, ed., *Orderly Books of the Fourth New York Regiment, 1778–1780,* [and] *the Second New York Regiment, 1780–1783* (Albany, N.Y.,

1932), 633, hereafter cited as *Orderly Books of the Fourth and Second N.Y. Regiments*.

19. Robert Howe, General Orders, Feb. 14, 1777, in Robert W. Gibbes, *Documentary History of the American Revolution* (New York, 1855–1857), III, 55.

20. Joel Barlow, *The Prospect of Peace* . . . (New Haven, Conn., 1778), 4.

21. *Providence Gazette; And Country Journal* (R.I.), Mar. 9, 1776; *Henry V*, IV, iii, 66. For the importance that revolutionaries attached to their future reputations, see Douglass Adair, "Fame and the Founding Fathers," in Trevor Colbourn, ed., *Fame and the Founding Fathers* (New York, 1974), 3–26.

22. Benjamin Franklin to William Strahan, Aug. 19, 1784, quoted in Bruce Ingham Granger, *Political Satire in the American Revolution, 1763–1783* (Ithaca, N.Y., 1960), 154.

23. *N.-Y. Gaz.*, Oct. 14, 1776.

24. Elizabeth Lichtenstein Johnston, *Recollections of a Georgia Loyalist*, ed. Arthur Wentworth Eaton (New York and London, 1901), 44–45.

25. Depositions against Cheshire County tories, June 3, 1777, Nathaniel Bouton, ed., *New Hampshire State Papers. Documents and Records Relating to the State of New-Hampshire during the period of the American Revolution, from 1776 to 1783*, VIII (Concord, N.H., 1874), 596.

26. William Dunlap, *History of the American Theatre* (London, 1833), I, 93.

27. *Dunlap's Pennsylvania Packet, or, the General Advertiser* (Philadelphia), Aug. 20, 1776.

28. Nicholas Street, *The American States acting over the Part of the Children of Israel in the Wilderness* . . . (New Haven, Conn., [1777]), 33.

29. [Lewis Nicola], *A Treatise of Military Exercise, Calculated for the Use of the Americans* (Philadelphia, 1776), 3, v.

30. David Fanning, *The Narrative of Colonel David Fanning* (New York, 1865), xxiii; I Samuel 15:23.

31. *South-Carolina and American General Gazette* (Charleston), Dec. 8, 1775.

32. Luke Swetland, *A Very Remarkable Narrative of Luke Swetland* (Hartford, Conn., [178–?]), 11. Punctuation added.

33. [Brackenridge], *Bunkers-Hill*, 49.

34. James 4:1.

35. Bailyn, *Ideological Origins*, chaps. 3–4; Bernard Bailyn, *The Origins of American Politics* (New York, 1968); Wood, *Creation of the American Republic*, Part I; Pauline Maier, *From Resistance to Revolution: Colonial Radicals and the Development of American Opposition to Britain, 1765–1776* (New York, 1972).

36. Oliver Noble, *Some Strictures Upon the Sacred Story Recorded in the Book of Esther* . . . (Newburyport, Mass., 1775), 18n.

37. *Reflections of a Few Friends of the Country, Upon Several Circumstantial Points* . . . (Philadelphia, 1776), 20.

38. Jonathan Trumbull to George Washington, Dec. 7, 1776, Peter Force, ed., *American Archives* . . . (Washington, D.C., 1837–1853), 5th Ser., III, 1111.

39. Entry of Mar. 13, 1776, *ibid.*, 4th Ser., V, 201–202.

40. *Independent Chronicle. And the Universal Advertiser* (Boston), Jan. 16, 1777.

41. [Jacob Green], *Observations on the Reconciliation of Great-Britain, and the Colonies* . . . (Philadelphia, 1776), 28.

42. Nathanael Greene to Catherine Littlefield Greene, June 2, 1775, George Washington Greene, *The Life of Nathanael Greene* . . . (New York, 1867–1871), I, 83.

43. Samuel Ward to Henry Ward, Nov. 11, 1775, Edmund C. Burnett, ed., *Letters of Members of the Continental Congress* (Washington, D.C., 1921–1936), I, 252.

44. For a fuller discussion of this subject, see chap. 4.

45. John Murray, *Nehemiah, Or the Struggle for Liberty never in vain* . . . (Newburyport, Mass., 1779), 35.

46. *An Address to General St. Clair's Brigade* . . . [Philadelphia, 1776], 4; entry of Oct. 20, 1776, "Journal of Lieut. Rufus Wheeler of Rowley," Essex Institute, *Historical Collections*, LXVIII (1932), 375.

47. Entry of Mar. 20, 1778, "Amos Farnsworths Journal," Massachusetts Historical Society, *Proceedings*, 2d Ser., XII (1898), 92.

48. Entry of July 4, 1779, "Journal of Rev. William Rogers, D.D.," Frederick Cook, ed., *Journals of the Military Expedition of Major General John Sullivan against the Six Nations of Indians in 1779* (Auburn, N.Y., 1887), 250.

49. Entry of June 30, 1775, "Journal of John Leach," Samuel Lane Boardman, ed., *Peter Edes: Pioneer Printer in Maine* (Bangor, Me., 1901), 116.

50. Ambrose Serle to the earl of Dartmouth, Mar. 20, 1777, B. F. Stevens, ed., *Facsimiles of Manuscripts in European Archives Relating to America, 1773–1783* (London, 1889–1895), XXIV, No. 2052.

51. On the place of ministers in the 18th century, see J. William T. Youngs, Jr., *God's Messengers: Religious Leadership in Colonial New England, 1700–1750* (Baltimore, 1976), and Donald M. Scott, *From Office to Profession: The New England Ministry, 1750–1850* (Philadelphia, 1978), chap. 1. See also "Note on the Printed Sermons of Massachusetts and Connecticut, 1740–1800," in Nathan O. Hatch, *The Sacred Cause of Liberty: Republican Thought and the Millennium in Revolutionary New England* (New Haven, Conn., 1977), 176–182. On religion and the revolution, see below, chap. 4.

52. Entry of Aug. 11, 1775, "Journal of Simeon Lyman of Sharon," Connecticut Historical Society, *Collections*, VII (Hartford, Conn., 1899), 113.

53. Entry of Apr. 30, 1775, "Farnsworths Journal," Mass. Hist. Soc., *Procs.*, 2d Ser., XII (1898), 79.

54. Joseph Hewes to James Iredell, May 17, 1776, Burnett, ed., *Letters of Congress*, I, 455.

55. Entry of July 20, 1775, Robert Greenhalgh Albion and Leonidas Dodson, eds., *Philip Vickers Fithian: Journal, 1775–1776* . . . (Princeton, N.J., 1934), 64.

56. Alan Heimert, *Religion and the American Mind from the Great Awakening to the Revolution* (Cambridge, Mass., 1966), esp. 214–218; Edmund S. Morgan,

"The American Revolution Considered as an Intellectual Movement," in Arthur M. Schlesinger, Jr., and Morton White, eds., *Paths of American Thought* (Boston, 1963), 16–23. Compare Joseph A. Conforti, "Samuel Hopkins and the New Divinity: Theology, Ethics, and Social Reform in Eighteenth-Century New England," *William and Mary Quarterly*, 3d Ser., XXXIV (1977), 572–589.

57. Entries of Sept. 2 3, 1775, "Journal of William Tennent," Gibbes, *Documentary History*, I, 233–234.

58. Israel Evans, *A Discourse Delivered near York in Virginia* . . . (Philadelphia, 1782), 38.

59. Nathaniel Whitaker, *An Antidote Against Toryism, Or the Curse of Meroz* . . . (Newburyport, Mass., 1777), 30–31.

60. Entry of Sept. 15, 1775, "Journal of Abner Stocking," in Kenneth Roberts, ed., *March to Quebec: Journals of the Members of Arnold's Expedition* (New York, 1938), 546; J. T. Headley, *The Chaplains and Clergy of the Revolution* (New York, 1864), 92–93, 105; [Samuel Peters], "Genuine History of Gen. Arnold, by an old Acquaintance," *Political Magazine*, I (1780), 746, in *The Works of Samuel Peters of Hebron, Connecticut*, ed. Kenneth Walker Cameron (Hartford, Conn., 1967), 164; Gardiner Spring, *Personal Reminiscences of the Life and Times of Gardiner Spring* . . . (New York, 1866), I, 25–26; John J. Currier, *History of Newburyport, Mass., 1764–1905* (Newburyport, Mass., 1906), 272–275. On Arnold's march to Quebec, see Christopher Ward, *The War of the Revolution*, ed. John Richard Alden (New York, 1952), I, chap. 13; Gustave Lanctot, *Canada and the American Revolution, 1774–1783*, trans. Margaret M. Cameron (Cambridge, Mass., 1967).

Chapter I
1775: Rage Militaire

1. *Lloyd's Evening Post and British Chronicle*, June 28–30, 1775, quoted in Margaret Wheeler Willard, ed., *Letters on the American Revolution, 1774–1776* (Boston and New York, 1925), 101–102.

2. [Charles Lee], *Strictures on a Pamphlet, Entitled, A "Friendly Address to All Reasonable Americans On The Subject of our Political Confusions,"* in *The Lee Papers* (New-York Historical Society, *Collections*, IV–VII [New York, 1872–1875]), I, 161, hereafter cited as *Lee Papers*.

3. Massachusetts, Records of the Great and General Court or Assembly for the Colony of the Massachusetts Bay . . . Records of the Council, May 1, 1776.

4. Timothy Pickering, Jr., *An Easy Plan of Discipline for a Militia* (Salem, Mass., 1775), preface, 11.

5. Dixon and Hunter's *Virginia Gazette* (Williamsburg), July 29, 1775.

6. [Janet Schaw], *Journal of a Lady of Quality*, ed. Evangeline Walker Andrews and Charles McLean Andrews (New Haven, Conn., 1921), 191.

7. Joseph H. Jones, ed., *The Life of Ashbel Green* (New York, 1849), 55.

8. Entry of Nov. 13, 1775, Albion and Dodson, eds., *Fithian: Journal, 1775–1776*, 131.

9. Robert Cooper, *Courage in a Good Cause; or The Lawful and Courageous Use of the Sword* . . . (Lancaster, Pa., 1775), 23–24.

10. Worthington C. Ford *et al.*, eds., *Journals of the Continental Congress* (Washington, D.C., 1904–1937), IV, 140.

11. See esp. Caroline Robbins, *The Eighteenth-Century Commonwealthman: Studies in the Transmission . . . of English Liberal Thought from the Restoration of Charles II until the War with the Thirteen Colonies* (Cambridge, Mass., 1961); J.G.A. Pocock, *The Machiavellian Moment: Florentine Political Thought and the Atlantic Republican Tradition* (Princeton, N.J., 1975); Perry Miller, "From the Covenant to the Revival," in *Nature's Nation* (Cambridge, Mass., 1967), 90–120; Heimert, *Religion and the American Mind*.

12. Entry of July 17, 1775, Albion and Dodson, eds., *Fithian: Journal, 1775–1776*, 59–60.

13. [Wheeler Case], *Poems, Occasioned by Several Circumstances and Occurrences, in the Present grand Contest of America for Liberty* (New Haven, Conn., 1778), 6.

14. *Pa. Packet*, June 12, 1775; *Va. Gaz.*, June 24, 1775, quoted in Frank Moore, ed., *Diary of the American Revolution from Newspapers and Original Documents* (New York, 1858), I, 71; *Pennsylvania Evening Post*, Aug. 10, 1776, quoted *ibid.*, 270; David Humphreys, *A Poem, Addressed to the Armies of the United States of America* (New Haven, Conn., 1780), 8; *N.-Y. Gaz.*, Aug. 12, 1776; *Connecticut Courant, and Hartford Weekly Intelligencer*, Feb. 19, 1776.

15. *N.-Y. Gaz.*, Oct. 2, 1775, in Moore, ed., *Diary of the Revolution*, I, 141; entry of Oct. 12, 1775, Daniel McCurtin, "Journal of the Times at the Siege of Boston," Thomas Balch, ed., *Papers Relating Chiefly to the Maryland Line during the Revolution* (Philadelphia, 1857), 22.

16. Lauber, ed., *Orderly Books of the Fourth and Second N.Y. Regiments*, 633.

17. Edward J. Lowell, *The Hessians and the Other German Auxiliaries of Great Britain in the Revolutionary War* (New York, 1884), 104.

18. Pinkney's *Virginia Gazette* (Williamsburg), Nov. 16, 1775.

19. *London Chronicle*, Aug. 19–21, 1775, quoted in Willard, ed., *Letters on the Revolution*, 168.

20. *Pennsylvania Journal*, July 30, 1777, quoted in Moore, ed., *Diary of the Revolution*, I, 466.

21. Robert Douthat Meade, "Patrick Henry: A Fresh Reappraisal," *The Cincinnati-Dance Lectures on the American Revolution* (n.p., 1976), 42.

22. Entries of Aug. 27–28, 1776, *The New-York Diary of Lieutenant Jabez Fitch*, ed. W.H.W. Sabine (New York, 1954), 31, 34.

23. Robert Douthat Meade, *Patrick Henry: Practical Revolutionary* (Philadelphia and New York, 1969), 167–168.

24. John Adams to James Warren, June 27, 1775, *Warren-Adams Letters: Being Chiefly a Correspondence among John Adams, Samuel Adams, and James Warren* (Mass. Hist. Soc., *Colls.*, LXXII–LXXIII [Boston, 1917–1923]), I, 67, hereafter cited as *Warren-Adams Letters*.

25. Thomas Pinckney to Harriott Pinckney Horry, June 11, 1776, "Letters of Thomas Pinckney, 1775–1780," *South Carolina Historical Magazine*, LVIII (1957), 69.

26. *Pennsylvania Magazine: or, American Monthly Museum*, I (1775), 220.

27. *To the Associators of the City of Philadelphia* [Philadelphia, 1775].

28. Richard Henry Lee to Arthur Lee, [Feb. 24, 1775], James Curtis Ballagh, ed., *The Letters of Richard Henry Lee* (New York, 1911–1914), I, 130–131.

29. [Nicola], *Treatise of Military Exercise*, 11.

30. Entry of July 3, 1781, Richard K. MacMaster, ed., "News of the Yorktown Campaign: The Journal of Dr. Robert Honyman, April 17–November 25, 1781," *Virginia Magazine of History and Biography*, LXXIX (1971), 407–408.

31. On rifles and riflemen, see Felix Reichmann, "The Pennsylvania Rifle: A Social Interpretation of Changing Military Techniques," *PMHB*, LXIX (1945), 3–14; Rhys Isaac, "Dramatizing the Ideology of Revolution: Popular Mobilization in Virginia, 1774 to 1776," *WMQ*, 3d Ser., XXXIII (1976), 379–382; Jac Weller, "Irregular but Effective: Partizan Weapons Tactics in the American Revolution, Southern Theatre," *Military Affairs*, XXI (1957), 122–127; Henry J. Young, "The Spirit of 1775: A Letter of Robert Magaw . . . with an Essay on the Background and the Sequel," *John and Mary's Journal*, I (1975), 15–50. Compare John William Ward, *Andrew Jackson: Symbol for an Age* (New York, 1955), 13–27.

32. Pocock, *Machiavellian Moment*; Lois G. Schwoerer, *"No Standing Armies!" The Antiarmy Ideology in Seventeenth-Century England* (Baltimore, 1974).

33. For a study of the American reception of the antiarmy ideology—a study that adopts a different interpretation from this one—see Lawrence Delbert Cress, "The Standing Army, the Militia, and the New Republic: Changing Attitudes toward the Military in American Society, 1768 to 1820" (Ph.D. diss., University of Virginia, 1976), chaps. 1–3.

34. Benjamin Hichborn, *An Oration, Delivered March 5th, 1777* . . . (Boston, 1777), 6–7.

35. Thomas Dawes, Jr., *An Oration Delivered March 5th, 1781* . . . (Boston, 1781), 15.

36. Stephen Saunders Webb, "Army and Empire: English Garrison Government in Britain and America, 1569 to 1763," *WMQ*, 3d Ser., XXXIV (1977), 1–31; Alan Rogers, *Empire and Liberty: American Resistance to British Authority, 1755–1763* (Berkeley and Los Angeles, Calif., 1974); John Shy, *Toward Lexington: The Role of the British Army in the Coming of the American Revolution* (Princeton, N.J., 1965).

37. Pocock, *Machiavellian Moment*; Robbins, *Commonwealthman*; Cress, "Standing Army."

38. Samuel Adams to James Warren, Nov. 20, 1780, Harry Alonzo Cushing, ed., *The Writings of Samuel Adams* (New York, 1904–1908), IV, 221.

39. John Adams to Samuel Cooper, May 30, 1776, Charles Francis Adams, ed., *The Works of John Adams, Second President of the United States: With a Life of the Author, Notes and Illustrations, by His Grandson Charles Francis Adams* (Boston, 1850–1856), IX, 382, hereafter cited as *Works of John Adams*; John Adams to Jonathan Mason, July 18, 1776, *ibid.*, 423.

40. John Shy, *A People Numerous and Armed: Reflections on the Military Struggle for American Independence* (London, Oxford, New York, 1976), chap. 6, "American Strategy: Charles Lee and the Radical Alternative," quoted at 161, 138.

41. William Gordon to Elizabeth Smith, July 30, 1775, to George Washington, Feb. 24, 1778, to Horatio Gates, Oct. 16, 1782, and to James Bowdoin, Sept. 28, 1786, in Worthington C. Ford, ed., "Letters of the Reverend William Gordon, Historian of the American Revolution: 1770–1799," Mass. Hist. Soc., *Procs.*, LXIII (1931), 316, 373, 475, 613.

42. Charles Lee to Benjamin Rush, Dec. 12, 1775, *Lee Papers*, I, 226.

43. Charles Lee to John Hancock, Feb. 22, 1776, *ibid.*, 321.

44. *Ibid.*

45. Charles Lee to George Washington, Feb. 29, 1776, *ibid.*, 336.

46. Charles Lee, Report on the Defense of New York, Mar. 1776, *ibid.*, 356; Charles Lee to William Moultrie, June 21, 1776, *ibid.*, II, 77.

47. Charles Lee to Primrose Kennedy, n.d., *ibid.*, 356.

48. The best study of Lee's character and career is John Richard Alden, *General Charles Lee: Traitor or Patriot?* (Baton Rouge, La., 1951).

49. Charles Lee to Patrick Henry, July 29, 1776, *Lee Papers*, II, 177; entry of Aug. 27, 1775, "Craft's Journal of the Siege of Boston," Essex Inst., *Hist. Colls.*, III (1861), 135; entry of Dec. 1, 1775, "Journal of Lyman," Conn. Hist. Soc., *Colls.*, VII (1899), 129.

50. "Anecdote," *American Museum*, V (1789), 452.

51. Charles Lee to Benjamin Rush, Sept. 19, 1775, *Lee Papers*, I, 207–208.

52. Entry of Dec. 2, 1775, "Journal of Lyman," Conn. Hist. Soc., *Colls.*, VII (1899), 129.

53. *Royal Gazette* (New York), Sept. 18, 1779.

54. Josiah Bartlett to John Langdon, Aug. 11, 1776, Burnett, ed., *Letters of Congress*, II, 47.

55. Jonathan Gregory Rossie, *The Politics of Command in the American Revolution* (Syracuse, N.Y., 1975); H. James Henderson, *Party Politics in the Continental Congress* (New York, 1974).

56. Dawes, *Oration Delivered March 5th, 1781*, 16.

57. *An Eulogium on Major General Joseph Warren . . . By a Columbian* (Boston, 1781), 11, 15.

58. *Boston-Gazette and Country Journal*, Oct. 16, 1775.

59. Entry of Apr. 8, 1776, "Diary of Samuel Cooper, 1775–1776," *American Historical Review*, VI (1901), 340.

60. Perez Morton, *An Oration; Delivered at the King's Chapel in Boston, April 8, 1776 . . .* (Boston, 1776), 10.

61. Joseph Warren to the Governor and Company of Connecticut, Apr. 26, 1775, *The Trumbull Papers* (Mass. Hist. Soc., *Colls.*, 5th Ser., IX–X, 7th Ser., II–III [Boston, 1885–1902]), II, 287, hereafter cited as *Trumbull Papers*.

62. [Brackenridge], *Bunkers-Hill*, 29. On Warren, see John Cary, *Joseph Warren: Physician, Politician, Patriot* (Urbana, Ill., 1961).

63. Benjamin Rush to John Adams, Oct. 1, 1777, L. H. Butterfield, ed., *Letters of Benjamin Rush* (Princeton, N.J., 1951), I, 156–157.

64. Henry Knox to Lucy Flucker Knox, Jan. 2, 1777, Francis S. Drake, *Life and Correspondence of Henry Knox . . .* (Boston, 1873), 38.

65. Richard Henry Lee to [George Washington], May 22, 1777, Ballagh, ed., *Letters of Richard Henry Lee*, I, 294.

66. Claude C. Robin, *New Travels through North-America: In a Series of Letters*, trans. Philip Freneau (Philadelphia, 1783), 19.

67. John Adams to James Warren, June [July] 6, 1775, *Warren-Adams Letters*, I, 76.

68. *Providence Gaz.*, Nov. 1, 1777.

69. Joseph Warren to Governor and Company of Connecticut, Apr. 26, 1775, *Trumbull Papers*, II, 287.

70. Joseph Hodgkins to Sarah Hodgkins, Oct. 13, 1778, Herbert T. Wade and Robert A. Lively, *This Glorious Cause: The Adventures of Two Company Officers in Washington's Army* (Princeton, N.J., 1958), 244.

71. James Duane, Notes of Debates, Feb. 22, 1776, Burnett, ed., *Letters of Congress*, I, 360–361.

72. Ford *et al.*, eds., *Journals of Congress*, VI, 1019.

73. Thomas Painter, *Autobiography of Thomas Painter* (n.p., [1910]), 16.

74. "Opinion of Brigadier-General Greene, in answer to Queries of October 5, 1775," in Force, ed., *American Archives*, 4th Ser., III, 1043.

75. *Pa. Packet*, July 15, 1776; George Gilmer, Address to the Inhabitants of Albemarle, *Papers, Military and Political*, Virginia Historical Society, *Collections*, N.S., VI (Richmond, Va., 1887), 126.

76. Otho Holland Williams to Nathanael Greene, Feb. 26, 1781, quoted in M. F. Treacy, *Prelude to Yorktown: The Southern Campaign of Nathanael Greene, 1780–1781* (Chapel Hill, N.C., 1963), 11.

77. George Washington to Patrick Henry, Apr. 13, 1777, John C. Fitzpatrick, ed., *The Writings of George Washington from the Original Manuscript Sources, 1745–1799* (Washington, D.C., 1931–1944), VII, 408.

78. [James Potter Collins], *Autobiography of a Revolutionary Soldier* [orig. publ. Clinton, La., 1859], in Mrs. S. G. Miller, *Sixty Years in the Nueces Valley, 1870 to 1930* (San Antonio, Tex., 1930), 236–237.

79. *Pennsylvania Gazette* (Philadelphia), June 18, 1777.

80. Charles Magill to Thomas Jefferson, Mar. 10, 1781, Julian P. Boyd *et al.*, eds., *The Papers of Thomas Jefferson* (Princeton, N.J., 1950–), V, 116.

81. See above, n. 77.

82. Nathanael Greene to Abner Nash, Dec. 6, 1780, Greene, *Nathanael Greene*, III, 552.

83. John Sullivan to Peter Colt, Nov. 10, 1778, Otis G. Hammond, ed., *Letters and Papers of Major-General John Sullivan* (New Hampshire Historical Society, *Collections*, XIII–XV [Concord, N.H., 1930–1939]), II, 428.

84. Richard H. Kohn, *Eagle and Sword: The Federalists and the Creation of the Military Establishment in America, 1783–1802* (New York, 1975), 38. See also Richard H. Kohn, "American Generals of the Revolution: Subordination and Restraint," in Don Higginbotham, ed., *Reconsiderations on the Revolutionary War: Selected Essays* (Westport, Conn., 1978), 104–123.

Chapter II
1776: The Army of Israel

1. Clifford K. Shipton, *Sibley's Harvard Graduates: Biographical Sketches of Those Who Attended Harvard College in the Classes 1761–63* (Boston, 1970), XV, 409–410; Irma B. Jaffe, *John Trumbull: Patriot-Artist of the American Revolution* (Boston, 1975); *Providence Gaz.*, Dec. 30, 1775; Solomon Williams, *The Greatness and Sovereignty of God . . . A Sermon, Delivered in the First Society in Lebanon, December 3, 1775. The next Lord's Day, after the News of the untimely Death of Mrs. Faith Huntington* . . . (Norwich, Conn., 1777); Jedidiah Huntington to Jabez Huntington, Sept. 21, 1775, *The Trumbull Papers* (Mass. Hist. Soc., *Colls.*, 5th Ser., IX–X, 7th Ser., II–III [Boston, 1885–1902]), I, 503, hereafter cited as *Trumbull Papers*; Jedidiah Huntington to Jonathan Trumbull, Oct. 5, 1775, Jan. 14 and Mar. 6, 1776, *ibid.*, 505–506, 509, 515; Jonathan Trumbull to Jedidiah Huntington, Feb. 26, 1776, *ibid.*, III, 3–4; entries of Nov. 24 and 28, 1775, Jabez Fitch, Jr., "A Journal," Mass. Hist. Soc., *Procs.*, 2d Ser., IX (1894), 84–86; Jedidiah Huntington to Jabez Huntington, Oct. 5, 9, 30, Nov. 2, 5, 9, 16, 23, Dec. 6, 1775, *The Huntington Papers* (Conn. Hist. Soc., *Colls.*, XX [Hartford, Conn., 1923], 245–253), hereafter cited as *Huntington Papers*; Andrew Huntington to Joshua Huntington, Oct. 24, 1775, *ibid.*, 247; Jedidiah Huntington to Joshua Huntington [erroneously headed "Andrew Huntington to Joshua Huntington"], Jan. 26, 1776, *ibid.*, 263; I. W. Stuart, *Life of Jonathan Trumbull, Sen., Governor of Connecticut* (Hartford, Conn., 1859), 41, 60–61, 195–196, 687n, 688; Jonathan Trumbull, *Jonathan Trumbull: Governor of Connecticut, 1769–1784* (Boston, 1919), 30, 176–177; David M. Roth, *Connecticut's War Governor: Jonathan Trumbull*, Connecticut Bicentennial Series, IX (Chester, Conn., 1974), 35–36; John Trumbull, *Autobiography, Reminiscences and Letters of John Trumbull, from 1756 to 1841* (New Haven, Conn., 1841), 2–3, 5, 22; Erastus Worthington, "The Dexter House during the Siege of Boston, 1775–

6," *Dedham Historical Register*, V (1894), 155–157; Israel Angell to Hope Angell, Dec. 1, 1775, quoted in Edward Field, ed., *Diary of Colonel Israel Angell Commanding the Second Rhode Island Continental Regiment during the American Revolution, 1778–1781* (Providence, R.I., 1899), x–xi; Daniel Barber, *The History of My Own Times*, Part III (Frederick, Md., 1832), 7–8; entry of Nov. 25, 1775, Nathan Hale, "Diary," in George Dudley Seymour, *Documentary Life of Nathan Hale* (New Haven, Conn., 1941), 192; *Political Magazine*, II (1781), 10, in Cameron, ed., *Works of Samuel Peters*, 167; Massachusetts, *A Proclamation for a Public Thanksgiving* (Watertown, Mass., 1775). For a description of the emotional effect of the Battle of Bunker Hill, see the diary of Chaplain David Avery, quoted in Headley, *Chaplains and Clergy of the Revolution*, 295.

2. Massachusetts Congress to George Washington, July 6, 1775, in *Pa. Packet*, July 17, 1775.

3. George Washington, General Orders, Aug. 30, 1776, Fitzpatrick, ed., *Writings of Washington*, V, 500.

4. Mass. Congress to Washington, July 6, 1775, in *Pa. Packet*, July 17, 1775.

5. George Washington, General Orders, Aug. 22, 1775, Fitzpatrick, ed., *Writings of Washington*, III, 440.

6. Entry of Mar. 9, 1777, "Revolutionary Diary Kept by George Norton of Ipswich, 1777–1778," Essex Inst., *Hist. Colls.*, LXXIV (1938), 339–340.

7. Entry of Nov. 16, 1776, Henry B. Dawson, ed., *Diary of David How* (Morrisania, N.Y., 1865), 36; entry of Jan. 8, 1779, Field, ed., *Diary of Angell*, 39; entry of Feb. 17, 1777, "Military Journal Kept in 1777, during the Rhode Island Expedition, by John Goodwin of Marblehead, Mass., First Lieutenant in Capt. Nathaniel Lindsey's Company in Col. Timothy Pickering's Regiment," Essex Inst., *Hist. Colls.*, XLV (1909), 208.

8. Entry of Apr. 30, 1776, "Journal of Bayze Wells of Farmington, May, 1775–February, 1777," Conn. Hist. Soc., *Colls.*, VII (Hartford, Conn., 1899), 296.

9. George Washington to Lund Washington, Aug. 20, 1775, Fitzpatrick, ed., *Writings of Washington*, III, 433.

10. Philip Schuyler to George Washington, July 18, 1775, quoted in Benson J. Lossing, *The Life and Times of Philip Schuyler* (New York, 1873), I, 359.

11. Nathaniel Folsom to New Hampshire Committee of Safety, July 1, 1775, Nathaniel Bouton, ed., *New Hampshire Provincial Papers: Documents and Records relating to the Province of New-Hampshire, from 1764 to 1776*, VII (Nashua, N.H., 1873), 557.

12. Daniel Barber, *The History of My Own Times* (Washington, D.C., 1827), 14. On homesickness, see Howard Lewis Applegate, "Remedial Medicine in the American Revolutionary Army," *Military Medicine*, CXXVI (1961), 451.

13. *Boston-Gaz.*, Apr. 22, 1776, and June 23, 1777; *Pa. Packet*, Apr. 8, 1776; Purdie's *Virginia Gazette* (Williamsburg), July 5 and Nov. 8, 1776, July 4, 1777.

14. Jedidiah Huntington to Jabez Huntington, Nov. 23, 1775, *Huntington Papers*, 252.

15. Jedidiah Huntington to Andrew Huntington, Oct. 5, 1775, *Huntington Papers*, 243.

16. Gilbert Saltonstall to Nathan Hale, Dec. 18, 1775, in Seymour, *Hale*, 64.

17. Jedidiah Huntington to Jabez Huntington, Nov. 23, 1775, *Huntington Papers*, 253.

18. Ford *et al.*, eds., *Journals of Congress*, III, 393.

19. *Conn. Courant*, Jan. 29, 1776.

20. Nathanael Greene letter, Sept. 28, 1776, quoted in William Johnson, *Sketches of the Life and Correspondence of Nathanael Greene, Major General of the Armies of the United States, in the War of the Revolution* (Charleston, S.C., 1822), I, 58.

21. Nathanael Greene to Samuel Ward, Oct. 16, 1775, Bernhard Knollenberg, ed., *Correspondence of Governor Samuel Ward, May 1775–March 1776* (Providence, R. I., 1952), 104.

22. Samuel Ward to Henry Ward, Dec. 31, 1775, *ibid.*, 160.

23. Elisha Porter to James Warren, Mar. 15, 1776, Force, ed., *American Archives*, 4th Ser., V, 240.

24. Samuel Adams to James Warren, May 12, 1776, Cushing, ed., *Writings of Samuel Adams*, III, 289.

25. George Washington to John Hancock, Sept. 24, 1776, Fitzpatrick, ed., *Writings of Washington*, VI, 107–108.

26. Among the useful studies of recruiting are Arthur J. Alexander, "How Maryland Tried to Raise Her Continental Quotas," *Maryland Historical Magazine*, XLII (1947), 184–196; Jonathan Smith, "How Massachusetts Raised Her Troops in the Revolution," Mass. Hist. Soc., *Procs.*, LV (1923), 345–370; John Robert Sellers, "The Virginia Continental Line, 1775–1780" (Ph.D. diss., Tulane University, 1968); Mark Edward Lender, "The Enlisted Line: The Continental Soldiers of New Jersey" (Ph.D. diss., Rutgers University, 1975); John David McBride, "The Virginia War Effort, 1775–1783: Manpower Policies and Practices" (Ph.D. diss., University of Virginia, 1977).

27. Lachlan McIntosh to George Washington, Apr. 28, 1776, Lilla M. Hawes, ed., "Letter Book of Lachlan McIntosh, 1776–1777," *Georgia Historical Quarterly*, XXXVIII (1954), 153.

28. George Washington to Joseph Reed, Apr. 28, 1780, Fitzpatrick, ed., *Writings of Washington*, XVIII, 310–311.

29. James H. Edmondson, "Desertion in the American Army during the Revolutionary War" (Ph.D. diss., Louisiana State University, 1971), 240.

30. Edmondson, "Desertion," esp. chap. 8; Lender, "Enlisted Line of New Jersey," chap. 7; Thaddeus W. Tate, Jr., "Desertion from the American Revolutionary Army" (M.A. thesis, University of North Carolina, 1948), 11.

31. Barber, *My Own Times* (1827), 16.

32. Artemas Ward, General Orders, Aug. 5, 1775, "Orderly Book for Capt. William Coits Company," Conn. Hist. Soc., *Colls.* (1899), VII, 86; General Orders, May 5, 1775, William Henshaw, "Orderly Book," Mass. Hist. Soc., *Procs.*, XV (1876), 96.

33. Daniel McCurtin, "Journal of the Times at the Siege of Boston," Balch, ed., *Papers Relating to the Maryland Line*, 12.

34. William Emerson to his wife, July 17, 1775, quoted in Allen French, *The First Year of the American Revolution* (Boston and New York, 1934), 301.

35. George Washington, General Orders, July 25, 1777, Fitzpatrick, ed., *Writings of Washington*, VIII, 465–466.

36. "Hissian": [Joseph Plumb Martin], *Private Yankee Doodle: Being a Narrative of Some of the Adventures, Dangers and Sufferings of a Revolutionary Soldier*, ed. George F. Scheer (Boston, 1962 [orig. publ. Hallowell, Me., 1830]), 82–83.

37. Entry of Sept. 28–29, 1776, Louise Rau, ed., "Sergeant John Smith's Diary of 1776," *Mississippi Valley Historical Review*, XX (1933–1934), 252.

38. Algernon Roberts, "A Journal of a Campaign from Philadelphia to Paulus Hook," *PMHB*, VII (1883), 461.

39. Entry of Jan. 23, 1777, "Journal of Sergeant William Young. Written during the Jersey Campaign in the Winter of 1776–7," *ibid*., VIII (1884), 272.

40. Regimental Court-Martial, Oct. 25, 1777, "The Journal and Order Book of Captain Robert Kirkwood of the Delaware Regiment of the Continental Line," Historical Society of Delaware, *Papers*, VI, No. LVI (Wilmington, Del., 1910), 216.

41. Entry of Nov. 17, 1776, "Diary of Lieut. James McMichael of the Pennsylvania Line, 1776–1778," Hazard *et al*., eds., *Pa. Archives*, 2d Ser., XV, 202.

42. Entry of Sept. 21–25, 1775, "Journal of Stocking," Roberts, ed., *March to Quebec*, 547.

43. Peter Muhlenberg, Brigade Orders, Sept. 5, 1777, "Orderly Book of Gen. John Peter Gabriel Muhlenberg, March 26–December 20, 1777," *PMHB*, XXXIV (1910), 455.

44. Benjamin Rush, "Result of some Observations made by Benjamin Rush, M.D.," *London Medical Journal*, VII (1786), 78.

45. Henry Knox to George Washington, Jan. 3, 1778, quoted in North Callahan, *Henry Knox: General Washington's General* (New York and Toronto, 1958), 134.

46. Ronald Hoffman, *A Spirit of Dissension: Economics, Politics, and the Revolution in Maryland* (Baltimore, 1973), 232.

47. Entry of Jan. 13, 1777, Ebenezer Elmer, "Journal Kept during an Expedition to Canada in 1776," New Jersey Historical Society, *Proceedings*, 1st Ser., III (1849), 55.

48. George Washington, General Orders, May 31, 1777, Oct. 21, 1778, July 29, 1779, Fitzpatrick, ed., *Writings of Washington*, VIII, 152–153, XIII, 118–119, XVI, 13.

49. Hezekiah Smith, Sermon to Nixon's Brigade, July 31, 1779, Reuben Aldridge Guild, *Chaplain Smith and the Baptists; or, Life, Journals, Letters, and Addresses of the Rev. Hezekiah Smith, D.D., of Haverhill, Massachusetts, 1737–1805* (Philadelphia, 1885), 256–257.

50. John Robert Shaw, *A Narrative of the Life and Travels of John Robert Shaw, The Well-Digger, Now Resident in Lexington, Kentucky* (Louisville, Ky., 1930 [orig. publ. Lexington, Ky., 1807]), 86.

51. Entry of Sept. 19, 1777, Theodore G. Tappert and John W. Doberstein, trans. and eds., *The Journals of Henry Melchior Muhlenberg* (Philadelphia, 1942–1958), III, 78.

52. *N.-J. Jour.*, Feb. 3, 1780.

53. Entries of Dec. 26 and 28, 1776, "The Revolutionary War Journal of Sergeant Thomas McCarty," N.J. Hist. Soc., *Procs.*, LXXXII (1964), 41.

54. Entry of Sept. 16, 1779, "Diary of Enos Hitchcock, D.D., A Chaplain in the Revolutionary Army," Rhode Island Historical Society, *Publications*, N.S., VII (Providence, R.I., 1899), 211.

55. John Smith Hanna, *A History of the Life and Services of Captain Samuel Dewees* (Baltimore, 1844), 203–204.

56. Entry of Aug. 3, 1776, Elmer, "Journal during Expedition to Canada," N.J. Hist. Soc., *Procs.*, 1st Ser., II (1847), 172.

57. Regimental Orders, July 2, 1777, "Journal and Order Book of Kirkwood," Hist. Soc. Del., *Papers*, VI, No. LVI, 95.

58. *Defensive Arms Vindicated; and the Lawfulness of the American War Made Manifest* (n.p., 1783), 5.

59. Orders, Aug. 11, 1779, "The Order Book of Lieut. Colonel Francis Barber," N.J. Hist. Soc., *Procs.*, LXV (1947), 199.

60. Entry of May 7, 1779, E. A. Benians and R. W. David, eds., *A Journal by Thos: Hughes . . .* (Cambridge, 1947), 65.

61. Capt. Gerard Irwin's men to Pennsylvania Council of Safety, n.d., Hazard *et al.*, eds., *Pa. Archives*, 2d Ser., III, 156.

62. Heitman, *Register of Officers*, 238.

63. Stuart L. Bernath, "George Washington and the Genesis of American Military Discipline," *Mid-America*, XLIX (1967), 88.

64. This narrative is reconstructed from the following conflicting sources: Douglas Southall Freeman, *George Washington: A Biography* (New York, 1948–1957), Volume V: *Victory with the Help of France*, 112 and n; William Irvine to Anthony Wayne, July 10, 1779, in George Morris Philips, comp., *Historic Letters from the Collection of the West Chester State Normal School* (Philadelphia, 1898), 11; "Anecdote," *American Museum*, VIII (1790), 200; Peter Ten Broeck to Cornelius Ten Broeck, July 9 [10?], 1779, *Magazine of American History*, II (1878), 169; William Gordon, *The History of the Rise, Progress, and Establishment of the Independence of the United States of America* (London, 1788), III, 270–271; Henry Lee, Jr., *Observations on the Writings of Thomas Jefferson* (New York, 1832), 143–144; George Washington, General Orders, Aug. 11, 14, 21, 1778, May 14 and July 8, 1779, Fitzpatrick, ed., *Writings of Washington*, XII, 313, 326, 348–349, XV, 72, 381; George Washington to Henry Lee, July 9 and 10, 1779, *ibid.*, XV, 388, 399; Henry Lee to George Washington, July 11, 1779, George Washington Papers, Library of Congress. On Reed, see Heitman, *Register of Officers*, 474.

65. John Hancock to Horatio Gates, Sept. 27, 1776, Force, ed., *American Archives*, 5th Ser., II, 561–562. Both sets of Articles of War are printed in Ford *et al.*, eds., *Journals of Congress*, II, 111–122, V, 788–807.

66. Entry of May 10, 1775, "The Revolutionary Journal of James Stevens of Andover, Mass.," Essex Inst., *Hist. Colls.*, XLVIII (1912), 44.

67. George Washington to Richard Henry Lee, Aug. 29, 1775, Fitzpatrick, ed., *Writings of Washington*, III, 451.

68. *Boston-Gaz.*, Jan. 1, 1781.

69. Joseph Johnson, *Traditions and Reminiscences Chiefly of the American Revolution in the South* . . . (Charleston, S.C., 1851), 86–87. See also Barnwell, anno., "Elliott's Journal," *S.C. Hist. and Gen. Mag.*, XVII (1916), 95–98.

70. Alexander Graydon, *Memoirs of His Own Time, with Reminiscences of the Men and Events of the Revolution*, ed. John Stockton Littell (Philadelphia, 1846 [orig. publ. Harrisburg, Pa., 1811]), 314.

71. George Washington, General Orders, June 7, 1777, Fitzpatrick, ed., *Writings of Washington*, VIII, 200.

72. George Washington, General Orders, Nov. 20, 1779, *ibid.*, XVII, 138.

73. Baron De Kalb to the comte [de Broglie], Nov. 2, 1777, Stevens, ed., *Facsimiles of Manuscripts*, VIII, No. 757; Lacey, "Memoirs," *PMHB*, XXV (1901), 353, 510–511; entry of Oct. 31, 1776, "Sergeant John Smith's Diary," *MVHR*, XX (1933), 259; Allen Bowman, *The Morale of the American Revolutionary Army* (Washington, D.C., 1943), 39–42; [Martin], *Yankee Doodle*, ed. Scheer, 41; Thomas Lynch to George Washington, Nov. 13, 1775, Burnett, ed., *Letters of Congress*, I, 253–254; Joseph Reed to a member of Congress, 1777, quoted in William B. Reed, *Life and Correspondence of Joseph Reed* . . . (Philadelphia, 1847), I, 240–241; Joseph Reed to Charles Pettit, Oct. 14, 1776, *ibid.*, 244; James Morris, "Memoirs of a Connecticut Patriot," *Conn. Mag.*, XI (1907), 450.

74. George Washington to George Weedon, Mar. 27, 1777, Worthington C. Ford, ed., *Correspondence and Journal of Webb*, I, 197.

75. Compare Lender, "Enlisted Line of New Jersey," chaps. 4, 6. See also the Appendix, pp. 373–378 below. The officers' aspiration to gentility has recently been discussed in Gerhard Kollmann, "Reflections on the Army of the American Revolution," Erich Angermann, Marie-Luise Frings, and Hermann Wellenreuther, eds., *New Wine in Old Skins: A Comparative View of Socio-Political Structures and Values Affecting the American Revolution* (Stuttgart, 1976), 153–176, and Don Higginbotham, "Military Leadership in the American Revolution," *Library of Congress Symposia on the American Revolution: Leadership in the American Revolution* (Washington, D.C., 1974), 91–111. See also Sidney Kaplan, "Rank and Status among Massachusetts Continental Officers," *AHR*, LVI (1951), 318–326.

76. Lacey, "Memoirs," *PMHB*, XXV (1901), 498.

77. George Washington to John Hancock, Oct. 4, 1776, Fitzpatrick, ed., *Writings of Washington*, VI, 153.

78. Quoted in Gordon, *History of the Independence of the United States*, II, 317.

79. Bernhard Knollenberg, *Washington and the Revolution: A Reappraisal* (New York, 1940), 111.

80. Entries of May 6 and June 8, 1778, Elisha Stevens, *Fragments of Memoranda Written by Him in the War of the Revolution* (Meriden, Conn., 1922), [12].

81. Barber, *My Own Times* (1827), 12.

82. Lacey, "Memoirs," *PMHB*, XXV (1901), 11.

83. Graydon, *Memoirs*, ed. Littell, 146–147.

84. Philip Brooks to New York Congress, Feb. 16, 1776, Force, ed., *American Archives*, 4th Ser., IV, 1163.

85. Entry of July 1, 1775, Albion and Dodson, eds., *Fithian: Journal, 1775–1776*, 44–45.

86. Nathanael Greene to John Brown, Sept. 6, 1778, Greene, *Nathanael Greene*, II, 135.

87. William Pierce to St. George Tucker, Feb. 6, 1782, *Mag. Am. Hist.*, VII (1881), 438.

88. Lacey, "Memoirs," *PMHB*, XXV (1901), 12.

89. William Richardson to William Smallwood, Apr. 12, 1777, Balch, ed., *Papers Relating to the Maryland Line*, 91.

90. Entry of Mar. 28, 1782, "Extracts from the Journal of Lieutenant John Bell Tilden, Second Pennsylvania Line, 1781–1782," *PMHB*, XIX (1895), 224.

91. Entries of Oct. 10, 1776, and Nov. 29, 1776, Lewis Beebe, "Journal of a Physician on the Expedition against Canada," *ibid.*, LIX (1935), 353, 359.

92. Lacey, "Memoirs," *ibid.*, XXV (1901), 197.

93. Nathanael Greene to John Sullivan, June 24, 1777, Otis G. Hammond, ed., *Letters and Papers of Major-General John Sullivan* (N.H. Hist. Soc., *Colls.*, XIII–XV [Concord, N.H., 1930–1939]), I, 400–401, hereafter cited as *Papers of Sullivan*; George Washington, General Orders, June 30 and July 4, 1777, Fitzpatrick, ed., *Writings of Washington*, VIII, 317, 349.

94. General Court-Martials, Sept. 23, 1776, Force, ed., *American Archives*, 5th Ser., II, 467–469; General Orders, Sept. 26, 1776, "Elisha Williams's Diary of 1776," *PMHB*, XLVIII (1924), 348; Graydon, *Memoirs*, ed. Littell, 178–180. Graydon evidently is listed as "Greaton" among the members of the court.

95. Jane Varick to Richard Varick, Apr. 11, 1777, Charles I. Bushnell, "Women of the Revolution. A Series of Letters Written by Distinguished Women of That Period," *Historical Magazine*, 2d Ser., V (1869), 107.

96. Graydon, *Memoirs*, ed. Littell, 178–180; Charles Biddle, *Autobiography of Charles Biddle* (Philadelphia, 1883), 143–147; Samuel Smith to Otho Holland Williams, Oct. 4, 1780, *Calendar of the General Otho Holland Williams Papers in the Maryland Historical Society* (Baltimore, 1940), 23; Edward Giles to Otho Holland Williams, June 1, 1781, *ibid.*, 46; "The Papers of General Samuel Smith. The General's Autobiography. From the Original Manuscripts," *Hist. Mag.*, 2d Ser., VII (1870), 85; William Wilmot to Benjamin Talbot, n.d., in

Francis B. Culver, "General Sullivan's Descent upon the British on Staten Island," *Md. Hist. Mag.*, VI (1911), 142; *Pa. Packet*, Apr. 8, 1780, Apr. 22, 1783; *South Carolina Gazette*, Mar. 29, 1783, quoted in *S.C. Hist. and Gen. Mag.*, VII (1906), 52; George Washington to Stephen Stewart, Mar. 24, 1790, Fitzpatrick, ed., *Writings of Washington*, XXXI, 27; entry of Mar.–Apr. 1783, "Military Journal of Major Ebenezer Denny, An Officer in the Revolutionary and Indian Wars," Historical Society of Pennsylvania, *Memoirs*, VII (Philadelphia, 1860), 255–256; David Humphreys, "Devices and inscriptions of American medals," *American Museum*, II (1787), 494–495; entry of Feb. 18, 1782, "Extracts from the Letter-Books of Reeves," *PMHB*, XXI (1897), 383–384; J. F. Loubat, *The Medallic History of the United States of America: 1776–1876* (New York, 1878), I, 15–19, II, 28, Plate V; Richard M. McSherry, "The National Medals of the United States," Md. Hist. Soc., *Fund-Publications*, No. 25 (1887), 18; Henry P. Johnston, *The Storming of Stony Point* (New York, 1900), 70, 183, 185, 197–198; Journal and Correspondence of the State Council of Maryland, June 16–17, 1781, William Hand Browne *et al.*, eds., *Archives of Maryland* (Baltimore, 1883–), XLV, 477–478; John Stewart to Thomas Sim Lee, recd. Aug. 23, 1781, *ibid.*, XLVII, 440; Nathanael Greene to John Stewart, Dec. 26, 1782, Walter Clark, ed., *The State Records of North Carolina* (Winston and Goldsboro, N.C., 1886–1905), XVI, 677–680; John Stewart to the secretary of war, Apr. 22, 1782, *ibid.*, 603–604; John Stewart to William Smallwood, July 11, 1782, and Oct. 23, 1782, Balch, ed., *Papers Relating to the Maryland Line*, 184–186, 196–197; John Stewart to Henry Lee, quoted in Thomas Boyd, *Light-Horse Harry Lee* (New York and London, 1931), 150; Frederick D. Stone, "Philadelphia Society One Hundred Years Ago, or the Reign of Continental Money," *PMHB*, III (1879), 367–368; John Sullivan to George Washington, Aug. 7, 1777, Hammond, ed., *Papers of Sullivan*, I, 426–427; Dixon and Hunter's *Va. Gaz.*, Sept. 12, 1777; Alexander Garden, *Anecdotes of the Revolutionary War in America, with Sketches of Character of Persons the Most Distinguished, in the Southern States, for Civil and Military Services* (Charleston, S.C., 1822), 399.

97. *Fresh News from Boston* . . . [New York? 1776].

98. *Pennsylvania Evening Post*, Mar. 30, 1776, in Moore, ed., *Diary of the Revolution*, I, 222–223.

99. Ford *et al.*, eds., *Journals of Congress*, IV, 248–249.

100. John Hancock to William Moultrie, July 22, 1776, Gibbes, *Documentary History*, III, 45.

101. Lanctot, *Canada and the American Revolution*, trans. Cameron; George F. G. Stanley, *Canada Invaded: 1775–1776* (Toronto, 1973); Charles H. Metzger, *The Quebec Act: A Primary Cause of the American Revolution* (New York, 1936); Charles H. Metzger, *Catholics and the American Revolution: A Study in Religious Climate* (Chicago, 1962); Sister Mary Augustine (Ray), *American Opinion of Roman Catholicism in the Eighteenth Century* (New York, 1974 [orig. publ. New York, 1936]).

102. Entry of Apr. 28, 1776, *Journal of the Rev. Ammi R. Robbins, A Chaplain in the American Army, in the Northern Campaign of 1776* (New Haven, Conn., 1850), 13.

103. Quoted in Eric Robson, *The American Revolution in Its Political and Military Aspects* (London, 1955), 158.

104. Caesar Rodney to Thomas Rodney, Feb. 4, 1776, George Herbert Ryden, ed., *Letters to and from Caesar Rodney, 1756–1784* (Philadelphia, 1933), 71.

105. Ford *et al.*, eds., *Journals of Congress*, IV, 387–388.

106. This casualty figure is given by Ward, *War of the Revolution*, ed. Alden, I, 384. It is based on Horatio Gates to George Washington, July 16, 1776, in Force, ed., *American Archives*, 5th Ser., I, 376, and includes deserters. The later deaths among the 3,000 sick at the time of Gates's letter probably pushed the total much higher. Gates's estimate is also accepted by Mark Mayo Boatner III, *Encyclopedia of the American Revolution*, Bicentennial Edition (New York, 1974), 178, by Don Higginbotham, *The War of American Independence: Military Attitudes, Policies, and Practice, 1763–1789* (New York, 1971), 115, and by Martin H. Bush, *Revolutionary Enigma: A Re-appraisal of General Philip Schuyler of New York* (Port Washington, N.Y., 1969), 61. I find this figure more convincing than the curiously precise guess of 1,872 wartime deaths in camp by southern irregulars, unreported state regiments, militia, and the Canadian expedition given in Howard H. Peckham, ed., *The Toll of Independence: Engagements and Battle Casualties of the American Revolution* (Chicago, 1974), 131–132. This valuable compilation of battlefield casualty figures may underestimate the deaths in camp and hospital due to disease. See Louis C. Duncan, *Medical Men in the American Revolution, 1775–1783*, Army Medical Bulletin No. 25 (Carlisle Barracks, Pa., 1931), 369–378.

107. Samuel Adams to Joseph Hawley, July 9, 1776, Cushing, ed., *Writings of Samuel Adams*, III, 295.

108. John Jay to the marquis de Lafayette, Jan. 3, 1779, Burnett, ed., *Letters of Congress*, IV, 1.

109. *Boston-Gaz.*, July 7, 1777.

110. George Washington to Henry Laurens, Nov. 11, 1778, Fitzpatrick, ed., *Writings of Washington*, XIII, 226–228; George Washington to John Sullivan, May 29, 1781, *ibid.*, XXII, 131. For a different evaluation of the invasion of Canada, see John R. Alden, *A History of the American Revolution* (New York, 1969), chap. 14.

111. Foner, ed., *Writings of Paine*, I, 21. This point is also made in Alden, *History of the Revolution*, 229.

112. Entry of [July] 21, 1776, *The Diary of Matthew Patten of Bedford, N.H.* (Concord, N.H., 1903), 361. On John Patten, see *History of Bedford, New Hampshire* (Concord, N.H., 1903), 1039.

113. Entry of Apr. 15–17, 1777, William H. W. Sabine, ed., *Memoirs of William Smith, 1776–1778* (New York, 1958), 115.

114. See below, chap. 4.

115. Joseph Montgomery, *A Sermon, Preached At Christana Bridge and Newcastle . . .* (Philadelphia, 1775), 29.

116. Micah 4:4.

117. Paine, *Common Sense*, in Foner, ed., *Writings of Paine*, I, 4.

118. [Charles Inglis], *The Deceiver Unmasked; or, Loyalty and Interest United: In Answer to a Pamphlet Entitled Common Sense* (New York, 1776), 14.

119. Micah 4:3.

120. See also below, chap. 4.

121. John Adams to John Winthrop, June 23, 1776, Adams, ed., *Works of John Adams*, IX, 409–410.

122. Entry of May 6, 1778, Victor Hugo Paltsits, ed., *Minutes of the Commissioners for Detecting and Defeating Conspiracies in the State of New York. Albany County Sessions, 1778–1781* (Albany, N.Y., 1909), I, 107.

123. Charles J. Hoadly, ed., *The Public Records of the State of Connecticut* (Hartford, Conn., 1894–1943), III, 141; entry of June 5, 1781, "News of the Yorktown Campaign: The Journal of Dr. Robert Honyman, April 17–November 25, 1781," *VMHB*, LXXIX (1971), 400–401. Compare John Bowater to Basil Feilding, earl of Denbigh, June 5–11, 1777, Marion Balderston and David Syrett, eds., *The Lost War: Letters from British Officers during the American Revolution* (New York, 1975), 131.

124. Shy, *People Numerous and Armed*, 216–219; Michael Kammen, "The American Revolution as a *Crise de Conscience*: The Case of New York," in Richard M. Jellison, ed., *Society, Freedom, and Conscience: The American Revolution in Virginia, Massachusetts, and New York* (New York, 1976), 125–189; James H. Kettner, "The Development of American Citizenship in the Revolutionary Era: The Idea of Volitional Allegiance," *American Journal of Legal History*, XVII (1974), 208–242.

125. Whitaker, *Antidote against Toryism*, 8.

126. Entry of Apr. 20, 1777, Sabine, ed., *Memoirs of William Smith, 1776–1778*, 117.

127. Joseph Hawley to Elbridge Gerry, July 17, 1776, Force, ed., *American Archives*, 5th Ser., I, 403–404.

128. Bailyn, *Ideological Origins*.

129. Nathanael Greene to Nicholas Cooke, July 22, 1776, "Revolutionary Correspondence of Governor Nicholas Cooke, 1775–1781," American Antiquarian Society, *Proceedings*, N.S., XXXVI, Part II (1927), 331.

130. George Washington to John Hancock, Sept. 2, 1776, Fitzpatrick, ed., *Writings of Washington*, VI, 4–5.

131. John Morin Scott to John Jay, Sept. 6, 1776, Johnston, ed., *Correspondence of Jay*, I, 82; John McKesson to George Clinton, Sept. 29, 1776, Hugh Hastings, ed., *Public Papers of George Clinton . . .* (New York and Albany, 1899–1904), I, 366; Proceedings of a Court-Martial, Oct. 7, 1776, Force, ed., *American Archives*, 5th Ser., II, 929.

132. Entry of Sept. 13, 1776, Albion and Dodson, eds., *Fithian: Journal, 1775–1776*, 231.

133. Nathanael Greene to Nicholas Cooke, Sept. 17, 1776, Force, ed., *American Archives*, 5th Ser., II, 370.

134. Nathanael Greene to Henry Knox, Nov. 17, 1776, quoted in Noah Brooks, *Henry Knox: A Soldier of the Revolution* (New York and London, 1900), 74.

135. Howard H. Peckham, ed., *Memoirs of the Life of John Adlum in the Revolutionary War* (Chicago, 1968), 22.

136. William Hooper to Samuel Johnston, Sept. 26, 1776, William L. Saunders, ed., *The Colonial Records of North Carolina*, X (Raleigh, N.C., 1890), 816–817.

137. George Washington to John Augustine Washington, Nov. 6, 1776, Fitzpatrick, ed., *Writings of Washington*, VI, 242–243.

138. Entry of Aug. 30, 1776 [Ewald Gustav Schaukirk], "Occupation of New York City by the British, 1776. Extracts from the Diary of the Moravian Congregation," *PMHB*, I (1877), 148.

139. Entry of Sept. 22, 1776, Albion and Dodson, eds., *Fithian: Journal, 1775–1776*, 241.

140. Joseph H. Jones, ed., *The Life of Ashbel Green* (New York, 1849), 122. On the invasion of New Jersey, see esp. Leonard Lundin, *Cockpit of the Revolution: The War for Independence in New Jersey* (Princeton, N.J., 1940).

141. George Washington to Lund Washington, Dec. 10–17, 1776, Fitzpatrick, ed., *Writings of Washington*, VI, 347.

142. John Hancock to New York Convention, Oct. 9, 1776, *Journals of the Provincial Congress . . . of New York* (Albany, N.Y., 1842), I, 675.

143. Compare Shy, *People Numerous and Armed*, chap. 9, "The Military Conflict Considered as a Revolutionary War."

144. Entry of Dec. 7, 1776, Franklin B. Dexter, ed., *The Literary Diary of Ezra Stiles* (New York, 1901), II, 94.

145. *Two Favorite Songs of the American Camp* [Boston, 1775?].

146. [Philip Morin Freneau], *American Liberty, A Poem* (New York, 1775), 9.

147. David Ramsay, *The History of the American Revolution* (London, 1793), I, 197.

148. Samuel Shaw to John Eliot, Nov. 18, 1776, Josiah Quincy, *The Journals of Major Samuel Shaw, The First American Consul at Canton, with a Life of the Author* (Boston, 1847), 27–28.

149. Winslow C. Watson, ed., *Men and Times of the Revolution; or, Memoirs of Elkanah Watson . . .* (New York, 1856), 24.

150. Charles Stedman, *The History of the Origin, Progress and Termination of the American War* (London, 1794), I, 206.

151. William Hooper to Dorothy Forbes, Apr. 2, 1776, in Nina Moore Tiffany, ed., *Letters of James Murray, Loyalist* (Boston, 1901), 238–239.

152. See also below, chap. 7.

153. Francis Johnston to Joseph Reed, May 18, 1779, Hazard *et al.*, eds., *Pa. Archives*, 1st Ser., VII, 412.

154. Thomas Burke to Charles Lee, June 11, 1776, *The Lee Papers* (N.-Y. Hist. Soc., *Colls.*, IV–VII [New York, 1872–1875]), II, 61.

155. Paine, "The American Crisis," No. II, Foner, ed., *Writings of Paine*, I, 69.

156. Benjamin Rush to Richard Henry Lee, Dec. 21, 1776 and Benjamin Rush to John Adams, Oct. 1, 1777, Butterfield, ed., *Letters of Rush*, I, 121, 156–157.

157. *Boston-Gaz.*, May 27, 1776.

158. Nathanael Greene to Jacob Greene, Jan. 3, 1778, Greene, *Nathanael Greene*, I, 545.

159. Ambrose Serle to the earl of Dartmouth, Aug. 12, 1776, Stevens, ed., *Facsimiles of Manuscripts*, XXIV, No. 2041.

160. Unknown correspondent to William Eden, [1778?], *ibid.*, No. 2102.

161. *Pa. Packet*, June 20, 1780.

162. Isaac J. Greenwood, ed., *The Revolutionary Services of John Greenwood of Boston and New York, 1775–1783* (New York, 1922), 40.

163. Edwin M. Stone, *The Life and Recollections of John Howland* (Providence, R.I., 1857), 70.

164. John Chester to Samuel B. Webb, Jan. 17, 1777, Henry P. Johnston, *Yale and Her Honor Roll in the American Revolution, 1775–1783* (New York, 1888), 61–62.

165. David Avery, *The Lord is to be Praised . . .* (Norwich, Conn., 1778), 24.

166. John Ross Delafield, ed., "Reminiscences Written by Janet Livingston, Widow of General Richard Montgomery," Dutchess County Historical Society, *Yearbook*, XV (1930), 45–76; Louise Livingston Hunt, "General Richard Montgomery," *Harper's Magazine*, LXX (1885), 350–359; Thomas P. Robinson, "Some Notes on Major-General Richard Montgomery," *New York History*, XXXVII (1956), 388–396; John Ross Delafield, "Montgomery Place," *ibid.*, XX (1939), 445–449; Julia Delafield, *Biographies of Francis Lewis and Morgan Lewis* (New York, 1877), I, 134–135, 183–184, 203–225, II, 147–149; issue of July 25, 1818, *Niles' Weekly Register*, XIV, 372–375; entries of July 1, 1777, Feb. 19 and Mar. 15, 1778, Sabine, ed., *Memoirs of William Smith, 1776–1778*, 170, 304–305, 324; George Washington to Sir Edward Newenham, July 29, 1789, Fitzpatrick, ed., *Writings of Washington*, XXX, 368; Sir Edward Newenham to George Washington, Oct. 10, 1789, Jared Sparks, ed., *Correspondence of the American Revolution; Being Letters of Eminent Men to George Washington, from the Time of His Taking Command of the Army to the End of His Presidency* (Boston, 1853), IV, 286–287; Charles Havens Hunt, *Life of Edward Livingston* (New York, 1864), 31–32, 43–45, 244–246, 355–356; Richard Dobbs Spaight to James Iredell, Mar. 10, 1785, Burnett, ed., *Letters of Congress*, VIII, 64; Janet Montgomery to Robert R. Livingston, Apr. 3, 1803, *American Historical Record*, II (1873), 180–182; Janet Montgomery to Montgomery Tappen, Apr.

1784, Bushnell, "Women of the Revolution," *Hist. Mag.*, 2d Ser., V (1869), 111; Janet Montgomery to Mrs. Tappen, Nov. 24, 1784, *ibid.*; Philip H. Smith, *General History of Duchess* [sic] *County* (Pawling, N.Y., 1877), 378–380; George Dangerfield, *Chancellor Robert R. Livingston of New York, 1746–1813* (New York, 1960), 243–245; Janet Montgomery to Stephen Van Rensselaer, Jan. 2, 1813, *Mag. Am. Hist.*, XV (1886), 612; Frederick Butler, *A Complete History of the Marquis de Lafayette*, in Roland Van Zandt, *Chronicles of the Hudson* (New Brunswick, N.J., 1971), 161–162, 172; Mercy Warren to Henry Knox, Mar. 9, 1789, *Warren-Adams Letters: Being Chiefly a Correspondence among John Adams, Samuel Adams, and James Warren* (Mass. Hist. Soc., *Colls.*, LXXII–LXXIII [Boston, 1917–1923]), II, 306; Peter Stephen Du Ponceau, "The Autobiography of Peter Stephen Du Ponceau," *PMHB*, LXIII (1939), 433; Arthur Lee to Anne Home Shippen Livingston, Sept. 22, 1784, Ethel Armes, comp. and ed., *Nancy Shippen, Her Journal Book* (Philadelphia, 1935), 214; Samuel White Patterson, *Horatio Gates: Defender of American Liberties* (New York, 1941), 348–351, 386; Hugh Henry Brackenridge, *The Death of General Montgomery, In Storming the City of Quebec. A Tragedy*, in Norman Philbrick, ed., *Trumpets Sounding: Propaganda Plays of the American Revolution* (New York, 1972), 230–231; William Smith, *An Oration In Memory of General Montgomery* . . . (Philadelphia, 1776), 24; *America Invincible. An Heroic Poem* (Danvers, Mass., 1779), 30–31; Mercy Otis Warren, *History of the Rise, Progress and Termination of the American Revolution* (Boston, 1805), I, 266–267; Janet Montgomery to Mrs. John Jay, Sept. 6, 1780, Henry P. Johnston, ed., *The Correspondence and Public Papers of John Jay* (New York, 1890–1893), I, 402–403; Elizabeth F. Ellet, *The Women of the American Revolution* (New York, 1969 [orig. publ. New York, 1850]), I, 89–92; Janet Montgomery to Aaron Burr, Mar. 7, 1779, Matthew L. Davis, *Memoirs of Aaron Burr*, I (New York, 1837), 169; Paul David Nelson, *General Horatio Gates: A Biography* (Baton Rouge, La., 1976), 282–283; *The Port-Folio*, VI (1818), 72–80; Edward Livingston, "Fragments of Unpublished Reminiscences of Edward Livingston," *United States Magazine and Democratic Review*, VIII (1840), 384; Pierre M. Irving, *The Life and Letters of Washington Irving* (New York, 1866), I, 283–284; Alf Evers, *The Catskills from Wilderness to Woodstock* (Garden City, N.Y., 1972), 242–243, 267–269, 288–289; Andrew Jackson to Edward Livingston, Aug. 2, 1828, John Spencer Bassett, ed., *Correspondence of Andrew Jackson* (Washington, D.C., 1926–1933), VI, 500; Greta G. Hughes and Richard Owen, trans., "A German Duke in America," *N.Y. Hist.*, XXV (1944), 63. On Richard Montgomery, see also Ward, *War of the Revolution*, I, 140–141, 181–195; Washington Irving, *Life of George Washington* (London, 1885 [orig. publ. New York, 1855–1859]), I, 382–383, II, 454–462; Report of Committee on Memorial to Richard Montgomery, Jan. 24, 1776, Burnett, ed., *Letters of Congress*, I, 328–329; entries of Dec. 31, 1775, and Jan. 1, 1776, "The Journal of Return J. Meigs," Roberts, ed., *March to Quebec*, 192; entry of Nov. 20, 1775, George Morison, "Journal of the Expedition to Quebec," *ibid.*, 534; Richard Montgomery to Philip Schuyler, Oct. 13, 1775, Sparks, ed., *Correspondence of the Revolution: Letters to Washington*, I, 469–470; Result of the Proceedings of a Council of War, held at St. John's, Oct. 13, 1775, *ibid.*, 470–471; General Montgomery's Answer to Articles of Capitulation of Montreal, Nov. 12, 1775, *ibid.*, 478–479; Richard Montgomery to Philip Schuyler, Oct. 31, 1775, Lossing, *Life of Schuyler*, I, 427; Nathanael Greene to John Adams, May 2, 1777, Bernhard Knollenberg, "The Revolutionary Correspondence of Nathanael Greene and John Adams," *Rhode Island History*, I (1942), 49–50; Willard, ed., *Letters on the Revolution*, 272; William Linn, *A Military Discourse, Delivered in Carlisle* . . . (Philadelphia, 1776), 10–11; Hugh Henry Brackenridge, *An Eulogium of the Brave Men who have Fallen in The Contest with Great-Britain* . . . (Philadelphia, [1779]), 13–14; *The Fall of Lucifer, an Elegiac Poem* [Hartford, Conn., 1781], 9–10; [David Humphreys], *The Glory of America; or Peace Triumphant Over War: A Poem* (Philadelphia, 1783), 6–7; *A Monody in Honor of the Chiefs who have Fallen in the Cause of American Liberty* . . . [Philadelphia, 1784], 4; Thomas Paine, "A Dialogue Between the Ghost of General Montgomery just arrived from the Elysian Fields; and an American Delegate, in a wood near Philadelphia," Foner, ed., *Writings of Paine*, II, 88–93; *Independent Chron.*, Mar. 27, 1777; *Conn. Courant*, Feb. 19, 1776, Aug. 4, 1777; *New-Jersey Gazette* (Burlington), Mar. 3, 1779; *Pa. Packet*, June 10, 1776, June 3, 1778, Nov. 4, 1780; *Pa. Gaz.* (Philadelphia), Feb. 21, 1776; Dixon and Hunter's *Va. Gaz.*, Mar. 16, 1776; New York Provincial Congress to New York Delegates in Congress, June 7, 1775, *Journals of the Provincial Congress, Provincial Convention, Committee of Safety and Council of Safety of the State of New-York, 1775–1776–1777* (Albany, N.Y., 1842), I, 33; entry of Feb. 19, 1776, Tappert and Doberstein, trans. and eds., *Journals of Muhlenberg*, II, 716; Ellet, *Women of the Revolution*, III, 26–30; John Marshall, *The Life of George Washington* . . . (Fredericksburg, Va., 1926 [orig. publ. Philadelphia, 1804–1807]), II, 110–111; entries of Jan. 18, 1776, Feb. 19 and 21, 1776, "Diary of Richard Smith in the Continental Congress, 1775–1776," *AHR*, I (1895–1896), 494, 503–505; Yale University, *Two Dialogues, on Different Subjects* . . . (Hartford, Conn., 1776), 23–24; John Joseph Henry, *An Accurate and Interesting Account of the Hardships and Sufferings of that Band of Heroes, Who Traversed the Wilderness in the Campaign Against Quebec In 1775* (New York, 1968 [orig. publ. Lancaster, Pa., 1812]), 98, 127–130, 179–180; see also *N.J. Gaz.*, Oct. 31, 1781, in Moore, ed., *Diary of the Revolution*, II, 520; *Boston-Gaz.*, Nov. 10, 1777, Feb. 2, 1778; *Conn. Courant*, Apr. 14, 1778; Jonathan Williams Austin, *An Oration, Delivered March 5th, 1778* . . . (Boston, 1778), 14; Simeon E. Baldwin, *Life and Letters of Simeon Baldwin* (New Haven, Conn., [1919]), 147.

Chapter III
Jericho

1. Isaac J. Greenwood, ed., *The Revolutionary Services of John Greenwood of Boston and New York, 1775–1783* (New York, 1922), 43–44; Joseph White, *An Narrative of Events, As They Occurred from Time to Time in the Revolutionary War* (Charlestown, Mass., 1833), 29–30.

2. Alexander Garden, *Anecdotes of the American Revolution, Illustrative of the Talents and Virtues of the Heroes and Patriots, Who Acted the Most Conspicuous Parts Therein. Second Series* (Charleston, S.C., 1828), 199–200.

3. See the Appendix, pp. 373–378 below.

4. Richard Henry Lee to [Thomas Jefferson], Apr. 29, 1777, Ballagh, ed., *Letters of Richard Henry Lee*, I, 286.

5. See, for example, entry of Sept. 10, 1775, Daniel McCurtin, "Journal of the Times at the Siege of Boston," in Balch, ed., *Papers Relating to the Maryland Line*, 16; entry of Nov. 14, 1775, "Craft's Journal," Essex Inst., *Hist. Colls.*, III (1861), 220.

6. William Hooper to Robert Morris, May 27, 1777, "Letters to Robert Morris, 1775–1782," N.-Y. Hist. Soc., *Colls.*, XI (New York, 1879), 429.

7. Caroline Gilman, ed., *Letters of Eliza Wilkinson, During the Invasion and Possession of Charlestown, S.C. by the British in the Revolutionary War* (New York, 1839), 17.

8. Foner, ed., *Writings of Paine*, I, 90.

9. [Baron de Kalb] to the comte [de Broglie], Aug. 10–15, [1778], Stevens, ed., *Facsimiles of Manuscripts*, VIII, No. 845.

10. *Conn. Courant*, June 30, 1777.

11. Entries of Jan. 7, 1777, and Feb. 4, 1777, Elmer T. Clark, ed., *The Journal and Letters of Francis Asbury* (London and Nashville, Tenn., 1958), I, 227, 229–230; John Coe to New York Provincial Convention, n.d., *Journals of the Provincial Congress, Provincial Convention, Committee of Safety and Council of Safety of the State of New-York, 1775–1776–1777* (Albany, N.Y., 1842), II, 477; James Tilton, *Economical Observations on Military Hospitals; and the Prevention and Cure of Diseases Incident to an Army* (Wilmington, Del., 1813), 29; William Van Horne to Joseph Hart, Oct. 6, 1778, "Revolutionary War Letters of the Reverend William Van Horne," *Western Pennsylvania Historical Magazine*, LIII (1970), 121–122; Thaddeus Maccarty, *Praise to God, a Duty of continual Obligation . . .* (Worcester, Mass., [1776]), 12; David Osgood, *Reflections on the Goodness of God . . .* (Boston, 1784), 8–9.

12. Ebenezer Baldwin, *The Duty of Rejoicing under Calamities and Afflictions . . .* (New York, 1776), 20–21.

13. Charles H. Lesser, ed., *The Sinews of Independence: Monthly Strength Reports of the Continental Army* (Chicago, 1976), 50.

14. Robert Morris to Commissioners for American Affairs in Europe, Mar. 28, 1777, Charles Isham, ed., *The Deane Papers* (N.-Y. Hist. Soc., *Colls.*,

XIX–XXIII [New York, 1887–1891]), II, 35, hereafter cited as *Deane Papers*.

15. Henry Knox to Lucy Flucker Knox, June 21, 1777, Drake, *Life and Correspondence of Knox*, 42.

16. Delaware Council to Assembly, May 10, 1777, *Minutes of the Council of the Delaware State*, Hist. Soc. of Delaware, *Papers*, VI (Wilmington, Del., 1887), 118.

17. Abigail Adams to John Adams, Aug. 12, 1777, L. H. Butterfield *et al.*, eds., *Adams Family Correspondence* (Cambridge, Mass., 1963–), II, 309.

18. Rush, "Observations," *London Medical Journal*, VII (1786), 80.

19. On loyalists in the Continental Army, see Lender, "Enlisted Line of New Jersey," 93–96.

20. *Conn. Courant*, June 30, 1777.

21. Entry of Apr. 25, 1777, Sabine, ed., *Memoirs of William Smith, 1776–1778*, 120–121.

22. Gilman, ed., *Letters of Eliza Wilkinson*, 22.

23. "Narrative of John Hempstead," William W. Harris, ed., *The Battle of Groton Heights: A Collection of Narratives, Official Reports, Records, Etc., of the Storming of Fort Griswold, the Massacre of Its Garrison, and the Burning of New London by British Troops under the Command of Brig.-Gen. Benedict Arnold, on the Sixth of September, 1781* (New London, Conn., 1870), 34.

24. Theodorick Bland, Jr., to Martha Daingerfield Bland, [Feb. 1777], Charles Campbell, ed., *The Bland Papers* (Petersburg, Va., 1840–1843), I, 48–49; William Irvine to Anne Callender Irvine, May 10, 1782, C. W. Butterfield, ed., *Washington-Irvine Correspondence* (Madison, Wis., 1882), 347.

25. Henry Harrison Metcalf, ed., *Laws of New Hampshire*, IV (Bristol, N.H., 1916), 75.

26. *Pa. Packet*, June 10, 1777.

27. Jonathan Trumbull to George Washington, July 25, 1777, *The Trumbull Papers* (Mass. Hist. Soc., *Colls*., 5th Ser., IX–X, 7th Ser., I–II [Boston, 1885–1902]), II, 86, hereafter cited as *Trumbull Papers*; Jonathan Trumbull to Philip Schuyler, July 26, 1777, *ibid*., III, 89; Jonathan Trumbull, Jr., to Jonathan Trumbull, July 11, 1777, *ibid*., 77–78.

28. *Boston-Gaz*., July 21, 1777. Compare Arthur St. Clair to James Bowdoin, July 9, 1777, *The Bowdoin and Temple Papers*, Mass. Hist. Soc., *Colls*., 6th Ser., IX (Boston, 1897), 407.

29. *New-York Journal, and the General Advertiser* (Kingston), Aug. 4, 1777, reprinted from *Independent Chron*., July 24, 1777.

30. Jonathan Trumbull to Meshech Weare, Apr. 25, 1777, Nathaniel Bouton, ed., *New Hampshire State Papers: Documents and Records Relating to the State of New-Hampshire during the Period of the American Revolution, from 1776 to 1783*, VIII (Concord, N.H., 1874), 547; Josiah Bartlett to Militia Colonels on the Connecticut River, May 3, 1777, *ibid*., 551.

31. Entry of Apr. 3, 1777, Fitch Edward Oliver, ed., *The Diary of William Pynchon of Salem* (Boston and New York, 1890), 27.

32. *Conn. Courant*, Sept. 1, 1777.

33. *N.Y. Jour.*, Aug. 4, 1777.

34. Arthur St. Clair to John Hancock, July 14, 1777, William Henry Smith, *The Life and Public Services of Arthur St. Clair . . . with His Correspondence and Other Papers*, I (Cincinnati, Ohio, 1882), 428.

35. Jeremy Belknap, *The History of New-Hampshire* (Boston, 1791), II, 321–322.

36. Horatio Gates to Joseph Trumbull, Apr. 29, 1777, quoted in Bush, *Revolutionary Enigma*, 107.

37. Entry of Dec. 26, 1776, James Thacher, *A Military Journal During the American Revolutionary War* (Boston, 1823), 82–83; entry of Dec. 25, 1776, Elmer, "Journal during Expedition to Canada," N.J. Hist. Soc., *Procs.*, 1st Ser., III (1848), 51.

38. [Nathanael Greene], Division Orders, Oct. 7, 1777, "Orderly Book of Muhlenberg," *PMHB*, XXXV (1911), 66.

39. [Martin], *Yankee Doodle*, ed. Scheer, 74.

40. John Brooks to ———, Jan. 5, 1778, Mass. Hist. Soc., *Procs.*, XIII (1874), 244.

41. Sergeant R——, "The Battle of Princeton," *PMHB*, XX (1896), 518. Compare White, *Narrative of Events*, 22.

42. Osmond Tiffany, *A Sketch of the Life and Services of Gen. Otho Holland Williams* (Baltimore, 1851), 23.

43. *Pa. Packet*, Aug. 18, 1778.

44. Entry of Apr. 21, 1775, Thacher, *Military Journal*, 16–17.

45. *N.-J. Jour.*, May 4, 1779, quoted in William S. Stryker *et al.*, eds., *Archives of the State of New Jersey: Documents Relating to the Revolutionary History of the State of New Jersey*, 2d Ser. (Trenton, N.J., 1901–1917), III, 308.

46. Ward, *War of the Revolution*, ed. Alden, I, 370–371. Compare Boatner, *Encyclopedia of the Revolution*, 430.

47. Benjamin Rush, "State and Disorders in the American army October 1777," in "Historical Notes of Dr. Benjamin Rush, 1777," *PMHB*, XXVII (1903), 147.

48. John Adams to Abigail Adams, Sept. 2, 1777, Butterfield *et al.*, eds., *Adams Family Correspondence*, II, 336; Samuel Adams to Richard Henry Lee, June 26, 1777, Cushing, ed., *Writings of Samuel Adams*, III, 379; George Williams to Timothy Pickering, Dec. 13, 1777, George Williams, "Revolutionary Letters Written to Colonel Timothy Pickering," Essex Inst., *Hist. Colls.*, XLII (1906), 325.

49. John Adams to Mercy Warren, Nov. 25, 1775, Adams, ed., *Works of John Adams*, IX, 369.

50. John Adams to Abigail Adams, Sept. 2, 1777, Butterfield *et al.*, eds., *Adams Family Correspondence*, II, 336.

51. Nathanael Greene to John Brown, Sept. 6, 1778, Otis G. Hammond, ed., *Letters and Papers of Major-General John Sullivan* (N.H. Hist. Soc., *Colls.*, XIII–XV [Concord, N.H., 1930–1939]), II, 312–313, 318.

52. [William Wolcott], *Grateful Reflections On the Divine Goodness vouchsaf'd to the American Arms . . .* (Hartford, Conn., [1779]), 48. On Gates, see Nelson, *Gates*.

Chapter IV
The Promised Land

1. Entry of Sept. 8, 1779, Eugene Parker Chase, trans. and ed., *Our Revolutionary Forefathers: The Letters of François, Marquis de Barbé-Marbois . . . 1779–1785* (Freeport, N.Y., 1969 [orig. publ. New York, 1929]), 98. Jonathan Trumbull to Silas Deane, Oct. 6, 1778, *Trumbull Papers*, III, 283.

2. Out of the extensive scholarly literature on this subject, I have been most directly influenced by Perry Miller, "From the Covenant to the Revival," in *Nature's Nation* (Cambridge, Mass., 1967), 90–120; Heimert, *Religion and the American Mind*; Robert Middlekauff, "The Ritualization of the American Revolution," in Stanley Coben and Lorman Ratner, eds., *The Development of an American Culture* (Englewood Cliffs, N.J., 1970), 31–43; Ruth Bloch, "Millennial Thought in the American Revolutionary Movement" (unpublished seminar paper, University of California, Berkeley, 1973); Henry F. May, *The Enlightenment in America* (New York, 1976); William G. McLoughlin, "Pietism and the American Character," in Hennig Cohen, ed., *The American Experience* (Boston, 1968), 39–63; William G. McLoughlin, "'Enthusiasm for Liberty': The Great Awakening as the Key to the Revolution," Amer. Antiq. Soc., *Procs.*, LXXXVII, Part I (1977), 69–95. This subject has also been usefully treated in Cedric B. Cowing, *The Great Awakening and the American Revolution: Colonial Thought in the Eighteenth Century* (Chicago, 1971); Cushing Strout, *The New Heavens and New Earth: Political Religion in America* (New York, 1974), esp. chap. 4; and John F. Berens, "Divine Providence and the American Enlightenment, 1740–1815" (Ph.D. diss., Marquette University, 1975). See also John F. Berens, *Providence and Patriotism in Early America, 1640–1815* (Charlottesville, Va., 1978). Some of the matters in this chapter are discussed from a different perspective in Philip Greven, *The Protestant Temperament: Patterns of Child-Rearing, Religious Experience, and the Self in Early America* (New York, 1977), esp. chap. 8. A number of recent studies have argued that evangelical religious ideas and attitudes, especially those about the millennium, did not have a consistent influence on the American Revolution. These works include Hatch, *Sacred Cause of Liberty*; James West Davidson, *The Logic of Millennial Thought: Eighteenth-Century New England* (New Haven, Conn., 1977); Albanese, *Sons of the Fathers*; Mark Allan Noll, "Church Membership and the American Revolution: An Aspect of Religion and Society in New England from the Revival to the War for Independence" (Ph.D. diss., Vanderbilt University, 1975); and Mark A. Noll, *Christians in the American Revolution* (n.p., 1977).

These studies, while differing with each other in subject and interpretation, all seem to follow, in part, Bernard Bailyn, "Religion and Revolution: Three Biographical Studies," *Perspectives in American History*, IV (1970), 85–172. Bailyn argues that whig political ideology, under the influence of individual temperament in times of crisis, more consistently explains conduct than does religious outlook. Some of the more recent studies suggest that religious ideas, images, and appeals were exploited by revolutionaries to dramatize analyses and goals that originated in secular political ideology. I have tried in this chapter and elsewhere in this book to suggest the ways in which one can see a fundamental influence on American revolutionary conduct, character, and ideals arising from a characteristically evangelical cast of mind.

3. Paine, *Common Sense*, appendix, Foner, ed., *Writings of Paine*, I, 45.

4. *New Hampshire Gazette*, Nov. 26, 1776, in Moore, ed., *Diary of the Revolution*, I, 328.

5. Israel Evans, *A Discourse, Delivered At Easton, On the 17th of October, 1779 . . .* (Philadelphia, 1779), 24.

6. See above, n. 2.

7. Yale University, *Two Dialogues*, 30; *A Discourse on Daniel vii, 27* ([Norwich, Conn.?] 1777), 19.

8. Linn, *Military Discourse*, 23.

9. See above, n. 2. See also Sacvan Bercovitch, "How the Puritans Won the American Revolution," *Massachusetts Review*, XVII (1976), 597–630.

10. William Stearns, *A View of the Controversy subsisting between Great-Britain and the American Colonies . . .* (Watertown, Mass., 1775), 33.

11. Entries of May 4–5, 1776, *Journal of Robbins*, 16.

12. Patrick Henry to Richard Henry Lee, June 18, 1778, H. R. McIlwaine, ed., *Official Letters of the Governors of the State of Virginia. The Letters of Patrick Henry* (Richmond, Va., 1926–1929), I, 292.

13. *N.J. Gaz.*, Oct. 31, 1781, in Moore, ed., *Diary of the Revolution*, II, 520.

14. David Ramsay, *An Oration on the Advantages of American Independence . . .* (Charleston, S.C., 1778), 15.

15. John Adams to Nathanael Greene, Mar. 18, 1780, Knollenberg, "Greene and Adams," *R.I. Hist.*, I (1942), 82. See also John C. Rainbolt, "Americans' Initial View of Their Revolution's Significance for Other Peoples, 1776–1788," *The Historian*, XXXV (1973), 418–433.

16. H. Trevor Colbourn, *The Lamp of Experience: Whig History and the Intellectual Origins of the American Revolution* (Chapel Hill, N.C., 1965), 4–6, 22, 101, 189.

17. *Massachusetts Spy or, American Oracle of Liberty* (Worcester), July 30, 1778.

18. See above, chap. 3, n. 29.

19. Entry of Sept. 8, 1779, Chase, trans. and ed., *Our Revolutionary Forefathers: Letters of Barbé-Marbois*, 104.

20. "Journal of Samuel Rowland Fisher, of Philadelphia, 1779–1781," *PMHB*, XLI (1917), 160.

21. John Jones to Mary Jones, Oct. 4, 1779, George White, *Historical Collections of Georgia . . .* (New York, 1854), 536.

22. Entry of May 9, 1776, "Farnsworths Journal," Mass. Hist. Soc., *Procs.*, 2d Ser., XII (1898), 92.

23. Entry of Oct. 15, 1775, Jabez Fitch, Jr., "A Journal," *ibid.*, IX (1895), 69.

24. Entry of July 21, 1776, Albion and Dodson, eds., *Fithian: Journal, 1775–1776*, 192. On the importance of eloquence, see Heimert, *Religion and the American Mind*, esp. chap. 4; Edwin Scott Gaustad, *The Great Awakening in New England* (New York, 1957), 107.

25. Entry of June 2, 1776, *Journal of Robbins*, 28.

26. Ebenezer David to Nicholas Brown, Feb. 3, 1778, Jeanette D. Black and William Greene Roelker, eds., *A Rhode Island Chaplain in the Revolution: Letters of Ebenezer David to Nicholas Brown, 1775–1778* (Providence, R.I., 1949), 76 and n.

27. Entries of Mar. 24, 1776, and Sept. 22, 1776, *Journal of Robbins*, 4, 41.

28. Entry of Sept. 30, 1776, *ibid.*, 43.

29. John Hurt, *The Love of our Country. A Sermon, Preached Before The Virginia Troops in New-Jersey* (Philadelphia, 1777), 21.

30. Entry of July 14, 1776, Beebe, "Journal of a Physician on the Expedition against Canada, 1776," *PMHB*, LIX (1935), 343.

31. Ebenezer David to Nicholas Brown, Aug. 31, 1776, Black and Roelker, eds., *Rhode Island Chaplain*, 27.

32. Ebenezer David to Nicholas Brown, Aug. 2, 1777, *ibid.*, 36.

33. Entry of Oct. 5, 1776, *Journal of Robbins*, 43.

34. Peckham, ed., *Memoirs of Adlum*, 126.

35. Ramsay, *American Revolution*, II, 164–165.

36. M. M. Quaife, ed., "A Boy Soldier under Washington: The Memoir of Daniel Granger," *MVHR*, XVI (1929–1930), 552n.

37. Entry of Dec. [5], 1780, James R. Nichols, ed., "The Doughboy of 1780: Pages from a Revolutionary Diary," *Atlantic Monthly*, CXXXIV (1924), 461.

38. Entry of Aug. 15, 1779, "Elijah Fisher's Journal While in the War for Independence," *Magazine of History*, II, Extra Number, No. 6 (1909), 31. On the importance of religion to soldiers, see also Walter F. Wallace, "'Oh, Liberty! Oh, Virtue! Oh, My Country': An Exploration of the Minds of New England Soldiers during the American Revolution" (M.A. thesis, Northern Illinois University, 1974), chap. 3.

39. Ebenezer David to Nicholas Brown, Aug. 31, 1776, Black and Roelker, eds., *Rhode Island Chaplain*, 27.

40. Graydon, *Memoirs*, ed. Littell, 232.

41. Entry of Sept. 13, 1776, *Journal of Robbins*, 39.

42. Hezekiah Smith to Hephzibah Kimball Smith, Mar. 11, 1776, Guild, *Chaplain Smith*, 171.

43. Entry of Oct. 29, 1780, "Diary of Lieut. Anthony Allaire, of Ferguson's Corps," in Lyman C. Draper, *King's Mountain and Its Heroes: History of the Battle*

of King's Mountain, October 7th, 1780, and the Events Which Led to It (Cincinnati, Ohio, 1881), 512.

44. John Gano, *Biographical Memoirs of the Late Rev. John Gano, of Frankfort, (Kentucky)* . . . (New York, 1806), 102.

45. Entry of Sept. 24, 1775, "Diary of Rev. Benjamin Boardman," Mass. Hist. Soc., *Procs.*, 2d Ser., VII (1892), 408.

46. Entry of Oct. 13, 1776, Beebe, "Journal," *PMHB*, LIX (1935), 353–354.

47. Evans, *Discourse Delivered Near York*, 40.

48. (Philadelphia, 1779); entries of Dec. 15–16, 1780, Harriette M. Forbes, ed., *The Diary of Rev. Ebenezer Parkman of Westborough, Mass.* (Westborough, Mass., 1899), 291–292.

49. [Martin], *Yankee Doodle*, ed. Scheer, 100–101; Luke 3:14.

50. Hezekiah Smith to Hephzibah Kimball Smith, July 14, 1780, Guild, *Chaplain Smith*, 269.

51. Entry of Aug. 6, 1775, "Craft's Journal," Essex Inst., *Hist. Colls.*, III (1861), 56. On chaplains, see also Charles H. Metzger, "Chaplains in the American Revolution," *Catholic Historical Review*, XXXI (1945–1946), 31–79; Eugene Franklin Williams, "Soldiers of God: The Chaplains of the Revolutionary War" (Ph.D. diss., Texas Christian University, 1972).

52. Shipton, *Sibley's Harvard Graduates*, XIV, 450–455; *Va. Gaz.*, Aug. 12, 1775, in Moore, ed., *Diary of the Revolution*, I, 117; *Pennsylvania Evening Post*, Mar. 30, 1776, *ibid.*, 222–223; entry of July 18, 1775, Caleb Haskell, "Diary at the Siege of Boston and on the March to Quebec," Roberts, ed., *March to Quebec*, 466; Abiel Leonard, *A Prayer, Composed For the Benefit of the Soldiery, in the American Army* . . . (Cambridge, Mass., 1775); Abiel Leonard to Samuel Blachley Webb, Aug. 22, 1775, Ford, ed., *Correspondence and Journal of Webb*, I, 97; entries of July 29, 1777, and Aug. 1, 1777, *ibid.*, 225; Israel Putnam to John Hancock, 1777, *ibid.*, 225n; John Chester to Joshua Huntington, Aug. 29, 1777, *The Huntington Papers* (Conn. Hist. Soc., *Colls.*, XX [Hartford, Conn., 1923]), 70; Jedidiah Huntington to Jabez Huntington, July 28, 29, 29–30, 1777, Aug. 1–2, 1777, *ibid.*, 356–359; entry of Aug. 1, 1777, "Diary of Hitchcock," R.I. Hist. Soc., *Pubs.*, N.S., VII (Providence, R.I., 1899), 125; *Boston-Gaz.*, Dec. 11, 1775, Mar. 25, 1776; Pinkney's *Va. Gaz.*, Aug. 10, 1775; entry of July 9, 1775, "Craft's Journal," Essex Inst., *Hist. Colls.*, III (1861), 53; entries of Sept. 3, Oct. 1, 8, 15, 1775, "Farnsworths Journal," Mass. Hist. Soc., *Procs.*, 2d Ser., XII (1898), 85–86; William Gordon to George Washington, Aug. 14, 1777, Ford, ed., "Letters of Gordon," Mass. Hist. Soc., *Procs.*, LXIII (1931), 357; entry of Oct. 21–22, 1775, Jeremy Belknap, "Journal of my Tour to the Camp, and the Observations I made there," *ibid.*, IV (1860), 82, 84; Alice M. Baldwin, *The New England Clergy and the American Revolution* (Durham, N.C., 1928), 161; Nathanael Greene to John Adams, May 2, 1777, Knollenberg, "Greene and Adams," *R.I. Hist.*, I (1942), 50; John Adams to Nathanael Greene, May 9, 1777, *ibid.*, 54; entry of Sept. 3, 1775, L. H. Butterfield *et al.*, eds., *The Diary and Autobiography of John Adams* (Cambridge,

Mass., 1961), II, 172; entry of July 9, 1776, "Diary of Ensign Caleb Clap, of Colonel Baldwin's Regiment, Massachusetts Line, Continental Army, March 29 until October 23, 1776," *Hist. Mag.*, 3d Ser., III (1874), 137–318; Ebenezer David to Nicholas Brown, Aug. 2, 1777, Black and Roelker, eds., *Rhode Island Chaplain*, 36–37; Clarence Winthrop Bowen, *The History of Woodstock, Connecticut* (Norwood, Mass., 1926), I, 146–150; George Washington to Jonathan Trumbull, Dec. 15, 1775, Fitzpatrick, ed., *Writings of Washington*, IV, 164; George Washington to John Hancock, May 29, 1777, and June 8, 1777, *ibid.*, VIII, 138–139, 203–204; Ford *et al.*, eds., *Journals of Congress*, VIII, 390–391, 609; Daniel Roberdeau to George Washington, May 26, 1777, Burnett, ed., *Letters of Congress*, II, 376; Robert C. Learned, "Congregational Churches and Ministers in Windham County, Ct.," *Congregational Quarterly*, III (1861), 350–351; Ellen D. Larned, *History of Windham County, Connecticut* (Worcester, Mass., 1874–1880), II, 179; entry of July 18, 1775, Paul Lunt, "Diary," Mass. Hist. Soc., *Procs.*, XII (1872), 195; William S. Baker, "Itinerary of General Washington from June 15, 1775, to December 23, 1783," *PMHB*, XIV (1890–1891), 121; *Conn. Courant*, Aug. 11, 1777; William Gordon, *The History of the Rise, Progress, and Establishment of the Independence of the United States of America* (London, 1788), II, 70; David Humphreys, *An Essay on the Life of the Honourable Major General Israel Putnam* (Boston, 1818), 100; William Abbatt, ed., *Memoirs of Major-General William Heath* (New York, 1901), 41; *Pa. Packet*, July 15, 1776.

53. [John P. Becker], *The Sexagenary: Or, Reminiscences of the American Revolution*, ed. Simeon De Witt Bloodgood (Albany, N.Y., 1866), 73.

54. Entry of Nov. 3, 1777, Sabine, ed., *Memoirs of William Smith, 1776–1778*, 253.

55. [Ezekiel Kellogg], *A Poem, on the Unsuccessful Measures, Taken [b]y the British Army; In order to Enslave and Destroy the United States* . . . (n.p., 1782), 11.

56. William Foster, *True Fortitude Delineated* . . . (Philadelphia, 1776), 19. On Americans' providential outlook, see Berens, "Providence and Enlightenment."

57. (n.p., 1777).

58. Ebenezer David to Nicholas Brown, Nov. 23–25, 1777, Black and Roelker, eds., *Rhode Island Chaplain*, 69.

59. John Adams to Samuel Chase, July 1, 1776, Adams, ed., *Works of John Adams*, IX, 416.

60. Samuel Adams to James Warren, Sept. 17, 1777, *Warren-Adams Letters* (Mass. Hist. Soc., *Colls.*, LXXII–LXXIII [Boston, 1917–1923]), I, 370.

61. Entry of Jan. 7, 1778, Duane, ed., *Diary of Marshall*, 159.

62. Jonathan Sergeant to James Lovell, quoted in Rossie, *Politics of Command*, 183.

63. Henry Laurens to John Laurens, Oct. 16, 1777, Burnett, ed., *Letters of Congress*, II, 521–522.

64. Richard Peters to Anthony Wayne, Jan. 29, 1778, quoted in Paul David Nelson, "Horatio Gates: Republican Soldier of the American Revolution, 1728–1806" (Ph.D. diss., Duke University, 1969), 189–190.

65. "Thoughts of a Freeman," Jan. 17, 1778, Jared Sparks, ed., *The Writings of George Washington*, V (New York, 1847), 499.

66. George Washington to Thomas Conway, Nov. 9, 1777, Fitzpatrick, ed., *Writings of Washington*, X, 29.

67. Nathaniel Chipman to Elisha Lee, Apr. 10, 1778, Johnston, *Yale and Her Honor-Roll*, 86.

68. *Independent Chron*., Feb. 26, 1778. Compare Ford, ed., "Letters of Gordon," Mass. Hist. Soc., *Procs*., LXIII (1931), 378–381; *Boston-Gaz*., Feb. 16, 1778.

69. The most influential study of the cabal controversy has been Knollenberg, *Washington and the Revolution*. Other accounts include Kenneth R. Rossman, *Thomas Mifflin and the Politics of the American Revolution* (Chapel Hill, N.C., 1952), 95–137; Rossie, *Politics of Command*, 179–201; Henderson, *Party Politics*, 118–120; Higginbotham, *War of American Independence*, 216–222; and Nelson, *Gates*, chap. 6. The existence of a cabal is accepted in Freeman, *Washington*, IV, 586–611.

70. Much of this correspondence is printed in Sparks, ed., *Writings of Washington*, V, 483–518. The best study of it is in Rossman, *Mifflin*, 95–137.

71. Benjamin Rush to Patrick Henry, Jan. 12, 1778, Butterfield, ed., *Letters of Rush*, I, 182–183; compare Benjamin Rush to George Washington, Feb. 25, 1778, *ibid*., 200–201; Patrick Henry to George Washington, Feb. 20, 1778, McIlwaine, ed., *Official Letters of Henry*, I, 245–246; Patrick Henry to George Washington, Mar. 5, 1778, Henry, *Patrick Henry*, I, 547–548; George Washington to Patrick Henry, Mar. 27, 28, 1778, Fitzpatrick, ed., *Writings of Washington*, XI, 160, 164–165; Benjamin Rush to John Adams, Oct. 21, 1777, Butterfield, ed., *Letters of Rush*, I, 159–160; William Gordon to George Washington, Feb. 25, 1778, Ford, ed., "Letters of Gordon," Mass. Hist. Soc., *Procs*., LXIII (1931), 373–374.

72. Paine, "The American Crisis," No. V, Foner, ed., *Writings of Paine*, I, 127.

73. Richard Henry Lee to Arthur Lee, Oct. 13, 1777, Ballagh, ed., *Letters of Richard Henry Lee*, I, 328.

74. Entry of Oct. 1, 1777, "Diary of Allen," *PMHB*, IX (1885–1886), 291.

75. George Washington to Charles Lee, Dec. 11, 1776, Force, ed., *American Archives*, 5th Ser., III, 1166.

76. *Independent Chron*., Feb. 26, 1778.

77. Entry of Jan. 19, 1778, "Diary of Joseph Clark," N.J. Hist. Soc., *Procs*., 1st Ser., VII (1855), 104.

78. Henry Laurens to Francis Dana, Mar. 1, 1778, Burnett, ed., *Letters of Congress*, III, 102–103.

Chapter V
Valley Forge

1. Samuel Shaw to John Eliot, Nov. 20, 1778, Quincy, *Journals of Shaw*, 52.

2. Entry of Dec. 22, 1777, "Valley Forge, 1777–1778. Diary of Surgeon Albigence Waldo, of the Connecticut Line," *PMHB*, XXI (1897), 311.

3. Lacey, "Memoirs," *ibid.*, XXV (1901), 345–346.

4. Du Ponceau, "Autobiography," *ibid.*, LXIII (1939), 208.

5. Freeman, *Washington*, IV: *Leader of the Revolution*, 575.

6. *Independent Chron.*, Mar. 26, 1778.

7. William North, "Baron Steuben," *Mag. Am. Hist.*, VIII, Part I (1882), 189; George Washington to John Cadwalader, Mar. 20, 1778, Fitzpatrick, ed., *Writings of Washington*, XI, 117; Marquis de Lafayette, *Memoirs, Correspondence and Manuscripts of General Lafayette* (New York, 1837), I, 35; John Laurens to Henry Laurens, Jan. 23, 1778, William Gilmore Simms, ed., *The Army Correspondence of Colonel John Laurens in the Years 1777–8* (New York, 1867), 112.

8. George Washington, General Orders, Feb. 22, 1778, Fitzpatrick, ed., *Writings of Washington*, X, 500.

9. Nathanael Greene to John Adams, Mar. 3, 1777, Nathanael Greene to John Brown, Sept. 6, 1778, Nathanael Greene to Thomas Jefferson, Dec. 6, 1780, Greene, *Nathanael Greene*, I, 336, II, 135, III, 553.

10. Nathanael Greene to George Washington, May 21, 1776, Sparks, ed., *Correspondence of the Revolution*, I, 207.

11. Henry Knox to George Washington, Mar. 27, 1781, *ibid.*, III, 276.

12. John Lamb to George Washington, Aug. 19, 1779, Isaac Q. Leake, *Memoir of the Life and Times of General John Lamb . . .* (Albany, N.Y., 1857), 226.

13. John Trumbull to John Hancock, Feb. 22, 1777, John Trumbull to James Lovell, Mar. 30, 1777, in Trumbull, *Autobiography*, 39, 46.

14. Psalm 75:5–7.

15. Thomas Burke, Abstract of Debates in Congress, Feb. 12–19, 1777, Clark, ed., *State Records of N.C.*, XI, 380.

16. Gouverneur Morris to George Washington, May 27, 1778, Burnett, ed., *Letters of Congress*, III, 264–265; also printed in Sparks, ed., *Correspondence of the Revolution*, II, 129–130.

17. George Washington to Henry Laurens, Mar. 24, 1778, Fitzpatrick, ed., *Writings of Washington*, XI, 139.

18. Entry of Dec. 29, 1777, "Diary of Waldo," *PMHB*, XXI (1897), 315.

19. Samuel Richards, *Diary of Samuel Richards: Captain of Connecticut Line, War of the Revolution, 1775–1781* (Philadelphia, 1909), 77.

20. William H. Glasson, *Federal Military Pensions in the United States*, ed. David Kinley (New York, 1918), 24.

21. George Washington to Henry Laurens, Apr. 10, 1778, Fitzpatrick, ed., *Writings of Washington*, XI, 237.

22. Roger Sherman, Samuel Huntington, Oliver Wolcott to Jonathan Trum-

bull, May 18, 1778, *Trumbull Papers* (Mass. Hist. Soc., *Colls*., 5th Ser., IX–X, 7th Ser., II–III [Boston, 1885–1902]), III, 231.

23. James Lovell to Samuel Adams, Jan. 13, 1778, Burnett, ed., *Letters of Congress*, III, 32.

24. *Ibid*.

25. Henry Laurens to James Duane, Apr. 7, 1778, *ibid*., 154.

26. Joseph Hodgkins to Sarah Hodgkins, Feb. 22, 1778, Wade and Lively, *This Glorious Cause*, 235–236. Officers' pensions and professionalism have been discussed recently in Cress, "Standing Army," chap. 5, and Gerhard Kollmann, "Reflections on the Army of the American Revolution," in Angermann *et al*., eds., *New Wine in Old Skins*, 153–176.

27. Isaac Sherman to Anthony Wayne, Aug. 22, 1779, Stillé, *Wayne and the Pennsylvania Line*, 408.

28. Joshua Hett Smith, *An Authentic Narrative of the Causes Which Led to the Death of Major André, Adjutant-General of His Majesty's Forces in North America* (London, 1808), 113.

29. Marshall, *Life of Washington*, IV, 66.

30. See above, chap. 2, n. 73.

31. *The Patriots of North-America: A Sketch* (New York, 1775), 47.

32. *Providence Gaz*., May 8, 1779.

33. *Proceedings of a General Court-Martial . . . For the Trial of Major General Howe, December 7, 1781 . . .* , N.-Y. Hist. Soc., *Colls*., XII (New York, 1880), 285–286.

34. Entry of Aug. 29, 1780, James Thacher, *Military Journal of the American Revolution* . . . (Hartford, Conn., 1862 [orig. publ. Boston, 1823]), 209–210.

35. Entry of Aug. 30, 1780, *ibid*., 210.

36. "Articles of War," Section VII, Ford, ed., *Journals of Congress*, V, 793–794.

37. Patrick Henry to George Washington, July 31, 1778, McIlwaine, ed., *Official Letters of Henry*, I, 302.

38. *N.-J. Gaz*. (Burlington), Mar. 17, 1779. See also Alden, *History of the Revolution*, 451; William Oliver Stevens, *Pistols at Ten Paces: The Story of the Code of Honor in America* (Boston, 1940), 14–15, 30.

39. Gérard de Rayneval to comte de Vergennes, Jan. 17, 1779, John Durand, trans. and ed., *New Materials for the History of the American Revolution* (New York, 1889), 187.

40. Samuel Shaw to John Eliot, Mar. 22, 1779, Quincy, *Journals of Shaw*, 55.

41. Entry of Jan. 1, 1778, "Diary of Waldo," *PMHB*, XXI (1897), 317.

42. Walter Stewart to Anthony Wayne, Dec. 24, 1781, Stillé, *Wayne and the Pennsylvania Line*, 285.

43. George Washington to the Committee of Correspondence, Jan. 20, 1779, Fitzpatrick, ed., *Writings of Washington*, XIV, 28.

44. James McHenry to Daniel McHenry, Aug. 15, 1778, in Bernard C. Steiner, *The Life and Correspondence of James McHenry* (Cleveland, Ohio, 1907), 24.

45. Brackenridge, *Six Political Discourses*, 43–44.

46. David Cobb to Henry Jackson, June 8, 1780, Gaillard Hunt, ed., *Fragments of Revolutionary History* (Brooklyn, N.Y., 1892), 151.

47. The major published studies of Steuben are Friedrich Kapp, *The Life of Frederick William Von Steuben, Major General in the Revolutionary Army* (New York, 1859), and John McAuley Palmer, *General Von Steuben* (New Haven, Conn., 1937). For an interpretation of Steuben's character and American career different from mine, see Philander Dean Chase, "Baron Von Steuben in the War of Independence" (Ph.D. diss., Duke University, 1972).

48. George Washington to Baron Steuben, Dec. 23, 1783, *Proceedings upon the Unveiling of the Statue of Baron Von Steuben* . . . ([Washington, D.C., 1913]), 6.

49. Horatio Gates to Baron Steuben, Nov. 1782, in Patterson, *Horatio Gates*, 334.

50. Baron Steuben to Benjamin Franklin, Sept. 28, 1779, quoted in Chase, "Baron Von Steuben," 143.

51. Chase, "Baron Von Steuben"; Higginbotham, *War of Independence*, 247; Shy, *People Numerous and Armed*, 155; Ward, *War of the Revolution*, ed. Alden, II, 552; Alvin R. Sunseri, "Frederick Wilhelm Von Steuben and the Re-Education of the American Army: A Lesson in Practicality," *Armor*, LXXIV (1965), 40–41, 45, 47; Broadus Mitchell, *Alexander Hamilton: The Revolutionary Years* (New York, 1970), 131. See also Peter Paret, "The Relationship between the Revolutionary War and European Military Thought and Practice in the Second Half of the Eighteenth Century," in Higginbotham, ed., *Reconsiderations on the War*, 144–157.

52. Jay Luvaas, trans. and ed., *Frederick the Great on the Art of War* (New York, 1966), 77–78.

53. Regimental Court-Martial, Nov. 27, 1777, Joseph Brown Turner, ed., "The Journal and Order Book of Captain Robert Kirkwood of the Delaware Regiment of the Continental Line," Hist. Soc. Del., *Papers*, VI, No. LVI (Wilmington, Del., 1910), 256.

54. George Washington, General Orders, May 17, 1783, Fitzpatrick, ed., *Writings of Washington*, XXVI, 439–440.

55. North, "Baron Steuben," *Mag. Am. Hist.*, VIII (1882), 191.

56. George Washington to Samuel Huntington, Aug. 20, 1780, Fitzpatrick, ed., *Writings of Washington*, XIX, 409.

57. Anthony Wayne, Division Orders, Apr. 9, 1778, "Orderly Book of the Second Pennsylvania Continental Line, Col. Henry Bicker," *PMHB*, XXXV (1911), 481.

58. Henry Bicker, Regimental Orders, Apr. 18, 1778, *ibid.*, XXXVI (1912), 36.

59. James Chambers, Regimental Orders, Aug. 21, 1778, "The Orderly Book of the First Pennsylvania Regiment," Hazard *et al.*, eds., *Pa. Archives*, 2d Ser., XI, 318–319.

60. Henry Laurens to John Laurens, Jan. 25, 1778, "Correspondence between Hon. Henry Laurens and his Son, John, 1777–1780," *S.C. Hist. and Gen. Mag.*, VI (1905), 49.

61. *N.J. Gaz.*, May 6, 1778.

62. Baron Steuben to Baron de Gaudy, 1787–1788, "Memorials of Baron Von Steuben: Unpublished and Forgotten Papers," *Deutsch-Amerikanische Geschichtsblatter*, XXX (1930), 135.

63. *Ibid.*

64. Ezra Selden to Samuel Mather, May 15, 1778, Johnston, *Yale and Her Honor-Roll*, 88.

65. Baron Steuben to Baron de Gaudy, 1787–1788, "Memorials of Steuben," *Deutsch-Amer. Geschichts.*, XXX (1930), 135. Punctuation revised.

66. David Griffith to Leven Powell, June 3, 1778, "The Leven Powell Correspondence—1775–1787," *The John P. Branch Historical Papers of Randolph-Macon College*, I (1901), 52–53.

67. [Martin], *Yankee Doodle*, ed. Scheer, 118.

68. North, "Baron Steuben," *Mag. Am. Hist.*, VIII (1882), 190–191.

69. Stephen Olney Manuscripts, quoted in [Catherine] Williams, *Biography of Revolutionary Heroes; Containing the Life of Brigadier Gen. William Barton, and also, of Captain Stephen Olney* (Providence, R.I., 1839), 277–278, 299; Broadus Mitchell, *Alexander Hamilton: Youth to Maturity, 1755–1788* (New York, 1957), 257–258.

70. Baron Steuben to Baron de Gaudy, 1787–1788, "Memorials of Steuben," *Deutsch-Amer. Geschichts.*, XXX (1930), 135.

71. [Baron Steuben], *Regulations for the Order and Discipline of the Troops of the United States* (Philadelphia, 1779), 121, 138, 141, 148, 149.

72. Entry of May 28, 1779, Thacher, *Military Journal* (1862 ed.), 163–164.

73. [Steuben], *Regulations*, 148.

74. *Pa. Packet*, Jan. 28, 1778.

75. Alexander Scammell to Abigail Bishop, June 8–23, 1777, in N.H. Hist. Soc., *Colls.*, IX (Concord, N. H., 1889), 198.

76. [Steuben], *Regulations*, 148–149.

77. Albigence Waldo, "Valley Forge: A Poem," *Hist. Mag.*, 1st Ser., VII (1863), 272.

78. Entry of May 28, 1779, Thacher, *Military Journal* (1862 ed.), 163.

79. John Burnham, "Recollections of the Revolutionary War from Bunker Hill to Yorktown," *Magazine of History*, Extra Number, No. 54 (1917), 15.

80. Entry of Aug. 19, 1780, Nichols, ed., "Doughboy of 1780," *Atlantic Monthly*, CXXXIV (1924), 459. See also entries of Sept. 5 and 6, 1779, in Robert C. Bray and Paul E. Bushnell, eds., *Diary of a Common Soldier in the American Revolution, 1775–1783: An Annotated Edition of the Military Journal of Jeremiah Greenman* (DeKalb, Ill., 1978), 139.

81. Baron Steuben to officers of the New Jersey Line, July 19, 1783, in *N.-J. Jour.*, Aug. 6, 1783; Steuben, Memorandum, "Memorials of Steuben," *Deutsch-*

Amer. Geschichts., XXX (1930), 81; Baron Steuben to Thomas Mifflin, Mar. 20, 1784, *Statue of Steuben*, 108–109.

82. Garden, *Anecdotes of the Revolution, Second Ser.*, 200.

83. John Nixon, J. Greaton, Rufus Putnam, Thomas Nixon, Hezekiah Smith to William Heath, June 27, 1779, *The Heath Papers*, II (Mass. Hist. Soc., *Colls.*, 7th Ser., IV [Boston, 1904]), 304, herafter cited as *Heath Papers*.

84. Cooper, *Courage in a Good Cause*, 24–25.

85. Entry of Sept. 12, 1777, Elisha Stevens, *Fragments of Memoranda Written by him in the War of the Revolution* (Meriden, Conn., 1922), [2].

86. Philip Vickers Fithian to Elizabeth Beatty Fithian, Aug. 26, 1776, in Philip Vickers Fithian, *Letters to His Wife* (Vineland, N.J., 1932), 34.

87. Peckham, ed., *Memoirs of Adlum*, 51–58, quoted at 51, 55–56.

88. *Pa. Gazette* (Philadelphia), Apr. 18, 1778.

89. Ramsay, *American Revolution*, I, 293; David Humphreys, *An Essay on the Life of the Honourable Major General Israel Putnam* (Boston, 1818), 17.

90. Pickering, *Plan of Discipline*, text, 10.

91. *Ibid.*, preface, 10–11, text, 10.

92. *Ibid.*, preface, 11.

93. Baron Steuben, *A Letter on the Subject of an Established Militia, and Military Arrangements, Addressed to the Inhabitants of the United States* (New York, 1784), 8.

94. Entries of Apr. 8, June 6, July 6, and July 8, 1781, Steven E. Kagle, ed., *The Diary of Josiah Atkins* ([New York], 1975), 19, 25, 38, 40.

95. Entry of May 28, 1779, Thacher, *Military Journal* (1862 ed.), 163–164.

96. [Martin], *Yankee Doodle*, ed. Scheer, 193.

97. [Steuben], *Regulations*, 131; George Washington, General Orders, Apr. 17, 1779, Fitzpatrick, ed., *Writings of Washington*, XIV, 400.

98. Baron Steuben, "Instructions for Training Soldiers," Mar.-May, 1778, Part I, quoted in Chase, "Baron Von Steuben," 65.

99. Entry of Sept. 15, 1781, "Military Journal of Denny," Hist. Soc. of Pa., *Memoirs*, VII (Philadelphia, 1860), 243–244.

100. Officers of the New Jersey Line to Baron Steuben, July 12, 1783, in *N.-J. Jour.*, Aug. 6, 1783.

101. Francis Bowen, *Life of Baron Steuben*, in Jared Sparks, ed., *The Library of American Biography*, IX (New York, 1848), 83.

102. Caron de Beaumarchais to M. D. Francy, Dec. 6, 1778, quoted in Joseph B. Doyle, *Frederick William Von Steuben and the American Revolution* (Steubenville, Ohio, 1913), 45.

103. See above, chap. 4, n. 32.

104. Anthony Wayne to George Washington, July 4, 1779, in Henry B. Dawson, *The Assault on Stony Point* (Morrisania, N.Y., 1863), 23.

105. Baron Steuben to Richard Peters, June 12, 1779, *PMHB*, XL (1916), 374. See also the discussion of Steuben's *Regulations* in Chase, "Baron Von Steuben," 130–135.

106. Baron Steuben to officers of the New Jersey Line, July 19, 1783, in *N.J. Jour.*, Aug. 6, 1783.

107. Lauber, ed., *Orderly Books of the Fourth and Second N.Y. Regiments*, 663.

108. James Chambers, Regimental Orders, June 26, 1779, "Orderly Book of 1st Pa. Regt.," Hazard *et al.*, eds., *Pa. Archives*, 2d Ser., XI, 457.

109. Lauber, ed., *Orderly Books of the Fourth and Second N.Y. Regiments*.

110. Mrs. Catesby Willis Stewart, *The Life of Brigadier General William Woodford of the American Revolution* (Richmond, Va., 1973), II, 1130–1131.

111. "William Whipple's Notes of a Journey from Philadelphia to New Hampshire, in the Summer of 1777," *PMHB*, X (1886–1887), 374.

112. "Side locks": Regimental Orders, Feb. 4, 1776, "Diary of Captain Barnard Elliott," in *Charleston, So. Ca. Yearbook–1889* [Charleston, S.C., 1889], 188.

113. Anthony Wayne, Division Orders, Apr. 6, May 16, 1778, in "Orderly Book of the Second Pennsylvania Continental Line, Col. Henry Bicker," *PMHB*, XXXV (1911), 474–475, XXXVI (1912), 249.

114. Benjamin Rush to Anthony Wayne, Sept. 29, 1776, Butterfield, ed., *Letters of Rush*, I, 117; Benjamin Rush, *Directions For Preserving the Health of Soldiers: Recommended To The Consideration of the Officers Of the Army of the United States* (Lancaster, Pa., 1778), 4.

115. Charles Cotesworth Pinckney, Regimental Orders, Jan. 22, 1778, "An Order Book of the 1st Regt., S.C. Line, Continental Establishment," *S.C. Hist. and Gen. Mag.*, VII (1906), 196.

116. Entry of Oct. 20, 1777, Albert Cook Myers, ed., *Sally Wister's Journal: A True Narrative* (Philadelphia, 1902), 84.

117. Francis Marion, Orders, Jan. 23, 1778, in Gibbes, *Documentary History*, III, 66.

118. Minutemen: entry of Mar. 31, 1775, Journal of Samuel Deane, in William Willis, ed., *Journals of the Rev. Thomas Smith, and the Rev. Samuel Deane, Pastors of the First Church in Portland* (Portland, Me., 1849), 336.

119. Abigail Adams to John Adams, June [16?], 1775, Butterfield *et al.*, eds., *Adams Family Correspondence*, I, 218–219.

120. George Washington, General Orders, July 3, 1778, Fitzpatrick, ed., *Writings of Washington*, XII, 154.

121. Anthony Wayne, Division Orders, Mar. 29, 1778, "Orderly Book of the 2d Pennsylvania Regiment," *PMHB*, XXXV (1911), 342.

122. St. George Tucker to Frances Tucker, July 5, 1781, quoted in Mary Haldane (Begg) Coleman, *St. George Tucker: Citizen of No Mean City* (Richmond, Va., 1938), 63–64.

123. Samuel Shaw to Francis Shaw, May 13, 1781, Quincy, *Journals of Shaw*, 92.

124. George Washington to John Mitchell, Feb. 17, 1779, Fitzpatrick, ed., *Writings of Washington*, XIV, 128–129.

125. *Macbeth*, V, ii, 19–20.

126. Chase, "Baron Von Steuben," chap. 5.

127. Richard Peters to John Montgomery, [1784], *Magazine of Western History*, IV (1886), 680.

128. Steuben, *Letter on Established Militia*, 10.

129. Quoted in Duncan, *Medical Men in the Revolution*, 234.

130. Burnham, "Recollections," *Mag. Hist.*, Extra Number, No. 54 (1917), 14–16.

131. [Thomas Marshall], Regimental Orders, May 27, 1777, "Orderly Book of Major William Heth of the Third Virginia Regiment," Va. Hist. Soc., *Proceedings*, N.S., XI (1892), 342.

132. White, *Narrative of Events*, 21.

133. Entry of Aug. 11, 1779, "Journal of Ensign Daniel Gookin," in Cook, ed., *Expedition of Sullivan*, 104.

134. Entry of Dec. 27, 1781, "Journal of Lieut. William McDowell, of the First Penn'a Regiment, In the Southern Campaign, 1781–1782," Hazard *et al.*, eds., *Pa. Archives*, 2d Ser., XV, 310.

135. Entry of Jan. 10, 1782, *ibid.*, 311.

136. Entry of Oct. 20, 1776, Thomas Ewing, ed., *George Ewing, Gentleman: A Soldier of Valley Forge* (Yonkers, N.Y., 1928), 7.

137. Marquis de Chastellux, *Travels in North America in the Years 1780, 1781 and 1782*, trans. and ed. Howard C. Rice, Jr. (Chapel Hill, N.C., 1963 [orig. publ. Paris, 1786]), I, 229.

138. Charles Knowles Bolton, *The Private Soldier under Washington* (New York, 1902), 22; William Heath to Samuel Adams, Aug. 27, 1777, *Heath Papers*, II, 148. On black soldiers, see esp. Benjamin Quarles, *The Negro in the American Revolution* (Chapel Hill, N.C., 1961). See also Pete Maslowski, "National Policy toward the Use of Black Troops in the Revolution," *S.C. Hist. and Gen. Mag.*, LXXIII (1972), 1–17; David O. White, *Connecticut's Black Soldiers, 1775–1783* (Chester, Conn., 1973).

139. Entry of [Apr. 14, 1782], "Diary Fragment," in Clark, ed., *State Records of N.C.*, XVI, 606.

140. Henry W. Archer to Anthony Wayne, July 28, 1779, Dawson, *Stony Point*, 121.

141. [Martin], *Yankee Doodle*, ed. Scheer, 254–255.

142. Entry of [Apr.] 13, [1782], "Diary Fragment," in Clark, ed., *State Records of N.C.*, XVI, 606.

143. Entry of Nov. 21, 1781, "Extracts from the Journal of Tilden," *PMHB*, XIX (1895), 212.

144. *Independent Chron.*, May 18, 1780.

145. Entry of Apr. 29, 1782, "Elijah Fisher's Journal," *Mag. Hist.*, II, Extra Number, No. 6 (1909), 49.

146. Ramsay, *American Revolution*, II, 317.

147. Entry of Mar. 21, 1782, "Extracts from Letter-Books of Reeves," *PMHB*, XXI (1897), 389; Lewis Morris, Jr., to Jacob Morris, Dec. 10, 1781,

"Letters to General Lewis Morris," N.-Y. Hist. Soc., *Colls.*, VIII (New York, 1876), 496; entry of June 6, 1781, Kagle, ed., *Diary of Atkins*, 24–25.

148. *Pa. Packet*, Sept. 28, 1782.

149. *Ibid.*

150. Ramsay, *American Revolution*, II, 314–322, quoted at 315–316.

151. Ramsay, *Oration on Independence*, 5.

152. Israel Evans, *A Discourse Delivered in New-York, Before a Brigade of Continental Troops, and Number of Citizens* . . . (New York, [1784]), 14.

153. Ramsay, *American Revolution*, II, 316.

154. George Williams to Timothy Pickering, Nov. 3, 1777, "Revolutionary Letters Written to Colonel Timothy Pickering," Essex Inst., *Hist. Colls.*, XLII (1906), 322.

155. Entry of Aug. 1779, Thacher, *Military Journal* (1862 ed.), 170–171.

156. John Singer Dexter to Samuel Blachley Webb, Nov. 2, 1782, Ford, ed., *Correspondence and Journal of Webb*, II, 429. The book in question probably was *Elegiac Epistles on the Calamities of Love and War Including a genuine Description of the Tragical Engagement between his Majesty's Ships the Serapis and Countess of Scarborough, and the Enemy's Squadron under the Command of Paul Jones, on the Twenty-third of September, 1779* (London, 1780).

157. Entry of Sept. 26, 1775, Fitch, "Journal," Mass. Hist. Soc., *Procs.*, 2d Ser., IX (1895), 61.

158. Entry of [Apr.] 16, [1782], "Diary Fragment," Clark, ed., *State Records of N.C.*, XVI, 607.

159. Entry of Jan. 28, 1779, Benians and David, eds., *Journal by Hughes*, 63.

160. Entry of Dec. 14, 1777, "Diary of Waldo," *PMHB*, XXI (1897), 307.

161. Lachlan McIntosh, General Orders, July 3, 1777, William Harden, ed., "Samuel Elbert, Order Book," Georgia Historical Society, *Collections*, V, Part II (Savannah, Ga., 1902), 42.

162. Entry of Feb. 20, 1782, Feltman, "Diary of the Pennsylvania Line," Hazard *et al.*, eds., *Pa. Archives*, 2d Ser., XI, 718.

163. Entry of Nov. 15, 1781, *ibid.*, 704.

164. Otho Holland Williams to Daniel Morgan, Jan. 25, 1781, quoted in James Graham, *The Life of General Daniel Morgan* . . . (New York, 1856), 323.

165. Entry of May 6, 1778, "Elijah Fisher's Journal," *Mag. Hist.*, II, Extra Number, No. 6 (1909), 19; entry of May 6, 1778, Ewing, ed., *George Ewing*, 48–51; Thacher, *Military Journal* (1862 ed.), 126–127; *N.Y. Jour.*, June 15, 1778, in Moore, ed., *Diary of the Revolution*, II, 50–51; John Laurens to Henry Laurens, May 7, 1778, Simms, ed., *Army Correspondence of Laurens*, 169; *N.J. Gaz.*, May 13, 1778; *Pa. Packet*, May 13, 1778; entry of May 6, 1778, "Diary of Lieut. James McMichael of the Pennsylvania Line, 1776–1778," Hazard *et al.*, eds., *Pa. Archives*, 2d Ser., XV, 217–218; entry of May 7, 1778, Tappert and Doberstein, trans. and eds., *Journals of Muhlenberg*, II, 149; entry of May 6, 1778, "The Journal of Ebenezer Wild [Ebenezer Tolman]," Mass. Hist. Soc., *Procs.*, 2d Ser., VI (1891), 107; John Hurt, "An Address to the first and

second Virginia Brigades at the feu de joye at Valley Forge," *VMHB*, XVII (1909), 213–214; Baron De Kalb to the comte [de Broglie], May 5–7, 1778, Stevens, ed., *Facsimiles of Manuscripts*, VIII, No. 821; Ellet, *Domestic History of the Revolution*, 129; George Washington, General Orders, May 5, 7, 1778, Fitzpatrick, ed., *Writings of Washington*, XI, 354–355, 362–363; Sparks, ed., *Writings of Washington*, V, 356–357n.

Chapter VI
Treason

1. This controversy is reviewed in Alden, *General Charles Lee*; Shy, *People Numerous and Armed*, chap. 6, "American Strategy: Charles Lee and the Radical Alternative"; Freeman, *Washington*, V, 18–43, 57–60, 89–91; Theodore Thayer, *Washington and Lee at Monmouth: The Making of a Scapegoat* (Port Washington, N.Y., 1976).

2. Heimert, *Religion and the American Mind*, 147–148.

3. For a study of the eulogies after Washington's death, see Robert P. Hay, "George Washington: American Moses," *Am. Qtly*., XXI (1969), 780–791. On the rhetoric about Washington, see also Marcus Cunliffe, *George Washington: Man and Monument* (Boston, 1958); Albanese, *Sons of the Fathers*, chap. 5; Berens, "Divine Providence and the American Enlightenment," 184–187, 235–244.

4. Ford *et al*., eds., *Journals of Congress*, XXV, 838.

5. *New England Chronicle*, Nov. 2, 1775, in Moore, ed., *Diary of the Revolution*, I, 159; *Essex Gazette*, Jan. 18, 1776, *ibid*., 192; *Pa. Packet*, Dec. 22, 1778; *Pennsylvania Ledger: Or the Virginia, Maryland, Pennsylvania, and New-Jersey Weekly Advertiser* (Philadelphia), Feb. 11, 1778; Pinkney's *Va. Gaz*., Oct. 5, 1775; Purdie's *Va. Gaz*., May 17, 1776; *Independent Chron*., Mar. 6, 1777.

6. Birthday: Entry of Mar. 3, 1779, Dexter, ed., *Diary of Stiles*, II, 324; *Boston-Gaz*., Feb. 18, 1782; *Pa. Packet*, Feb. 27, 1783; Dixon and Nicolson's *Va. Gaz*., Feb. 19 and 26, 1780; Hayes's *Va. Gaz*. (Richmond), Feb. 15, 1783, Feb. 14 and 21, 1784; David Meade Randolph, "Journal," *Southern Literary Messenger*, I (1835), 340.

7. Entry of Aug. 30, 1781, "Journal of Fisher," *PMHB*, XLI (1917), 455–456.

8. Evans, *Discourse Delivered in New-York . . .* , 21; entry of Sept. 13, 1781, "General Richard Butler's Journal of the Siege of Yorktown," *Hist. Mag*., 1st Ser., VIII (1864), 105; Nathanael Greene to his brother, Feb. 7, 1778, quoted in Rossman, *Mifflin*, 97; *Providence Gaz*., July 15, 1780; John Murray, *Jerubbaal, or Tyranny's Grove Destroyed, and the Altar of Liberty Finished . . .* (Newburyport, Mass., 1784), 44, 51; Josiah Meigs, *An Oration Pronounced Before a Public Asembly in New-Haven, On the 5th Day of November 1781 . . .* (New Haven,

Conn., 1782), 11; entry of May 29, 1780, Thacher, *Military Journal*, 235; Elisha Boudinot to George Washington, Apr. 1783, quoted in Elias Boudinot, *The Life, Public Services, Addresses and Letters of Elias Boudinot, L.L.D. . . .*, ed. J. J. Boudinot (Boston and New York, 1896), I, 305–306; Mathieu Dumas, *Memoirs of His Own Time; Including the Revolution, the Empire, and the Restoration* (Philadelphia, 1839), I, 30; [Chevalier de Fleury], "Summary of the political and military Condition of America," Nov. 16, 1779, Stevens, ed., *Facsimiles of Manuscripts*, XVII, No. 1616.

9. Elias Boudinot, *Journal or Historical Recollections of American Events during the Revolutionary War* (Philadelphia, 1894), 68–69; Ezekiel Cornell to William Greene, May 30, 1780, John Russell Bartlett, ed., *Records of the State of Rhode Island and Providence Plantations in New England*, IX (Providence, R.I., 1864), 113.

10. Lewis Morris, Jr., to Lewis Morris, Sept. 14, 1776, "Letters to General Lewis Morris," N.-Y. Hist. Soc., *Colls.*, VIII (New York, 1876), 445–446.

11. Jonathan Mitchell Sewall, *Miscellaneous Poems* (Portsmouth, N.H., 1801), 53.

12. William Tudor, *An Oration Delivered March 5th, 1779 . . .* (Boston, 1779); entry of Mar. 5, 1779, William Tudor, ed., *Deacon Tudor's Diary* (Boston, 1896), 75–76.

13. John Sullivan to George Washington, Dec. 1, 1779, Otis G. Hammond, ed., *Letters and Papers of Major-General John Sullivan* (N.H. Hist. Soc., *Colls.*, XIII–XV [Concord, N.H., 1930–1939]), III, 168–171.

14. Luzerne to Vergennes, Apr. 16, 1780, and Jan. 28, 1781, Durand, trans. and ed., *New Materials*, 219–220, 234–235; Edwin M. Stone, *The Life and Recollections of John Howland . . .* (Providence, R.I., 1857), 92–93.

15. Jonathan Mason, *An Oration, Delivered March 6, 1780 . . .* (Boston, 1780), 15–16.

16. Luzerne to Vergennes, Apr. 16, 1780, Durand, trans. and ed., *New Materials*, 219.

17. *Boston-Gaz.*, Jan. 1, 1781.

18. J.F.D. Smyth, *A Tour in the United States of America* (Dublin, 1784), II, 179.

19. [Chalmers], *Plain Truth*, 126–127; [James Chalmers], *Additions to Plain Truth . . .* (Philadelphia, 1776), 126–128.

20. Entries of Jan. 23, Apr. 8, and July 19, 1778, Sabine, ed., *Memoirs of William Smith, 1776–1778*, 290, 343, 420; entries of Jan. 14 and Feb. 15, 1779, William H. W. Sabine, ed., *Historical Memoirs from 26 August 1778 to 12 November 1783 of William Smith* (New York, [1971]), 64, 74; William Heron's Information, Sept. 4, 1780, Stevens, ed., *Facsimiles of Manuscripts*, VII, No. 733; entry of Oct. 24, 1779, Benians and David, eds., *Journal by Hughes*, 74; George Washington to Henry Laurens, Nov. 11, 1778, Fitzpatrick, ed., *Writings of Washington*, XIII, 227–228; Bernhard A. Uhlendorf, trans. and ed., *Revolution in America: Confidential Letters and Journals, 1776–1784, of Adjutant*

General Major Baurmeister of the Hessian Forces (New Brunswick, N.J., 1957), 150; Charles Stedman, *The History of the Origin, Progress, and Termination of the American War* (London, 1794), I, 310; Cornelius Stagge, Intelligence, Feb. 18, 1780, E. B. O'Callaghan and B[erthold] Fernow, eds., *Documents Relative to the Colonial History of the State of New-York . . .* , VIII (Albany, N.Y., 1857), 787; Dumas, *Memoirs*, I, 65; Baron Steuben to Congress, Jan. 28, 1780, quoted in Palmer, *General Von Steuben*, 222; Charles Inglis to Joseph Galloway, Feb. 25, 1779, "Letters to Joseph Galloway, from Leading Tories in America," *Hist. Mag.*, 1st Ser., VI (1862), 238; Whitmel Hill to Thomas Burke, n.d., Clark, ed., *State Records of N.C.*, XIV, 3.

21. William Thompson to Richard Butler, Oct. 5, 1778, Hazard *et al.*, eds., *Pa. Archives*, 1st Ser., VII, 65.

22. William Waller Hening, ed., *The Statutes at Large; Being a Collection of All the Laws of Virginia . . .* , X (New York, 1823), 337, 433–434.

23. See the Appendix, pp. 373–378 below.

24. On the Carlisle Commission, see Weldon A. Brown, *Empire or Independence: A Study in the Failure of Reconciliation, 1774–1783* (University, La., 1941), chap. 10; Carl Van Doren, *Secret History of the American Revolution* (New York, 1941), 63–116.

25. Elisha P. Douglass, "Thomas Burke, Disillusioned Democrat," *North Carolina Historical Review*, XXVI (1949), 150–186. See also Roger J. Champagne, *Alexander McDougall and the American Revolution in New York* (Schenectady, N.Y., 1975).

26. E. James Ferguson, *The American Revolution: A General History, 1763–1790* (Homewood, Ill., 1974), 145.

27. *N.-Y. Jour.*, Feb. 22, 1779.

28. Ford *et al.*, eds., *Journals of Congress*, XV, 1432–1433.

29. Ferguson, *American Revolution*, 145; entry of Oct. 17–20, 1780, *The Journal of Claude Blanchard, Commissary of the French Auxiliary Army Sent to the United States during the American Revolution, 1780–1783*, trans. William Duane and ed. Thomas Balch (Albany, N.Y., 1876), 71.

30. Moore Furman to [Nathanael Greene?], Nov. 15, 1779, Anne deB. MacIlvaine *et al.*, eds., *The Letters of Moore Furman: Deputy Quartermaster General of New Jersey in the Revolution* (New York, 1912), 39.

31. Furman to Greene, June 9, 1779, *ibid.*, 8.

32. Lowell, *Hessians and Other German Auxiliaries*, 210.

33. Benjamin Franklin to John Jay, Oct. 4, 1779, Francis Wharton, ed., *The Revolutionary Diplomatic Correspondence of the United States* (Washington, D.C., 1889), III, 365. See, for example, Elizabeth Cometti, "Morals and the American Revolution," *South Atlantic Quarterly*, XLVI (1947), 62–71.

34. Curtis P. Nettels, *The Emergence of a National Economy, 1775–1815* (New York, 1962), 14, 17, 20.

35. Edmund Pendleton to William Woodford, Nov. 1, 1779, quoted in Stewart, *Life of Woodford*, II, 1111.

36. Ferguson, *American Revolution*, 146–147. See also Anne Bezanson, *Prices and Inflation during the American Revolution: Pennsylvania, 1770–1790* (Philadelphia, 1951), 296–297; Charles Christopher Crittenden, *The Commerce of North Carolina, 1763–1789* (New Haven, Conn., 1936), 133–135; Nettels, *National Economy*, 12, 14–22; Robert A. East, *Business Enterprise in the American Revolutionary Era* (New York, 1938), 31–32, 35–36, 51–53, 62, 74–77, 149–150; Lee Nathaniel Newcomer, *The Embattled Farmers: A Massachusetts Countryside in the American Revolution* (New York, 1953), 131–132.

37. See esp. Edmund S. Morgan, "The Puritan Ethic and the American Revolution," *WMQ*, 3d Ser., XXIV (1967), 3–43; J. E. Crowley, *This Sheba, Self: The Conceptualization of Economic Life in Eighteenth-Century America* (Baltimore, 1974), chap. 5.

38. Josiah Bartlett to William Whipple, Apr. 24 and May 29, 1779, quoted in Henderson, *Party Politics*, 239.

39. Tench Tilghman to James McHenry, Jan. 25, 1779, quoted in Steiner, *McHenry*, 26.

40. Clarence L. Ver Steeg, *Robert Morris: Revolutionary Financier* (Philadelphia, 1954), 50–51, 53. See also Richard Buel, Jr., "Time: Friend or Foe of the Revolution?" in Higginbotham, ed., *Reconsiderations on the Revolutionary War*, 139–143.

41. *N.-J. Jour.*, June 19, 1782.

42. William Livingston to Henry Laurens, June 18, 1778, quoted in Theodore Sedgwick, Jr., *A Memoir of the Life of William Livingston* . . . (New York, 1833), 294.

43. Wood, *Creation of the American Republic*, 107–114.

44. Ford *et al.*, eds., *Journals of Congress*, X, 132.

45. Entry of Apr. 9, 1778, Tappert and Doberstein, trans. and eds., *Journals of Muhlenberg*, III, 141.

46. Ford *et al.*, eds., *Journals of Congress*, XVII, 756–757.

47. Roger Sherman to Jonathan Trumbull, Apr. 23, 1777, *The Trumbull Papers* (Mass. Hist. Soc., *Colls.*, 5th Ser., IX–X, 7th Ser., II–III [Boston, 1885–1902]), III, 46.

48. Robert Munford, *The Patriots*, in Philbrick, ed., *Trumpets Sounding*, 290; [Benjamin Gale], *Brief, Decent, But Free Remarks, and Observations* . . . (Hartford, Conn., 1782), 7; [Martin], *Yankee Doodle,* ed. Scheer, 150; Nathanael Greene to Nicholas Cooke, July 4, 1775, quoted in Greene, *Nathanael Greene*, I, 96–98; Murray, *Jerubbaal,* 49; *Boston-Gaz.*, Nov. 29, 1779; George Williams to Timothy Pickering, Feb. 28, 1779, "Revolutionary Letters Written to Colonel Timothy Pickering," Essex Inst., *Hist. Colls.*, XLIII (1907), 202.

49. Tench Tilghman to James McHenry, Jan. 25, 1779, quoted in Steiner, *McHenry*, 25–26.

50. Entry of Sept. 28, 1775, George Morison, "Journal of the Expedition to Quebec," Roberts, ed., *March to Quebec*, 512.

51. On King's Mountain, see esp. Draper, *King's Mountain and Its Heroes*;

Ward, *War of the Revolution*, ed. Alden, II, chap. 67; Franklin and Mary Wickwire, *Cornwallis: The American Adventure* (Boston, 1970), chap. 9.

52. "Colonel Robert Gray's Observations on the War in Carolina," *S.C. Hist. and Gen. Mag.*, XI (1910), 153.

53. Aedanus Burke to Arthur Middleton, Jan. 25–Feb. 5, 1782, "Correspondence of Hon. Arthur Middleton, Signer of the Declaration of Independence," *ibid.*, XXVI (1925), 192.

54. Nathanael Greene to Alexander Hamilton, Jan. 10, 1781, Harold C. Syrett *et al.*, eds., *The Papers of Alexander Hamilton* (New York, 1961–), II, 529–530.

55. William Pierce to St. George Tucker, July 20, 1781, *Mag. Am. Hist.*, VII (1881), 434.

56. Charles O'Hara to the duke of Grafton, Jan. 6, 1781, George C. Rogers, Jr. [ed.], "Letters of Charles O'Hara to the Duke of Grafton," *S.C. Hist. and Gen. Mag.*, LXV (1964), 171. See also Clyde R. Ferguson, "Carolina and Georgia Patriot and Loyalist Militia in Action, 1778–1783," in Jeffrey J. Crow and Larry E. Tise, eds., *The Southern Experience in the American Revolution* (Chapel Hill, N.C., 1978), 174–199; Richard Maxwell Brown, *Strain of Violence: Historical Studies of American Violence and Vigilantism* (New York, 1975), chap. 3, "South Carolina Extremism and Its Violent Origins: From the Regulator Movement to the Edgefield Tradition, 1760–1960."

57. Compare John Shy, "The Loyalist Problem in the Lower Hudson Valley: The British Perspective" and Catherine S. Crary, "Guerrilla Activities of James DeLancey's Cowboys in Westchester County: Conventional Warfare or Self-Interested Freebooting," in Robert A. East and Jacob Judd, eds., *The Loyalist Americans: A Focus on Greater New York* (Tarrytown, N.Y., 1975), 3–24; Adrian C. Leiby, *The Revolutionary War in the Hackensack Valley: The Jersey Dutch and the Neutral Ground, 1775–1783* (New Brunswick, N.J., 1962), esp. 125; Robert McCluer Calhoon, *The Loyalists in Revolutionary America, 1760–1781* (New York, 1973), 326.

58. Timothy Dwight, *Travels In New-England and New-York* (New Haven, Conn., 1823), III, 491–492.

59. William Pierce to St. George Tucker, Feb. 6, 1782, *Mag. Am. Hist.*, VII (1881), 438–439.

60. *Royal South-Carolina Gazette* (Charleston), Dec. 19, 1780.

61. Shy, *People Numerous and Armed*, 215–219; John Richard Alden, *The American Revolution, 1775–1783* (New York, 1954), 86–87; Jackson Turner Main, *The Sovereign States, 1775–1783* (New York, 1973), 269.

62. William Livingston, Speech to New Jersey Legislature, Feb. 25, 1777, quoted in Bradley Chapin, *The American Law of Treason: Revolutionary and Early National Origins* (Seattle, Wa., 1964), 49.

63. "Petition and Memorial of Sundry Militiamen of the Tenth Division of Amherst County to Virginia House of Delegates," Nov. 9, 1780, Virginia State Library, Richmond, Va. I owe this reference to the work of John D.

McBride. For accounts of the battle of Camden, see Ward, *War of the Revolution*, ed. Alden, II, chaps. 64–65; Wickwire and Wickwire, *Cornwallis*, chap. 7; Nelson, *Gates*, chap. 8.

64. Warren, *History of the Revolution*, II, 173–174. On the siege of Charleston, see Ward, *War of the Revolution*, ed. Alden, II, chap. 61; Alden, *History of the Revolution*, 414–415; George Smith McCowen, Jr., *The British Occupation of Charleston, 1780–1782* (Columbia, S.C., 1972), chap. 1.

65. John Rutledge to the South Carolina delegates in Congress, May 24, 1780, "Letters of John Rutledge," *S.C. Hist. and Gen. Mag.*, XVII (1916), 133–134; Sir Henry Clinton to William Eden, May 30, 1780, quoted in Sir Henry Clinton, *The American Rebellion*, ed. William B. Willcox (New Haven, Conn., 1954), 175n; Paul H. Smith, *Loyalists and Redcoats: A Study in British Revolutionary Policy* (Chapel Hill, N.C., 1964), 128–130; Ferguson, "Carolina and Georgia Militia in Action," in Crow and Tise, eds., *Southern Experience*, 185.

66. J[edidiah] Huntington to Jeremiah Wadsworth, May 5, 1780, *Huntington Papers* (Conn. Hist. Soc., *Colls.*, XX [Hartford, Conn., 1923]), 150. Gordon S. Wood has commented on this nostalgia in *Creation of the American Republic*, 102.

67. *Pa. Gazette* (Philadelphia), Apr. 7, 1779; Luke 1:17.

68. *Pa. Packet*, June 20, 1780.

69. Benjamin Rush, *Medical Inquiries and Observations, Upon the Diseases of the Mind* (New York, 1962 [orig. publ. Philadelphia, 1812]), 78–83, 95, 114–115; Benjamin Rush, "Influence of the American Revolution," Dagobert D. Runes, ed., *The Selected Writings of Benjamin Rush* (New York, 1947), 332.

70. Henry Lee to Anthony Wayne, Sept. 27, 1780, Henry B. Dawson, ed., *Papers concerning the Capture and Detention of Major John André* (Yonkers, N.Y., 1866), 71.

71. The most valuable studies of Arnold are Willard M. Wallace, *Traitorous Hero: The Life and Fortunes of Benedict Arnold* (New York, 1954); Willard M. Wallace, "Benedict Arnold: Traitorous Patriot," in George Athan Billias, ed., *George Washington's Generals* (New York, 1964), 163–192; Van Doren, *Secret History*; James Thomas Flexner, *The Traitor and the Spy: Benedict Arnold and John André* (New York, 1953). On Arnold's treason, see also Richard J. Koke, *Accomplice in Treason: Joshua Hett Smith and the Arnold Conspiracy* (New York, 1973).

72. *Boston-Gaz.*, Feb. 16, 1778.

73. Wallace, *Traitorous Hero*, 198, 253; Benedict Arnold to Horatio Gates, Oct. 1, 1777, quoted in James Wilkinson, *Memoirs of My Own Times*, I (Philadelphia, 1816), 259; United States, *Proceedings of a General Court Martial . . . For the Trial of Major General Arnold* (Philadelphia, 1780), 40, 51; Benedict Arnold to George Washington, Sept. 25, 1780, Dawson, ed., *Papers concerning André*, 26–27.

74. Van Doren, *Secret History*, 387.

75. Samuel Shaw to John Eliot, Oct. 1, 1780, Quincy, *Journals of Shaw*, 81.

76. Nathanael Greene to ———, Oct. 15, 1780, *Hist. Mag.*, 2d Ser., I (1867), 204.

77. *Pa. Packet*, Sept. 25, 1781.

78. Alexander Scammell to Col. Peabody, Oct. 3, 1780, Dawson, ed., *Papers concerning André*, 66.

79. Andrew Elliott to William Eden, Oct. 4–5, 1780, Stevens, ed., *Facsimiles of Manuscripts*, VII, No. 739.

80. On Deane, see Flexner, *Traitor and Spy*, 237–238; Van Doren, *Secret History*, 170–171; Silas Deane to Barnabas Deane, Jan. 31, 1782, Charles Isham, ed., *The Deane Papers* (N.-Y. Hist. Soc., *Colls.*, XIX–XXIII [New York, 1887–1891]), V, 31; Silas Deane to Benjamin Franklin, Oct. 19, 1783, *ibid.*, 213–214; Smith, *Death of André*, 290; Benjamin Franklin to Robert Morris, Mar. 30, 1782, Wharton, ed., *Revolutionary Correspondence*, V, 279. On the origins and significance of Deane's exile, see esp. Morgan, "Puritan Ethic," *WMQ*, 3d Ser., XXIV, 25–34; E. James Ferguson, *The Power of the Purse: A History of American Public Finance, 1776–1790* (Chapel Hill, N.C., 1961), 90–94, 102–104, 110; Henderson, *Party Politics*, chap. 8.

81. Marquis de Lafayette to Madame de Lafayette, Feb. 2, 1781, *Memoirs, Correspondence and Manuscripts of Lafayette*, I, 386.

82. George Washington to Henry Lee, Oct. 20, 1780, Fitzpatrick, ed., *Writings of Washington*, XX, 223–224; Thomas Jefferson to Peter Muhlenberg, Jan. 31, 1781, Boyd *et al.*, eds., *Papers of Jefferson*, IV, 487–488; Aaron Ogden, "Autobiography of Col. Aaron Ogden, of Elizabethtown," N.J. Hist. Soc., *Procs.*, 2d Ser., XII (1892), 23–24; James Robertson to Henry Clinton, Oct. 1, 1780, quoted in Winthrop Sargent, *The Life and Career of Major John André, Adjutant-General of the British Army in America* (Boston, 1861), 379.

83. *N.J. Jour.*, Aug. 1, 1781; *Providence Gaz.*, Aug. 11, 1781; *N.-J. Gaz.*, July 25, 1781.

84. *N.J. Jour.*, Nov. 21, 1781.

85. Thacher, *Military Journal*, 579–580; *Pa. Packet*, Oct. 3, 1780, Jan. 16, 1781; *A Representation of the Figures exhibited and paraded through the Streets of Philadelphia, on Saturday, the 30th of September 1780* [Philadelphia, 1780]; Samuel Adams to Elizabeth Wells Adams, Oct. 10, 1780, Cushing, ed., *Writings of Samuel Adams*, IV, 210; James Madison to Thomas Jefferson [c. Oct. 5, 1780], William T. Hutchinson *et al.*, eds., *The Papers of James Madison* (Chicago, 1962–), II, 112; *Boston-Gaz.*, Oct. 23, 1780, Nov. 12, 1781; *Conn. Courant*, Dec. 12, 1780, Nov. 6, 1781; Clarkson and Davis's *Va. Gaz.*, Oct. 21, 1780; entry of Oct. 4, 1780, Henry D. Biddle, ed., *Extracts from the Journal of Elizabeth Drinker* (Philadelphia, 1889), 129; Wallace, *Traitorous Hero*, 269; entries of Sept. 29–30, 1780, "Journal of Fisher," *PMHB*, XLI (1917), 311, 314–315.

86. Johnson, *Traditions and Reminiscences*, 255.

87. *Fall of Lucifer*, 7–8.

88. *Pa. Packet*, Oct. 7, 1780.

89. Eleazer Oswald to John Lamb, Dec. 11, 1780, Leake, *Memoir of Lamb*, 266–267.

90. Van Doren, *Secret History*, preface.

91. For related studies, see Albanese, *Sons of the Fathers*, 94–95; David R. Johnson, "Benedict Arnold: The Traitor as Hero in American Literature" (Ph.D. diss., Pennsylvania State University, 1975), chaps. 2, 7; Bernard Bailyn, *The Ordeal of Thomas Hutchinson* (Cambridge, Mass., 1974), esp. chap. 7; Peter Shaw, "Their Kinsman, Thomas Hutchinson; Hawthorne, The Boston Patriots, and His Majesty's Royal Governor," *Early American Literature*, XI (1976), 183–190; Winthrop D. Jordan, "Familial Politics: Thomas Paine and the Killing of the King, 1776," *Journal of American History*, LX (1973), 294–308; Robert Middlekauff, "The Ritualization of the American Revolution," in Coben and Ratner, eds., *Development of an American Culture*, 31–43.

92. E. B. Hillard, *The Last Men of the Revolution*, ed. Wendell D. Garrett (Barré, Mass., 1968 [orig. publ. Hartford, Conn., 1864]), 34–35.

Chapter VII
Division

1. One-fifth: Return J. Meigs to Titus Hosmer, Dec. 26, 1778, *The Trumbull Papers* (Mass. Hist. Soc., *Colls.*, 5th Ser., IX–X, 7th Ser., II–III [Boston, 1885–1902]), III, 327; Rhode Island, *At the General Assembly of . . . Rhode Island . . . February 1783* [Providence, R.I.? 1783], 15. Compare Lesser, ed., *Sinews of Independence*, 244.

2. *Conn. Courant*, Sept. 8, 1777.

3. Eliphalet Wright, *A People Ripe for an Harvest . . .* (Norwich, Conn., [1776]), 10.

4. Petition to the General Assembly from Ann Glover, widow of Samuel Glover, Jan. 10, 1780, Clark, ed., *State Records of N.C.*, XV, 187–188.

5. Alexander McDougall's notes delivered to the committee of Congress, Aug. 1780, quoted in Champagne, *McDougall and the Revolution*, 162.

6. George Washington to Samuel Huntington, May 27, 1780, Fitzpatrick, ed., *Writings of Washington*, XVIII, 428–432; [Martin], *Yankee Doodle*, ed. Scheer, 182. See also Committee at Headquarters to Samuel Huntington, May 10 and 28, 1780, Burnett, ed., *Letters of Congress*, V, 132–133, 174; Committee at Headquarters to the States, May 25, 1780, Bartlett, ed., *Records of R.I.*, IX, 108–112.

7. Return J. Meigs to George Washington, May 26, 1780, quoted in S. Sydney Bradford, "Discipline in the Morristown Winter Encampment," N.J. Hist. Soc., *Procs.*, LXXX (1962), 28; John Henderson to Mr. Nicholson, May 27, 1780, in Stan. V. Henkels, comp., *Thos. Birch's Son's Catalogue No. 683* (n.p., n.d.), 79.

8. *Ibid.*
9. *Ibid.*
10. [Martin], *Yankee Doodle*, ed. Scheer, 185.
11. Henderson to Nicholson, May 27, 1780, Henkels, *Catalogue No. 683*, 79.
12. [Martin], *Yankee Doodle*, ed. Scheer, 186–187.
13. *Ibid.*
14. *Ibid.*
15. Washington to Huntington, May 27, 1780, Fitzpatrick, ed., *Writings of Washington*, XVIII, 430–431.
16. *Ibid.*
17. [Martin], *Yankee Doodle*, ed. Scheer, 182.
18. Ezekiel Cornell to William Greene, May 30, 1780, Bartlett, ed., *Records of R.I.*, 113.
19. Alexander Hamilton to Nathanael Greene, June 11, 1779, Syrett *et al.*, eds., *Papers of Hamilton*, II, 73.
20. Entry of Jan. 26, 1780, Sabine, ed., *Memoirs of William Smith, 1778–1783*, 218.
21. Arthur St. Clair to Joseph Reed, Feb. 21 and July 25, 1779, Smith, *Life of St. Clair*, I, 461, 481.
22. The standard account is Carl Van Doren, *Mutiny in January* (New York, 1943).
23. Entry of Jan. 2, 1781, "Extracts from the Letter-Books of Reeves," *PMHB*, XXI (1897), 72–76; John Sullivan to the French minister, Jan. 13, 178[1], Otis G. Hammond, ed., *Letters and Papers of Major-General John Sullivan* (N.H. Hist. Soc., *Colls.*, XIII–XV [Concord, N.H., 1930–1939]), III, 177; entry of Jan. 6, 1781, "The Diary of William S. Pennington," N.J. Hist. Soc., *Procs.*, LXIV (1946), 34.
24. Ford *et al.*, eds., *Journals of Congress*, XIX, 83.
25. Joseph Reed to Committee of Congress, Jan. 6, 1781, quoted in Reed, *Joseph Reed*, II, 320.
26. *Ibid.*
27. Anthony Wayne to George Washington, Jan. 2, 1781, quoted in Stillé, *Wayne and the Pennsylvania Line*, 242.
28. Joseph Reed to William Moore, Jan. 12, 1781, "Diary of the Revolt in the Pennsylvania Line," Hazard *et al.*, eds., *Pa. Archives*, 2d Ser., XI, 672.
29. Joseph Reed to ———, [Jan. 1781], Campbell, ed., *Bland Papers*, II, 49.
30. Entries of Jan. 20 and 25, 1781, "Sir Henry Clinton's Original Secret Record of Private Daily Intelligence," *Mag. Am. Hist.*, X (1883), 333, 337, 497.
31. Entry of Jan. 25, 1781, *ibid.*, 497; entries of Jan. 25 and Feb. 4, 5, 20, 1781, "Journal of Fisher," *PMHB*, XLI (1917), 406, 411, 415.
32. Among the most important studies of the nationalist movement are Merrill Jensen, "The Idea of a National Government during the American Revolution," *Political Science Quarterly*, LVIII (1943), 356–379; Merrill Jensen, *The New Nation: A History of the United States during the Confederation, 1781–1789* (New York, 1950); E. James Ferguson, *The Power of the Purse: A History of*

American Public Finance, 1776–1790 (Chapel Hill, N.C., 1961); Jackson Turner Main, *The Antifederalists: Critics of the Constitution, 1781–1788* (Chapel Hill, N.C., 1961); Henderson, *Party Politics*; Wood, *Creation of the American Republic*; and Ver Steeg, *Robert Morris*. The relationship between the nationalist movement and the Continental Army has been discussed in Kohn, *Eagle and Sword*, and Cress, "Standing Army."

33. Diary entry, Sept. 11, 1781, E. James Ferguson *et al.*, eds., *The Papers of Robert Morris, 1781–1784* (Pittsburgh, Pa., 1973–), II, 244.

34. Robert Morris to the Governors of the States, Oct. 19, 1781, *ibid.*, III, 85.

35. Robert Morris to Benjamin Franklin, Nov. 27, 1781, *ibid.*, 282.

36. Robert Morris, Diary, Jan. 26, 1782, and Robert Morris, Memorandum, Feb. 1782, *ibid.*, IV, 115–116, 328. This arrangement is discussed in Eric Foner, *Tom Paine and Revolutionary America* (New York, 1976), 188–192.

37. Robert Morris to James Lovell, June 16, 1782, Wharton, ed., *Revolutionary Correspondence*, V, 495.

38. Joseph Reed to Nathanael Greene, Nov. 1, 1781, Reed, *Joseph Reed*, II, 374.

39. Alexander Hamilton to John Laurens, June 30, 1780, Syrett *et al.*, eds., *Papers of Hamilton*, II, 347–348.

40. Alexander McDougall to George Clinton, Apr. 3, 1779, Hastings, ed., *Papers of Clinton*, IV, 688–689.

41. *Pa. Packet*, Apr. 8, 1780.

42. Joseph Reed to Anthony Wayne, June 13, 1781, quoted in John F. Roche, *Joseph Reed: A Moderate in the American Revolution* (New York, 1957), 187. See also Robert Levere Brunhouse, *The Counter-Revolution in Pennsylvania, 1776–1790* (Harrisburg, Pa., 1942), esp. 84–85; William A. Benton, "Pennsylvania Revolutionary Officers and the Federal Constitution," *Pennsylvania History*, XXXI (1964), 419–435.

43. Joseph Reed to Nathanael Greene, Sept. 2, 1780, quoted in Johnson, *Life and Correspondence of Greene*, I, 166–167.

44. Nathanael Greene to Joseph Reed, Sept. 8, 1780, *ibid.*, 167.

45. Alexander Hamilton to James Duane, Sept. 3, 1780, Syrett *et al.*, eds., *Papers of Hamilton*, II, 401–417.

46. Henry Jackson to Henry Knox, Feb. 28, 1782, quoted in Louis Clinton Hatch, *The Administration of the American Revolutionary Army* (New York, 1904), 116–117.

47. Ebenezer Huntington to Andrew Huntington, July 7, 1780, "Letters of Ebenezer Huntington, 1774–1781," *AHR*, V (1900), 725–726.

48. Samuel Shaw to John Eliot, Nov. 18, 1776, Quincy, *Journals of Shaw*, 26.

49. Louise Burnham Dunbar, *A Study of "Monarchical" Tendencies in the United States from 1776 to 1801* (Urbana, Ill., 1923).

50. Richard H. Kohn, "American Generals of the Revolution: Subordination and Restraint," in Higginbotham, ed., *Reconsiderations on the Revolutionary War*, 104–123.

51. Alexander Graydon to Joseph Reed, Oct. 5, 1780, Hazard *et al.*, eds., *Pa. Archives*, 2d Ser., III, 437–438.

52. Nathanael Greene to Samuel Blachley Webb, Dec. 21, 1779, Ford, ed., *Correspondence and Journal of Webb*, II, 231.

53. Jackson Turner Main, *Political Parties before the Constitution* (Chapel Hill, N.C., 1973), 149, 172, 360–361, 385; Main, *Antifederalists*, 191, 198–200, 209, 219, 263; Benton, "Pennsylvania Officers," *Pa. Hist.*, XXXI (1964), 419–435; Edwin G. Burrows, "Military Experience and the Origins of Federalism and Anti-federalism," in Jacob Judd and Irwin H. Polishook, eds., *Aspects of Early New York Society and Politics* (Tarrytown, N.Y., 1974), 83–92; Forrest McDonald, *We the People: The Economic Origins of the Constitution* (Chicago, 1958), 262–263. A separate question, the role of military policy in the debate over the Constitution, is discussed in Kohn, *Eagle and Sword*, chap. 5, and Cress, "Standing Army," chap. 7.

54. See esp. Stanley Elkins and Eric McKitrick, "The Founding Fathers: Young Men of the Revolution," *Pol. Sci. Qtly.*, LXXVI (1961), 181–216; Sidney Kaplan, "Veteran Officers and Politics in Massachusetts, 1783–1787," *WMQ*, 3d Ser., IX (1952), 29–57; Higginbotham, *War of American Independence*, 449; Kohn, "Generals of the Revolution," in Higginbotham, ed., *Reconsiderations on the War*, 104–123.

55. Out of the large literature on the politics of the early national period, I am especially indebted to Kohn, *Eagle and Sword*; Pocock, *Machiavellian Moment*, chap. 15; Gerald Stourzh, *Alexander Hamilton and the Idea of Republican Government* (Stanford, Calif., 1970); John R. Howe, Jr., "Republican Thought and the Political Violence of the 1790s," *Am. Qtly.*, XIX (1967), 147–165; Richard Hofstadter, *The Idea of a Party System: The Rise of Legitimate Opposition in the United States, 1780–1840* (Berkeley and Los Angeles, Calif., 1969); James M. Banner, Jr., *To the Hartford Convention: The Federalists and the Origins of Party Politics in Massachusetts, 1789–1815* (New York, 1970); David Hackett Fischer, *The Revolution of American Conservatism: The Federalist Party in the Era of Jeffersonian Democracy* (Chicago, 1965); Richard Buel, Jr., *Securing the Revolution: Ideology in American Politics, 1789–1815* (Ithaca, N.Y., 1972); Lance G. Banning, *The Jeffersonian Persuasion: Evolution of a Party Ideology* (Ithaca, N.Y., 1978); Drew R. McCoy, "The Republican Revolution: Political Economy in Jeffersonian America, 1776–1817" (Ph.D. diss., University of Virginia, 1976).

56. Nathanael Greene to Thomas Sumter, Jan. 8, 1781, quoted in Edward McCrady, *The History of South Carolina in the Revolution, 1780–1783* (New York, 1902), 61. See also Wickwire and Wickwire, *Cornwallis*, 145–147, 169–185, 250, 269–270.

57. William Moultrie, *Memoirs of the American Revolution* (New York, 1802), II, 245.

58. Entry of Nov.–Dec. 1781, Journal of Jean-Baptiste-Antoine de Verger, in Howard C. Rice, Jr., and Anne S. K. Brown, trans. and ed., *The American Campaign of Rochambeau's Army*, I (Princeton, N.J., 1972), 152.

59. Daniel Morgan to Nathanael Greene, Feb. 20, 1781, quoted in Graham, *Life of Morgan*, 370.

60. Wickwire and Wickwire, *Cornwallis*, 169–171, 185; Don Higginbotham, *Daniel Morgan: Revolutionary Rifleman* (Chapel Hill, N.C., 1961), 132–133; Hugh F. Rankin, *Francis Marion: The Swamp Fox* (New York, 1973), 298–299; John Richard Alden, *The South in the Revolution, 1763–1789*, in Wendell H. Stephenson and E. Merton Coulter, eds., *A History of the South*, III (Baton Rouge, La., 1957), 267; Robert C. Pugh, "The Revolutionary Militia in the Southern Campaign, 1780–1781," *WMQ*, 3d Ser., XIV (1957), 154–175; Shy, *People Numerous and Armed*, 217–219; McBride, "Virginia War Effort"; Clyde R. Ferguson, "Carolina and Georgia Patriot and Loyalist Militia in Action, 1778–1783," in Crow and Tise, eds., *Southern Experience*, 174–199.

61. Samuel McDowell to Thomas Jefferson, Apr. 20, 1781, Boyd *et al.*, eds., *Papers of Jefferson*, V, 507.

62. McDowell to Jefferson, May 9, 1781, *ibid.*, 621–622.

63. Nathanael Greene to Thomas Nelson, quoted in Greene, *Life of Greene*, III, 341.

64. George Moffett to Thomas Jefferson, May 5, 1781, Boyd *et al.*, eds., *Papers of Jefferson*, V, 603–604.

65. Entry of June 8, 1781, "Clinton's Intelligence," *Mag. Am. Hist.*, XI (1884), 250.

66. Nathanael Greene to Baron Steuben, Feb. 3, 1781, quoted in Friedrich Kapp, *The Life of Frederick William Von Steuben, Major General in the Revolutionary Army* (New York, 1859), 399.

67. George Washington to James McHenry, Mar. 12, 1782, Fitzpatrick, ed., *Writings of Washington*, XXIV, 63–64; Robert Morris and Richard Peters to George Washington, Aug. 13, 1781, Ferguson *et al.*, eds., *Papers of Morris*, II, 51; John Armstrong to Joseph Reed, Nov. 27, 1779, Hazard *et al.*, eds., *Pa. Archives*, 1st Ser., VIII, 32; James Duane to George Washington, Oct. 10, 1780, Burnett, ed., *Letters of Congress*, V, 414. See also Appendix.

68. John Paterson to William Heath, Mar. 31, 1780, *The Heath Papers*, III (Mass. Hist. Soc., *Colls.*, 7th Ser., V [Boston, 1905]), 44.

69. Paterson to Heath, Oct. 23, 1780, *ibid.*, 114.

70. Entry of Aug. 26, 1783, Nathanael Greene's Journal, in Greene, *Nathanael Greene*, III, 501.

71. R. Wooding to William Davies, July 21, 1781, William P. Palmer, ed., *Calendar of Virginia State Papers and Other Manuscripts* (Richmond, Va., 1875–1893), II, 234.

72. Joshua Beall to Thomas Sim Lee, Aug. 21, 1781, Browne *et al.*, eds., *Archives of Maryland*, XLVII, 434–435.

73. [Martin], *Yankee Doodle*, ed. Scheer, 232; entry of Oct. 8–9, 1781, Thacher, *Military Journal*, 339.

74. George Washington to Philip Schuyler, Jan. 30, 1780, Fitzpatrick, ed., *Writings of Washington*, XVII, 465. Compare diary entry, Nov. 3, 1781, Ferguson *et al.*, eds., *Papers of Morris*, III, 131.

75. Ramsay, *American Revolution*, II, 273.

76. Nathan Fiske, *An Oration Delivered at Brookfield, Nov. 14, 1781* . . . (Boston, [1781]), 6.

77. *Pa. Packet*, Dec. 4, 1781.

78. *N.-Y. Gaz.*, Dec. 31, 1781; *Pa. Gaz.*, Apr. 9, 1783; Representation of the Quakers to the President and Supreme Executive Council, Nov. 22, 1781, Hazard *et al.*, eds., *Pa. Archives*, 1st Ser., IX, 450–451; entry of Oct. 1781, Biddle, ed., *Journal of Drinker*, 137; entry of Oct. 24, 1781, Jacob Cox Parsons, ed., *Extracts from the Diary of Jacob Hiltzheimer, of Philadelphia* (Philadelphia, 1893), 46; entry of Oct. 25, 1781, Anna Rawle, "Diary," *PMHB*, XVI (1892), 105–107.

Chapter VIII
The Legacy

1. Dumas, *Memoirs*, I, 65; entry of Sept. 22, 1782, Jean-François-Louis, comte de Clermont-Crevecoeur, Journal, Rice and Brown, trans. and ed., *American Campaigns of Rochambeau's Army*, I, 78; entry of Sept. 22, 1782, Jean-Baptiste-Antoine de Verger, Journal, *ibid.*, 166–167; Gerard Shelley, trans., *The Memoirs and Anecdotes of the Count de Ségur* (New York, 1928), 143; entries of Sept. 14 and 21, 1782, Acomb, trans. and ed., *Journal of Von Closen*, 239–240, 242; M.W.E. Wright, trans., *Memoirs of the Marshal Count de Rochambeau, Relative to the War of Independence of the United States* (Paris, 1838 [orig. publ. Paris, 1808]), 89–90; *Pa. Packet*, Oct. 24, 1782.

2. George Washington, General Orders, Aug. 7, 1782, Fitzpatrick, ed., *Writings of Washington*, XXIV, 487–488.

3. George Washington, General Orders, Aug. 3, 1782, Fitzpatrick, ed., *Writings of Washington*, XXIV, 459–460.

4. See above, chap. 5.

5. *Ibid.* On Steuben, see Washington, General Orders, June 18, 1782, *ibid.*, 359.

6. Robert Howe to Baron Steuben, Nov. 1782, quoted in Dana Bigelow, "Baron Steuben," Oneida Historical Society, *Year Book*, XI (1910), xxi.

7. George Washington to William Heath, Aug. 19, 1781, Fitzpatrick, ed., *Writings of Washington*, XXIII, 22.

8. Roger Welles to his father, Apr. 13, 1782, Johnston, *Yale and Her Honor-Roll*, 141. Number of soldiers computed from Lesser, ed., *Sinews of Independence*, 220.

9. These proposals are fully discussed in Kohn, *Eagle and Sword*, chap. 3, and Cress, "Standing Army," chap. 6. See also Marcus Cunliffe, *Soldiers and Civilians: The Martial Spirit in America, 1775–1865* (Boston, 1968), 52.

10. *Independent Chron.*, Dec. 19, 1782. Compare William R. Staples, *Rhode Island in the Continental Congress* . . . , ed. Reuben Aldridge Guild (Providence, R.I., 1870), 428.

11. George Washington to Benjamin Lincoln, Oct. 2, 1782, Fitzpatrick, ed., *Writings of Washington*, XXV, 226–228.

12. Kohn, *Eagle and Sword*, chap. 2. Exhaustive discussion of the Newburgh crisis may be found in Richard H. Kohn, "The Inside History of the Newburgh Conspiracy: America and the Coup d'Etat," *WMQ*, 3d Ser., XXVII (1970), 187–220; Paul David Nelson, "Horatio Gates at Newburgh, 1783: A Misunderstood Role," *ibid.*, XXIX (1972), 143–151; Richard H. Kohn, "Rebuttal," *ibid.*, 151–158; C. Edward Skeen, "The Newburgh Conspiracy Reconsidered," *ibid.*, XXXI (1974), 273–290; Richard H. Kohn, "Rebuttal," *ibid.*, 290–298; Nelson, *Gates*, chap. 10. See also Freeman, *Washington*, V, chap. 26.

13. The addresses are reprinted in Ford *et al.*, eds., *Journals of Congress*, XXIV, 295–299.

14. Rufus King, Memorandum, in Charles R. King, *The Life and Correspondence of Rufus King*, I (New York, 1894), 621–622.

15. John Armstrong, Jr., to Horatio Gates, Apr. 29, 1783, quoted in Hatch, *Administration of the Army*, 208–209.

16. Henry Knox, Draft of Reply to Newburgh Addresses, Mar. 15, 1783, *ibid.*, 205–208.

17. Samuel Shaw to John Eliot, Apr. 1783, Quincy, *Journals of Shaw*, 104.

18. Ford *et al.*, eds., *Journals of Congress*, XXIV, 295–299.

19. *Conn. Courant*, Jan. 20, 1778. Typographical errors corrected.

20. Samuel Shaw to John Eliot, Dec. 22, 1782, Quincy, *Journals of Shaw*, 99–100.

21. Charles Thomson, Notes of Debates, July 31, 1782, Burnett, ed., *Letters of Congress*, VI, 407–408.

22. Notes on Debates, Mar. 17, 1783, Hutchinson *et al.*, eds., *Papers of Madison*, VI, 348.

23. Gouverneur Morris to John Jay, Jan. 1, 1783, quoted in Max M. Mintz, *Gouverneur Morris and the American Revolution* (Norman, Okla., 1970), 158.

24. See above, chap. 7, n. 55.

25. Howe, "Republican Thought and Political Violence," *Am. Qtly.*, XIX (1967), 147–165.

26. Elias Boudinot to the ministers plenipotentiary at Paris, July 15, 1783, Burnett, ed., *Letters of Congress*, VII, 221.

27. Kenneth R. Bowling, "New Light on the Philadelphia Mutiny of 1783: Federal-State Confrontation at the Close of the War for Independence," *PMHB*, CI (1977), 419–450.

28. Entry of Jan. 7, 1778, Sabine, ed., *Memoirs of William Smith, 1776–1778*, 282.

29. William Franklin to Lord George Germain, Nov. 12, 1778, K. G. Davies, ed., *Documents of the American Revolution, 1770–1783* (*Colonial Office Series*), XV (Dublin, 1976), 251.

30. Stephen Bayard to William Irvine, Apr. 15, 1783, Butterfield, ed., *Washington–Irvine Correspondence*, 412.

31. Quoted in Greene, *Nathanael Greene*, I, 573.

32. *Conn. Courant*, Jan. 20, 1778. Punctuation added.

33. Arthur St. Clair to Thomas Fitzsimmons, Jan. 21, 1783, Smith, *Life of St. Clair*, I, 579.

34. Windsor Brown to George Muter, Dec. 12, 1781, Palmer, ed., *Calendar of Va. State Papers*, II, 655.

35. Stephen Olney to Dutee J. Pearce, Dec. 29, 1828, quoted in Williams, *Revolutionary Heroes*, 290.

36. [William?] de Galvan to [Matthew Clarkson?], James Minor Lincoln, comp., *Papers of Captain Rufus Lincoln of Wareham, Mass.* (Cambridge, Mass., 1904), 101. See also Biddle, *Autobiography*, 172n; Garden, *Anecdotes of the Revolution, Second Series*, 148–149.

37. *Conn. Courant*, July 29, 1783.

38. *Independent Chron.*, Mar. 14, 1782.

39. *Conn. Courant*, July 29, 1783.

40. *Ibid.*, May 13, 1783.

41. *Ibid.*

42. *Ibid.*, June 24, 1783.

43. *Ibid.*, Oct. 14, 1783.

44. *Ibid.*, July 29, 1783.

45. *Boston-Gaz.*, Dec. 29, 1783, Jan. 12, 1784; *N.-J. Gaz.*, Dec. 16, 1783.

46. *Conn. Courant*, June 3, 1783.

47. *Boston-Gaz.*, Oct. 20, 1783.

48. *Conn. Courant*, Sept. 30, 1783. For discussion of the pension controversy, see Cress, "Standing Army," chap. 5; Sidney Kaplan, "Pay, Pension, and Power: Economic Grievances of the Massachusetts Officers of the Revolution," *Boston Public Library Quarterly*, III (1951), 15–34; Larry R. Gerlach, "Connecticut and Commutation, 1778–1784," Conn. Hist. Soc., *Bulletin*, XXXIII (1968), 51–58; Glasson, *Military Pensions*, ed. Kinley, 24–51; Christopher Collier, *Roger Sherman's Connecticut: Yankee Politics and the American Revolution* (Middletown, Conn., 1971), 213–217; Roth, *Jonathan Trumbull*, 72–73, 75–76.

49. Arthur St. Clair to Alexander McDougall *et al.*, Dec. 1782, in Smith, *Life of St. Clair*, I, 575–576.

50. *Conn. Courant*, Sept. 2, 1783.

51. *Ibid.*, Sept. 30, 1783.

52. Samuel Adams to Noah Webster, Apr. 30, 1784, Cushing, ed., *Writings of Samuel Adams*, IV, 303–305.

53. Granger, *Political Satire in the Revolution*, 202; *Boston-Gaz.*, June 23, 1783, Oct. 13 and 20, 1783; *Conn. Courant*, June 3, 1783, Aug. 5, 12, 19, 26, 1783, Sept. 2, 16, 1783, Oct. 7, 14, 21, 1783; *N.-J. Jour.*, Sept. 3, 1783; *Pa. Gaz.*, Dec. 31, 1783; Noah Webster, "Sketches of the Rise, Progress and Consequences of the late Revolution," in *A Collection of Essays and Fugitiv Writings on Moral, Historical, Political and Literary Subjects* (Boston, 1790), 184–188.

54. Morris, "Memoirs of a Connecticut Patriot," *Conn. Mag.*, XI (1907), 454.

55. Ebenezer Huntington to Andrew Huntington, Aug. 12, 1783, *Letters Written by Ebenezer Huntington during the American Revolution* (New York, n.d.), 106.

56. Anthony Wayne to William Irvine, May 18, 178[4], "Letters of General Wayne to General Irvine, 1778–1784," *Hist. Mag.*, 1st Ser., VI (1862), 340–341.

57. *Conn. Courant*, July 29, 1783.

58. [Martin], *Yankee Doodle*, ed. Scheer, 280–281.

59. *Pa. Packet*, July 22, 1783.

60. Baron Steuben to [William North?], 1783, Kapp, *Life of Steuben*, 687.

61. *Ibid.*, 686. Compare Baron Steuben to George Washington, Apr. 26, 1783, *ibid.*, 511–512.

62. Entry of Apr. 10, 1783, "Fisher's Journal," *Mag. Hist.*, II, Extra Number, No. 6 (1909), 58. See also Hugh F. Rankin, *The North Carolina Continentals* (Chapel Hill, N.C., 1971), 390–391; Memorial to the Maryland General Assembly, June 3, 1782, *Otho Holland Williams Papers*, 65.

63. Thacher, *Military Journal* (1862 ed.), 347–348. See also Freeman, *Washington*, V, 465–468.

64. Jethro Sumner to William Heath, Oct. 28, 1783, quoted in Curtis Carroll Davis, *Revolution's Godchild: The Birth, Death, and Regeneration of the Society of the Cincinnati in North Carolina* (Chapel Hill, N.C., 1976), 5. The most thorough study of the beginnings of the Society of the Cincinnati is Richard Frank Saunders, Jr., "The Origin and Early History of the Society of the Cincinnati: The Oldest Hereditary and Patriotic Association in the United States" (Ph.D. diss., University of Georgia, 1969). See also Wallace Evan Davies, "The Society of the Cincinnati in New England, 1783–1800," *WMQ*, 3d Ser., V (1948), 3–25; Edgar Erskine Hume, "Early Opposition to the Cincinnati," *Americana*, XXX (1936), 597–638.

65. Thomas Jefferson, The Article on the United States in the *Encyclopédie Méthodique*, Jefferson's Observations on Démeunier's Manuscript, Boyd *et al.*, eds., *Papers of Jefferson*, X, 50. Burke's pamphlet was titled *Considerations on the Society or Order of Cincinnati* . . . (Charleston, S.C., 1783).

66. Thomas Jefferson to George Washington, Apr. 16, 1784, Boyd *et al.*, eds., *Papers of Jefferson*, VII, 106–107.

67. Thomas Jefferson, Anas, Paul Leicester Ford, ed., *The Writings of Thomas Jefferson*, I (New York, 1892), 157–159; Jefferson, Observations on Démeunier's Manuscript, Boyd *et al.*, eds., *Papers of Jefferson*, X, 51.

68. Henry Knox to Baron Steuben, Feb. 21, 1784, quoted in Hume, "Opposition to Cincinnati," *Americana*, XXX (1936), 601.

69. Steuben to Knox, Nov. 11, 1784, *ibid.*, 602–603.

70. Warren, *History of the Revolution*, III, 278–297.

71. Entry of May 5, 1784, Winthrop Sargent, *Journal of the General Meeting of the Cincinnati in 1784*, Hist. Soc. Pa., *Memoirs*, VI (Philadelphia, 1858), 26–28.

72. Jefferson, Observations on Démeunier's Manuscript, Boyd *et al.*, eds., *Papers of Jefferson*, X, 51.

73. Arthur Campbell to William Davies, Mar. 13, 1782, Palmer, ed., *Calendar of Va. State Papers*, III, 99.

74. Steuben, *Letter on Established Militia*, 16.

75. Murray, *Jerubbaal*, 7.

76. Levi Frisbie, *An Oration Delivered at Ipswich* . . . (Boston, 1783), 20; entry of Apr. 29, 1783, William Parker Cutler and Julia Perkins Cutler, *Life, Journals and Correspondence of Rev. Manasseh Cutler, LL.D.*, I (Cincinnati, Ohio, 1888), 94–95.

77. Henry Phelps Johnston, ed., *Memoir of Colonel Benjamin Tallmadge* (New York, 1904), 99–100.

78. St. George Tucker to Frances Tucker, Sept. 15, 1781, quoted in Coleman, *St. George Tucker*, 70.

79. *N.-J. Jour.*, Feb. 16, 1780.

80. Massachusetts, Journal of the House of Representatives of the Commonwealth of Massachusetts, Sept. 28, 1781, (MS), 266. See also Cecelia Tichi, "Worried Celebrants of the American Revolution," in Everett Emerson, ed., *American Literature, 1764–1789: The Revolutionary Years* (Madison, Wis., 1977), 275–291.

81. Benjamin Rush to John Adams, Feb. 12, 1812, Butterfield, ed., *Letters of Rush*, II, 1123; George W. Corner, ed., *The Autobiography of Benjamin Rush* (Princeton, N.J., 1948), 155; J. Thomas Scharf and Thompson Westcott, *History of Philadelphia, 1609–1884*, I (Philadelphia, 1884), 274; Kenneth R. Bowling, "Good-by 'Charle': The Lee-Adams Interest and the Political Demise of Charles Thomson, Secretary of Congress, 1774–1789," *PMHB*, C (1976), 314–315, 334–335.

82. Evans, *Discourse Delivered in New-York*, 13.

83. George Washington, Circular to the States, June 8, 1783, Fitzpatrick, ed., *Writings of Washington*, XXVI, 485.

84. Jonas Clark, *A Sermon Preached* . . . *May 30, 1781* . . . (Boston, [1781]), 74.

85. Ellet, *Domestic History of the Revolution*, 73.

86. Joseph Buckminster, Jr., *A Discourse Delivered in the First Church of Christ at Portsmouth, on Thursday December 11, 1783* . . . (Portsmouth, N.H., 1784), 20–21.

87. Ezra Stiles, *The United States Elevated to Glory and Honor* . . . (New Haven, Conn., 1783), 36.

88. Nathaniel Niles, *The American Hero: A Sapphic Ode* (Norwich, Conn., 1775), 2.

Appendix
A Note on Statistics and Continental Soldiers' Motivation

1. Papenfuse and Stiverson, "Smallwood's Recruits," *WMQ*, 3d Ser., XXX (1973), 117–132; Lender, "The Enlisted Line of New Jersey"; Lender, *New Jersey Soldier*; Mark E. Lender, "The Mind of the Rank and File: Patriotism and Motivation in the Continental Line," in William C. Wright, ed., *New Jersey in the American Revolution, III, Papers Presented at the Seventh Annual New Jersey History Symposium* (Trenton, N.J., 1976), 21–38; John R. Sellers, "The Common Soldier in the American Revolution," in Stanley J. Underdal, ed., *Military History of the American Revolution: Proceedings of the Sixth Military History Symposium, USAF Academy*, 1974 [Washington, D.C., 1976], 151–166; Robert A. Gross, *The Minutemen and Their World* (New York, 1976), 146–153.

2. Lender, "Enlisted Line of New Jersey," iv, 133, 302.

3. Papenfuse and Stiverson, "Smallwood's Recruits," *WMQ*, 3d Ser., XXX (1973), 131.

4. Sellers, "Common Soldier," in Underdal, ed., *Military History Symposium*, 165.

5. Charles William Royster, "The Continental Army in the American Mind: 1775–1783" (Ph.D. diss., University of California, Berkeley, 1977).

6. Lender, "Enlisted Line of New Jersey," 3, 297; Lender, *New Jersey Soldier*, 5; Papenfuse and Stiverson, "Smallwood's Recruits," *WMQ*, 3d Ser., XXX (1973), 117.

7. Lender, "Enlisted Line of New Jersey," 203, 133, 149.

8. Lender, "Enlisted Line of New Jersey," 150; Papenfuse and Stiverson, "Smallwood's Recruits," *WMQ*, 3d Ser., XXX (1973), 127, 131.

9. Lender, "Enlisted Line of New Jersey," 302, iv; Gross, *Minutemen*, 152.

10. Lender, "Enlisted Line of New Jersey," 129.

11. *Ibid.*, 258.

12. Papenfuse and Stiverson, "Smallwood's Recruits," *WMQ*, 3d Ser., XXX (1973), 127–131; Lender, "Enlisted Line of New Jersey," chap. 8; Sellers, "Common Soldiers," in Underdal, ed., *Military History Symposium*, 158–161.

13. Lender, "Enlisted Line of New Jersey," vi, 224; Lender, *New Jersey Soldier*, 27.

14. Sellers, "Virginia Continental Line."

15. Edmondson, "Desertion during the Revolutionary War."

16. Lender, "Enlisted Line of New Jersey," 143; Lender, *New Jersey Soldier*, 29–30; Lender, "Mind of Rank and File," in Wright, ed., *New Jersey in the American Revolution*, 22–23.

17. Gross, *Minutemen*, 151.

18. Peckham, ed., *Toll of Independence*, 132–133. Compare Duncan, *Medical Men in the Revolution*, 369–378.

19. See Charles H. Metzger, *The Prisoner in the American Revolution* (Chicago,

1971), esp. 135–136; William R. Lindsey, *Treatment of American Prisoners of War during the Revolution*, Emporia State Research Studies, XXII (Emporia, Kansas, 1973); Larry G. Bowman, *Captive Americans: Prisoners during the American Revolution* (Athens, Ohio, 1976), esp. 93–96. See also Jesse Lemisch, "Listening to the 'Inarticulate': William Widger's Dream and the Loyalties of American Revolutionary Seamen in British Prisons," *Journal of Social History*, III (1969), 1–29.

20. Lender, "Enlisted Line of New Jersey," 163.

21. Peckham, ed., *Toll of Independence*, 132.

22. See, for example, Robert Middlekauff, "Why Men Fought in the American Revolution," *Huntington Library Quarterly* (forthcoming).

Index

A

B

J

K

L

M

W

Y